◆

Wrestling with Angels
and Singing with Dragons

Note: For an explanation of the title, see page 373.

Wrestling with Angels
and Singing with Dragons

THE MAKING OF A GARDEN ACROSS 45 YEARS

2015 by William H. Frederick, Jr., ASLA, VMM

Publisher: William H. Frederick, Jr., Hockessin, DE

Author: William H. Frederick, Jr.
Editor: Douglas Brenner
Editor: Thomas Christopher
Production: Verve Marketing & Design

Wrestling with Angels and Singing with Dragons
Copyright © 2015 by William H. Frederick, Jr.

ISBN 978-0-692-32853-8

Printed In China

Library of Congress Cataloging –in –Publication Data
2015904560

Paul Skibinski
1958-2013

This book was written to make a record of how our garden happened, and to convey the pleasure it has brought to its creators and its many visitors. My wife, Nancy, joins me in dedicating the book to Paul Skibinski, head gardener and superintendent of the Ashland Hollow garden for 28 years (1985-2013). The place described here would have been impossible without him. Paul was a keen observer of everything around him. His passion for science and art was expressed in his nurturing of plants, students, and employees. He was a consummate craftsman. His optimism arose from a clarity of understanding and an insight into past experience that pierced many kinds of fog. He was a rare and wonderful human being. Nancy and I count ourselves extremely fortunate to have been Paul's employers, associates in horticulture and art, and friends.

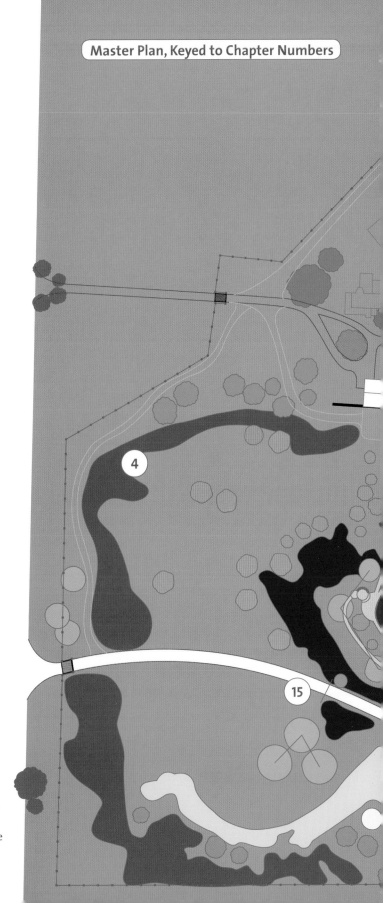

Master Plan, Keyed to Chapter Numbers

This plan does not reference Chapters 1, 13, and 14, because those chapters discuss areas and subjects outside the physical boundaries of the Ashland Hollow garden.

Let the Journey Begin

Garden Chronology

Building the Garden at Ashland Hollow

1963	Acquisition of Land
1965	Completion of House
1966	Entrance Garden
	Studio Garden
	Vegetable Garden
1966-67	Stream Valley Garden
1967	Conifer Windbreak Planting
1969	Orchard
1971	Swimming Pool Garden
1976	Hillside Meadow
	Torreya Grove
	American Holly Grove
1981	Wisteria Lawn
1982-83	Rose Path
1986	Winter Garden
1988	Quince Hillside
1989	Green and White Path
1990	Frog Steps
	Lilac Planting along Drive
1995-96	Priapus Path

1 Two Passions and An Adventure in Education

The garden we started at Ashland Hollow in 1964 has a history that begins in 1934, when I was eight. It is a story about an early passion for plants and design as well as a growing passion for color. The passions at times were blocked, at many times stimulated, and frequently in conflict with each other. This garden embodies the harmonious flowering of these passions.

Also part of my life during those 30 years were two other gardens; the education I received in nontraditional ways at the Arthur Hoyt Scott Horticultural Foundation (now the Scott Arboretum), during my four years at Swarthmore College, and in one postgraduate year at Cornell University; marriage; the founding of a nursery/landscape contracting firm (Millcreek Nursery); garden visits in California, Spain, Brazil, the Netherlands, and England; and the publication of two important books on contemporary garden design. From all of this I got many glimpses of original, nontraditional, site-appropriate gardens of great artistic merit that enhanced the contemporary lifestyles of their owners. Wonderful new friendships were made along the way, and very generous support was received from many quarters.

The blank slate at Ashland Hollow in 1964—in fact, a rich and varied canvas. Our kids and some friends race downhill from what is now the Orchard toward the site of today's Winter Garden.

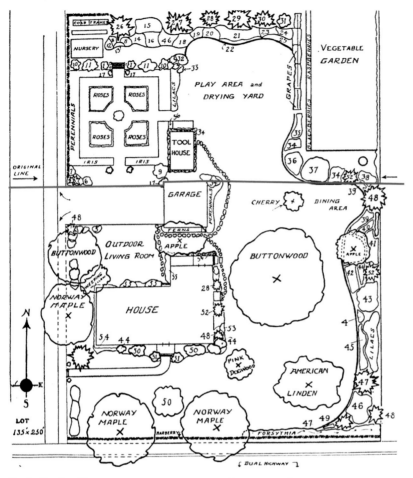

This plan shows the relationship of Garden #1 (above the red line) to my parents' existing garden. The plant list covers both gardens. The plan originally illustrated an article I wrote for *Plants & Gardens Magazine* (Spring 1948).

Key to Planting Plan

1. *Spiraea vanhouttei*
2. Mock orange (*Philadelphus*)
3. Dwarf Japanese quince (*Chaenomeles japonica*)
4. *Weigela*
5. Lilac 'Charles Joly'
6. Father Hugo's rose or golden rose of China (*Rosa hugonis*)
7. Japanese maple (*Acer palmatum*)
8. Firethorn (*Pyracantha*)
9. Weeping Japanese cherry
10. Flowering dogwood (*Cornus florida*)
11. Flowering crab apple
12. Scotch broom (*Cytisus scoparius*)
13. Swiss mountain pine (*Pinus mugo* var. *mugo*)
14. Beauty bush (*Kolkwitzia amabilis*)
15. European white birch (*Betula pendula*)
16. Snowberry (*Symphoricarpos albus*)
17. Japanese box (*Buxus microphylla* var. *japonica*)
18. *Syringa microphylla*

19. *Euonymus yedoensis*
20. Beautyberry (*Callicarpa japonica*)
21. Japanese yew (*Taxus cuspidata*)
22. Azalea—Kurume hybrid
23. *Viburnum* x *burkwoodii*
24. Fringe tree (*Chionanthus virginicus*)
25. Spreading cotoneaster (*Cotoneaster divaricatus*)
26. Atlas cedar (*Cedrus atlantica* 'Glauca')
27. China fir (*Cunninghamia lanceolata*)
28. Carolina hemlock (*Tsuga caroliniana*)
29. Deodar cedar (*Cedrus deodara*)
30. Austrian pine (*Pinus nigra*)
31. *Cryptomeria japonica* 'Lobbii'
32. *Viburnum carlesii*
33. American arborvitae (*Thuja occidentalis*)
34. *Forsythia*
35. Rhubarb
36. *Cotoneaster salicifolius*
37. Hawthorn (*Crataegus*)
38. Kousa dogwood (*Cornus kousa*)
39. Snow azalea (*Rhododendron mucronatum* [syn. *Azalea ledifolia* var. *alba*])

40. *Rhododendron caucasicum* 'Boule de Neige'
41. Rosebay (*Rhododendron maximum*)
42. Flame azalea (*Rhododendron calendulaceum*)
43. *Magnolia* x *soulangeana* 'Lennei'
44. Hicks yew (*Taxus* x *media* 'Hicksii')
45. Bridal wreath (*Spiraea prunifolia*)
46. Winged euonymus (*Euonymus alatus*)
47. Blue spruce (*Picea pungens*)
48. American holly (*Ilex opaca*)
49. Tiger-tail spruce (*Picea polita*)
50. Dwarf Japanese yew (*Taxus cuspidata* 'Nana')
51. Japanese holly (*Ilex crenata*)
52. Hemlock (*Tsuga canadensis*)
53. Hemlock (*T. canadensis*)
54. Japanese barberry (*Berberis thunbergii*)
55. *Hydrangea*
56. Privet (*Ligustrum vulgare*)

Garden #1

Around 1942, when I was 15 or 16 years old, I made my first garden on a 135-by-100-foot plot of pasture adjoining my mother and father's backyard in Delaware. The garden was carved out of my grandfather's farm, the same way my parents' yard had been set apart when they married, in 1924. I had exhausted the possibilities for gardening on their parcel because it lacked sunny space. Like the designs of many first gardens, mine was based on traditional formal principles: Within an enclosure of eight-foot-deep perennial borders, four square beds surrounded a specimen "dwarf English" boxwood (*Buxus sempervirens* 'Suffruticosa'). The four beds, edged in smaller box, contained hybrid tea roses, and climbing roses covered a wooden arbor directly behind the central boxwood.

The "display" part of the garden, which occupied about one-third of the parcel, connected with part of my parents' lawn leading to the rear hall door of their house. The other two-thirds of the plot contained a toolshed, a vegetable garden, a propagating bed, a small nursery area, and an informal lawn enclosed by a *Cunninghamia lanceolata*, a *Cedrus atlantica* 'Glauca', and a collection of shrubs "on trial" (i.e., new to me). My father and I grew enough boxwood from cuttings to plant the low hedges around the rose beds, and we started *Lilium formosanum* from seed.[1.1] The lilies flowered six to eight feet high the next year, *after* I had left for Navy boot camp. Tremendously enthusiastic letters from my father reached me, about this and other garden matters. That, however, was the end of my intimate association with Garden #1, as college and law school followed close on the heels of the Navy.

I had learned that shaded, root-filled beds in mature gardens offer very limited gardening encouragement; that so-called invasive plants, such as *Physostegia virginiana* and *Oenothera perennis*, have their uses where growing conditions are tough; and that there is very little monetary outlay when you grow your perennials from seed, raise your boxwood from cuttings, and buy rooted cuttings of the less common trees.

My time in Naval ROTC was cut short by the end of the war, and I was able to continue and complete my college education at Swarthmore.

The Scott Arboretum and Cornell

I had not known until then that Mrs. Arthur Hoyt Scott had established an arboretum on the Swarthmore campus in memory of her late husband, the founder of the Scott Paper Company and, like her, an avid gardener and breeder of peonies and iris. The arboretum's mission was to grow and display all of the desirable woody and herbaceous plants known to be hardy in the Philadelphia suburbs, as both an aid and an inspiration to homeowners in that area.

When the arboretum's founding director, John C. Wister, became aware of my enthusiasm, I was assigned a series of jobs (in my spare time and during the summer of 1947) that gave me a chance to follow an enormous plant palette throughout its seasons of interest. This also provided the opportunity to get to know and learn from John as well as Harry Wood, the superintendent of buildings and grounds, and John's wintertime assistant, Gertrude Smith. Harry had trained as a gardener in the British tradition, on the great Lowther estate in the English Lake District; Gertrude ran her own garden-maintenance business in Montclair, New Jersey, from spring through fall. What a trio! They all upheld the highest-quality standards and were happy to fan the flames of my passion for plants.

John Wister, a Harvard graduate in landscape architecture, saw his job as that of collector, assembler, and evaluator of all the best garden plants in every appropriate genus. Incredibly thorough and diligent, he included every species, variety, and—most significant—every cultivar, whether it had occurred as a mutation or seedling variant, or had emerged from the work of a dedicated plant breeder. Annual travels kept him in touch with plant introductions from the wild, both domestic and international, and with specialty breeders of plants such as viburnums, hollies, tree peonies, and iris.

To display the resulting collection, he planned each planting on campus and directed and maintained a labeling system for visitors to use. One of my jobs was checking and replacing labels as needed. The bonus was an immersion in the best of the world's magnolias, rhododendrons, azaleas, hollies, tree peonies, and other genera. I could not have arrived at a better time.

Harry Wood made certain that the planting and pest control were done well, and he was responsible for propagation. He also saw to it that John Friel, a propagator for the arboretum, learned the then new method of grafting the woody scion of a tree peony onto a herbaceous root, the herbaceous part serving as a nurse plant until the scion sent out its own roots. Harry showed a genuine desire to ensure that I was properly educated. We became great friends. Insistent that I see British gardens, he organized, and conducted me on, my first trip to England.

Gertrude Smith had a great mind and a great sense of humor, and she was extremely articulate. The author of a book on bulbs, she also made major contributions to John Wister's books and articles. Outstanding, to my mind, is his privately published *Swarthmore Plant Notes*.[1,2] This five-volume work assembled records of all of the plants in the Scott collections, including their botanical names, the dates of their introduction into the arboretum, the locations where they had been collected, and background on breeders. Much of that valuable information would otherwise have been lost. These volumes still make very good reading today.

Questions put to Gertrude by a novice like me provoked an engagement of minds—the kind that happens only rarely. She made you think. Sometimes, you momentarily felt like a fool. Always, you came away with much more than you had expected, and always thanking God that such people existed.

The title page of the introductory volume of *Swarthmore Plant Notes*; the Arthur Hoyt Scott Horticultural Foundation is now the Scott Arboretum.

Opposite: From the table of contents

SWARTHMORE PLANT NOTES

(Third Typewritten Edition 1955-1956)

A RECORD OF ALL PLANTS GROWN BY

THE ARTHUR HOYT SCOTT HORTICULTURAL FOUNDATION

SWARTHMORE COLLEGE, SWARTHMORE

DELAWARE COUNTY, PENNSYLVANIA

IN ITS FIRST TWENTY-FIVE YEARS

1930 - 1954

JOHN C. WISTER, DIRECTOR

INTRODUCTORY VOLUME

GENERAL PURPOSE AND ARRANGEMENT

i

S W A R T H M O R E   P L A N T   N O T E S

INTRODUCTORY VOLUME

GENERAL PURPOSE AND ARRANGEMENT

TABLE OF CONTENTS

- - - - - - - -

The Plant Descriptions are divided as follows:-

VOLUME I

TREES, SHRUBS and VINES

PART ONE: Trees; Shrubs from the Yew Family to the Dogwood Family

PART TWO: Shrubs from the Heath Family to the Composite Family; Vines

VOLUME II

HERBACEOUS PLANTS

(Tree Peonies are included in the Peony Chapter)

ii

After a three-year postgraduate detour to law school and summer work in a law office, I finally felt secure in the decision that my life's work would have to do with gardens. In 1951 my very patient fiancée, Nancy Greenewalt, and I were married. We persuaded the head of the Plant Science Department in Cornell University's College of Agriculture to let both of us attend classes for a year as special students. Between us, we essentially took the entire curriculum that an individual student might have taken in a two-year program.

Nancy had graduated from Bryn Mawr College in 1950 with a major in biology. At Swarthmore I had majored in political science and minored in botany (yes, back then the college taught taxonomic botany). We decided that she would take all of the Cornell courses in plant pathology and entomology, as well as those on woody and herbaceous plants, while I would sign up for the ones in nursery and landscape contracting and management and in garden design.

Unexpected encounters with three gifted men at Cornell that year would later play a significant part in my resolution of the perpetual plants-versus-garden-design question—and in the making of the Ashland Hollow garden.

A young Chuck Cares, not long out of graduate school in landscape architecture, was one of my instructors. He taught me the essence of making a good garden plan; but, even more important, he helped convince me of the need for such expertise among present-day homeowners. (Three years earlier I had reneged on accepting my admission to Harvard's Graduate School of Design, because members of a prominent Boston landscape architectural firm had warned me that my only pos-sible future in the field lay in highway and subdivision design.)

While working for John Wister, I had heard many references to Liberty Hyde Bailey and the Bailey Hortorium at Cornell. A brilliant younger man, George Lawrence, was in the process of assuming leadership of this institution when we were in Ithaca. He taught a course in taxonomy, which Nancy had the good fortune to take.

This was the start of a friendship that influenced our lives in many ways. George's facile mind had no trouble plowing through the complexities created by other botanists, as when he presided over the birth of the International Code of Nomenclature for Cultivated Plants. A short time after Nancy and I left Cornell, George was literally bought away to direct funding and development for the Hunt Botanical Library in Pittsburgh. It is George who deserves credit for the system we use, to this day, for keeping records of what is planted at Ashland Hollow and where it is planted, as well as when it arrived here and from where. Even more important, of course, he convinced us of the need for nomenclatural accuracy. Fortunately, in my opinion, he took a conservative approach to name changes proposed by publicity-seeking botanists!

During our year at Cornell, a hometown friend was attending the university's School of Architecture, which in those days also gave degrees in landscape architecture. Our friend introduced us to a fellow student there, a Brazilian by the name of Conrad Hammerman, who invited us to attend a slide show he presented about his mentor and countryman, Roberto Burle Marx. A real eye-opener for me, this was in many ways the beginning of my search for an appropriate approach to contemporary garden design in our part of the world. Conrad has remained a highly valued friend ever since. He was responsible for our visits to see and understand Roberto's work in Brazil, and he gave us the opportunity to entertain and get to know Roberto during his many visits to the United States.

Architects, a Landscape Architect, and Millcreek Nursery

After Nancy and I returned to Delaware, in 1952, two life-defining events occurred: a meeting with Sam and Vicky Homsey and the founding of Millcreek Nursery.

The Homseys were Wilmington's outstanding architects by several measuring sticks. In the first place, Vicky held degrees in both architecture and landscape architecture; secondly, even though most of their work was cutting-edge contemporary, they could also, on request, produce extremely competent designs for Georgian and other classical contexts; and finally, they had received a lot of carriage-trade residential commissions. Getting cold feet over my lack of design experience, I wondered if I should go back for more schooling. The Homseys seemed like the right people to ask for advice, and with alacrity and great good cheer they agreed to see Nancy and me.

As soon as I had described my background and my quandary, they said, "No more school! Go to work and do it!" To which Sam added, "Spend as much time as you can visiting other gardens and looking at photographs of gardens. You are probably already used to analyzing what is wrong with a garden you don't like. Spend more time looking at gardens you do like and deciding what it is that makes them good."

Nancy and I got going at once with a pretty intensive program of visiting gardens and investing in books with plates of gardens that we could study at leisure. It would take twelve more years and three garden-visiting trips—one to California, one to Spain, Holland, and England, and one to Brazil—before we began our garden at Ashland Hollow. But thanks to encouragement from the Homseys and others, in 1952 we founded Millcreek Nursery on 50 acres of fertile, rolling Piedmont terrain in Millcreek Hundred, Delaware. We wanted to promote and sell the much larger palette of plants we had come to realize would thrive here—and to encourage homeowners to enrich their lives by making appropriately designed garden installations.

Nancy and I grew only plants that we could not obtain from wholesalers, in addition to specimen sizes of a few kinds of plants that were likewise unavailable. The nursery operated four or five landscape crews, mostly installing gardens designed by myself and two other designers.

An early aerial photograph of Millcreek Nursery shows young field plantings in the upper right quadrant. At far left, a curved drive leads to landscape loading docks with propagation areas at lower left.

The entrance to Garden #2 (Sunset Hills); *Arundo donax* (giant reed) frames this view of the fountain and bench. See "A" on plan, page 16.

A detail of the fountain with fragrant white blossoms of *Datura metel* (Hindu datura) in the background

Garden #2

During the nursery's first 12 years, Nancy and I lived in a rental property called Sunset Hills, and the garden there became my second garden.

Our home was a somewhat modernized frame farmhouse on top of a windy hill. Two elderly Norway maples stood on the west, entrance side, framing the views of many glorious sunsets. At some distance behind the house were an aged orchard and two large trees: a silver poplar (*Populus alba*, or one of its varieties or cultivars), quite close to the building where it flanked our view of the orchard, and, in the middle distance, a blowsy Kwanzan cherry (*Prunus serrulata* 'Kwanzan').

Having so much shade near the house, we decided on a sunny spot next to the cherry for our garden. An inviting stepping-stone path connected this garden to the rest of our life. Because it was enclosed with shrubs, the garden had a very intimate feel. The shrubs hid a four-foot fence, which kept dogs out and could keep children in.

One entered through a wooden gate. From this point one had a view of the fountain framed by a four-to-five-stem clump of giant reed (*Arundo donax*) on the right.

The fountain consisted of three woks of different sizes placed at different elevations. Water came from a spout in the side of a roughly five-inch-square teak post and flowed from pan to pan until it disappeared through the free-form ground cover of pebbles in the central part of the garden. The height of the whole composition was probably no more than 40 inches, the spread no more than 45 inches.

Behind the fountain, a backless teak bench—approximately 20 inches wide, 14 feet long, and 6 inches thick—rested on an attractive rock at one end and a sturdy "leg" at the other. This seat followed the gentle curve of the free-form pebbled area on that side of the garden.

Behind that area was a handsome, lively green-foliaged, narrow columnar incense cedar (*Calocedrus decurrens*). As one looked through the entrance, the fountain, the bench, and the incense cedar were occultly balanced in a striking way.[1.3] The pebbled space was not large, its curvilinear form surrounded primarily by a bed of varying width, which contained perennials and a few tender bedding plants. Seated on the bench during warm weather, one faced north, away from the sun, while the flowers looked toward the sun—and toward the sitter. The sounds were entirely peaceful and it all had a great deal of magic, making this a hard place to leave.

Note the attraction to the boldly textured foliage of the *Arundo*, the fascination with water, the carefully studied shape of the pebbled area, as well as the importance of occult balance. These concerns would all play significant roles in my third garden, at Ashland Hollow.

Plan of Garden #2 (Sunset Hills). For a view of detail A, see page 14, top photo.

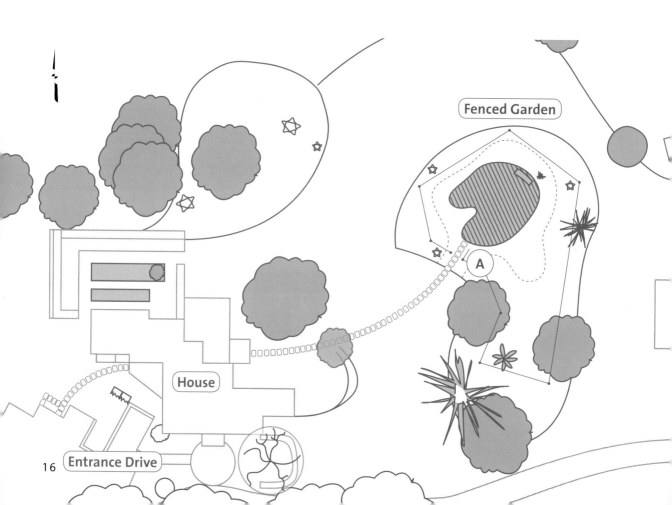

Fenced Garden

A

House

Entrance Drive

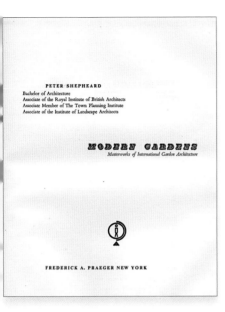

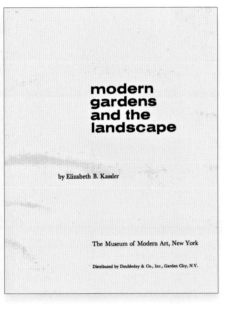

Garden Design: A Bubbling Cauldron

The field of garden design was undergoing a wonderful ferment at that time.

In 1954 the British architect, planner, and landscape designer Sir Peter Shepheard compiled his survey *Modern Gardens* (New York: Frederick A. Praeger). The list of designers with work illustrated in the book includes **Roberto Burle Marx, Thomas Church, Brenda Colvin, Mien Ruys, Peter Shepheard** himself, C. Th. Sørensen, Christopher Tunnard, and André and Paul Vera. I avidly studied all of these photographs and the accompanying notes. Over the years to come I got to visit gardens designed by those whose names appear in boldface above, and I was fortunate enough to count Roberto, Tommy, and Peter as good friends. It was not until much later that I met Mien Ruys and fell in love with her and her work. Unfortunately, she died just a few years after conducting Nancy and me around her own incredibly beautiful garden on the former site of the Ruys family's famous Moerheim Nursery.

In 1964 the Museum of Modern Art released a volume, somewhat similar to Shepheard's, by Elizabeth B. Kassler: *Modern Gardens and the Landscape* (New York: Doubleday; a revised edition appeared in 1984). Among the designers Kassler presented were Luis Barragán, Burle Marx, Church, **Alden B. Dow**, Gabriel Guevrekian, **Philip Johnson**, Le Corbusier, **Edwin Lutyens**, **Isamu Noguchi**, Tunnard, and **Frank Lloyd Wright**. This book, of course, provided another feast for study (as above, I have boldfaced the names of those whose gardens I was able to visit).[1.4]

Top: Sir Peter Shepheard's 1954 photographic essay on contemporary gardens awakened the rest of the horticultural world to the stimulating variety of garden design then under way.

Bottom: A decade later, New York City's Museum of Modern Art followed up with further exciting photographs and news in *Modern Gardens and the Landscape.*

California

Tommy Church was a personal friend of Sam and Vicky Homsey. Sometime between 1952 and 1954 he came to Wilmington to visit them. The Homseys very kindly invited Nancy and me to dinner with Tommy, and that was the beginning of a wonderful friendship, which lasted until his death. He invited us to California so that he could show us some of his gardens. This we did in 1954. Tommy had trained at Harvard, he belonged to a small group then revolting against a traditionalist regime. For that group, fresh ideas about such things as close indoor-outdoor relationships, the design strength of curvilinear forms, and occult balance had become more important. Tommy went to California where architects were designing houses with open floor plans and walls of glass on what were, by East Coast standards, very small lots. Thanks to the moderate climate out West, homeowners could spend much more of the year in their gardens. The absence of a strong regional tradition in garden design left them open to new ideas.

Tommy quickly developed a following. Even people of modest means (and this was during the Great Depression) were not turned away. He would ask for a budget, and although this might pay his design fee for only one day, he was at least able to give clients a concept, if not the details. As times got better, his practice grew and prospered.

Nancy and I were, of course, totally unfamiliar with the plants being used in California—and totally unprepared for the highly dramatic and beautiful garden designs. These usually included swimming pools and a seamless continuity of life indoors and out, a real mind-stretcher for us. In particular, the fact that free-flowing forms of paving, lawn, and beds of plants could equal in strength the best of traditional rectilinear garden design was the message we brought home.

Gardens by Thomas Church, ASLA, mostly in California, were first opened to us by the designer in 1954. Their beautiful flowing, organic relationships between indoors and outdoors were stunning!

Gardens of Many Rooms

In 1960 we took our first garden-visiting trip to Europe. This included Spain, the Netherlands, and England. From our time in Spain it is Granada—above all the Generalife—that stands out in my mind. The variety of ways in which water is used there was a great inspiration. I particularly remember a right-angle turn in a path "marked" by a bowl of water about two feet in diameter and only a few inches above the paving. A single two-inch bubbler in the center sent circular wavelets radiating from it. So very refreshing!

In the Netherlands we went to see the first Floriade, held in Rotterdam. This was an outdoor garden exhibition (planted, in some parts, two or three years earlier), which stayed open from mid-spring to early fall. Supported financially by the nursery and travel industries, it became part of the municipal park system at the end of the year. That exhibition proved sufficiently successful to be repeated in different Dutch cities in 1972, 1982, and at ten-year intervals ever since.

Although the first Floriade included individual commercial displays, much of the acreage comprised well-designed parks and gardens, usually involving newly introduced plants and design ideas. This and other early Floriades displayed a high level of taste and impeccable maintenance. As we have visited Floriades over the years, Nancy and I have always come home invigorated and with lots of notes on usable plants and ideas.

During our 1960 trip, we were joined at the Floriade by my Swarthmore mentor Harry Wood and then, in England, by his wife, Anne Wertsner Wood. Although Harry had been trained as a gardener up in the Lake District, he made sure that we saw the best and most important gardens, farther south, on this, our initial trip. We spent time at, among other gardens, Lawrence

Johnston's Hidcote, the Harold Nicolsons' Sissinghurst, and the Lloyd family's Great Dixter. I would not make a different selection now if I were starting over to see traditional English gardens for the first time. These are not the oldest, the largest, or the grandest. They are all 20th-century. They all have strong bones and innovative design. They are horticulturally rich. And they received their starts with the personal passions of their owners.

The important image that I carried home was the garden of more than one room, each of which provides a different horticultural experience, making it possible to walk a circuit through the garden and never see the same room twice.

Lawrence Johnston accomplished this at Hidcote on a site with considerable grade changes. Harold Nicolson and his wife, Vita Sackville-West, did it at Sissinghurst on an essentially level site with the added charm of an ancient multibuilding country house scattered about the garden. Great Dixter has the advantage of a handsome architectural design by Edwin Lutyens, upon which Christopher Lloyd, the original owners' son, superimposed a lively planting design.

In England, the gardens at Great Dixter, Hidcote, and Sissinghurst impressed us with their division into many rooms. Here we saw the Far Eastern principle of the stroll garden adapted to accommodate British horticultural richness. Each room is unique for the single color of its flowers or the season of bloom, its specialized purpose, or another distinctive feature. These four of Sissinghurst's garden rooms illustrate the point very well.

Right: The Lime Walk
Below: The Cottage Garden

Opposite
Top: The Herb Garden
Bottom: The White Garden

23

Brazil

During the same year, 1964, that plans for the Ashland Hollow house were completed and construction began, Nancy and I took a third trip of major importance to my emerging garden design philosophy. The goal of this journey, to Brazil, was our first meeting with Roberto Burle Marx. From an aesthetic viewpoint, I feel that he is the most important landscape architect of the second half of the 20th century. I say this 40-plus years after that trip, and after subsequent visits to many more of his gardens than we saw then.

In '64 we saw the recently completed garden adjoining the new Museum of Modern Art in Rio de Janeiro with its curvilinear pattern of two clones of Bermuda grass (dark green and yellow). We were also taken to Petropolis, to see the garden of Roberto's friend and (in later years) travel companion Odette Monteiro. There, sophisticated curvilinear forms were used in an incredibly beautiful, breathtaking setting. The house faces up a narrow valley where a stream becomes ponds of various sizes and a curvilinear path takes the visitor through rich plantings, very painterly in nature. It features *Tibouchina* trees loaded in season with purple splendor. This design serves a dual purpose, as both a foreground to and an enhancement of the view toward a striking, well-worn sugar-loaf mountain in the distance.

Roberto was a man of many other talents: painter, sculptor, jewelry designer, decorator, and music lover with a great tenor voice, even late in life. His generous hospitality included an invitation to his *sitio*[1.5] for a garden visit and Sunday brunch. This one-story converted farmhouse complex includes its own chapel nearby. The expansion of dramatic gardens in the surround was just beginning, but high artistry infused everything the owner

An early color rendering of the Odette Monteiro garden plan, designed by Roberto Burle Marx. The carefully studied organic forms fit beautifully into the Brazilian mountain valley of Petropolis, north of Rio de Janeiro.

24

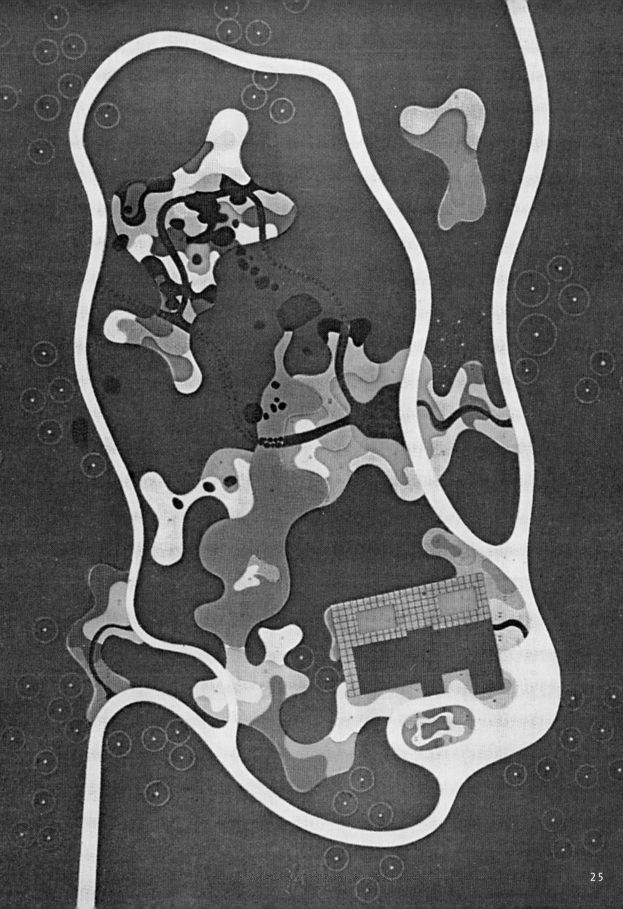

touched: the flower arrangements, the display of primitive sculpture, the food, the multinational guest list, and the entertainment. No one could forget the warmth of Roberto's welcome.

I came home, as I had from California, with a realization of the potential of curvilinear forms for gardens. In addition, I now strongly respected the use of color, especially large sweeps of a single color, as a key structural element.

Falling upon a totally open but selective mind, the observations I made while working for Millcreek clients, reading about and looking at photographs of cutting-edge work, and visiting a wide range of international gardens turned out to be the best possible post-Cornell preparation I could have received.[1.6]

Of course, my education has continued. Before the mid 1960s I was unaware of the early-20th-century geometric, yet asymmetrical, Bauhaus-influenced garden designs of Northern Europe,[1.7] but they struck a chord as soon as I discovered them. The same would hold true for the occult balance[1.8] of Noguchi's gardens and sculpture, and the "Chinese cup garden" of Walter Beck's landscape at Innisfree. Although those pleasures were still unknown to me, I was more than ready to entertain them.

I had never before heard the word "Fauvist" applied to color. However, I realized that I had been starved for the intense hues that emanated from that group of painters, and I hungered to find uses for that palette in my own designs.

The journey begins.

NOTES

1.1. Known in those days as *Lilium philip-pinense* var. *formosanum*.

1.2. This was a very limited mimeographed edition. Copies are available at the Scott Arboretum of Swarthmore College, in Swarthmore, Pennsylvania.

1.3. For more about occult balance, see Chapter 3, pages 63-65.

1.4. In 1968 Susan Jellicoe, a British garden designer, and Geoffrey Jellicoe, an architect and landscape architect, published *Modern Private Gardens*, another important record of contemporary gardens. Besides covering designs by the authors, the book included gardens by Arne Jacobsen (in Denmark); John Brookes, Russell Page, and Lanning Roper (England; Roper was an American expatriate); Thomas Church (the United States); Mien Ruys (the Netherlands); and Roberto Burle Marx (Brazil). By the time that this book came out, I had toured gardens by the designers whose names appear in boldface on page 17. I visited work by Susan Jellicoe, Lanning Roper, and John Brookes. John is a heroic figure in the world of British landscape architecture, a lone torchbearer for good contemporary garden design as it was emerging in Europe and the United States. This did not occur emphatically until well after the midpoint of John's career. He received overdue recognition only recently, when Queen Elizabeth appointed him an MBE. I met Mien Ruys in 1984, on a trip that also took me to Arne Jacobsen's personal garden and to one that C. Th. Sørensen did for his daughter.

1.5. A small farm, roughly an hour's drive from the city.

1.6. Travel focused on garden visiting has continued to play an important part in our lives. We made two more trips to see Tommy Church, one more to Roberto in Brazil, and three more to Floriades. The major feature of the 1982 Dutch exhibition was a breathtaking meadow of great sweeps of *Prunella* (different color forms) and heather with occasional clumps of dramatically sculptural plants, such as Himalayan rhubarbs. For the most part, what I saw on these trips and other garden visits in 1970 and 1984 either confirmed—brilliantly—conclusions I had reached by 1964 or strengthened notions that arose later in the course of my professional design work.

1.7. In particular, gardens by Arne Jacobsen and C. Th. Sørensen, as well as paintings and furniture by Gerrit Rietveld.

1.8. For further discussion of geometry and occult balance, see Chapter 3.

2 The Land, the House, and the Challenge

Finding a Valley

Bridge Across the Stream

Site-Specific Design

Opposite: The return of the waterway to its original narrow course, as it flows eastward from the ponds we created upstream of the house

The decision to move our family away from Sunset Hills was fired by the fact that we now had four wonderful kids. Nancy's doctor had told her "no more"; the six of us were living off of one bathroom; and we all definitely needed more space. It was time to buy or build a larger house.

Our specifications for the site focused on finding a valley. There were two reasons for this: First, we wanted privacy and the ability to control our view; real estate developments were creeping over the hills in every direction, a disturbing state of affairs for two people who had spent all of their lives "in the country." Second, and equally important, we had had enough of gardening on windy, cold hilltops. A valley, especially one running east and west, would offer the north- and south-facing slopes that provide appropriate growing conditions for a wide palette of plants.

We started working with our real estate agent around 1960-61, on what must have seemed to him an impossible assignment. As our search began, Nancy's parents, who owned a fairly sizable farm assembled from several smaller properties many years earlier, asked, "Have you looked at the Walker Farm?" We said, "Yes, but that is not the kind of place we had in mind." And so, the search for a site plodded on.

The Land

Thank heavens Nancy's parents asked the same question again in 1963. After some discussion we realized that she and I had misunderstood the location of the Walker Farm. We went and looked and found a valley with a springhouse at its head and a stream flowing through from west to east!

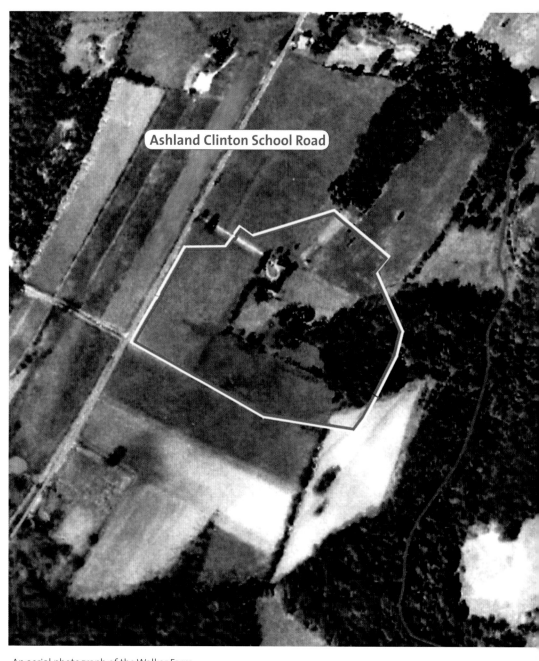

Ashland Clinton School Road

An aerial photograph of the Walker Farm
taken in 1961, from Delaware Data MIL
maintained by the Delaware Geological
Survey. The red line (following the deer
fence we built later) marks the shape of
our parcel, Ashland Hollow, amid a totally
agricultural landscape.

With a change in grade of 64 feet—from just off the public road to what has since become the floor level of our single-story house—this piece of land, Ashland Hollow, truly was a hidden valley. We would have the privacy we sought as well as complete control over our views.

In addition, the landforms were gorgeous; they would never cease to please the eye. Open pasture covered the south- and east-facing slopes, and the north-facing one was wooded. Several groves of beech with pure silvery trunks grew in the woods. A much smaller valley just uphill from the springhouse had a slightly different compass orientation, which gave it a special charm of its own. From the area we selected as the house site a view opens onto a larger valley below. Its meadow follows a wider, sycamore-lined stream called Burrows Run, into which our stream flows. Burrows Run empties into Red Clay Creek, which in turn empties into the Christina River. Near Wilmington, the Christina reaches the Delaware River on its way to the Atlantic Ocean. This would come to make us feel firmly connected to the sea and the rest of the world.

The site has, of course, had a tremendous influence on the development of our garden, and yet the land's natural beauty continues to unfold—and enchant us—51 years later. I have come to believe that there is probably no greater tangible gift that parents can give their children than a piece of land. Which is exactly what Nancy's mother and father did for us, shortly after our momentous discovery in 1963.

Typical landscapes in the region around Ashland Hollow: (1) a brick farmhouse and its part-frame hillside "bank" barn; (2) lush mid-May pasture with buttercups and trees limbed up by cattle seeking shade in hot weather; (3) the gradual descent of a wide, rock-strewn creek

The House

There was no question about who should be our architects for the house. Douglass Buck and Theodore Fletcher had designed two other buildings for us. We admired their work. We worked well together.

After examining the site thoroughly, Doug and Ted asked, "How would you feel about building the house as a bridge across the stream?" This thought had not occurred to us, but they gave some pretty convincing arguments: the best views up and down the valley, and cool breezes in the summer, thanks to natural cross-ventilation. To test the idea, we built a wooden footbridge, just wide enough for one person, 15 feet above the stream (the proposed floor level of the house) along what would be the centerline of the main room. This gave us several months, through changing seasons, to walk back and forth and see for ourselves how great it would be. We said, "Go."

The whole experience of designing and building the house was one of the best of our lives. When Doug and Ted came back with their concept plans, we felt only two changes were needed—a tribute to the architects' sensitivity to our needs. The first change, in the part of the house immediately over the stream, called for combining the separate living room, dining room, and foyer (which Nancy and I had put on our want list) into one big room. Here too, it turned out, Doug and Ted had anticipated our desire: their design divided these spaces with nonbearing partitions, in hopes that we would eventually decide to remove them.

As a trial run for the main living area, we constructed this temporary footbridge 15 feet above water level in the stream.

Left: The completed house as bridge, viewed from the south-facing hillside

Below left: "Lights on" in the Big Room. Beneath its wide balcony, the western arch spans the stream.

Bottom left: The return of the waterway to its original narrow course, as it flows eastward from the ponds we created upstream of the house

Opposite: Wooden topographic model prepared by Nancy G. Frederick. Note the beautiful landforms in the center. Under these slopes are several good springs, one of which supplies water to the 1860 springhouse. Together, they provide the source of our stream.

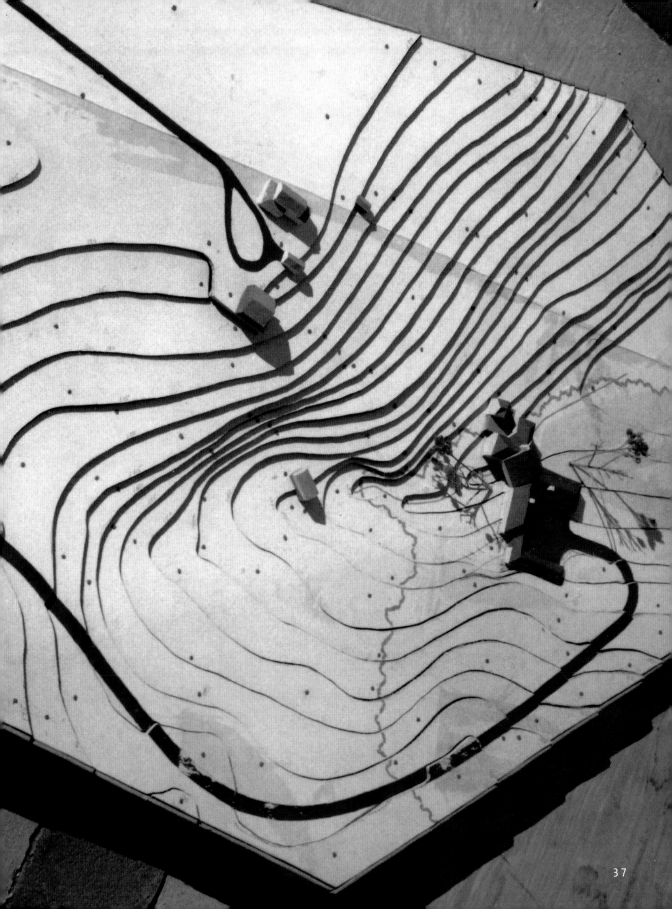

37

The second change we asked for involved flipping the entrance courtyard to bring in the drive on a more gradual descending grade.

At our request, the entire house is on one story, and it fits the site beautifully. I have always thought that the roof's low pitch and wide overhangs show the influence of Frank Lloyd Wright. The exterior walls are a warm tan stucco, and the roof is of dark gray Ludovici ceramic tiles, which look for all the world like weathered cedar shingles.

Diagonally off the north side of the central "Big Room," the living-dining space, the master bedroom and guest room wings form a Y whose fork encloses two sides of a square garden tied into the south-facing hillside. Our studio stands within the square.

Mirroring this configuration, the kids' wing and kitchen wing extend southward from the Big Room to frame two sides of the entrance courtyard. Our garage and workshop compose the third side. Just off this courtyard, a small space between the kids' wing and kitchen wing contains our Entry Garden and the entrance

Floor plan of the house with the entrance courtyard to the left (south), and the studio and Studio Garden to the right (north)

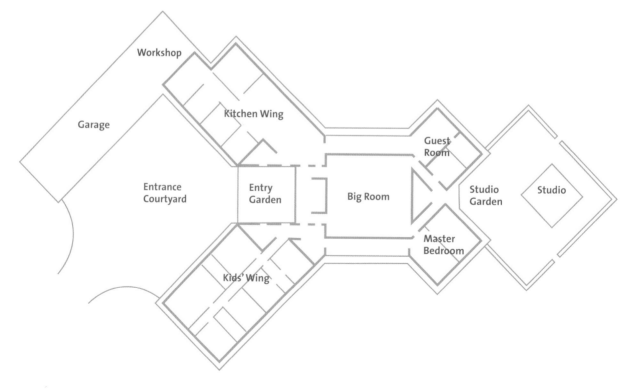

hall. The hall also connects both wings, providing a route for back-and-forth traffic that bypasses the Big Room.

This is only one part of a sound floor plan that successfully achieves the architects' objectives. They conceived the Big Room as the most "social" area of the house; the most personal and private activities take place at the ends of the four wings. A breezeway connects Nancy's workshop to the end of the kitchen wing. The kids' playroom occupies the end of their wing. And, as noted above, the studio that Nancy and I share is a freestanding structure at the end of the master bedroom-guest room complex. This entire layout has worked extremely well.

Construction started in 1964 with Doug's beautiful driveway hugging the contours of the former farm fields and then descending a bit more precipitously through the woods to the courtyard. Just a little over a year later, in October 1965, the house was ready and we moved in.

We appreciated our good fortune, having always hoped that we could start a garden when we were young enough for it to mature by the time we reached retirement age—and had plenty of time to really enjoy it. On moving day, Nancy was 37 and I was 39. Another dream had come true.

The Challenge

Any consideration of the planning and development of our garden should keep in mind that Nancy and I both have deep roots in the surrounding area. We were born and raised just outside of Wilmington. Ashland Hollow is only five miles from the former homes of Nancy's maternal grandparents and both sets of her maternal great-grandparents; it is eight miles from where my paternal grandparents lived, six miles from my maternal grandparents' home, and three miles from those of both sets of paternal great-grandparents and one set of maternal great-grandparents.

An aerial photograph taken a few years after our house had been built and the Conifer Windbreak had been established

This matters because a love of the local 19th-century agricultural landscape is firmly embedded in our lives. Most of the farms established on this rolling Piedmont terrain ranged from 100 to 400 acres, and they usually comprised a mixture of field crops, meadows, and wood lots. Fields and pastures were separated by fences and hedgerows, which in general consisted of native dogwoods, hawthorns, blackhaw viburnum, and red cedars (*Juniperus virginiana*). Some farmers used the "living fence" of that time, Osage orange (*Maclura pomifera*). Since trimming spiny Osage oranges can be impractical, they often grew into trees, mingling with the native plants. The scenic character of such a landscape, with its "organized variety" and ever-changing content is, we think, quite beautiful.

Our major challenge lay in making a garden that would sensitively combine this heritage with the exciting, sophisticated, global plant palette that had enthralled us, as well as the design ideas then crackling on the international scene. Fortunately, we had an excellent example to study nearby where something similar had been done with great success a generation earlier. This is Winterthur,[2.1] the home and world-renowned garden of Henry Francis du Pont.

40

Another essential design influence, stemming primarily from my Swarthmore years, was the concept that there should be something of interest going on in the garden every month of the year: blossoms, ornamental fruit, colored twigs, exfoliating or mottled bark, and so on. And I had no doubt that we could achieve this.

An array of plant-palette options started going through my mind from the moment the site became ours and the design of the house firmed up. In 1964, as has happened at other times in my life when the path ahead seemed unclear, I sat down and wrote a letter to a friend—six pages that outlined my thinking so far. I attached a list of 430 kinds of ornamental plants I wanted to use in the garden. The breakdown was:

Major trees	30
Secondary trees	35
Shrubs	200
Vines	15
Herbaceous plants and ground covers	125
Edibles	25

Combine this objective with our rather steep-sided valley, the pastures on the south- and east-facing slopes, and the woodland on the north-facing slope, and it all seems daunting—even to me decades later! My correspondent replied that it sounded like an arboretum, which was certainly not my intention. I envisioned a work of art that would draw from an exceptionally large palette. It was at this point that the landforms, the handsome two-story springhouse, the stream, the existing mature trees, and a white frame farmhouse and red barn atop the south-facing hill started speaking to me.

Because we deliberately regarded much of the design input and the emerging plant palette as experimental, we decided not to make a master plan. Instead, the garden would take shape as a series of building blocks.

Early on, I concluded that the most workable scheme would be a series of many outdoor "rooms," linked harmoniously by a path in such a way that (as at Hidcote) a visitor walking the full circuit from beginning to end would not pass through the same room twice. In principle, it would recall a Japanese "stroll garden," but the experiences en route would be horticultural events rather than set scenes involving rocks, sand, and trimmed plants. I felt that this would provide the maximum opportunity to enjoy a full year of rich seasonal interest from the plant palette I had begun to assemble.

Nancy and I were so enamored with existing features of our property, both large and small, that I approached each new part of the garden with the premise that landforms and existing trees and buildings would inspire its design, and that I would make no grade changes unless they were absolutely necessary. Largely instinctive, this procedure probably deserves the label "site-specific design."

As my roughly chronological narrative unfolds, the reader will encounter many ways in which our garden shows a debt to the 19th-century agricultural landscape around it.

The springhouse warrants special mention. Centrally located at the head of the stream valley, where it is visible from most other parts of the garden, this simple landmark built by farmers who once lived here serves as both a reference point and a reminder of the site's heritage. It is a beautiful and unique piece of architecture. The lower of its two stories, built of local field-

A northward view from the future orchard site, taken in the mid-1960s, shows the springhouse at the head of the stream valley. It marks the center of the 17 acres then being converted from hayfields and meadows to garden. To the right of the springhouse stands a cluster of native red cedars, most of which we later replaced with a grove of Japanese umbrella pines.

Near the entrance drive, I use a walkie-talkie to direct my sons, Dixie and Peter, as they position stakes for new planting on the south-facing hillside.

stone, is half-buried six feet below grade. Inside this cellarlike area, butter crocks and milk cans once sat in 18 to 24 inches of cool spring water, a natural source of refrigeration.

Back then, a curious mechanical device known as a ram delivered water uphill to the farmhouse. Gravity conducted water from the spring into a large cup on one end of a rocker arm. When the cup was full, the liquid weight lowered the rocker arm, forcing a pulse of water into a pipe to the house. The water would have accumulated in a tank, from which the farm family could draw it. This hydraulic system worked entirely without electricity, a reminder of how important mechanical devices were before the advent of modern technology.

Vertical boards and battens side the springhouse's upper story, which has a wood-shingled roof. It is only the bottom story that dates to the mid-19th century. The top floor was added in the 1890s, to provide temporary living quarters for the family after the original farmhouse burned down and while its replacement was under construction. Today the springhouse is very much the hub of our garden.

The springhouse in snow with the Springhouse Woods behind it on our steepest hillside. The fieldstone lower story was built in two stages around 1860. The frame story above it dates to around 1890. We eventually sacrificed the large swamp maple at left to make room for a swimming pool.

NOTE

2.1. I made my first recorded visit to Winterthur, to see the Azalea Woods at its peak, in the spring of 1959. It was around then that I also became acquainted with Henry Francis du Pont. My respect for his design ability has steadily increased over the years. Mr. du Pont's mastery of color and plant choreography ensured a lasting place for Winterthur among the world's top-ranked garden designs.

The south-facing hillside with the house roof in the foreground, the red barn and farmhouse at top of hill. Visible just below the crest of the hill is part of the recently planted Conifer Windbreak.

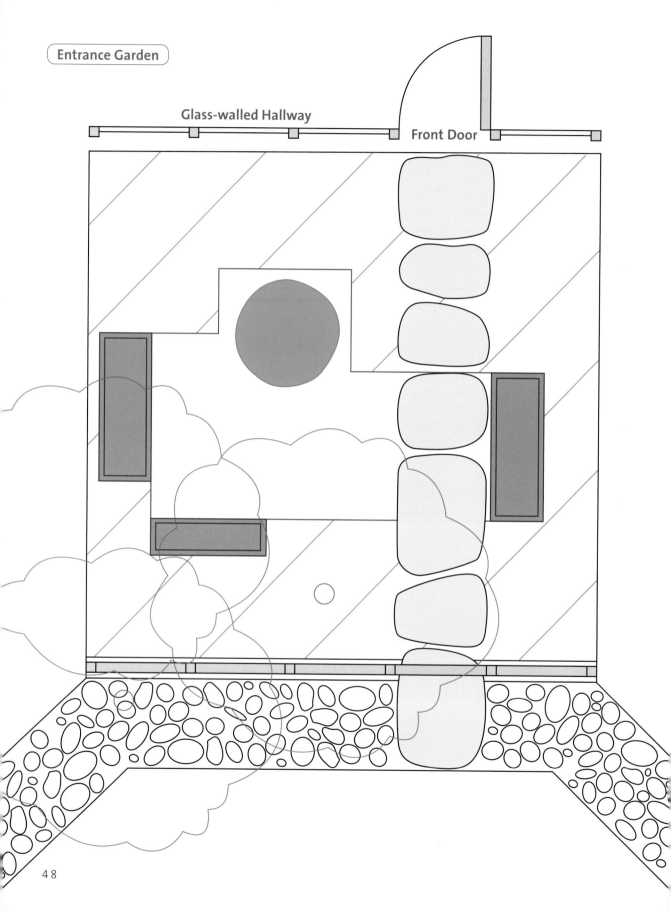

Entrance Garden

Glass-walled Hallway

Front Door

48

3 The Entrance Garden and The Studio Garden

Hot on the heels of the contractor, we moved into our new house in October 1965—excited, but also exhausted (from packing, moving, keeping up with four lively kids, and running our rapidly expanding nursery/landscape business). Somehow, we found time and energy to host a square dance for the builders and find a 12½-foot tree to trim for our first Christmas here. Nancy and I could look out at our potential garden, although what we saw, at least close to the house, was a sea of mud. The seasonal restraint on garden building was probably a good thing.

By the following spring we had plans in order for the Entrance Garden and the Studio Garden.

Decompression

The Entrance Garden is part of a series of spatial changes that enhance visitors' first sight of the garden proper. Having followed the driveway in from the public road, they park their cars in a vehicular courtyard (72 by 72 feet) in full view of the front door. The clearly marked path to the door, and the glass-walled hall (27 by 6 feet) into which it opens, leads straight through the Entrance Garden (27 by 24 feet). Stepping from the front hall into the Big Room—our 40-by-40-foot living/dining room, which truly is the largest space in the house—prepares visitors for their first panorama of the landscape that lies beyond. The vantage point is a western balcony overlooking the

Opposite: Passage through a sequence of enclosed and open spaces gives visitors a welcoming experience of decompression.

Top left: As they round the driveway's big bend, visitors look down on the automobile courtyard, flanked by the trellis-framed Entrance Garden and the angled wings of the house.

Bottom left: The Entrance Garden path aligns with the front door, which faces out from a glass-walled entry hall.

Top right: Double doors on the east and west sides of the Big Room open onto balconies with panoramic views.

Middle and bottom right: The west balcony surveys two very different vistas of the Stream Valley Garden.

Stream Valley Garden (100 by 260 feet), one of the largest areas in our entire stroll garden.

The vehicular courtyard is severely architectural.[3.1] On three sides it is enclosed by wings of the house (including the garage), whose warm, light tan stucco walls set off the shapes and colors of nearby plantings. The courtyard is paved with the same black bituminous surface as the driveway, except for a four-foot-wide band of "dinosaur eggs"—giant smooth, water-worn pebbles at the base of the walls.

Our Entrance Garden opens off this space, cutting into the courtyard's northeast corner on a diagonal. Both areas share a clump of three swamp magnolias (*Magnolia virginiana*), which emerge partly from among the dinosaur eggs and partly from the Entrance Garden soil.

The other permanent plants in the courtyard, which enjoy winter warmth from heat reflected off the stucco walls, are a pomegranate (*Punica granatum*), far to the right of the garden's entry; a wintersweet (*Chimonanthus praecox*), closer in on the right; and a Sargent's hydrangea (*Hydrangea aspera* subsp. *sargentiana*), along the east-facing wall to the left of the entry.

The pomegranate is listed as hardy in Zone 7-8 (i.e., unable to withstand winter temperatures below 0°F). Although Delaware is said to be satisfactory for plants requiring temperatures above 10°F, our valley holds the cold; we have recorded winter lows of -20°F (Zone 5). Therefore, growing our pomegranate, which is small and has endured only a few winters so far, is a true experiment. We hope that the milder microclimate of the courtyard will make the crucial difference, because it would be lovely to have the pomegranate's diminutive shiny foliage and wonderfully crinkled orange flowers.

Wintersweet (*Chimonanthus praecox*)

Sargent's hydrangea
(*Hydrangea aspera* subsp. *sargentiana*)

Wintersweet too is supposedly hardy to Zone 7, but for many years now, ours has come through what registered as Zone 5 winters in other parts of Ashland Hollow. The shrub's spicily fragrant flowers, which open in relays on warm days throughout the winter, are right at nose level as one enters the path to the front door.

Sargent's hydrangea is likewise listed as Zone 7, and it has thrived here for a number of years. It came as a gift, and the donor told me that the plant needed full shade. It languished, however, in the shady location I picked. Then I read an article in a British garden magazine that raved about this hydrangea's performance against an east wall. After I moved our Sargent's to the east wall of the courtyard, it has never turned back. Each year, in late June/early July, its gorgeous violet-colored lacecap flowers stand out against its large, velvety olive green leaves.

The Entrance Garden is one of the smallest spaces in our entire landscape, but it is extremely rich in both architectural and horticultural detail. The architectural elements had been completed with the construction of the house, and by the spring of 1966 we had our planting plans in order. Only one step down from the floor level of the house, the garden would be even with the courtyard paving.

A Bowl, a Jet, and Fragrance
In front of the Entrance Garden, six heavy square posts, stained dark brown, support the ends of six matching beams evenly spaced at right angles to the courtyard and the front hall's glass façade (white paint outlines the coordinating geometry of its sturdy timber frame).

Florida pinxter bloom (*Rhododendron canescens* (syn. *Azalea canescens*). Behind it are the fountain and front-hall façade.

The Entrance Garden's beams continue under the ceiling of the front hall (actually a sort of gallery measuring 27 by 6 feet) and penetrate its rear wall, which is finished in the same tan stucco used outside. Except where the front path begins, the intervals between the posts on the courtyard side of the garden support airy wooden screens in variations on a Chinese Chippendale pattern. Their delicate design provides the trellis for a large-flowered blue clematis.

Nancy and I asked Conrad Hammerman[3.2] to help with the balance of the hardscape—above all, a small fountain to remind us of a recent trip to Granada and the Generalife, where there seemed to be a water feature spouting at every intersection.

Recognizing that the Entrance Garden and the front hall are essentially one space, despite the glass wall that divides them, Conrad wisely located our fountain approximately halfway between the trellises and the hallway's rear wall.

Top: Winter color in the front hall.

Above: Ernest Wilson's Chinese house lemon, which bears large yellow fruit at Christmastime, occupies a place of honor in the hall. It can be seen both from outside and from the short hallway leading into the Big Room.

Below: An unknown *Clematis* cultivar climbs the trellises; it flowers in May.

Above: Chinese Chippendale-style trellis-work (variations on a theme) separates the Entrance Garden from the courtyard.

The fountain is a simple bowl, 4 feet in diameter and 15 inches high. A single jet of water rises 15 to 24 inches above the little pool inside the basin, almost lapping its brim. The gentle splashing sound and sparkling light that the jet gives off are continual sources of pleasure to us both. Nancy is the faithful tender of the fountain, making sure that it is at its best for visitors.

Conrad also had three backless wooden benches of equal size built into this garden. With one seat parallel to the trellises, and the others to the side walls, they are ideally arranged for watching the fountain and listening to its music. This has turned out to be a wonderful place for us to relax, and to prepare visitors' senses for the much larger water feature—the stream valley—they are about to experience from the Big Room just inside. The fountain and benches rest on a freestanding rectilinear platform of brick pavers laid in a basket-weave pattern, which is momentarily interrupted by the front path passing through.

To our delight, Conrad recommended that instead of making the path brick, we should use oversize gray "stepping-stones"—a brilliant idea. The seven poured-concrete "stones" are roughly quadrilateral. They measure a uniform 53 inches across, so that the sides of the path run parallel from courtyard to door, but they vary in width (from 25 to 55 inches) and the angles of these lines crossing the center vary as well. All of the corners are beautifully rounded.

Each slab consists of two layers poured in place with some drying time in between: a substratum of standard concrete and a 1½-inch surface tinted with a light gray dye. Most visitors assume they are walking on "real" stone unless we reveal the fraud. They simply feel a reassuring "country" texture underfoot.

At night this path is illuminated by the glow from the front hall and by two ceramic hanging lanterns made in California. These disperse light downward from many small openings topped by protruding hoods, and when a lantern sways, the "pieces of light" flicker slowly.

The plantings in this garden are partly permanent and partly seasonal. A few plants in large tubs always stay in the hall. The rotation of seasonal plants, in pots and tubs, usually reaches a crescendo from Christmas until whenever our attention refocuses outdoors. Heavy beams over the garden let us add or subtract the lath laid across them, as we need more or less shade for plants that have been forced into bloom elsewhere and placed in the hall "holding house." It turns out that we have never needed more than a small amount of lath. This is partly because the clump of three swamp magnolias (*Magnolia virginiana*) straddling the southwestern corner of the garden and the courtyard provide both a canopy for the plantings below and a summer sunshade for the whole entry area, outside the hall as well as within it.

Our outdoor plantings are permanent and in the ground, except for tubbed and potted plants occasionally brought in during the growing season.

The choice of swamp magnolia, with its vanilla-scented flowers, exemplifies our main criterion in selecting hardy plants for this part of the garden. Fragrance, we decided, would best produce the physical and emotional effect we hoped to achieve. Except for the evergreen ground covers between the stepping-stones, *Ophiopogon japonicus* and *O. japonicus* 'Nanus', all of the plants here have aromatic blossoms. Our goal was to enjoy fragrance during as many months of the year as possible. Here are the plants that realize this desire, in order of bloom times:

Above: One of a pair of hanging ceramic lanterns, which emit just the right amount of light for the stepping-stone path to the front door

Above: We often decorate the path with potted plants. Paul **Skibinski** created these pyramids of hedge apples, also known as monkey balls, for a fall party. (For more about hedge apples, see *Maclura pomifera*, page 410).

Late December to late February: Wintersweet (*Chimonanthus praecox*), in the courtyard

April: Burkwood's hybrid osmanthus (*Osmanthus burkwoodii* [syn. x *Osmarea burkwoodii*])

Late April to early May: *Daphne* x *burkwoodii* 'Carol Mackie'

Early May: Florida pinxter bloom (*Rhododendron canescens* [syn. *Azalea canescens*])

May: Hardy orange (*Poncirus trifoliata*), espaliered on the west-facing wall

Late May to early August: Swamp magnolia (*Magnolia virginiana*)

Above: An espalier of hardy orange (*Poncirus trifoliata*) has only begun its upward growth along the training wires (held in place by brass eyes and lead anchors) that surround a utility-room ventilator.

Below: The full-grown espalier in bloom

Above: True to its name, hardy orange produces an orange blossom-like flower.

Right: The fruit at maturity

Early to mid-June: *Rhododendron arborescens* (syn. *Azalea arborescens*)

Late June: Chinese woodbine (*Lonicera tragophylla*)

September: Fragrant olive (*Elaeagnus pungens* 'Fruitlandii'), espaliered on the east-facing wall

During the growing season, pots and tubs of seasonal plants are sometimes clustered on either side of the opening for the front path in the courtyard. Our head gardener, Paul Skibinski,[3.3] keeps the mix of what goes here—and what is visible year-round through the entrance hall's glass wall—in a perpetually dynamic state.

This 40-some-year-old *Elaeagnus pungens* 'Fruitlandii' espalier has small, white gardenia-scented flowers in the fall. A *Rhododendron arborescens* (syn. *Azalea arborescens*) grows between the espalier and the fountain bowl.

The Studio Garden

The Studio Garden, which forms the transition from house to 17 acres of garden, is itself an important room of the house. Here, *Tulipa* 'King's Blood' rises above the chartreuse foliage of *Hosta sieboldii* f. *kabitan.* Behind them is a halo of *Chaenomeles* x *superba* 'Rowallane' with a mixture of shaded azalea blossoms in the distance.

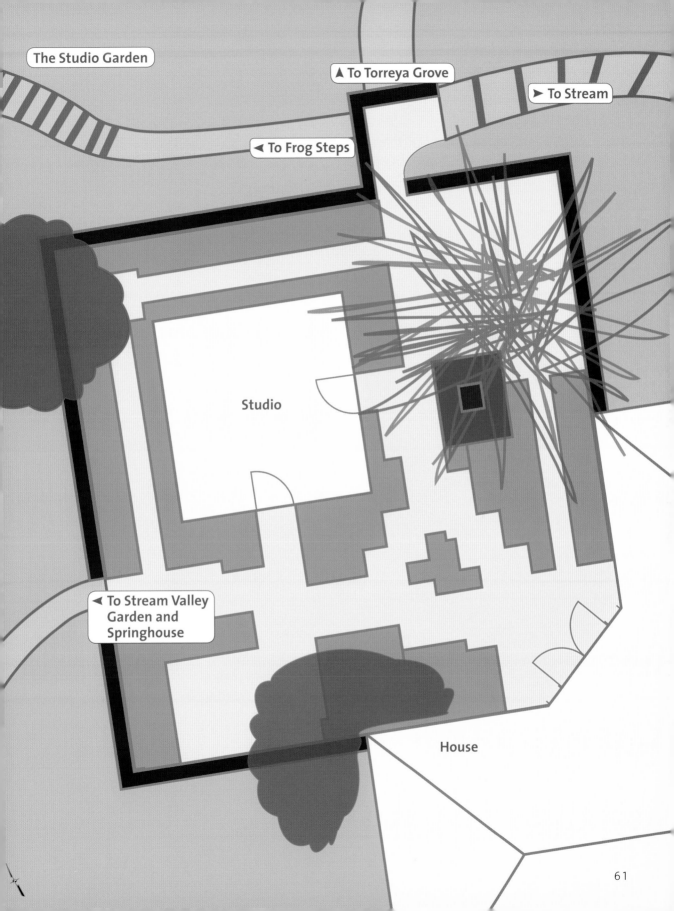

The Studio Garden

▲ To Torreya Grove

► To Stream

◄ To Frog Steps

Studio

◄ To Stream Valley Garden and Springhouse

House

The Studio Garden: A Level Place

The first fully experiential step from our house into the world of the garden, the Studio Garden is indeed one step down from the double hall off the Big Room. This walled outdoor space—enclosing a level 66-foot-square plot—really functions as another room of the house, in addition to providing a pass-through to the studio and (by means of two exits, east and west) to the rest of Ashland Hollow's 17-acre garden.

On the two corners immediately adjacent to the house, the walls are low, sitting-height (16 to 19 inches). These seats command downhill views, westward into the Stream Valley Garden and eastward into the meadows of the Burrows Run valley. The rest of the enclosure consists of retaining walls, which enable the whole northern end of the house-garden-studio complex to hook comfortably into the south-facing hillside (just as the garage wall links the southern end of the complex into the north-facing hillside). Where it passes the studio's side windows, the wall steps up to a height of 34 inches and then rises another 20 inches to meet the higher hillside grade in the north corner.

Because of this agreeable accommodation to different grades, the level plateau of the Studio Garden can feel quite intimate, even though its views into the rising south-facing slope allow for the experience of rich, layered plantings over a much larger area.

An example is the making of the important path to the west that connects our house to the springhouse. We constructed this path, a gift from my maternal grandmother, on the south-facing hillside shortly after the house was finished. Besides positioning the grassy path to capture surface water during heavy rains and slow it down, we designed the path to a minimum width of 6 feet, so that people could easily stroll side by side (a similar path farther uphill comes into its own later in this narrative).[3,4]

A landmark of the Studio Garden in winter is this blue tub covered by a British garden cloche. English and European market gardeners traditionally used such glass bells to protect tender plants from late frosts and to provide extra warmth, which accelerated growth for early sales. We utilize this one to experiment with early-flowering plants and bulbs.

Geometry and Occult Balance

(Bauhaus Influence)

The first stage in creating the Studio Garden, the design and laying of its brick paving, began in 1966. By then I had made two key decisions about the level areas in this garden:

- To use rectilinear geometry instead of free-form curves
- To rely on occult balance, rather than symmetry, for both two- and three-dimensional forms

At the start, we stretched strings as diagrammed below:

- From the back hall door to the studio door
- From the back door to the west garden exit (onto the grass path to the springhouse)
- From the back door to the east exit (onto a landing at the head of a grass path to the Torreya Grove and two sets of steps—one set leading down to the stream valley, and the other, uphill to the Frog sculpture)
- From the studio door to the east exit

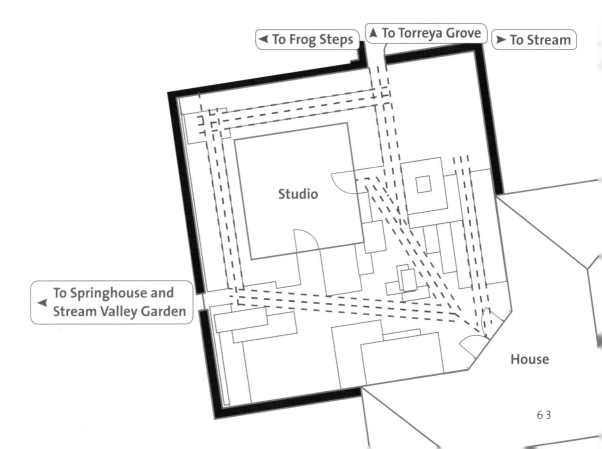

◄ To Frog Steps

▲ To Torreya Grove

► To Stream

Studio

To Springhouse and
Stream Valley Garden ◄

House

These string lines designated areas for foot traffic. In the same fashion, we laid out additional straight paths between the two rear walls of the studio closest to the south-facing hillside and the nearby garden retaining walls.

Figuring that all paths would be at least 41 inches wide, we could now see how much space remained for planting beds and places to sit. We reserved paved seating spaces in three different sizes:

- 6 by 6 feet, behind the studio, for a two-seater bench
- 12 by 18 feet, in the southwest corner of the garden, for a small circular table and three butterfly chairs—to enjoy a view of the island in the Stream Valley Garden
- 24 feet by 24 feet, in the southeast corner, for a large round table and five chairs with meadow views

The path on the northeast side of the studio leads to a copy we had made of a wooden bench in the Winterthur garden.

We settled on grayed red paving brick, laid in a basket-weave pattern, for all of the paving. That color appealed to us because it harmonizes with the sandy tan stucco on the house and studio walls. We liked the pattern because it is nondirectional. For geometric consistency, we decided that the patterns of brickwork throughout the entire garden should be rectangular and parallel to the house and studio (which are parallel to each other), regardless of the directional layouts that various paths might take. Working with the basket-weave brick module let us simply refrain from invading any of the 41-inch-wide surfaces "stringed out" for paths or seating areas. What was left could now become the garden beds.

Above: The medium-sized seating area accommodates a circular slate table and three butterfly chairs.

Opposite: From here, the view into the Stream Valley Garden focuses on a moss-covered island.

Left: Moss that volunteered to grow on a ceramic piece has become a permanent resident of the table.

The Third Dimension

The next stage of design work concentrated on the vertical aspects of the Studio Garden. Before describing this phase, however, I must explain that the inspiration for it almost certainly came from Arne Jacobsen's own garden in Klampenborg, Denmark. Susan and Geoffrey Jellicoe had discussed and illustrated that landscape in their book *Modern Private Gardens*, which came out in 1968, two years after we started planning our Studio Garden and 18 years before I saw Jacobsen's design in the flesh. But I must have seen a photograph of his garden somewhere by 1966, because I already had a vivid image of it in my mind at that time.

The Dane's work, like that of many other garden designers in his country, Northern Germany, and the Netherlands, was an offshoot of Bauhaus design. This interpretation insisted that the ground plan, walls, and hedges all embody geometry and occult balance, though the rigid patterns were to be blurred by dense, apparently casual planting similar to that of a traditional market

The personal garden of the Danish landscape architect Arne Jacobsen

gardener's plot or an English cottage dooryard. Vita Sackville-West has well described her sophisticated version of this type of planting as: "Profusion, even extravagance and exuberance, within the confines of the utmost linear severity."

One can best understand the concept of occult balance by contrasting it to the classically balanced plans of Italian Renaissance gardens and later French and English versions of similar classical designs. Their geometric layouts are bilaterally symmetrical, with beds, plantings, and ornaments duplicated in matching mirror-image formation on either side of a straight axial path.

Occult balance, however, achieves equilibrium in the ground plan and three-dimensional features *without* exact duplication. The viewer's eye is satisfied nonetheless by evenly weighted pairings of different elements—a lawn, for example, offset by an equal weight of planting beds or paving. Similarly, although three-dimensional objects on opposite sides of a given area may not be identical in number or form, they counterbalance each other in visual mass or aesthetic heft.[3.5]

For a simple demonstration of occult balance, place an odd number (five works well) of various small objects on a tabletop and ask several people to take turns moving these things into an eye-pleasing arrangement. Tell them, however, that nobody is allowed to duplicate anyone else's move. The more turns the participants take, the likelier they are to compose a grouping that everyone likes.

Inside our Studio Garden we have three hedges, none higher than the stone-topped sitting walls and each composed of a different kind of plant:

- Japanese red maple (*Acer palmatum* 'West Grove'), 27 inches high
- The Sheridan hybrid boxwood *Buxus* 'Green Gem' (ideal for small hedges because this shrub naturally grows broader than it is tall), 17 inches high
- The dwarf form of English yew *Taxus baccata* 'Fowle', 15 inches high

A low hedge of red-leaf Japanese maple (*Acer palmatum* 'West Grove') backs up a sculpture by Henry Loustau.

The hedges divide the garden into separate spaces (especially where they help to designate the sitting areas) without totally blocking views of the rest of the garden.

Living geometry also appears at the corner of the studio, in the form of a single sheared ball of 'Green Gem' boxwood. This same shape recurs in a bronze sculpture by Henry Loustau, this garden's man-made center of interest: a globe, 12 inches in diameter, topped by a 6-inch-high "house" within a tiny fence. The base for this composition—a 15-inch-square marble slab edged by a 1-inch metal rim projecting upward to form a tray— rests on a 27-inch-tall cylindrical post set in a rectangular bed of dark green *Vinca minor* 'Aurea'.

Like much of Loustau's work, this sculpture presents a surprising twist. When poked ever so slightly with a finger, the sphere rolls helter-skelter on its tray, never tipping over far enough for the house to touch the edge, never falling off the tray. This, of course, sends a timeless message: the globe we all inhabit, including our own little worlds of domesticity, is less secure than we might like.[3.6]

Plants on Walls

The sandy tan walls of our house and studio make ideal spots for vines and espaliers:

Hedera helix 'Buttercup'

- Plantings of *Hedera helix* 'Buttercup' climb the retaining walls behind the studio at two locations. This ivy's new growth, a vibrant chartreuse, turns dark green with age.
- A horizontal, five-branched cordon espalier of *Viburnum macrocephalum* forma *macrocephalum*, which flowers in late April to early May, occupies one wall of the house.

- *Clematis* 'Betty Corning' (Viticella Group), with its silvery violet bells in late May, is at home on the other wall of our house.
- A very fine winter-blooming witch hazel (*Hamamelis* x *intermedia* 'Pallida') turns out to be happy at the corner of the studio nearest the door from the house, because of the warmth it receives there from the winter sun. The witch hazel wraps itself around the corner from west to east, providing a long display of light, bright yellow blossoms (which open on warmer days and close on chillier ones). Some years this show starts in January and continues through March.

Top left: *Viburnum macrocephalum* forma *macrocephalum* grows as a five-cordon espalier against a northwest-facing wall.

Above: The Asiatic witch-hazel hybrid *Hamamelis* x *intermedia* 'Pallida', as it looked two years after planting

Left: We have continued to train that witch hazel as an informal espalier around the corner of the studio.

- The climbing "blue" rose, *Rosa* 'Veilchenblau', wraps itself around the back (north) corner of the studio and runs along the top of the northeast-facing window. This rose bears its blossoms in clusters very much like one of its parents, *R. multiflora*. Remarkably, when 'Veilchenblau' has a northern exposure like this,[3-7] its flowers open pink, although they eventually turn blue within 24 hours. Of course, in horticultural parlance, "blue" often signifies purple or violet with just a tinge of true blue, as is the case here.

- *Vitis vinifera* 'Purpurea', a grape with small, light maroon leaves that yields little bunches of "baby" fruits, grows up one side of the west-facing studio window and across an aluminum wire trellis above it. In the fall, a nearly white "bloom" creeps over the foliage, turning the leaves a softer pastel and giving the whole vine an extraordinarily attractive shimmer.

- A modern form of the old-fashioned rose of Sharon, *Hibiscus syriacus* 'Blue Bird', has been trained into a single 44-inch stem on the southwest corner of the studio. We have allowed the stem to branch in a number of directions, and we have trained a few of these branches to round the corner to the northwest. Seen from the back hall door, this vegetation creates an informal "fuzz" (roughly three feet wide and four feet high) that softens the sharp line of the stuccoed corner. This gentle intervention contributes to the intimacy of the Studio Garden while still allowing glimpses through to the hillside of plumbago and butterfly bushes beyond. Blue blossoms (with sexual parts a pristine white) cover the rose of Sharon throughout most of the late spring, summer, and early fall.

Top: We fastened the climber *Rosa* 'Veilchenblau' to the studio's north wall.

Middle: Supported by an aluminum trellis, the ornamental red-leaf grape (*Vitis vinifera* 'Purpurea') climbs the north side of the other large window and crosses its top. The leaves and fruit are quite diminutive.

Above: Our *Hibiscus syriacus* 'Blue bird' grows on one tall stem. Branches spreading around the studio's southwest corner make a desirable puff of blue, which keeps wandering eyes in the garden.

- An informal evergreen espalier of *Elaeagnus pungens* 'Maculata' grows against the high south-facing retaining wall behind the studio. The shiny, dark olive green leaves are variegated with a brighter green and splashes of gold. Typical small, white, gardenia-scented *E. pungens* blossoms emerge in September.

Below: *Elaeagnus pungens* 'Maculata' makes a stunning informal espalier.

Left: The woody plant's gold, olive green, and bright green leaf variegation

Shrubs

Two shrubs of considerable importance distinguish the Studio Garden:

- *Chaenomeles* x *superba* 'Rowallane' grows in a bed of chartreuse-leaved *Hosta sieboldii* f. *Kabitan* at the southwest corner and hangs over the adjacent sitting wall. Its carmine bloom in mid-April coincides with the flowering of the unexcelled white trumpet *Narcissus* 'Beersheba'.
- Relatively compact *Adina rubella* has attractive small, shiny, pointed leaves and, in late August and early September, white Telstar-shaped blossoms. Because its wood is not hardy here, we cut it to the ground each spring. It rebounds to a height and spread of approximately four feet by bloom time.

A flowering quince (*Chaenomeles* x *superba* 'Rowallane') has been trained over a portion of the sitting wall. It blooms with *Narcissus* and tulips.

Trees

In addition to the 'Red Jade' crab apple just outside the garden, two trees live within the garden itself.

• The native American fringe tree (*Chionanthus virginicus*), has always been a favorite of ours. Its fragrant white flowers (which usually appear just as the tulips are going off and the *Allium* 'Purple Sensation' and *Iris germanica* are nearing their peak) have such an entrancing configuration that a fringe tree needs to be seen in an intimate area like this for full enjoyment. Each threadlike blossom roughly resembles the branching of a deer antler (held upside down). You have to examine it up close to appreciate it. We planted our specimen amid the paving of the smaller sitting area where it enhances the sense of structure by forming a partial roof.

Right: One of our favorites, American fringe tree (*Chionanthus virginicus*) casts a limited amount of shade and produces exceptionally beautiful white blossoms in May.

Above: Structurally, the flowers are reminiscent of deer antlers.

- Much larger than dainty, deciduous *Chionanthus virginicus*, the blue Atlas Mountains cedar (*Cedrus atlantica* 'Glauca') is a handsome needle evergreen. We have trained ours into tree form, to shade the Studio Garden's larger sitting area. This cedar also serves another purpose in the greater landscape: rising between the house and studio roofs, and taller than either one, it is visible from other points at Ashland Hollow as a marker for the Studio Garden. The tree's blue gray needles and the roofs' warm gray tile shingles sing a pretty tune together.

Appropriately, the largest tree growing in the Studio Garden—the conifer *Cedrus atlantica* 'Glauca'—shades this garden's largest gathering area.

Heavy Maintenance

The plantings around the studio require higher maintenance than any other part of our entire garden at Ashland Hollow.

- The espaliers, climbers, hedges and topiaries demand special pruning at various times of year. In addition to the woody plants here, we have a wide range of herbaceous plants, including perennials, bulbs, and tender annuals and tropicals.
- We deal with time-consuming seasonal changes:

   Each fall, the planting of bulbs competes with leaf cleanup, cutbacks, and mulching.

   In spring, after tulip and *Muscari* blooms have finished, we take on bulb removal, soil preparation, and planting the array of tender ornamentals.

- The numerous pots and tubs we use in this garden are moved in and out periodically, from tulip time until frost.
- Weekly deadheading, weeding, and other tasks glue everything together.

Mondrian, Rietveld, and Tulips

Our spring display of tulips, grape hyacinths (*Muscari armeniacum*), and pansies is substantial. And from the very beginning, the layout of the tulip plantings has been distinct from the rest of the garden in its two-dimensional patterning and color design. I have superimposed a series of geometric forms—rectangles and circles of varying sizes—within the garden's bed layout. Most of these shapes are freestanding, but a few rectangles bite into circles and, in one case, two rectangles intersect at right angles. Each form is solidly planted with orderly rows of closely spaced bulbs, and each contains flowers of a single color, different from that in any adjoining geometric form. It is as if the tulips' highly saturated colors paint these geometric forms within the square canvas of the Studio Garden. The colors (as listed by the tulip breeders) include:

Soft Yellow	Yellow Orange
Lemon Yellow	Tangerine
Golden Yellow	Orange Red
Peach	Poppy Red
Lavender	Burgundy
Deep Garnet	Dark Maroon Red

These are surrounded by drifts of light blue and dark blue pansies and rich blue grape hyacinths (*Muscari armeniacum*).

A few years before this bulb planting became a possibility, I had fallen in love with the work of painter Piet Mondrian (1872-1944) and architect-designer Gerrit Rietveld (1888-1964), which I had probably seen during an early visit to the Museum of Modern Art in New York City. I am sure that these Dutch modernists' geometric compositions inspired me to celebrate high spring with this floral layout, even though I used colors much warmer than theirs.

The beds' geometric patterns draw upon a brilliant palette of bulbs. Above: Orange *Tulipa* 'Day Dream', yellow *T.* 'West Point'

Below: Black *T.* 'Queen of the Night', blue *Muscari armeniacum*, orange *T.* 'Lightning Sun', orange red *T.* 'Day Dream', yellow *T.* 'West Point'

Below: Blue *M. armeniacum*; orange *T.* 'Lightning Sun'; orange red *T.* 'Day Dream'; yellow *T.* 'West Point'

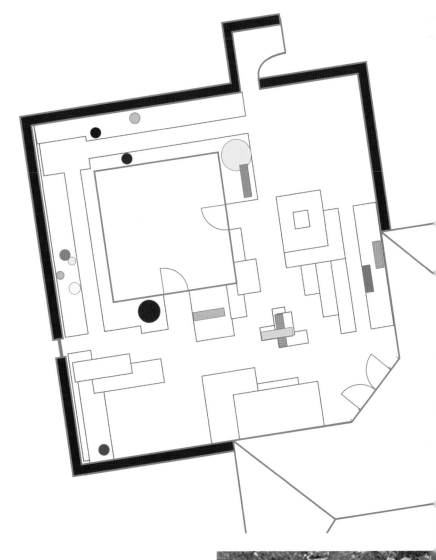

Above: Orange *T.* 'Lightning Sun' (planted with yellow *T.* 'Sancerre', not shown)

Below: Lively pink *T.* 'Temple of Beauty'; lavender *T.* 'Cum Laude'

Above: *T. linifolia* with dwarf *Iris* 'Grapesicle' in the Studio Garden's "window bed," six inches higher than the windowsills. We feature diminutive flowering plants here.

Left: *Muscari azureum* 'Album' and *T. kolpakowskiana*

Expanding Color Palette

The design of our first herbaceous plantings in the Studio Garden beds posed a major challenge. I had never before faced such an opportunity to combine broad brushstrokes of color and intriguing details within a large variety of exposures. My enthusiasm for experimentation, of course, ran high. In April 1977 I became captivated by a color scheme illustrated in that month's issue of *The Garden*, the Royal Horticultural Society journal. What caught my eye was a photograph taken in the British garden designer John Codrington's personal garden. The colors I noticed there—cantaloupe, turquoise blue, and dark purple—seemed like a winning complement to the tan stucco of our house and studio.

Keeping this palette in mind over the years, I have learned how difficult it is to find plants whose flowers provide these exact colors throughout the gardening season. Cantaloupe and turquoise blue are the hardest to come by, but by using flowers that unite components of these tones, I have achieved some delightful effects. From early on I added the requirement that this scheme incorporate a minimal flash of scarlet. The result is just lively enough.

Above: I conducted my early color experiments using a mockup of the studio and garden walls as a background for watercolor samples of floral hues.

Above: Late spring, early summer-blooming *Oxypetalum caeruleum* fills the bill for turquoise. Unfortunately, few other flowers do this so well in other seasons.

Left: The small but electric flash of scarlet in this composition came from a sun-loving *Impatiens*.

The color combination in John Codrington's English garden (seen here in a 1997 magazine photograph) became the basic palette for the Studio Garden, carried out with plants more suitable to our climate. Codrington used a hybrid cultivar of mossy saxifrages for its cantaloupe-tone flowers. The blue behind them (closer to turquoise in the original publication) is Spanish squill (*Hyacinthoides hispanica* [syn. *Endymion hispanicus*]), and the burgundy is probably the foliage of a cut-back shrub or tree, perhaps *Prunus cerasifera* 'Pissardii', a flowering plum.

Another important conclusion I have reached here has to do with choosing the right "mixers" for intense colors. Many books recommend dabs of white. This is a snare and a delusion! When using saturated hues such as those that appeal to me, I find that white only punches holes in the composition and does no blending at all. I far prefer light blue and chartreuse, which is readily available in the foliage of various plants.

It would take another book to describe all of the plants involved in the Studio Garden (See Appendix 1). Suffice it to say that our attention constantly focuses on scale, texture, and form, *as well as* color. For harmony, the size of flowers and foliage must be proportional to the size of the garden, which in the case of our studio plot, is relatively small.

Over the years this garden has become more shaded, due to the growth of surrounding trees. This means that each year more shade-tolerant plants enter our palette, and spots that still receive sun become more precious. Nearness to the house means that, in warm weather, this garden gets daily use; its intimacy and evolving color refinement make it forever magical.

Above: A rich cacophony of colors surrounds the white late-summer blossoms of *Allium tuberosum*. Up front, *Impatiens auricoma* 'Jungle Gold' is backed by coleus (*Solenostemon scutellarioides* 'Sedona') and *Hamelia patens*. Beyond the path, New Guinea *Impatiens* 'Tango' spreads beneath a tree-form hibiscus with peach-colored blossoms.

Two plants have proved to be especially useful at filling in the mauve and lavender bands of the spectrum: *Lathyrus vernus*, above, a member of the Pea family whose bicolor flowers appear at early tulip time; and *Tricyrtis* 'Sinonome', left, which for a long period in the fall bears flowers reminiscent of certain species orchids.

The continuing challenge for improvement has led to discoveries. I have come to realize, for example, that small amounts of vibrant deep mauve and carmine create a lively mixture with chartreuse. "Almost black" burgundy and maroon add depth to the picture. And touches of orange tinged with true pink bring a richness to the warmer shades of cantaloupe, peach, and orange.

This chronological color chart shows how the Studio Garden scheme developed over time (sequentially from top to bottom). The broad, unlabeled swaths of sandy tan represent the color of the house and studio's stucco walls.

COLOR Palette   Studio Garden

ORIGINAL color Palette:

cantaloupe

turquoise blue

dark purple

MiXers, added

chartreuse

caerulean blue

accent

Cadmium Red-light

EXTENDED palette

MauVE shades

Romney rose

Planting on the South-facing Hillside around the Studio Garden

Plantings on the downhill side of the Springhouse Path include the white-flowered shrub *Fothergilla gardenii*, **A1** (on plan, opposite), which is essential to the early-May color composition of the Studio Garden. On the uphill side stand two untrimmed aged *Taxus cuspidata* 'Nana', **A2**. The black-green foliage borne on their widely spaced, slightly ascending branches is very handsome in winter. Repeating their color and textures in ground-hugging form, a single horizontal *Taxus*, **A3**, sprawls on the downhill side of the path immediately next to a studio sitting wall. A friend and I found this Weston Nursery selection[3.8] growing in Arnold Arboretum ground-cover trials at the Case Estates in 1985.[3.9]

Left: White *Fothergilla gardenii* and, at right, dark green dwarf Japanese yew (*Taxus cuspidata* 'Nana') help to compose an attractive picture to the west of the studio.

Above: A closer look at the strong character of *T. cuspidata* 'Nana' and, just below it, the even lower spreading habit of Weston Nurseries' horizontal *T. cuspidata* selection

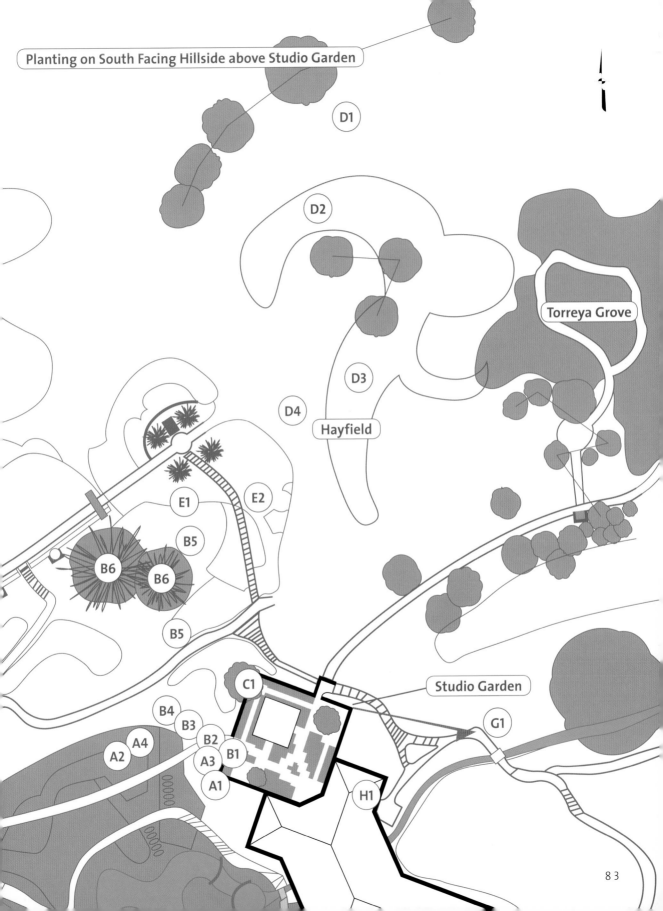

Planting on South Facing Hillside above Studio Garden

D1

D2

Torreya Grove

D3

D4

Hayfield

E1

E2

B5

B6

B6

B6

B5

C1

Studio Garden

B4

B3

G1

A4

B2

A2

A3

B1

A1

H1

For many years *Ribes odoratum*, **A4**, an old-time farmhouse dooryard plant with a superb fragrance reminiscent of clove, has thrived among the branches of this *T. cuspidata* 'Nana'. Native from South Dakota and Minnesota to Texas and Arkansas, *R. odoratum* has sharp-yellow tubular blossoms with reddish flecks at their bases. These appear in pendulous clusters of five to ten flowers, overlapping the bloom time of the white *Fothergilla*.

The west-facing studio window looks out onto the near hillside, which is covered by a low sweep of dark green broadleaf foliage (*Euphorbia amygdaloides* var. *robbiae*), **B1**. Above that area, another swath of ground cover, plumbago (*Ceratostigma plumbaginoides*), **B2**, provides rich cobalt blue blossoms from late August into October.

Interrupting both ground covers in five locations, from mid to late May, are the spiky foliage clumps and elegant long-stemmed, salmon-to-cantaloupe blossoms of *Iris* 'Happy Birthday' (Tall Bearded Group), **B3**. One more clump hops the wall into the Studio Garden.

All summer long, the ground covers complement the display of butterflies on three *Buddleja davidii* cultivars, **B4**: 'Black Knight' (deep purple), 'Opera' (electric mauve), and 'Princeton Purple' (lively bright purple). Another *B. davidii* cultivar, 'Potter's Purple', recurs inside the Studio Garden.

The vista uphill from these plantings includes a small bit of our tree-wisteria planting, as well as two mature golden larches (*Psuedolarix amabilis* [syn. *P. kaempferi*]), **B6**, with an elderly horizontally spreading *Euonymus alatus* 'Montrosus', **B5**, in the immediate foreground. This plant is enjoyable enough in the fall for its rich range of foliage colors—scarlet and shades

Top: Clove currant (*Ribes odoratum*)

Middle: *Iris* 'Happy Birthday' (Tall Bearded Group)

Bottom: *Buddleja davidii* 'Opera'

of pink—but even more so for the extra-large "wings" on its branches. When *E. alatus* 'Monstrosus' is leafless, the display of accumulated snow is extremely dramatic.

A weeping crab apple (*Malus* 'Red Jade'), **C1**, which bears shiny red pendant fruits in the fall, overhangs the northern corner of the retaining wall from the hillside behind the studio.

Top left: The red fall foliage of *Euonymus alatus* 'Monstrosus' in front of golden larch (*Pseudolarix amabilis*)

Top right: *E. alatus* 'Monstrosus' after leaf fall

Left: The weeping crab apple *Malus* 'Red Jade' covered with spring bloom

Above: The same tree's red-jadelike autumn fruit

To the right of the crab apple, a view extends northward over part of the original hayfield. This changes appearance after each of its three annual mowings. A concave curve of maroon-foliaged English beech (*Fagus sylvatica* 'Riversii'), **D1**, stops one's eye at the top of the hill. In front of the beeches, and about two-thirds of the distance to the studio, stands a charming grove of three *Aesculus pavia* (syn. *A. splendens*), **D2**. This small horse chestnut was seedling selected[3.10] for its deep coral red flowers, which our specimens have produced abundantly every May since an early age. The beeches' deep maroon helps to play up this color.

In April, a large, fingerlike planting of *Narcissus* occupies a significant portion of this field. The cultivars are yellow 'Carlton', **D3**, on the lower ground, and predominately white 'Mrs. Ernst H. Krelage', **D4**, higher up. This planting looks more extensive than it is because the warmth of the yellow optically advances toward the viewer, while the cooler white seems to recede. At the same time, association with the horse chestnuts visually "fastens" the massed *Narcissus* to the hillside's slope.

Left: An arc of burgundy-foliaged English beech (*Fagus sylvatica* 'Riversii') delineates the top of the hayfield (in May), behind three horse chestnuts (*Aesculus pavia*) selected for their contrasting red blooms.

Above: The horse chestnuts' flowers

Below: Our hayfield above the Studio Garden to the north helps to glue together much of this planting of trees and shrubs. The first of the season's three mowings has just been completed.

In April, naturalized *Narcissus* colors the same meadow. The yellow is *N.* 'Carlton'; the white is *N.* 'Mrs. E. H. Krelage'.

The aforementioned view is framed by plantings adjacent to the Frog Steps on the left-hand side of the hayfield. When the steps are seen from the Studio Garden, the following evergreens play especially important roles:

> A horizontally branching straight *Euonymus alatus*, E5
> Four bright green, narrowly vertical thujas (*Thuja occidentalis* 'Hetz Wintergreen'), E1
> A weeping hemlock (*Tsuga canadensis* 'Pendula'), E2
> A dense, predominantly horizontal bird's-nest spruce (*Picea abies* 'Nidiformis'), E3

The four thuja spires signal a hidden destination at the top of the steps. The other evergreens' distinctive profiles are particularly important to this view in wintertime, when deciduous trees and shrubs have shed their leaves, and herbaceous plants have disappeared. Then, these horizontal and weeping forms draw the eye slowly and seductively uphill, through a series of experiences.

Components of the picture to the left of the hayfield include Sargent's weeping hemlock (*Tsuga canadensis* 'Pendula'), left, and bird's-nest spruce (*Picea abies* 'Nidiformis'), below.

87

The Torreya Grove stands to the right of the hayfield.

A mature black walnut tree (*Juglans nigra*) and original woodland on the north-facing hillside frame the view, G1, that descends from the Torreya Grove to the Burrows Run meadow.

A planting, H1, set against the same background but nearer to the house includes a handsome *Viburnum carlesii*, my favorite of all fragrant viburnums. It is large enough to contribute to the Studio Garden's April splendor.

Besides enhancing the character of various seasons within the Studio Garden, these outlying eye-catchers invite to visitors to explore other parts of Ashland Hollow.

Left: To the right of the hayfield and the Torreya Grove, the view from the Studio Garden to the Burrows Run meadow is framed by a native black walnut tree (*Juglans nigra*).

Below: The flowers on this *Viburnum carlesii*, immediately downhill and east of the Studio Garden, perfume the spring air.

3.1. The charm of this simplicity is all the more striking because it contrasts with the lively experience the visitor has had coming in the drive. For more about that approach route, see Chapter 15.

3.2. By this time, Conrad Hammerman had earned his degree in landscape architecture from Cornell, had settled in Philadelphia, and was starting his practice. We ended up asking for his help with, among other things, two areas of the garden where hardscape design and construction would be necessary.

3.3. For more about Paul Skibinski, see Chapters 13 and 14.

3.4. See Chapter 9.

3.5 Some friends and I had exactly this experience on a visit to Innisfree, the garden of Walter and Marion Beck near Millbrook, New York (by then, both of the Becks had died). This is a "Chinese Cup Garden," which Walter Beck had laid out. We were received by his friend and consulting landscape architect, Lester Collins. Mr. Beck, he told us, had felt that the principle of occult balance was essential to an understanding of his garden, as well as to its continuing maintenance. Many evenings after dinner, he would use the tabletop exercise I describe here to "educate" his wife and Collins. The landscape architect did the same with us while we waited out a thunderstorm inside the Becks' former home. (Their garden was subsequently, and unfortunately, much diminished when the house—the viewpoint from which most of the garden had been designed to be seen—was torn down to save money on upkeep.) This principle is, of course, integral to modern art. The sculpture and gardens of Isamu Noguchi are especially good examples.

3.6. A 46-inch-tall clipped topiary spiral, created from a conical form of *Taxus cuspidate* 'Capitata', initially occupied this space. Increasing shade in the area, however, stunted the shrub's growth on one side of the shrub to such an extent that, with regret, we had to remove it.

3.7. As is the case at Sissinghurst where I first saw this rose.

3.8. We seldom trim this plant, except to limit its spread. It rarely exceeds a height of 30 inches. As new growth emerges from the top center, it weighs down the longer existing branches.

3.9. These arboretum trials have since been discontinued.

3.10. A selection by Princeton Nurseries. The type is native from southern Illinois and Missouri to Texas and eastern North Carolina.

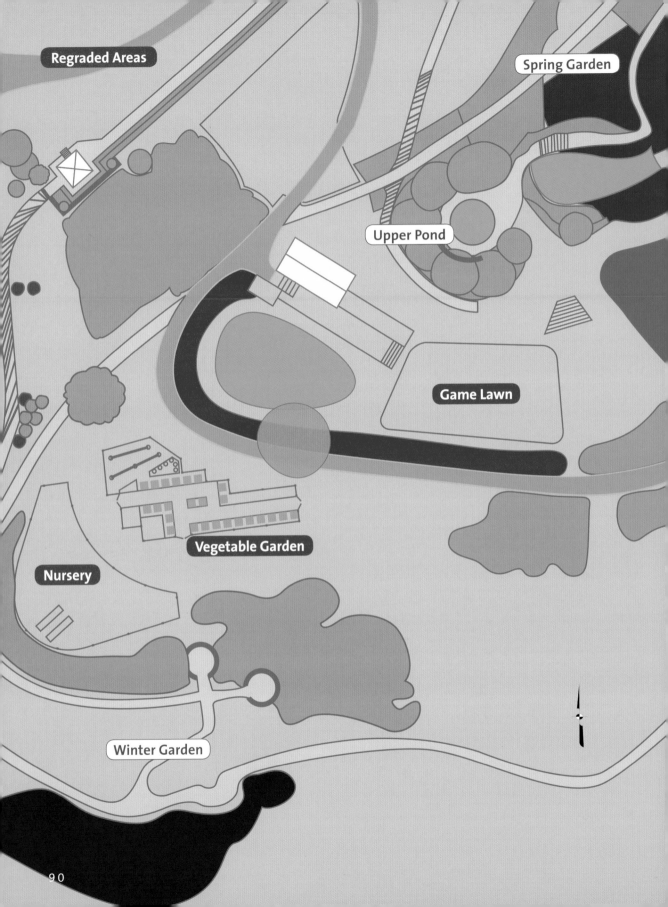

Regraded Areas

Spring Garden

Upper Pond

Game Lawn

Vegetable Garden

Nursery

Winter Garden

4 Grading, Construction, and First Tree Planting

Game Lawn, Nursery, and Vegetable Garden

First Tree Planting

Stream Valley Garden Construction

Game Lawn, Nursery, and Vegetable Garden

In addition to paving and partially planting the Entrance Garden and Studio Garden in 1966, our first full year in the new house, we carried out two other important projects:

- Regrading three areas
- Planting a few very important trees

The main obstacle to starting a garden amid the beautiful landforms here was the lack of any level ground. With the help of our friend Dick Vogel,[4.1] who did sensitive cut–and–fill drawings for this work, we made a Game Lawn (approximately 66 by 144 feet), an area for a small nursery, and another for our Vegetable Garden. After we had completed necessary soil preparation and seeding, Nancy started on the Vegetable Garden, and the nursery was ready to begin its role as a temporary home for various ornamental plants. Over the years, the Vegetable Garden has tremendously enhanced our menus with both fresh and frozen produce. Eating summer-picked succotash in midwinter is a sheer delight! (See Chapter 12.)

We use the nursery to test new plants that become available from commercial sources, botanical explorers, or breeders. It is also a safety valve for potential strains on the garden's design. Well-meaning visitors bring gift plants, and like any plant enthusiast, I am occasionally guilty of impulse purchases. Acquisitions in both categories also go into the nursery, to be observed and eye-tested for possible garden use. If a plant doesn't pass muster, we give it to friends who have a use for it or we donate it to a fund-raiser auction (see pages 391-393).

The Game Lawn, looking toward the
springhouse and swimming pool

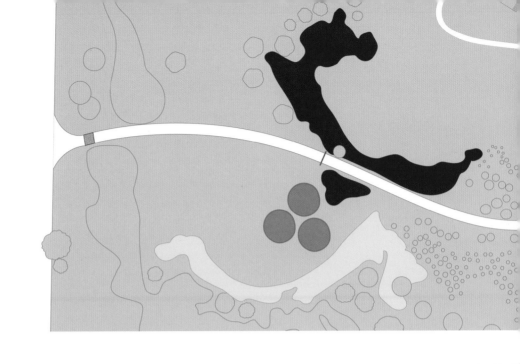

First Tree Planting

Nancy and I felt a sense of urgency about planting certain trees. For example, we knew that white oak (*Quercus alba*) takes more time to mature than most trees do—and we had the perfect knoll on the west side of the drive to plant a grove of these oaks, leaving their lower branches intact. This meant that we could pass them daily and watch them mature into giants with flaring trunks and long, nearly horizontal branches rising above. Forty-seven years later, the drama is in full swing.

From the long-range plan in my mind, I knew the point at which a projected path at the east end of the upper swale would meet future steps up the south-facing hillside from the Studio Garden. The urge to mark this juncture (later the site of the Frog sculpture too) with four vertical evergreens was strong. I had admired the planting of incense cedars (*Calocedrus decurrens*) along Conservatory Road at Longwood Gardens for many years, and we had several specimens in our inventory at Millcreek Nursery. Because these cedars are also slow-growing, early planting seemed imperative. We placed four of the evergreens at the chosen location, hoping that we would be here long enough to see them reach their handsome maturity.

Opposite
Top: The plan shows the relationship between the three white oaks (*Quercus alba*), the driveway, the dark green grove of American hollies (*Ilex opaca*), and the yellow of the *Forsythia* planting.

Bottom: A current view of the white oaks, which were planted in 1966 on a high knoll along the driveway

The last, but not least, of the 1966 plantings were 13 wisteria (cultivars of *Wisteria floribunda*). These had been started, probably four years earlier, as almost untrained vines purchased from the famous Clark Nursery in San Jose, California (the nursery had only roughly trained the plants on single stakes). If they were to be part of our garden, they needed to move immediately to their final home on the Wisteria Lawn (on the south-facing hillside) and commence more refined training on metal supports (diagram opposite; for training details, see pages 353-355).

The quantities and colors of selected cultivars were:
- Five *Wisteria floribunda* 'Shiro-noda' (syn. 'Alba'), white
- Three *W. floribunda* 'Honbeni' (syn. 'Rosea'), pink
- Five *W. floribunda* 'Royal Purple', purple

The motivation for this project came from a group of Japanese wisteria trained as small trees by an avid gardener of our grandparents' generation in Wilmington, Mrs. William K. du Pont. The extraordinary result accomplished by her method was that the blossoms hung below three sets of branches, clear of any foliage that might obstruct a view of the flowers. I had admired this effect in Mrs. du Pont's garden where the venerable wisteria trees—some with hollow trunks—were still putting on a spectacular show every year. We were anxious to start training ours.

Diagram of galvanized-pipe armatures for
training the first 13 wisterias planted in the
garden. As they grow up these supports,
the vines take on the form of small trees.

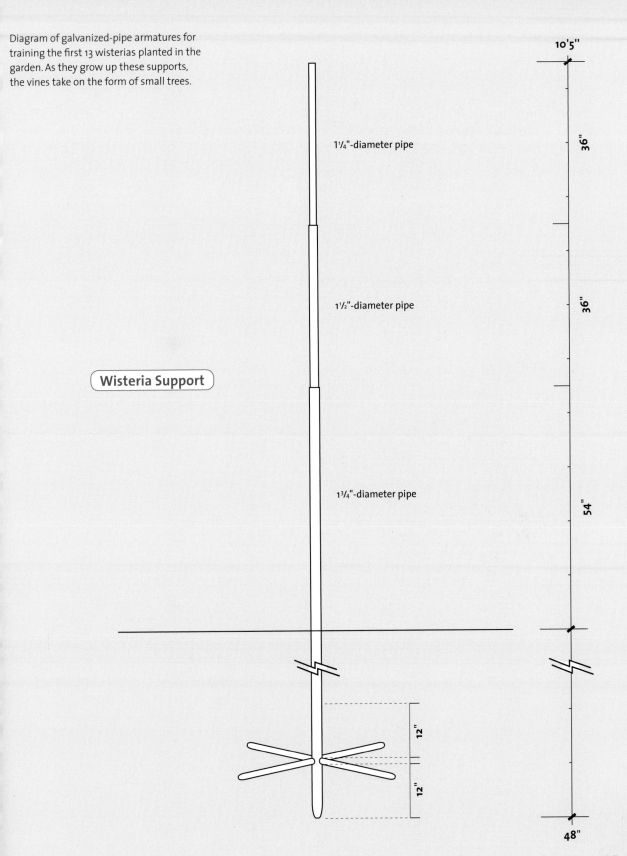

10'5"

1¼"-diameter pipe

36"

1½"-diameter pipe

36"

Wisteria Support

1¾"-diameter pipe

54"

12"

12"

48"

Stream Valley Garden Construction

Our largest project in 1966 was the construction of dams and ponds upstream (west) of the house. An existing grove of handsome native red cedars (*Juniperus virginiana*), a short distance downstream from the springhouse, gave us a natural starting point for the water garden. The ending would, of course, be the house itself—the bridge across the stream.

In between, we were blessed with beautiful trees: semimature tulip poplars (*Liriodendron tulipifera*), American beech (*Fagus grandifolia*), swamp maple (*Acer rubrum*), and red oak (*Quercus rubra*). But this whole stretch from springhouse to house could be merely glimpsed as patches of water shining here and there, not viewed as a continuous stream. Even less showed in the summer, when vegetation clothed the ground. This presented an exciting opportunity to not only reveal the partially hidden waterway, but also enlarge its apparent extent by making a series of wide ponds.

This project became known as the Stream Valley Garden. We asked Conrad Hammerman to prepare a design. As a student of Roberto Burle Marx and the Cornell architecture school, Conrad had ideal qualifications for the job. We all saw how exactly the organic forms of Roberto's early work suited the land forms of this valley and satisfied our desire to retain, as much as possible, the feeling of Delaware's 19th-century agricultural landscape.

Saving the large trees was a top priority. To that end, we strove to keep heavy equipment away from tree trunks and roots, and we shot grades at the base of each tree and at the extant stream-water level nearest to it. Conrad then made sure that the water contained by any new adjacent pond did not exceed that level. Over all, this meant that we created ponds by removing, or

Top: A view from the west balcony of the house upstream toward the springhouse, prior to construction of the five ponds

Above: Four tulip poplars (*Liriodendron tulipifera*) upstream, after pond construction. The smallest tree replaced a large one killed by vibration from heavy equipment running over its roots.

Pages 98-99: Ancient *Wisteria* trained as a tree, one of four or five in the former garden of Mrs. William K. duPont, inspired our own similar planting.

House

Layout for ponds and dams in the Stream Valley Garden. This brilliant design was by our friend Conrad Hammerman.

"cutting," soil rather than by the conventional process of cutting and filling.

We lost only one tree, a tulip poplar, as a construction casualty, and that was because heavy equipment damaged small roots by repeatedly running over them.

Fortunately, we cut the ponds into clay of such good quality that no lining was necessary.

Conrad's brilliant design comprises one large pond with an island at the center (the Stream Valley Garden's main feature), two smaller ponds above it, and another two below it. Both the uppermost and lowest ponds (the latter just upstream of our Big Room's west balcony) form perfect circles. The other three bodies of water have organic forms dictated by the site.

The carefully studied shapes of these three ponds and the grading of the surrounding Stream Valley Garden demonstrate that the design impact of refined organic forms is every bit as great as that of more traditional geometry—a strength that had already been confirmed for us on recent visits to Burle Marx and Church landscapes.

In both concept and detail, the design was a thing of great beauty. It was also pragmatic. None of the ponds went any deeper than two-and-a-half feet, at that time the shoulder height of our youngest child, Rebecca. If she happened to fall in, she could always touch bottom.

Conrad presented his plan both on paper and in the form of a Plasticine model, which proposed a cluster of water jets of varying height in the uppermost, circular pond (within the red-cedar grove) We decided against this feature because it seemed too much of a stretch from the agricultural landscape we hoped to honor. However, we enthusiastically accepted the rest of his scheme, including suggestions that:

- The garden should terminate in a grove of vertical evergreens.
- A grouping of attractive, very large vertical rocks should be built into the face of the upper, double-spillway retaining wall.

This same area posed interesting engineering problems, which Dudley Willis, a registered civil engineer worked with Conrad to solve. Now, thanks to their ingenuity, all of the springs in that part of the property either flow naturally into the upper-most pond—which we call the Upper Pond—or are captured and piped there.

In order to conduct water from the Upper Pond to the big retaining wall, where it would divide into major and minor streams feeding two separate spillways, Dudley ran a horizontal pipe in from the center of the Upper Pond. (A large-diameter circular well screen, secured by a reinforced concrete frame, prevents organic matter from clogging the pipe.) This pipe runs on true level to a reinforced concrete box on the back of the fieldstone double-spillway wall. After water fills the box, it runs over the major spillway at the top. Meanwhile, lower down and to the north, five narrow horizontal pipes set side by side carry a smaller runoff from the box through the wall to flow over the minor spillway's stone shelf. (The major spillway, of course, sets the water level for the Upper Pond.)

Unlike the three pond dams below it, which hold water back, the double-spillway wall does not function as a true dam. It is, however, a crucial retaining wall, supporting a massive seven-foot grade change. Where the wall curves to the south, considerably beyond the falling water, blue lacecap hydrangeas trail from "pockets" left in the masonry specifically for that purpose.

The uppermost spillways

Immediately beyond the wall's northern end, 10 steps made from old granite curbstones rise from the stone path in the lower part of the Stream Valley Garden to the Upper Pond. That pond is hidden from the house and lower garden by the steep change of grade and the planting just in back of the spillway wall.

The other grade changes between the double waterfall and the house are much more gradual:

- 3 feet 6 inches
- 1 foot 2 inches
- 1 foot 8 inches

Consequently, the west balcony surveys four ponds and three waterfalls, as well as the double-spillway wall. For a visitor walking through the garden and up the steps, the Upper Pond and its vertical enclosure planting come as an intimate surprise.

From the time we moved in, the springs kept the stream flowing even during very dry spells—until a serious summer drought in 2002 brought it to a halt from early August until late October. We feared that our water table had gone down for good. To our relief, we have not had a similar occurrence since then. Recently, however, I found a note describing trouble with wells in the area two years before we arrived. Maybe this is simply a sometime thing.

The dams were all built of either Avondale Quarry stone or fieldstone or a mix of the two. According to Conrad, the exceptionally skillful masons, Barney and his assistant, Emilio, were both "wonderfully patient about the whole job." The final product looks like it belongs there.

Opposite: In the foreground, water flows over the two lowest spillways, feeding the round pond beneath the west balcony. Upstream, a third spillway to the left of the island overhangs a 3½-foot drop.

Spillway Design

Longitudinal and cross-section drawings (top left and right) and plan (bottom) of Conrad Hammerman's prototype for cut-stone slabs to channel pond overflow. The actual contours and dimensions differ from one spillway to the next.

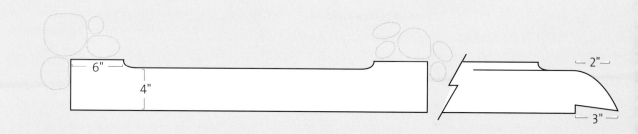

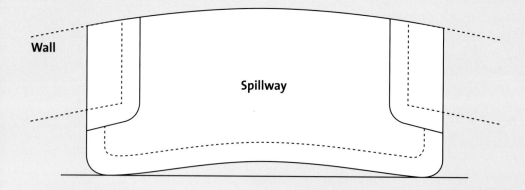

Wall

Spillway

The design of the cut-stone spillways is not only practical but elegant. These monoliths all have small raised shoulders that abut the stone retaining walls or dams, to keep the water flow from "running around the corner." Their sloped fronts, which project slightly farther at the bottoms than at the tops, descend from a gentle roll or curve to a razor edge. Recessed two to three inches from this edge on the underside of the stone, a small semicircular indentation arcs inward to catch any moisture running back from the edge and redirect it forward to the smooth, linear cascade.

These details provide us with beautiful sheets of water that vary in form because no two spillways have identical shapes. Each one follows the curve of its dam or retaining wall, which helps to contour the pond it contains. Thus, the waterfall into the lowest pond is concave, echoing the inward bend of the dam it overflows; the next fall upstream is convex, like the bowed rim of its dam; and in rhythmic progression, the next fall and its barrier are also convex.

At the time of construction we chose sandstone rather than more expensive granite for the spillways. This turned out to be a false economy when, about 20 years later, the soft, porous sandstone began to spall (break off in thin chips). We had to replace all five spillways with granite.

Of course, owning a series of ponds is not unlike owning a wooden boat. In both cases, there are inevitably leaks to be repaired—albeit, with ponds one is trying to keep the water *in*. I believe our annual chores in this regard would be fewer if the stone dams extended another four or five feet farther into the bank on each side. Also, it would have been better to construct the dams with stone-veneered reinforced-concrete cores instead

of with solid stone. It is difficult to make a veneered wall simu-
late load-bearing stone convincingly, but a talented mason can
pull this off. It just takes longer!

The pyramidal island in the center of the big pond was constructed of soil mounded atop a base of large stones under the
water. An enchanting piece of sculpture that vaguely resembles
a young mountain peak, it holds the eye from any viewpoint
(each of its three facets differs slightly in shape from the others).
As soon as the soil was firmly in place, we planted the entire
surface with moss from the woods. Unbeknownst to us, though,
small bits of liverwort (*Marchantia polymorpha*) and *Selaginella
apoda* must have been mixed in with the moss, because a year or
so later we noticed patches of both growing amid the moss. To
our amazement, the three plants assorted themselves according
to whichever compass direction each preferred. Since they are
all low and ground-hugging, we have let them have their way.
A water line runs under the pond bottom from the "mainland"
to the top of the little mountain where it terminates in a small,
inconspicuous oil-burner nozzle. This sprays a fine mist over
the island during droughts, so that it remains green even when
much of the garden around it turns brown.

The island, seen from upstream.

All of the regrading in the Stream Valley Garden presented
us with banks that needed immediate planting, to prevent any
erosion of Conrad's beautiful forms.

Our overall planting plan for this garden called for simplicity
and serenity—shades and textures of green. The only exceptions
to this would be flushes of other colors appearing in the first
two weeks of May and, to a lesser extent, in early August.

Vast in scale, the color-saturated display in early May is a cluster of "evergreen" azaleas north, west, and south of the ponds. Early August brightens the palette with a significant grouping of red cardinal flower (*Lobelia cardinalis*) on the northwest bay of the biggest pond.

After considerable debate and study, we decided to put masses of *Hedera helix* 'Baltica' on the banks of the ponds; 14,000 plants went in right after construction. Many other plantings came later, but that initial blanket of ivy tucked everything in as we closed down for the winter in 1966.

This had been a major year for construction. We welcomed the chance to catch our breath, confident that 1967 would be calmer, with just a few planting projects to work on as time allowed.

The ground cover on the steepest banks is Baltic ivy (*Hedera helix* 'Baltica').

4.1. Richard Vogel is a landscape architect
with special expertise in landscape
construction and grading.

As it flows under the house to the east, the
gardenesque stream returns to its original
rivulet form. It eventually joins the series
of streams that connects us with Delaware
Bay and the Atlantic Ocean.

5 Stormy Weather, Happy Planting

Stormy Weather

Grove of Japanese Umbrella Pines

A Conifer Windbreak Planting

Cacophony in the Valley

Opposite: During a heavy downpour on March 3, 1967, surface water buildup from the broad hillside above destroyed much of the beautiful grading and seeding of the prior year.

Stormy Weather

The winter of 1966-67 was peaceful, but on the third of March a torrential rainstorm pushed Burrows Run over its banks and across its meadows up and down the valley below ours. At the same time, water rushed down our southwest hillside, across the newly graded and seeded Game Lawn, down a low point between that lawn and the Beech Grove, and down the south side of the largest pond, cutting deep channels into the newly planted ivy banks. Anyone who has ever watched a foot-deep surge of water scour a flat, newly seeded lawn will understand the power involved.

It was at this point that my faith in civil engineers crashed. Before constructing the ponds, I had consulted with a supposedly reliable civil engineer about the need to control or manage moving surface water during storms. I recalled learning how this had been done at Valley Garden, a former estate turned public park near Wilmington,[5.1] where a series of ponds, smaller than ours, had been built in an existing stream. Before pond construction began there, a sizable storm-water line had been laid down the center of the valley and linked with laterals serving inconspicuous catch basins for the overflow. When I asked the civil engineer whether something similar might make sense for us, he answered, "You'll never need it."

After our storm catastrophe proved otherwise, we again sought Dick Vogel's help. This was a good test for his acumen at solving water problems, and he passed with flying colors. A swale was built at the bottom of the west hillside, to carry surface water southward where a catch basin collects it. From there a 30-inch pipe conducts the water underground through the woods, beneath the kitchen breezeway and the entrance courtyard, and then through more woods beyond the house until

Rainwater from the same storm flowed in heavy rivulets just downhill from the Game Lawn, washing out our plantings of Baltic ivy on the newly graded banks of the largest pond.

it empties out into the meadow below. It works extremely well. What could have been less complicated, and considerably less expensive, if done in advance of pond construction now turned into a major project. There was no choice but to regrade, reseed, replant ivy, and move on. Once this remedial construction was complete, we could focus on two important and interesting planting projects:

- The Grove of Japanese Umbrella Pines
- The Conifer Windbreak Planting

Grove of Japanese Umbrella Pines

We had built a mound to the south of the Upper Pond that hooked into the south-facing bank to the north. Approximately 44 inches high and 30 inches wide at the top, this rise was necessary for the preservation of the three red cedars (*Juniperus virginiana*) already there, because it reinforced the preexisting ground level at the base of each tree. It would also promote good drainage for the Japanese umbrella pines (*Sciadopitys verticillata*) we wanted to plant there and prevent surface water from flushing through that area from the direction of the springhouse.

We had a simple bench made for the mound from slabs of Conshohocken stone that had previously capped an overlook retaining wall on an old estate across Crum Creek from Swarthmore College.[5.2] Our mound curves to fit the circular pond and the paving around it; the bench curves to fit the mound.

Fifteen Japanese umbrella pines, ranging from 2 ½ to 6 inches in caliper were moved from Millcreek Nursery where we had started them from seed—an extremely slow process. When the seedlings are small they grow a mere ¼ to ½ inch per year. Only after they reach 15 to 18 inches do they start to stretch out at a normal growth rate for a conifer. After ours had been in place for

The grove of Japanese umbrella pines (*Sciadopitys verticillata*) with a light green ground cover of *Sedum kamtschaticum*. These trees are now three times as tall and completely grown together.

House

Grove of Japanese Umbrella Pines

Springhouse

Opposite: Outlined in red on this plan, our grove of Japanese umbrella pines (*Sciadopitys verticillata*) terminates the Stream Valley Garden.

Above: Foliage of Japanese umbrella pine

a while, we began to see interesting seedling variants: some are tall and narrow; some are short and fat; some are faster growing; others could almost be called dwarfs.[5.3]

I suspect that this tree was first introduced into our area by Bill Phelps, who founded Guyencourt Nursery (in operation from c.1923 to 1939). To this day, a stand of these pines screens a former boundary of his land. A grove of *Sciadopitys* from the nursery still probably survives on an old estate near Granogue, Delaware. When Bill was going out of business, the owner of this property bought a major portion of his stock to use in landscaping her then new home.

The beauty of the umbrella pines' light, bright green, almost fleshy needles causes them to stand out when compared with other conifers. In this region, if *S. verticillata* is given a site to its liking, it usually does well. The spot where Nancy and I planted ours meets those requirements. Besides having apparently fertile soil, it is free of heavy wind, thanks to buffering by the hill to the north and the two-story springhouse to the west. For a time in the morning, the woods shields the pines from the sun, which in the late afternoon sinks behind the springhouse and the north hill, and yet there is always light from overhead. Unfortunately, ice and heavy snow can break these pines' branches, although low winter temperatures down to -10°F have not bothered them.[5.4]

Where a visitor reaches the top of the steps to the upper pond area, on the right just before the first umbrella pine, we wanted to plant an early-flowering cherry. I consulted my Scott Arboretum mentor Gertrude Smith Wister (she and John had married in 1960) for advice on which cherry would have buds hardy enough to withstand our valley's characteristic winter temperature lows and late spring freeze. She immediately recommended *Prunus* x *subhirtella* 'Autumnalis'. Given its name, of course, I had always assumed that this cultivar would complete its bloom in the fall. Not so, it turned out, in the conditions we have here. We followed Gertrude's advice, and the tree has faithfully flowered every spring for many years as an important participant in the whole garden's "Cherry Moment."

Just opposite the cherry tree, where the stone steps meet the Upper Pond paving at the top of the high retaining wall, we added another key part of the permanent planting: *Stranvaesia davidiana* var. *undulata* 'Prostrata' (syn. *Photinia*). This member of the Rose family has semi-evergreen leaves, clusters of white flowers in spring, and gorgeous matte red berries hanging from long stems in the fall. The fact that some of the narrow, bright apple green leaves turn red in the fall greatly enhances the beauty of these berries. When the plant grows in a wind-free location, these leaves do not usually burn during the winter, and so they stay red until spring.[5.5] In the location we gave this *Stranvaesia*, its undulating and pendulous branches effectively soften the corner where stone steps meet stone wall.

To cover the ground beneath the umbrella pines we selected *Sedum kamtschaticum*, because it is a light yellow green that makes the *Sciadopitys* foliage seem darker than it actually is. This completed the architectural part of the planting in the upper pond area. We subsequently added many more plants here, to amplify this area's all-season interest.

Beneath the cherry tree, amid the granite treads of the steps and between the stones in the path below, a number of diminutive flowering plants found their homes later. We collected and planted a few Quaker ladies (*Houstonia caerulea* [syn. *Hedyotis caerulea*]) from a nearby meadow. Before the neighboring trees grew large enough to cast too much shade, these wildflowers

Above: The umbrella pines very shortly after they were planted around the uppermost pond. Today, these evergreens completely screen the springhouse from the granite curbstone steps.

Below: At the same time we planted the pines and sedum, we also put in a shrub ground cover of crimson pygmy barberry (spaced four feet on center) on the steep bank above the uppermost pond. This barberry carpet was later extended around the swimming pool and the Game Lawn where the same bank continues.

multiplied, furiously filling crevices over quite an area and leaping up into the step treads. Along the path as it approaches the steps, the bank to the right is solid with crested iris (*Iris cristata*) from the Smoky Mountains.

People walking through the garden see the area under the cherry tree nearly at eye level. Successful experimentation has yielded colonies of *Cyclamen hederifolium*; *C. purpurascens* (syn. *C. europaeum*); *Galanthus reginae-olgae* (fall flowering); *G. nivalis* 'Ophelia' (double, and more green than white—wonderfully outrageous); *Fritillaria assyriaca*; *F. meleagris* 'Alba'; *Erythronium* 'Pagoda' (a beautiful yellow form of the West Coast trout lily); and two shooting stars, *Dodecatheon jeffreyi* (native from Alaska to Southern California, Idaho, and Montana) and *D. meadia* (from southern Wisconsin and Pennsylvania to East Texas and Alabama). Of these shooting stars, the second species definitely likes Ashland Hollow better.

Top: Paul Hluchan's 2006 painting (gouache on paper, 11 x 14 in.) depicts the granite steps and the stone path leading to them.

Above: In between these magnificent stones, native Quaker ladies (*Houstonia caerulea*) flourish.

Right: *Prunus* x *subhirtella* 'Autumnalis' normally blooms in the fall. In our cold valley, however, this cherry tree waits until spring to flower.

About halfway up the granite staircase, one step has a beveled front carved with a simple inscription:

W. FREDERICK

My uncle Robert Frederick gave me this piece when he saw me assembling the salvaged curbstones for these steps. His present was a relic from the nearby cemetery at Lower Brandywine Church, which like other old graveyards had pipe railings around many of its burial plots. The entrance to each plot was customarily marked by a stone "threshold" like this. But as the cost of mowing and trimming rose, the managers of this cemetery required the removal of all enclosures. Which is how this fragment ended up in my uncle's barn. Since I was a William, he felt that I should have it, and that my garden stairway was its perfect new resting place.

This generous transfer coincided with Conrad's work on the retaining wall and the steps. Just one step down from the *W. Frederick* carving, he incorporated an upright stone into the step (along with numerous vertical pieces in the wall). It is exceptionally eye-catching with a jagged top jutting three or four feet above the inscription. Very few visitors miss the tall stone, or fail to ask about my namesake riser.

As if to play up this little bit of theater, a fascinating hosta (*Hosta clausa*) grows among several step treads in the same area. Hal Bruce, Winterthur's curator of plants, called it to my attention when I was picking his brain about suitable perennials for ground covers, a subject of ever greater interest to me as more and more perennials became available. *H. clausa*, I discovered, is stoloniferous (spreading underground by horizontal branches at the base of the plant), an uncommon trait in the hosta clan. Hal and I both felt that breeders should work with this plant to develop desirable matlike ground covers, which could prove more horticulturally useful than adding

Below: The flowers and foliage of *Hosta clausa*, a stoloniferous member of its clan

Opposite
Top: This West Coast dog's-tooth violet (*Erythronium* 'Pagoda') is quite happy under the cherry tree.

Middle: Northwest of the steps, on a bank just outside the cherry's shade, the lovely *Iris cristata* (a native of the Smokies) flourishes. In springtime it blooms regularly with the azaleas. In the fall its fresh yellow foliage complements the season's warm colors.

Bottom: The white form of the guinea-hen flower (*Fritillaria meleagris* 'Alba') also resides in the cherry's shade.

further variations to the plethora of hosta leaf color patterns.[5,6] *H. clausa* is quite striking all by itself in this location. With their spread restricted by the step treads' straight edges, the stems stand at attention in almost military rows. These organized ranks bear vertical clusters of large purple buds. A few buds may open, but most remain furled for all of the hosta's "bloom period." This effect is exceedingly attractive here where the upright inflorescences contrast with the horizontal lines of the gray granite steps. During the growing season, the dark green leaves contribute handsomely to Conrad's masterful composition of stone against stone.

A Conifer Windbreak Planting

Another major planting project we initiated and completed in 1967 was the Conifer Windbreak. We had decided that this should consist of needle evergreens, rather than deciduous trees or a mix of evergreen and deciduous, for several reasons:

- To slow the harsh winter winds from the northwest that normally hit us hard
- To provide privacy from Ashland Clinton School Road
- To act as a partial sound barrier
- To screen out the farmhouse from our house and garden (the tall narrow Victorian building looks attractive from the public road, but not from below in our valley)

Our broad palette of conifers represented the best performers I had observed as an undergraduate at the Scott Arboretum and then later at places like the Cutting Arboretum, on the south shore of Long Island. *Abies nordmanniana* ranked high on the list because it is tolerant of our hot, muggy summers. This fir stands out in the landscape of Easton, Maryland, where E. Sam Hemming, a nurseryman of my grandfather's generation who discovered the evergreen's merits, made extensive plantings. Also, during our first two years of married life in Delaware, Nancy and I lived in a small hilltop house surrounded by a mature grove of these shiny, dark green-needled trees (put there many years earlier by another keen plantsman, a Mr. Vogel). That hilltop, not far from Ashland Hollow, is close to being the state's highest elevation, which speaks well of *A. nordmanniana's* endurance.

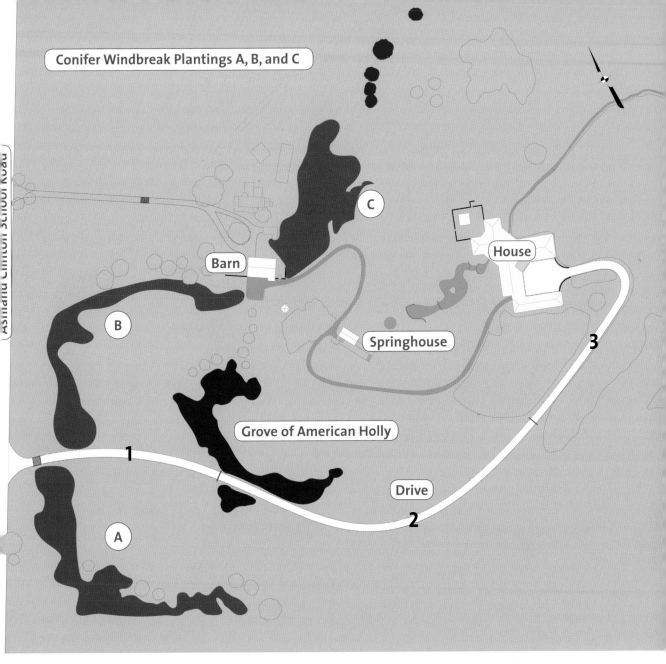

Conifer Windbreak Plantings A, B, and C

Ashland Clinton School Road

C

Barn

B

Springhouse

House

3

Grove of American Holly

1

Drive

2

A

Our windbreak planting commences on the western boundary and swings 90° where that line meets Ashland Clinton School Road. It follows the road past our driveway and then heads east to skirt the backs of the barn and the farmhouse.

Because of the number of botanical taxa involved here, and our desire to organize them for maximum visual appeal, we again asked Conrad to help. He astutely devised an aesthetic discipline that kept the windbreak from looking like an institutional pinetum.

The planting is two-to-three trees deep, informally staggered; and we have generally grouped multiple specimens of each kind of conifer together, intermingling different kinds where they meet. In the plan on page 123, see the dark green serpentine with segments labeled (in red) A, B, and C. Start at the bottom of the plan (A) and follow the dark green area to the left until it reaches the driveway entrance. The windbreak's *dramatis personae* are listed below, roughly following the curvature of the serpentine through each section:

Below: Cedar of Lebanon
(*Cedrus libani* subsp. *stenocoma*)

Bottom: Nordmann fir
(*Abies nordmanniana*)

A

Cedrus libani subsp. *stenocoma* (cedar of Lebanon)

Selected form, hardy at Arnold Arboretum in Boston. Found in 1938 in southwestern Anatolia. Hardier than the type, it can be counted on for winter survival here.

Pinus strobus (white pine)

Native to eastern North America

Picea abies (Norway spruce)

Native to Europe. Because it starts to lose limbs fairly early and remaining branches take on a funereal droop, I plan to remove this when the more desirable *P. orientalis* needs extra space.

P. orientalis (Oriental spruce)

Native to Caucasus, Asia Minor

Above: Tanyosho pine
(*Pinus densiflora* 'Umbraculifera')

Below: Japanese white pine
(*P. parviflora* 'Glauca')

Abies nordmanniana (Nordmann fir)
   Native to Greece, Caucasus, Asia Minor
Pinus strobus (white pine)
   Native to eastern North America
P. cembra (Swiss stone pine)
   Native to Europe and northern Asia

B

Pinus strobus (white pine)
P. koraiensis (Korean pine)
   From Japan and Korea
P. cembra (Swiss stone pine)
P. flexilis sdlgs (limber pine)
   Native from Alberta to California and Texas
P. strobus (white pine)
P. densiflora 'Umbraculifera' (Tanyosho pine)
   A form of Japanese red pine
P. bungeana (lacebark pine)
   From northwestern China
P. strobus 'Fastigiata'
   A form of our native white pine with a narrow conical head
Picea orientalis (Oriental spruce)

C

Pinus strobus (white pine)
P. parviflora 'Glauca'
   A form of Japanese white pine selected for its attractive
   bluish foliage
Abies nordmanniana (Nordmann fir)
P. strobus (white pine)
P. ayacahuite (Mexican white pine)
   Native to mountains from British Columbia to California.
   Grown from seed by a great plantsperson, Polly Hill

We have enlivened each of these three planting areas with a selection of special interest. In area A, the last plants to the south—four widely spaced cedars of Lebanon—ease the visual transition from the tightly organized windbreak into the rural hayfield-and-orchard complex. The intervals between the cedars also show off their mature form, which is a charming open, horizontally branched narrow cone. With age, the very tops of these trees often lean over to one side a little, and the branch tips take on a slightly weeping character (and, of course, it is a tree mentioned in the Bible for its venerable stance).

At the other end of planting area A (farthest from the cedars), a few Swiss stone pines step forward, so that their elegantly narrow forms and bluish needles can lend grace to the utilitarian barrier erected by their neighbors.

In area B, five Tanyosho pines stand upstage to show off their flat-top multistem profiles, which contrast delightfully with the slim verticals of the Swiss stone pines and the stout pillars of the fastigiate white pines behind them. (The Tanyosho pines have the added allure of trunks highlighted in orange.)

In area C, a pair of glaucous Japanese white pines, placed at slightly different elevations, serve as occultly balanced sculptures that contrast with their neutral backdrop. These Japanese white pines' widely spaced branches—thrust diagonally upward and clothed in clusters of very short needles—are a delight to behold.

The eastern end of this planting, which concludes with a trio of fat Mexican white pines, is anchored to the hillside by several randomly dispersed dark green specimens of native red cedar (*Juniperus virginiana*), here before we came. Over time, evergreens that started out as pristine verticals have taken on stronger personalities as the impact of snow, ice, and wind has poked a few holes, left the occasional branch askew, and revealed expanses of beautiful trunks. This is indeed a happy ending.

This schematic plan, based on Conrad Hammerman's design cartoon, lays out the planting of "evergreen" azaleas by color, as well as a solid bank of crimson pygmy barberry.

Cacophony in the Valley

During Conrad's work on the Stream Valley Garden we made an agreement: if he specified the azalea colors, I would find azalea plants to match. To that end he submitted a cartoon showing the colors and their relation to one another. This involved large patches of single tones interlocking with each other. My only restraint on his scheme was "No white." As noted in Chapter 3, when I am dealing with wonderfully saturated colors like those of the so-called evergreen azaleas, I feel that white punches serious, disturbing holes in the picture. I was enthusiastically

Opposite: The south-facing hillside of azaleas (with three tree-form *Wisteria floribunda* in the background) rises beyond the island.

Overleaf, page 130
Top Left: A view from the south side of the pond includes the azaleas 'Stewartstonian' (red) in the foreground and *Kaempferi* "Salmon Seedling" near the studio.

Top Right: *Kaempferi* "Salmon Seedling" with *Fothergilla gardenii* in the background

Bottom Left: Ascending steps from the west arch under the house with, mostly, *Kaempferi* "Salmon Seedling"

Bottom Right: South-facing hillside with *Kaempferi* "Salmon Seedling" in the foreground, and 'Amoenum' (mauve) and 'Stewartstonian' behind it and at the top

Page 131
Top Left: Along the lower path on the south-facing hillside, pale pink 'Bo-Peep' (center) blooms amid other azaleas.

Top right: 'Pink Pearl' occupies the center of another swath of that hillside. The diagonal path goes from the studio to the springhouse. High above it, two tree-form *Wisteria floribunda* are in flower.

Bottom left: The azalea 'Amoenum' stands to the right of the grass path linking the Studio Garden to the springhouse. 'Pink Pearl', at left, and 'Bo-Peep', far left

Bottom right: More 'Pink Pearl' accompanies a bank of crested iris (*Iris cristata*) and *Prunus subhirtella* 'Autumnalis' along a path to the house with Quaker ladies (*Houstonia caerulea*) growing between the stones.

in favor of Conrad's notion that this should be a modernist, cacophonous color scheme.

From 1968 through 1975 I collected names of candidates to match the agreed-upon colors, visiting all of the local gardens that had azalea displays (Winterthur, Wendy Heckert's private garden, and the Scott Arboretum, among others). Then came the problem of finding nurseries where my choices might be available. We started planting in 1969, and with one exception, every azalea was in place in 1975. These were the final choices, listed by selection and pigmentation:

'Pink Pearl'
Kurume selection or hybrid; Rowney rose plus a little white
'Amoenum'
Rhododendron (azalea) *obtusum* selection or hybrid; magenta
Salmon Selection
From the seedling population of *R. kaempferi* at the Scott Arboretum (Crum Woods, behind Swarthmore's Lang Music Building); cadmium yellow deep plus white plus a little alizarin
'Herbert'
Gable hybrid; purple/magenta
Stewartstonian
Gable hybrid; cadmium red light and white
'Chloe'
Glenn Dale hybrid; Rowney rose
'Bo-Peep'
Glenn Dale hybrid; pale pink

The cacophony of Conrad's cartoon had, and still has, a tremendous appeal for me. The near clashes produce a very desirable excitement—the same effect created at Winterthur by H. F. du Pont's hand in both the Azalea Woods and the primula plantings in the Quarry Garden

131

Most visitors to Wintherthur's Azalea Woods are unaware that a large planting of soft pink azaleas has some orange ones in its midst—just as visitors to Winterthur's Quarry Garden may not notice how warm tangerine is used to make the cool pinks and purples sparkle. It is the same deliberate straying from harmony that pleased me in the work of many Fauvist painters. For a while I thought of all of this as a "modern thing." Now, however, I realize there is a strong similarity between our azaleas and the color schemes in many fine oriental rugs!

After most of these azaleas were planted, we discovered that all except one bloomed together as we intended. The out-of-kilter variety was 'Sambo', a Glenn Dale whose enchanting color is described as pomegranate purple to Bordeaux (a brownish red). 'Sambo' bloomed one to two weeks later than the rest, so in the final palette we replaced it with 'Stewartstonian'.

While the lengthy process of azalea selection, sourcing, and planting was going on, we installed a planting of *non*-evergreen azalea, *Rhododendron vaseyi*, on the bank above the lowest pond and below our breakfast area window. This delicate shell pink beauty starts blooming just a few days ahead of the pack and overlaps them.

Five years after completing the main planting, we put a group of non-evergreen azaleas from northeast Asia and northern Japan, *Rhododendron mucronulatum*, at the head of the valley just above the big retaining wall. These are mostly seedlings that in early April produce light, stunning flowers in shades of warm purple and pink, tying in with the cherry blossoms and *Crocus tomasinianus* of the same season. They also signal the big display to come in early May.

5.1. Designed and built by Robert Wheelwright, ASLA, for Mrs. Eugene du Pont.

5.2. A friend called to say that I could have these if I had a truck there at eight o'clock the next morning. I didn't waste any time getting there. A smaller bench of the same material overlooks the largest pond.

5.3. We did try to root cuttings. Our success rate was low, however, and those pines that did take had difficulty growing into attractive, saleable plants in the fields.

5.4. In 1982 we first noticed occasional dead branches in the *Sciadopitys*. With the help of the University of Delaware's plant pathology department (primarily Bob Mulrooney), we determined that this was due to cankers caused by Diploidia (or, in the university's opinion, Botryosphaeria). Our sanitation spray program started immediately. We had the problem pretty well under control by 1990 and stopped spraying by 1992.

5.5. This form and cultivar of the plant, which is normally much larger and less pendulous, was introduced by Don and Hazel Smith of Watnong Nursery. Don was a former high school principal who turned what had been his hobby into a business when he retired. After he and Hazel died, this *Stranvaesia* continued to be available from Environmentals, Inc., Jim Cross's remarkable Long Island nursery. Jim was a disenchanted denizen of Wall Street who fell for the charms of the rare-plant world. He put his skills as a propagator and marketer to good use—for the benefit of us all—with passion and gusto.

5.6. Happily, this is now occurring.

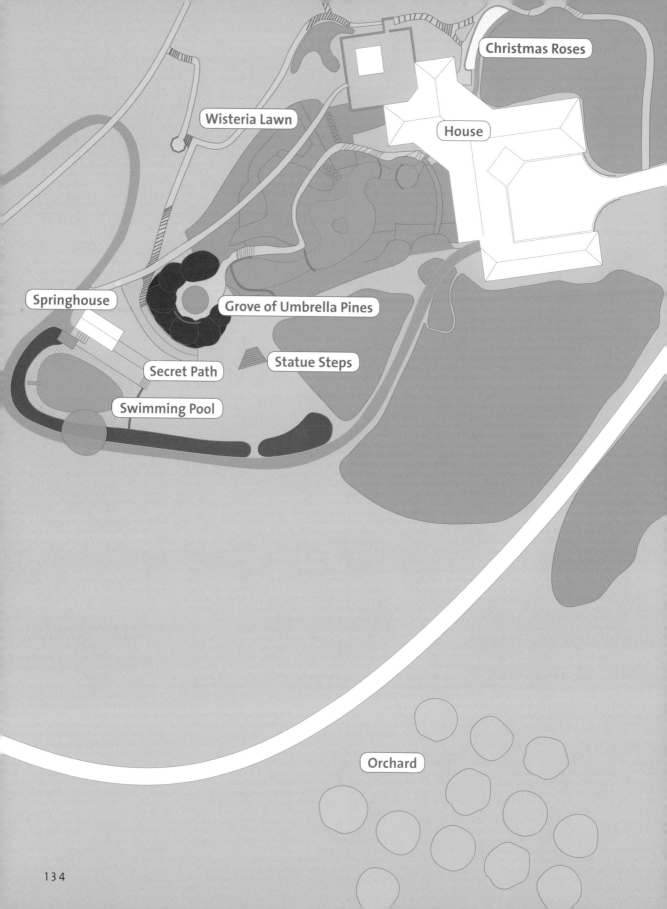

Christmas Roses

Wisteria Lawn

House

Springhouse

Grove of Umbrella Pines

Secret Path

Statue Steps

Swimming Pool

Orchard

6 Orchard, Swimming Pool, and Secret Path

A Daffodil Orchard

Christmas Roses

Country Swimming Pool (Read "Pond")

Secret Path

A Daffodil Orchard

Planting an orchard was our next large project in 1969. The site we chose, on one of our highest knolls (to the right of the drive as you enter), accords with Robert Frost's advice: "Keep cold, young orchard. Good-bye and keep cold." Air circulation up there is good; the buds harden off promptly for winter, and they do not blossom until the danger of spring frosts has passed.

We planted the portion of the Orchard nearest the drive with one of each of the following apple trees:

Malus 'Early Harvest'

M. 'Golden Delicious'

M. 'Jonathan'

M. 'Smokehouse'

M. 'Winesap'

And to enhance the visible "presence of orchard," these trees alternate with five specimens of a highly floriferous ornamental crab apple from Japan, *M. floribunda*. Farther back in the Orchard are the ever-popular pie cherry *Prunus* 'Montmorency', one seckle pear tree, and two sand pears (*Pyrus* 'Seuri' and *P.* 'Chojuro').

When Nancy and I first conceived of the Orchard, we resolved to do without a spray program, not only to avoid the expense, but also as part of our tribute to the 19th-century agricultural landscape. Early on, we pruned the trees annually. Now, we do nothing but occasionally prune for structure and enjoy the spring blossoms. Whatever fruit the Orchard yields is gathered above by birds and, below, by mammals on the ground.

Narcissus 'Pomona' blooms amid the apple and crab apple trees alongside the drive.

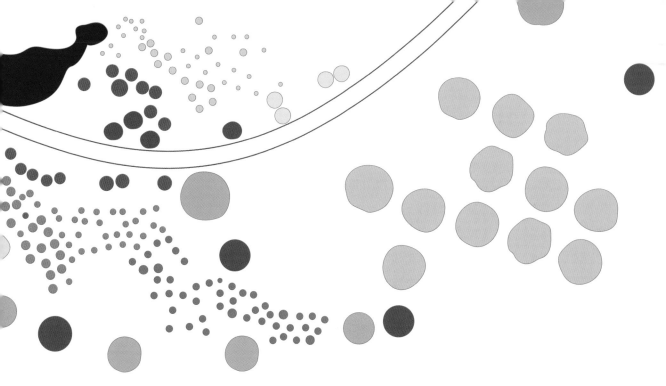

This schematic plan, which represents the Orchard in pink, shows its importance as a feature of plantings along the drive (parallel black lines).

The idea of naturalizing *Narcissus* in the stretch of orchard most visible from the drive had been in our minds from the beginning. When I asked my friends and mentors at the Scott Arboretum to tell me their favorite daffodils for naturalizing, these were the answers I got:

Narcissus 'Hera' (recommended by Mrs. Scott).

N. 'Loch Fyne' (John Wister).

N. 'Pomona' (Gertrude Smith Wister)

To these I added my own favorite, *N.* 'Trevithian'. All four have flourished in this area. Each spring, friends come with buckets of water in hand to cut the glorious blossoms, as do we.

Here are some bits of history about these selections:

N. 'Hera' was introduced by the de Graaff Brothers (De Gebroeders de Graaff) of Noordwijk, the Netherlands, in 1908.

Narcissus 'Loch Fyne' was introduced by The Brodie of
    Brodie Forest, Scotland, in 1920.
N. 'Trevithian' was introduced by P. O. Williams of
    Cornwall, England, in 1927.
N. 'Pomona' was introduced by De Graaff Brothers,
    Nordanijk, Holland in 1936.

Of the four cultivars, *N.* 'Trevithian' is, I believe, the only one still
available in the bulb trade. The absence of the others is very
unfortunate. They are all good naturalizers. They bloom and mul-
tiply well with absolutely no attention, requiring only that their
foliage be allowed to die down naturally. They raise no objection
to growing in field grass. They have a desirable "wild" look. And
N. 'Trevithian' gives off an absolutely delicious fragrance.

The Dutch flower breeder Jaap Leenen is currently engaged
in a project aimed at producing improved *Narcissus* for naturalizing. Of the dozen we have received "on trial," two show
promise of doing well under our tough conditions. Both have
upward-facing flowers, an objective that is extremely desirable
and seldom found. Both last well. It seems to us that these are
all commendable breeding objectives.[6.1]

The total bloom sequence for trees and bulbs in the Orchard
lasts probably three weeks, providing a great drive-by experience.

Top: *Narcissus* 'Pomona'

Middle: *N.* 'Trevithian', the most fragrant
daffodil in the Orchard

Above: *N.* 'Loch Fyne'

Opposite
Top: *N.* 'Trevithian' in front of apple trees
alternating with crab apples (*Malus
floribunda*), which beef up the bloom

Middle: *N.* 'Ara', one of the stars from Dutch
breeder Jaap Leenen

Bottom: *N.* 'Gouache', also from Leenen

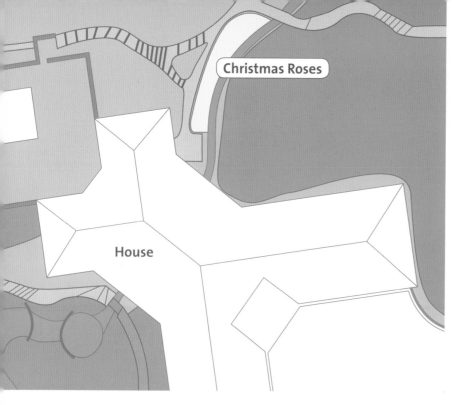

Christmas Roses

House

The tan area, just downstream from the house, starts off its early spring display with Christmas roses (*Helleborus niger*).

Christmas Roses

Another planting made the same year as the Orchard, but more intimate in mood, centered on hellebores, the first members of their genus (as far as we know) to come to this former farm. Four decades later, they still captivate us in early spring. We planted 300 seedlings of *Helleborus niger* (Christmas rose), a native European species, along the steep southeast-facing stream bank beyond where the stream flows eastward from underneath the house. At first glance, this spot might seem less than ideal. The area is rather heavily shaded by a large American beech (*Fagus grandifolia*) on the opposite side of the stream. Nevertheless, the hellebore seedlings took off like gangbusters. And year after year, they break the end-of-winter gloom when they push their buds up, sometimes through snow and melting ice, and open their glossy white flowers in mid-March.

Opposite
Top: After flowing under the house, the stream passes the south-facing bank at right where the Christmas roses thrive.

Middle: In response to the warmth of the spring sun, our planting of *H. niger* opens even when the ambient air temperature may still not appeal to humans.

Bottom: The fully open flowers of *H. niger*

We subsequently added another 175 Christmas roses, and their numbers have increased steadily as batches of young seedlings pop up on their own. The opening of the flowers is triggered by the early spring sun's precious warmth beaming through the leafless trees and striking the bank at right angles.

The blossoms, of course, face south across the stream. To enjoy this spectacle all the more, we placed a backless stone bench on the far side of the stream. From there one gazes directly into the yellow-spotted, gleaming white flowers—a magical picture. Upon observing this arrangement, a Japanophile friend of ours commented, "But where are your hellebore-viewing robes?" The Big Room and east balcony above afford equally satisfying vantage points. The dramatic dark green leaves and white blooms stand out against the tannish leaf cover of the forest floor.

The success of our Christmas Roses sparked other plantings for early spring in the same area. Heading the list of seasonal companions that have done well here are three kinds of skunk cabbage, aroids (members of the Arum family) with their toes in the water:

> *Symplocarpus foetidus* (our own native); opens to greet spring's first flies, which pollinate it.
>
> *Lysichiton camtschatcensis* (from Kamchatka, Sakhalin, and the Kurile Islands, western Japan); has glistening white sheaths with yellow on the spadix.
>
> *L. americanus* (Alaska to California and east to Idaho and Montana); its greenish yellow sheaths are the most dramatic of them all.

Another aroid, diminutive by comparison, *Acorus gramineus* 'Ogon' has golden variegated foliage that persuaded us to make it a focal point in the hellebore planting. We partnered it with *Leucojum vernum*, a bulb in the Amaryllis family. Although its plump white bells are some of the smallest flowers in that clan, they dwarf those of the snowdrops colonizing nearby with winter aconites (their flower segments are yellow-edged). The double-flowered, nonspreading form of *Ranunculus ficaria*, *R. ficaria* 'Flore-Pleno', hugs the ground exposed by gaps in the heavy-foliaged cover of hellebores.

The early blossoms of two perennials that gardeners most often grow for their foliage hold a special charm for me. I planted the first of these, *Trachystemon orientalis*,[6.2] as a ground cover a little way uphill from the hellebores. Its large, attractive heart-shaped leaves do a good job of shading out undesirables in their territory. But before the leaves emerge (at the same moment *Scilla siberica* blooms), spikes of exquisite starlike violet flowers delight us for a very short time. The second charmer, *Darmera peltata*, initially caught my attention when I came across its enormous glossy foliage in England, edging the pond at the bottom of Newby Hall's rock garden. In fact, *D. peltata* is native to the Pacific Northwest where our own specimen comes from. We planted it on the bank directly across the stream from the hellebores. But each year it moved closer to the water, until now it stands right at midstream. As this shift occurred, the leaves' decorative qualities lasted progressively longer from spring into summer. Now the foliage stays with us for the entire frost-free season. I might never have noticed the blossoms, however, if I hadn't gone faithfully to this area every year to see the hellebores. From the magic spot in the middle of the stream

Opposite
Top: An exotic skunk cabbage (*Lysichiton camtschatcensis*) has made itself at home here, just downstream from the hellebores and blooming a little later.

Left: *Lysichiton camtschatcensis*

Right: *Leucojum vernum*

sprout several gangly, leafless stems about two-to-three feet long, which branch in an unaccountable, angular way. Clusters of minute light pink flowers emerge at the tips of these branches. Unlike the leaves (up to 18 inches across), the flowers themselves are not showy. It is the extraordinary style of their presentation that I would not want to miss.

The climax of early spring in the Christmas rose area comes as the hellebore blossoms disappear and the Brandywine bluebells (*Mertensia virginica*) take over. As with so many good blues in our gardens, *M. virginica* belongs to the Borage family (*Boraginaceae*).

It is native to our area but was not present in this valley until we introduced it. Since then, the bluebell has spread rapidly wherever it finds good soil near the streams. Its lettucelike stems and foliage give little indication of strength and structure—the flowers are the thing! The buds are often pink or pinkish, but they open to reveal a glorious cool blue.

Above: The early broadleaf foliage of *Trachystemon orientalis*

Left: This plant's even earlier delicate violet blossom

Opposite
Top left: Long-stem *Darmera peltata* blooms very early, shortly before its huge, shiny, pleated leaves appear in the stream.

Top right: Fond of alluvial bottom land, the Brandywine bluebell (*Mertensia virginica*) is the queen of local spring wildflowers.

Bottom: After this bench on the south side of the stream has served as a vantage point for hellebore viewing, New York ferns take over as a splendid ground cover for the balance of the growing season.

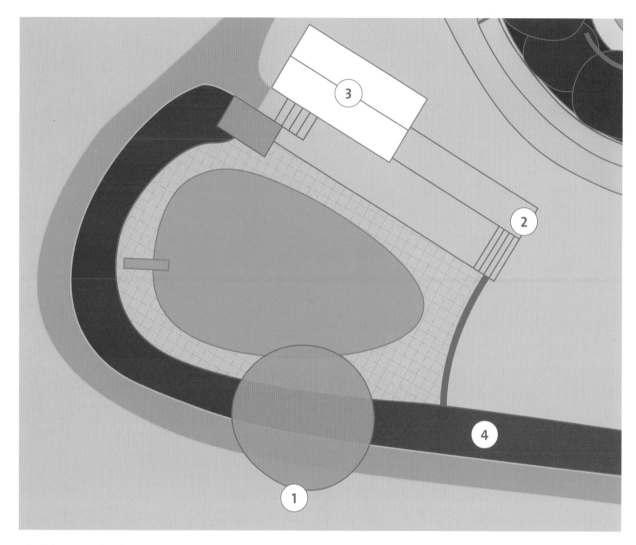

1. English weeping beech
2. Grape Arbor
3. Springhouse
4. Bank planting of crimson pygmy barberry

Country Swimming Pool (Read "Pond")

Talk about having a swimming pool probably started even before we moved here. As soon as the site for the house had been selected, further discussion ensued, along with considerable debate about where the pool should go—*if* we decided to put one in. By the time house plans matured, two sites had emerged as the best possibilities:

- On the west side of the springhouse
- To the east of the house and far enough away for a good view of Burrows Run valley (a grove of trees to be added)

Both locations met the double requirement of lying within convenient walking distance of the house while being invisible from it, especially in wintertime. There was no need for further decision at that time. Just in case, though, we did provide a route to the eastern site for electrical service, which the springhouse area already had.

By 1971 the oldest of our four children was 17, the youngest, 9. It was time to fish or cut bait. The springhouse option won easily, because it combined the scenic enclosure of surrounding landforms with the historic character of the building itself.

New construction presented a fine opportunity to reinforce such ties to the utilitarian simplicity of a 19th-century farm. We made the pool oval, a shape reminiscent of a millpond. After testing various paint colors to see how they looked underwater, we chose an olive green. Reflections of the sky turn the pool water an attractive blue refreshingly unlike the usual screaming aqua. A natural wood arbor erected between the pool and the springhouse partially shades stone paving around the water. We crafted the arbor posts from trunks of red cedar trees (*Juniperus virginiana*; bark left in place) saved when fencerows were cleared from the south-facing hillside. The crossbeams are seasoned white oak, which Amos Norton—part owner of James W. Flaherty & Co. and superintendent of all construction adjacent to our pool—had been keeping for just such a use. Amos had a special fondness for the historical moment we sought to evoke, and his painstaking care showed itself in numerous ways.

He made sure, for example, that a new two-foot retaining wall at the south end of the pool area matched the fieldstone of the springhouse. Paving stone came from the nearest quarry, in Avondale, Pennsylvania. Fortunately, the vein of stone accessible then yielded the appropriate thin flat stones (rather than so-called house-building chunks). Unfortunately, the quarry owner was breaking the large pieces of flat stone into smaller ones for veneering cinder block. Amos somehow convinced him to reserve large pieces for this job. Then Amos stood over his excellent Ethiopian mason to see that these were all fitted with consistently narrow joints.

For me, building the arbor counted as more than a utilitarian project. It was a sentimental journey. My grandfather Frederick, whom I adored, had an arbor very much like this, on which he grew Concord grapes (*Vitis labrusca* 'Concord'). We planted exactly the same variety, adding one each of *V. labrusca* 'Golden Muscat' and *V. labrusca* 'Steuben'. Just as in my grandfather's time, we pick ripe grapes, squeeze them into our mouths, and sidestep any of the fallen fruit being enjoyed by wasps (which gets cleaned up weekly). The crop also goes into homemade grape-hull pie and grape jelly.[6.3]

Our arbor delivers an unanticipated bonus. On late summer afternoons, sunlight bounces off the pool's gently rippling surface and onto the underside of the arbor where it bursts into moving particles as it strikes the big fat bunches of blue. They couldn't look more luscious.

Anyone who relaxes in the sitting area at the south end of the pool has a view of the steep Hillside Meadow to the northwest of the lovely rising terrain on two sides of this area. Framing the view on the right is the springhouse, and, on the left, a weeping European beech (*Fagus sylvatica* 'Pendula'). Ten to twelve feet tall when we planted it, this tree almost died to the ground during its first winter at Ashland Hollow.

Only one live branch remained near ground level, wandering off horizontally with no apparent purpose. We faced the choice of taking out this tree and planting a new one or leaving what was there for a year or two, to see whether the lone branch might eventually shape up into a strong leader. We chose the latter course. Today the beech has a 48-foot spread (extending five feet over the pool) and stands nearly twice as tall as the two-story springhouse! The poolside branches shelter a small, secret space with a bench for two.

Ripening Concord grapes are lighted from below by reflections off moving water in the swimming pool.

Exuberant Planting (Red, White, Blue, and Yellow)

Because of its dedicated season of use—swimming-pool time—and its lack of heavy shade (except under the arbor), this area is brilliantly colorful. All bloom here, and around the Game Lawn, adheres to a red-white-blue-and-yellow palette appropriate for high summer's principal holiday, the Fourth of July.

Structure

Two major plantings—one lemon yellow and one burgundy red—compose a framework for more detailed play with color close to the pool. The bold strokes of yellow and burgundy are very much in the manner of Roberto Burle Marx, who used color as a structuring element in garden design.

From 1960 on, we have planted 460 *Hemerocallis* 'Hyperion' in two groups on ground slightly higher than the Game Lawn and the pool. These daylilies, which have been spaced about three feet apart, now contribute two solid yellow masses as a radiant landscape backdrop.

The burgundy counterpart relies on a ground cover of crimson pygmy barberry (*Berberis thunbergii* 'Atropurpurea Nana'), planted three to four feet on center.

At the time Conrad Hammerman was designing the ponds in the Stream Valley Garden, he originated this scheme as a structural element to link the uppermost pond, the swimming pool, and the Game Lawn. The essentially even height of the bank above those three areas bends a unifying horseshoelike curve around them.

The burgundy foliage of crimson pygmy barberry (*Berberis thunbergii* 'Autropurpurea Nana') and the lemon yellow blossoms of daylilies (*Hemerocallis* 'Hyperion') structure our pool plantings.

Opposite
Top: An aerial view of the swimming pool area highlights the barberry ground cover's defining role.

Bottom: The significant size and volume of the weeping English beech (*Fagus sylvatica* 'Pendula') balances the volume of the springhouse across the pool. The tree and building frame the view of the Hillside Meadow from the sunny poolside sitting area.

This slope's ground cover of dwarf red barberry maintains its great structural importance year round—not only in spring (the fresh leaf color looks especially vibrant while the azaleas bloom) and in summer (at swimming-pool time), but even in winter, when the plant is a mellow nut brown.

Contrasting Textures

We have sought unusually strong textural contrasts in this area, strong enough to engage visitors who might be looking down from the driveway.

At the southern end of the Game Lawn, our multistem *Aralia elata* has extraordinary compound leaves more than 30 inches long, which are made up of 72 or more blue green leaflets. The leaves project horizontally or at a downward slope. During the summer, 18-inch inflorescences of small white flowers decorate the foliage. The contrast with the absorbing woodland foliage behind this plant is complete and dramatic.

A 180° turn away from the *Aralia*, at the opposite end of the swimming pool, a clump of giant reed (*Arundo donax*) looms against the Springhouse Woods. The multiple 12-to-18-foot-tall stems of this member of the Grass family often lean gracefully toward the strongest light, showing off 18-inch-long gray green leaf blades. The overall effect, which suggests a cross between bamboo and corn, has a captivating charm. Herbaceous in our climate, *A. donax* reaches full height during the swimming season, when 2-foot silvery panicles top the foliage. Again, this surprisingly bold texture has no trouble making an emphatic contrast with the dark green woods.

The most successful textural combination of all occurs roughly halfway between the two I have just described. Every year—along the way from the Game Lawn to the swimming pool (to the right, just before the steps down to the pool)—we plant three wonderfully bold-foliaged *Ricinus communis* 'Zanzibariensis', a form of castor oil bean[6.4] that skyrockets to 15 feet in one season. The individual palmate leaves, offered to view on waxy red branches emerging from waxy red trunks, can grow as large as 36 inches across. They are a shiny rich green with as many as 12 lobes, each marked by a nearly white midrib.

Behind the three *Ricinus*,[6.5] a clump of yellow-groove bamboo (*Phyllostachys aureosulcata*) stands against the end of the springhouse, slightly taller than its roof peak. The bamboo's small, narrow, sharply pointed leaves look as if they have been sprinkled onto its twigs at many different angles. They provide a delightful mist through which the vertical stems (in shades of green to yellow) can peek.

Viewed from a distance, the combination of castor oil bean and bamboo contrasts nicely with the broadleaf foliage of the Springhouse Woods to the north. The success of this textural feature can best be seen from a distance, on the Game Lawn or the driveway, where the sequential layers unfold as:

Castor oil bean (broad) against
Bamboo (fine) against
Springhouse Woods (solid, light-absorbing medium texture)

Top: Across the Game Lawn from the pool, a Japanese angelica tree (*Aralia elata*) presents its coarse leaves against a background of smaller woodland foliage.

Above: Black fruit on pink stems is a distinctive feature of this tree.

Top: The large leaves of castor oil bean (*Ricinus communis* 'Zanzibariensis'), an annual, provide a striking counterpoint to the fine foliage of yellow-groove bamboo (*Phyllostachys aureosulcata*), a permanent woody plant.

Below: *R. communis* 'Zanzibariensis' leaves and their contrasting red stems

Bottom: Giant reed grass (*Arundo donax*) at the northwest end of the pool area against the Springhouse Woods

Water's Edge, Country Meadow

To carry out the "country" theme, we have used fine-textured ornamental grasses at the edge of our "pond," and meadowlike plants around the diving-board area.

In addition to giant reed grass, described above, the grasses include two right beside the pool: *Calamagrostis* x *acutiflora* 'Karl Foerster', which flowers early in the swimming season, and *Pennisetum alopecuroides*, which blooms near the season's end.

"Grasslike" describes the aforementioned yellow-groove bamboo (*Phyllostachys aureosulcata*), as well as dwarf golden variegated bamboo (*Arundinaria viridistriata* [syn. *Pleioblastus viridistriatus*]), growing in a pocket in the stone paving just to the right of the springhouse door. Never taller than three feet, this plant has narrow (one-inch-wide) seven-inch-long leaves striped longitudinally with narrow bands of dark green, yellow green, and butter yellow. The width of the bands varies for different colors on a single leaf, and no two leaves have exactly the same pattern. The effect at a distance is quite different, as the variegations blur together into a vibrant, cheerful chartreuse. This color is always useful for lighting up a shady area, as it does here under the grape arbor.

The diving-board end of the pool owes its meadowlike feeling to the lance-shaped foliage and yellow fleur-de-lis blossoms of *Iris orientalis* 'Shelford Giant', which blooms in June. This is surrounded by the later blooming daisy-type flowers of *Heliopsis helianthoides* 'Karat' and *Rudbeckia fulgida* var. *deamii*. We grow a very special denizen of this area, *Verbascum* 'Harkness Hybrid', from seed that originally came from Ben Blackburn at Willowwood Arboretum in Gladstone, New Jersey. I have never been able to get confirmation of this, but I like to think that the hybrid was named for Bernard E. Harkness (a taxonomist famed

Top: Water's-edge grasses *Pennisetum alopecuroides* (foreground) and *Calamagrostis acutiflora* 'Karl Foerster'

Above: A very short (18 to 24 inches) bamboo, *Arundinaria viridistriata* (syn. *Pleioblastus viridistriatus*)

Opposite
Top left: *Iris orientalis* 'Shelford Giant' in the country meadow landscape

Top right: *I. orientalis* 'Shelford Giant', close up

Middle left: The poolside meadow later in the season

Middle right: Meadow landscape up to the diving-board end of the pool

Bottom left: *V.* 'Harkness Hybrid' with *C. acutiflora* 'Karl Foerster'

Bottom right: *Verbascum* 'Harkness Hybrid' in front of crimson pygmy barberry

for his work with lilacs), of the Rochester, New York, Department of Parks.[6.6] A dozen or more of these verbascums are grown from seed in our greenhouse each spring (they are biennial) and set out in gravelly pockets in early July. The following year they grow taller than my head by mid-June, when they display their soft yellow blossoms. These snuggle against the gray green of small, furry leaves on stems that rise from clusters of large feltlike leaves at the base. Repetition of verticals always makes for an attractive incident. The verbascum spires are stunning, especially when seen against the burgundy foliage of the crimson pygmy barberry behind them.

Country Cottage Theme

Closer to the springhouse, the plantings take on a more cottagey personality.

One hundred and eighty degrees from the steps up to the Game Lawn, a similar set of steps leads to rustic, solid wooden gates that open onto our service road. At the bottom of these steps to the left—in front of a fieldstone wall and the huge, textured blue green leaves of *Hosta sieboldiana* 'Caerulea'— stands a large terra-cotta oil-jarlike urn, which Paul fills annually with some wonderful treasure(s) he has found. [6,7]

At the south end of the springhouse, running parallel with the Grape Arbor, a sizable bed contains the most colorful planting in the pool area. The perennials we grow here include *Liriope muscari* 'Monroe White', *Inula helenium*, and a Stout hybrid day-lily, *Hemerocallis* 'Autumn Prince', whose small, trumpet-shaped lemon yellow flowers begin their long season of bloom in late August to early September. Their presentation is seductive: wiry stems lean towards the light and move gracefully in even the slightest breeze. Each year we supplement these perennials with a different mix of annuals and tropicals selected from Paul's current palette.

Above: *Hemerocallis* 'Autumn Prince'

Right: The cottagey bed seen through the grape arbor

Opposite: A painting by the author, *Summer from the Grape Arbor*, 2000. Oil on canvas, 18 x 23 in. Collection Nancy G. Frederick

Tubs, Pots, and Urns

The cottagey effect is further enhanced by a number of plants in pots, tubs, and urns, which we arrange in groups around the stone-paved terrace, mostly at the south end of the pool. These come and go during the swimming season.

Vines

We probably use more vines here than in any other part of the garden, and I feel that they epitomize this particular area's distinct character.

County law requires that a swimming pool be enclosed within a four-foot-high childproof fence. Our chain-link fence is painted an unobtrusive dark green, and the foliage of trees and shrubs screens it from view. However, the fence also offers a perfect support for experimenting with some of the vines.

The following vines are grouped according to planned associations with other plants:

Vines—Woody

Bignonia capreolata (syn. *Anisostichus capreolata*) (cross vine)—Orange red flowers in late May. Evergreen leaves. Also a good climber on wood and stone. The form 'Tangerine Beauty' is exceptionally floriferous and long blooming

Clematis 'Mrs. Cholmondeley'—Large light blue flowers up to eight inches across

Clematis 'Ramona'—Pale lavender blue flowers

Lonicera periclymenum 'Serotina'—Cerise pink buds that open white and fade to yellow

Wisteria frutescens 'Amethyst Falls'—Recently introduced form of a native wisteria. Closely spaced violet flowers,less pendulous than Asian forms because inflorescences are held at several different angles

Top: *Colocasia* 'Black Magic' above *Isolepis Cernua*

Middle: Gray *Teucrium fruticans* with *Salvia coccinea* 'Lady in Red'

Above: *Durantia elegans* 'Grandiflora' (foreground) and *Pentas lanceolata* 'Cranberry Punch' (center left)

With smaller leaves and flowers, and less "wisteria-like" aggressiveness than other forms, *W. frutescens* 'Amethyst Falls' has followed the top rail of the pool fence seven to eight feet in both directions from its point of origin. In several places it has also spread seven to eight feet uphill or down from the fence and over adjoining shrubs, creating the effect of a wave or cascade. "Waterfall" is aptly named.

Vines—Tender

Each year we augment these permanent vines by planting a few tender climbers. In 2007, for example, we used:

Cardiospermum halicacabum (balloon vine; love-in-a puff)
Cobaea scandens (cup-and-saucer vine)
Dolichos lablab (syn. *Lablab purpureus*) (hyacinth bean)
Ipomoea purpurea 'Kniola's Purple-black'
Mina lobata

Vines—Most Important of All

On the arbor, of course, the grapevines dominate our vine palette, but the rich orange flowers of the very ornamental trumpet vine *Campsis* x *tagliabuana* 'Madame Galen' come a close second. These dangle from the arbor directly above the chartreuse foliage of the dwarf bamboo. For a long period of time, this orange-and-chartreuse combination forms the centerpiece of the whole arbor area.

Top left: *Bignonia capreolata*

Second from top: *Clematis* 'Mrs. Cholmondeley'

Third from top: *Wisteria frutescens* 'Amethyst Falls'

Bottom: *Campsis* x *tagliabuana* 'Madame Galen'

Secret Path

On the far side of the springhouse from the pool (the east side) lies what I have come to call the Secret Path (see plan, page 134). Hidden from the rest of the garden, it does not provide a main route to or from any destination. There is no reason to go this way unless one likes horticultural surprises and intimate spaces. The grass path can be entered from either end: at the foot of railroad-tie steps from the Wisteria Lawn (which cross the springhouse path as they descend) or from a grassy patch between the Grove of Umbrella Pines and the Statue Steps. Entered from this end, the Secret Path quietly disappears, curving sharply between the grove and the springhouse. It widens just behind the grove and then narrows upon reaching the steps back up to the Wisteria Lawn. The climb to the top reveals that these steps are directly on axis with the steps from the western part of the Wisteria Lawn.

We have tucked extra-special plant treasures along the way, each discoverable—during its particular season of interest—by the inquisitive eye.

On the Game Lawn bank (to the left when it is approached from the east, or downstream), one encounters a specimen of the lilac *Syringa laciniata*.[6.8] Our plant started out as a cutting of a very special form growing in the former garden of the distinguished American gardener Louise Crowninshield.[6.9] *S. laciniata* (the type originated in northwestern China) flowers in early May. The inflorescences comprise clusters of small violet flowers, which are held tightly against a single branch. In typical plants, an inflorescence may be 12 inches long. In the Crowninshield plant and ours, however, many inflorescences measure up to 36 inches long. The length holds particular importance because the flowers of well-known *Syringa* hybrids develop close to and

Syringa laciniata from Louise Crowninshield

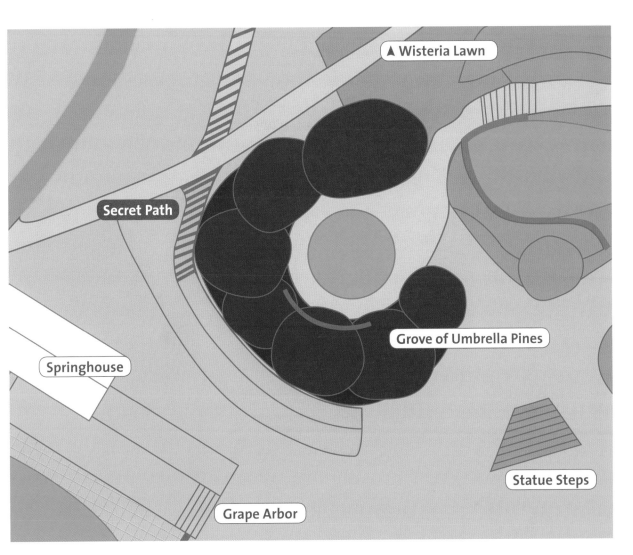

Detail of Secret Path

often slightly within the foliage. Blossoms on *laciniata* normally project above the leaves of the plant. When its inflorescences reach 36 inches, as often happens with the Crowninshield plant, it has a distinctively spiky form, which is very, very pleasing. Here it consorts with other shrubs, such as a mass planting of the double-barreled charmer *Itea virginica* 'Henry's Garnet'. This bears six-inch pendulous white blossoms during late June and early July, as well as consistently good fall foliage, coloring murrey, maroon, and scarlet in late October and early November.

Also, on the left are background plantings for the swimming-pool bed directly above. This includes the summer bloomers *Inula helenium* and *Heliopsis helianthoides* 'Venus'. Both contribute yellow daisies, the latter most deliciously refined.

Just before the low stone wall containing the large clump of bamboo,[6.10] one comes upon the supremely handsome tree peony *Paeonia* 'Joseph Rock'.[6.11] Its blossoms are huge (seven to eight inches across, minimum) with several layers of crinkled, shiny white petals that are tinted an almost-black maroon at the base. These dark areas compose a band inside each flower, surrounding and enhancing the "large boss of golden fluff in the flower's heart."[6.12]

This form of *P. suffruticosa* was introduced from southwest Kansu, China, by the American plant explorer Dr. Joseph Rock, who discovered it and sent seed to the Arnold Arboretum. In 1936, one of the offspring distributed from there a few years earlier was planted by Sir Frederick Stern in his famous garden of rarities at Highdown, in the south of England. By 1959, we are told, that plant stretched eight feet high and twelve feet wide. I have never seen a tree peony this large in the United States, but we have made sure to leave sufficient space around our plant, should it ever need it.

Paeonia 'Joseph Rock'

Just beyond this, to the left of the ascending steps, are three plants of the deciduous azalea *Rhododendron* x *mortierii*. Like many others in the group, they bear bicolor flowers: orange and pink in this case. Words are lacking to adequately convey each shade, because the colors change as the flowers age. Suffice it to say that orange and pink do not necessarily work well together. However, in cases where there is a major amount of one (in this case, pink) and a minor amount of the other, what might have been a very disturbing discord becomes something especially exciting. My friend Doug Reed would probably refer to it as Fauvist! These shrubs grow out of the deep burgundy ground cover of crimson pygmy barberry, and the blossoms are seen against the shaded fieldstone wall of the springhouse, giving momentary glory to that little corner.

The Ghent azaleas (*Rhododendron* x *gandavense*) play an important and romantic part in the history of plant breeding. They are a happy outgrowth of the plant exploration conducted from the 18th century into the early 20th century.

In 1738 John Bartram introduced American azaleas into England. In 1793 *Rhododendron luteum* (syn. *Azalea pontica*) reached England from the Black Sea region.

Two azaleas (*Rhododendron* x *mortierii*) bloom above a ground cover of crimson pygmy barberry. False Solomon's seal (*Smilacina racemosa* [syn. *Maianthemum racemosum*]), in the foreground, completes the picture.

In 1825, P. Mortier, a master baker of Ghent, raised the first hybrids between two North American azaleas, *Rhododendron calendulaceum* (the flame azalea of our Smokies) x *R. nudiflorum* (the pinxter bloom we know in our woods; its Latin name is now *R. periclymenoides*). The plants to the left of our steps, seedlings from the above cross, are named after Mortier.

The Belgian breeder then created some of the other seedlings from the above cross with *R. luteum* (native to the Black Sea Region). This added the excitement of more yellow. Seedlings selected from the cross were called Ghent azaleas (*Rhododendron x gandavense*), after Mortier's hometown. One of these is the cultivar *Coccinea speciosa*, which appears in Chapter 10.

Mortier's breeding program posed an obvious challenge. The azaleas he set out to hybridize had different bloom dates, but in order to make a cross, the flowers of both parents had to be in bloom at the same time. It is said that Mortier solved this problem by keeping the early bloomers in the coolest place he could find, while putting the late bloomers next to his ovens, to force them into early bloom.

I feel especially entranced to have this plant named after him in my garden—not just because of its singular beauty but also because its breeder's work has been carried on by a succession of others, including Lionel de Rothschild. On his great estate at Exbury, in England, the breeding of deciduous azaleas continues to this day.

In our hot, humid climate, many of the newer hybrids carrying larger and more spectacular flowers do not do as well as the original Ghent azaleas. Only a few of these (including the two in our garden) are grown any longer in the United States. This is a marketing error that some enterprising American nurseryman should correct.

These three special spring events—the flowering of Louise Crowinshield's lilac in early May, of Mortier's azalea in mid-May, and of Rock's tree peony in late May or early June—are reason enough to enter the Secret Path. One more reason occurs months later, however, and seasonally speaking, it brings the path to a splendid conclusion. In late September, *Sternbergia lutea*, another delightful member of the Amaryllis family, opens its rich yellow blossoms at the point where the steps rise to cross the springhouse path. *S. lutea* is frequently called fall crocus; and it does look very much like *Crocus*; but, since *Crocus* belongs to the Iris family, this is a misnomer. Some gardeners advocate the name "fall daffodil," because daffodils are fellow members of the Amaryllis family. The latter, ill-fitting alias has never stuck, and I prefer to go with the Latin *Sternbergia*.

Sternbergia lutea

A bigger surprise than the plant's common name is the timing of its blossoms, which are more glamorous and beautiful than any spring- or fall-blooming crocus. (Yes, there are true *Crocus* that bloom in the fall as well.) At this time in the fall our minds are attuned to things like asters, chrysanthemums, and colorful foliage, when along come dark green, strap-shaped leaves, and stunning yellow cups. We have tried growing *Sternbergia lutea* elsewhere in the garden, always selecting sites that stay dry and sunbaked in the summer (supposedly simulating the plant's native haunts in southern Europe, Asia Minor, and Central Asia), but to no avail. It apparently feels at home only in the steep, narrow strip just above the grass line of the springhouse path and just below the ground cover of crimson pygmy barberry. After the golden flowers pass, the handsome foliage remains until spring—and then, in preparation for next year's surprise, it finally dies down.

6.1. To the best of my knowledge, none of these has come on the market yet.

6.2. This was a significant gift from John Elsley, then curator of hardy plants at the Missouri Botanical Garden.

6.3. RECIPE FOR GRAPE HULL PIE
    7 cups stemmed Concord grapes
    3 tablespoons cornstarch (instant tapioca better —1 tablespoon not enough)
    1 cup sugar
    1 teaspoon salt
    Grated rind of 1 orange

    Pastry for 9-inch double-crust pie

Preheat the oven to 450°F. Wash grapes, slip skin from pulp, reserve skins. Heat pulp to boiling and rub through colander (or use Foley food mill) to take out seeds. Add other ingredients to pulp and cook on low heat, stirring until thickened. Add skins (maybe not all of them). Pour mixture into a 9-inch pie pastry, and top with a lattice crust.

Bake at 450° for 10 minutes; reduce temperature to 350° and bake 25 minutes longer. Cool.

6.4. The cultivar names of this plant are thoroughly mixed up in the trade. We are not absolutely certain that 'Zanzibariensis' is correct. Nevertheless, we are sure that the description given here accurately describes what we have, and that it is the showiest and most wind-resistant of the many cultivars we have tried.

6.5. This plant's seeds are extremely poisonous, and they should be kept out of children's reach.

6.6. This seems very likely, because Blackburn and Harkness were college classmates. Harkness was modest but tremendously important and a highly regarded horticulturist. His passion for ornamental plants led him into incredibly forward-looking corners of the horticultural world. Technically the taxonomist for the Rochester Department of Parks, he specialized in lilacs, expanding the collection to 900 different cultivars. His many achievements included running an evaluation (with five other professionals) to select the 10 best lilacs. Harkness died after a long life, one of the most respected horticulturists of his generation.

6.7. During the summer of 2007 our list of tender plants was as follows:
    Caladium 'Tom-Tom'
    Alocasia 'Calidora'
    Hibiscus acetosella 'Red Shield'
    Impatiens balsamina (magenta form)
    Salvia farinacea 'Victoria Blue'
    Salvia guaranitica
    Talinum paniculatum 'Kingswood Gold'
    Tibouchina macrophylla
    Torenia 'Summer Wave'

6.8. Gift of Peter Lindtner, garden fruit specialist at the E. I. du Pont Garden.

6.9. Starting in the mid-1920s, she and her husband, Frank Crowninshield, created what was probably in its time the world's most romantic garden. They built it on the south side of the Brandywine River among the hillside ruins of buildings originally used by Mrs. Crowninshield's family to manufacture black powder.

6.10: Described earlier: *Phyllostachys aureosulcata.*

6.11. Also known as 'Rock's Variety' and *Paeonia suffruticosa* subsp. *rockii.*

6.12. From the writings of British plant explorer Reginald Farrer.

Under the arbor

7 Beech Grove, Birds, Statues, and a Circular Pond

Beech Grove

Goldfinches and Redbud Blossoms

Statue Steps and the Wedding Tree

Upper Pond

Opposite: Beech grove with *Crocus tommasinianus*

Beech Grove

The beautiful American beech (*Fagus grandifolia*) is a common part of our region's woodland mix, but one hardly ever finds a "pure" stand of trees comprising only this species. Fortunately for us, Ashland Hollow has one of these rare stands, just south of the garden's ponds and waterfalls and at the bottom of our stream valley's north-facing slope. Predating our arrival, the grove is roughly 90 by 110 feet and contains 18 trees, randomly spaced. They all appear to be roughly the same age. The larger ones measure 18 to 20 inches in diameter (at breast height); the smaller ones, 7 to 8 inches. There is one clump of five trees, another of four, and one of three. Six specimens are loners.

Left: Groves of American beech (*Fagus grandifolia*) are common in our local forests. This one occupies an important place in upstream views from our house.

Below: We underplanted the grove with bulbs of *Crocus tommasinianus*, which have multiplied prodigiously.

Because of their closeness to one another, trees at the outer edge of the grove have normally spreading branches on the sides exposed to sunlight. The remainder, inside the grove, branch only near the top, and unevenly at that, as they compete for light. This results in a domed effect inside the grove. It is, of course, the trunks—totally smooth, branchless, and a medium silver gray—that matter when we look out from the house or stroll through the garden. They are stunning in different light conditions and at many different times, but especially when the low late-day sun catches them sideways! The interior of the grove is free of woody or herbaceous undergrowth, although a few native herbaceous plants, including the wonderful late-blooming aster *Symphyotrichum cordifolium* (syn. *Aster cordifolius*), grow near the edge.

We did a trial planting of *Crocus tommasinianus*, which is native to Yugoslavia, in 1971 (the same year the swimming pool went in). This crocus blooms very early, depending on the season, of course, usually in mid-March. Almost silver on the outside, the bud opens to a lovely violet inside. The beech bark contains both of these colors, producing our hoped-for harmony.

The first 750 "tommies" were so successful, both culturally and aesthetically, that we planted another 1,800 bulbs in 1972 and 1,000 more two years later. They rapidly started seeding themselves in all directions, and before long there were many thousands among the beeches.

The bulbs we used for these early plantings had probably been collected in the wild (central Yugoslavia), because we soon began to notice color variation. We also found named cultivars on bulb vendors' lists, and in 1980 we added a few 'Ruby Giant' and 'Taplow Ruby'. Both fall on the darker side of the seedling variations.

Trouble struck paradise late in the winter of 1986-87. Ice lay on the ground under the beech trees for at least two months. When it melted and bloom time came, not a crocus emerged where the ice had been: a lack of oxygen had killed the mature bulbs. Sadly, we concluded that the garden had lost one of its principal glories. But the following year, a scattering of blossoms appeared, along with many small leaves of tommy seedlings. And in two or three years, our friends were back! The seeds already in the ground had survived.

This plant's ability to self-seed is quite remarkable. Even before the Great Ice we had noticed seedlings coming up near the end of the 30-inch pipe that carries storm water from a catch basin near the Beech Grove under the drive courtyard and through the woods southeast of the house, before emptying into Burrows Run Meadow. That crocus colony at the edge of the woods continues to expand.

The year of the big freeze brought an unexpected windfall when we discovered *Crocus tommasinianus* growing in the treads of stone-fronted steps that lead from the western opening of the arch under the house partway up a south-facing slope; i.e., on the *opposite* side of the valley from the Beech Grove. Obviously, these crocus had arrived there as seed, but how? We can only speculate that this trick was pulled off by mice or by our gardener at the time, who enjoyed creating surprises.

New colonies turn up in other locations every year. Some must start out as seeds unwittingly mixed into leaf cleanup, hauled with it to the compost pile and then sown again by chance, as compost is spread about the garden.

Many thousand strong today, our multitude of "tommies" started out in 1971 with a planting of 750 bulbs.

The Beech Grove is visually linked to many parts of the Stream Valley Garden by more beeches growing on that garden's banks: several ancient specimens as well as two young ones we planted to replace a pair that died of old age. All winter long, the youngsters hold onto their leaves, which the cold bleaches almost white—a tremendous asset to the seasonal picture we view from the house.

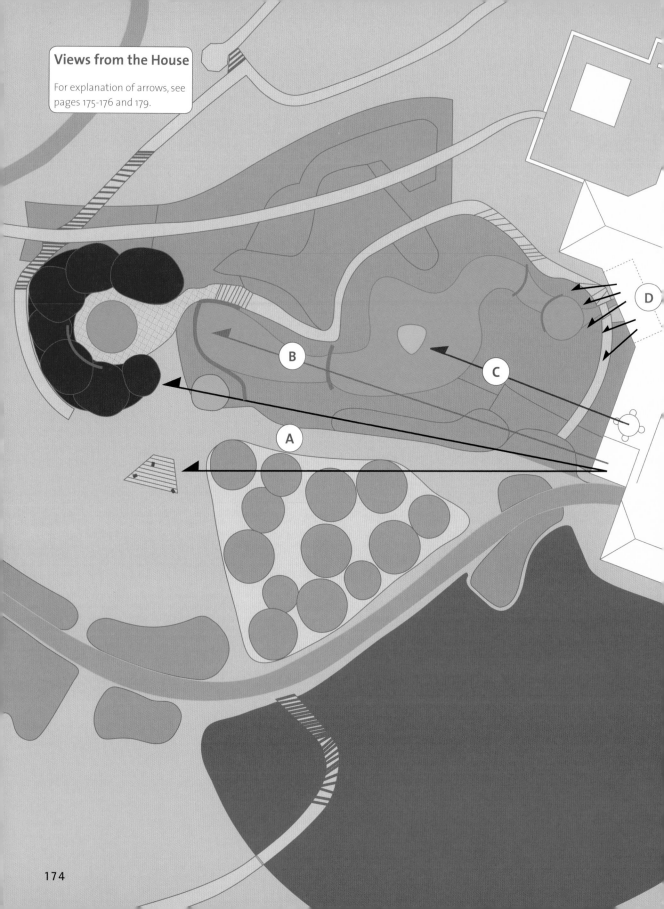

Views from the House

For explanation of arrows, see pages 175-176 and 179.

A

B

C

D

Goldfinches and Redbud Blossoms

Even though our house has no porch in front, the screened one just off of our kitchen is known simply as the back porch. We enjoy eating almost every meal here in the warm seasons, but we also value this airy space for the relationship it establishes between our house and the stream valley. One is "in" the garden here in several unique and exciting ways.

Dead ahead of the porch, the sight line splits in two. On the left stretches out the longer, broader, and more pastoral view, **A**. On the right is the shorter but more dramatic tree-focused vista, **B**, of the big retaining wall with its two marvelous waterfalls in the Stream Valley Garden.

Framed by our schoolhouse bell[7.1] and the Beech Grove, View **A** surveys a carefully calculated zigzag of lawn, which leads the onlooker's eye out to the sun-drenched Game Lawn and Statue Steps (on the left) and connects visually with the Upper Pond (on the right).

View A, from the back porch to the left

A shrub planting immediately to the left of the porch continues onto a steep north-facing bank. Near the top of the bank, a weeping form of the Japanese snowbell (*Styrax japonicus* 'Carillon') bears delicate, pendulous, bell-shaped white flowers in June, when the porch is in full swing. Above and to the left of the *Styrax*, the horizontally spreading branches of three corkbark euonymus (*Euonymus alatus*) emphasize the snowbell's pendulous quality by contrast. Ferns cover the bank below. At the bottom of the bank, close to a wall of the house, a true aristocrat of shrubs, America's native oakleaf hydrangea (*Hydrangea quercifolia*), thrives without ever having been pruned. Its handsome 11-inch-long, cone-shaped, white flower heads appear in mid-June. These in fact consist of two kinds of blossoms, arranged as if by a jeweler's hand. The outer flowers, relatively few and large (1½ inches across), are sterile. The more numerous, small (⅛ inch across), and densely crowded inner flowers are fertile. Because the substantial heads terminate the branches, their weight causes a mildly pendulous effect. In July the flower heads mature to splendid shades of green and chartreuse. And the entire season's performance takes place against the background of generous (9- by-9-inch) dark green leaves roughly the shape of oak foliage.

Thanks to their exemption from pruning, the branches have attained an impressive size. Their shapely structure and attractive exfoliating bark are bonuses during the winter, when the hydrangea can be seen through a window in the kitchen door.

At the base of the porch screens, hay-scented ferns (*Dennstaedtia punctilobula*) rise above ground-hugging wild lily-of-the-valley (*Maianthemum canadense*), which came with the ferns; *Sedum ternatum*, another shade-tolerant native; and a clump of the taller, exquisite light blue-flowered *Amsonia tabernaemontana*.

Nancy and I made sure, of course, that various parts of our house have good visual connections with the landscape. The Big Room has six sets of French doors on each side: one set looking eastward, downstream, into woodland with pasture beyond; the other set, westward (see five short arrows on plan) onto the ponds and waterfalls of the Stream Valley Garden. Especially in the summer, when the doors are open and we spend a lot of time on the Big Room's west balcony, this view is a huge part of life in our garden.

The other indoor-outdoor connection, probably even more important to us, occurs in the kitchen dining area, the part of the room that is closest to the back porch.

Below: Oakleaf hydrangea (*Hydrangea quercifolia*), a close companion to anyone on the porch

Bottom: View B, from the porch, in midsummer

Opposite
Top: Looking across the largest pond from the kitchen dining table

Bottom left: View C, showing the ponds almost completely covered in fallen leaves. Note the stone bench (lower right) and Game Lawn (upper left).

Bottom right: Our daughter Rebecca with autumn leaves in the lower pond, seen from the west balcony

Alongside the circular dining table in our kitchen, a large but shallow bay window that is three double casements wide faces west. Nine feet across and five-and-a-half feet tall[7.2] (two panes lower than our other windows and only 16 inches off the floor), the bay is a half-casement deep.

The central axis of the view, **C**, from the kitchen table and across the bluestone windowsill, extends down onto the largest pond. Just below the window are the deciduous pinxter bloom azaleas, and in the middle distance, slightly off-axis to the left, stand three beech trees of different sizes but all young enough still to be sprinkled with nearly white leaves in the fall. Beyond them to the right lie a small peninsula, covered in the summer with Japanese silver ferns (*Athyrium goeringianum* 'Pictum' [syn. *Athyrium niponicum* var. *pictum*]), and farther back near the center, the mossy pyramidal island.

From our high nest inside the bay window, we keep track of seasonal changes: spring's evergreen azalea display encircling the ponds; fall colors all around; the comings and goings of mallards, wood ducks, and herons; snapping turtles and frogs. Our Norwich terriers, Plato and Socrates, spend hours on the windowsill helping us out.

A redbud (*Cercis canadensis*), growing against the wall of the house, flanks this view on the left. There is a magical moment in early spring when the goldfinches, which have just gotten their bright yellow plumage, argue over access to thistle seed at the vertical feeder, and the redbud's sharp mauve blossoms reappear on its almost black branches.

Above: Male goldfinch

Opposite: Redbud (*Cercis canadensis*)

Statue Steps and the Wedding Tree

The back porch and other vantage points on that side of the house offer glimpses of "inhabited" steps climbing the grassy bank that slopes gently upward to the north side of the Game Lawn. This stairway took its name, the Statue Steps, from the three bronze figures we placed on it.

The eight steps are old granite curbstones from the streets of Wilmington, which had ended up in a junkyard. With risers 5 to 6 inches high and treads approximately 20 inches deep, they provide a comfortable transition on a grade change of approximately 4 feet over a 13-foot distance. In plan, the stairway resembles a truncated wedge with its narrow end at the bottom and its wide end (27 feet) at the top.

The bronzes, made in 1961 (before we moved to Ashland Hollow) by the Wilmington sculptor Charles Cropper Parks, are life-size portraits of our three oldest children: Dixie, then seven; Peter, five; and Margaretta, two. Rebecca, born later, became the subject of a half-size likeness that Cropper made in 1963-64 for display inside our house.

Above: The step sculpture of our son Peter reading. During the summer *Emilia flammea* (syn. *E. coccinea*) and other plants enclose the bronze boy.

These statues actually got started back when Nancy and I discussed the possibility of having the kids' portraits *painted*. It then occurred to us that young children's most appealing and attractive characteristic is their lovely bodies, which can best be captured in three dimensions.

Cropper chose to portray Dixie holding a wiggling box turtle and Peter reading a picture book about trucks. Ironically, it turns out, these accessories should have been reversed. It is Dixie whose life has been involved with trucks, mostly in conjunction with farming and contracting. As I write, he is restoring a Ford pickup for recreation. Peter should be holding the turtle, because his life has focused on field biology.

The heads of all three statues face downward. Visitors often assume that this is because the bronzes were created expressly for this location, in order to meet the gaze of anyone climbing the steps. Not so! Our early talks with Cropper centered on how nice it would be to gather the sculptures around a tiny pond that could reflect their faces. We never found the right place for such a pond, but as soon as these steps were constructed, it became clear that the statues had their spot.

Above: Charles Cropper Parks, *Rebecca*, 1963-64. Bronze

Right: Steps with Parks's statues of our three older children (Beech Grove in background)

Opposite: Statue Steps with Game Lawn and bank ground cover of crimson pygmy barberry beyond

We left plant pockets in the steps for some softening growth, but to avoid overwhelming the statues, only very small-scale plants were selected. All are herbaceous, with each bulb or perennial a special gem in its own right:

Hosta venusta
Tiny leaves (about 3 ½ inches); very short flower scapes (about 7 inches) with charming small lavender blossoms

Coreopsis verticillata 'Moonbeam'
Leaves like soft, short needles; soft, pale yellow blossoms 1-to-1½ inches across; entire plant only 9-to-10 inches tall

Dodecatheon jeffreyi (bulbous)
Rosette of leaves about 6 inches across; individual mauve blossoms, like scared rabbits, on scapes 7-to-8 inches tall

D. meadia
Almost identical to *D. jeffreyi* except flowers are white and a little taller

Hemerocallis minor
Dainty funnel-shaped, lemon yellow flower on a plant no taller than 14 inches when in blossom. We have two forms: one blooming in early June; the other, in late August.

Each year Paul adds some sort of fine-textured, diminutive tender plants such as scrimlike *Verbena bonariensis*.

Below: *Dodecatheon meadia*

Bottom: The azalea *Rhododendron* 'Stewartstonian' beside Upper Pond paving; the Statue Steps are behind the viewer.

Below: Viewed from the Game Lawn, the small, light green Wedding Tree (*Cornus alternifolia*, right) seems to lean toward the statues'. Beyond them, through the Grove of Umbrella Pines, one sees *Rhododendron* 'Stewartstonian' and tree wisterias in bloom on the south-facing hillside.

Bottom right: Our daughter Margaretta and Michael Martin exchange vows under the Wedding Tree.

The three statues catch one's eye from various parts of the garden. They mark a sort of pedestrian intersection between the back porch, the Upper Pond, the Secret Path, the swimming pool area, and the path to the Winter Garden. Photographs of the statues have appeared in garden publications with sufficient frequency that first-time visitors come looking for them.

To the north of the Statue Steps and behind the retaining wall and double spillways of the highest waterfall (umbrella pines screen the Upper Pond), stands the only mature native red cedar (*Juniperus virginiana*) that remains from the time of our arrival in 1965. Its trunk now has an impressive diameter of 14 inches at breast height.

Six feet to the left of this venerable specimen and closer to the steps, the trunk of another native, the stately pagoda dogwood (*Cornus alternifolia*), leans to the southwest, displaying its beautiful widely spaced, distinctly horizontal branches against the dark green of the red cedar. Our elder daughter and both of our sons have been married in the dogwood's shade as guests stood or sat on the steps, the bank, and the grass to witness the event. For us, this particular *C. alternifolia* will forever be the Wedding Tree.

Overleaf: Snow highlights the nearly horizontal branching habit that distinguishes pagoda dogwood (*Cornus alternifolia*).

184

Upper Pond

Proceeding into the Grove of Umbrella Pines, one comes to a favorite part of the garden for many visitors, and certainly my favorite spot: the Upper Pond. Here we have gathered all of the springs in and around the springhouse to provide a concentrated source for the Stream Valley Garden's waterway. The 30-foot-diameter circular pond is ringed by a planting area: a gently sloping bank only about three feet wide. In recent years, the soil has been kept moist by seepage from the pond through an underwater, "dry" (mortarless) stone wall installed to prevent the original clay bank from eroding into the pond. Informal paving made up of relatively large flat stones from the Avondale Quarry surrounds the bank.

This narrow planting area is surprisingly unique in our stream valley, being the only waterside place that has rich soil and is neither steep nor heavily shaded.

The most extensive paving adjoins the head of the granite stairway up from the stream valley. Roughly 18 feet from the top step to the pond and 30 feet across, this paved arrival area reaches its widest point at water's edge. Visitors pause here to take in the sunniness at this altitude, so different from the stream valley out of which they have just ascended. On either side, as the paving nears the pond, it narrows to a 30-inch-wide stepping-stone path.

Both paths follow the arc of the pond until they reach the ends of the curved stone bench at the base of the mound where the three red cedars and the Japanese umbrella pines grow. There the stepping-stones scatter into a slightly wider paved area between the bench and a vertical stone at water's edge.

Looking across the Upper Pond from the stone bench, one catches sight of the house at the lower end of the Stream Valley Garden.

This upright stone is another of Conrad's characterful standing monoliths. It echoes the verticality of the umbrella pines and the red cedar triad, as well as the rock near the *W. Frederick* inscription in the granite approach steps and the larger vertical stones Conrad built into the retaining wall just downstream from here.

All of this verticality, of course, sharply contrasts with the 24-foot-long backless bench and—the largest horizontal in the whole picture—the surface of the pond itself. Conrad has emphasized the latter by his deployment of another two extremely interesting rocks in the water. Although each of these has a distinctive configuration, they both show smooth, flat tops very close to the pond surface. As the water moves, continually wetting the rocks, they take on an attractive sheen. On one rock we have placed a handsome ceramic frog. He retires to the warmth of the house in winter, and with the help of quite a lot of glue to repair accidents, he has served as a pond-garden focal point for probably 40 years.

Speaking of frogs, an abundance of live ones has called the pond home from the moment we first filled it with water. There is no shortage of frogs in the lower, shadier ponds, but it is up here that their presence is most dramatic. They enjoy sunning on the verdant rim, a safe jump away from the water should an intruder arrive. A regular symphony of plops begins when they wake up and exit. Our terriers, who like to accompany visitors, rush after any frog they see, but as far as I know, they have never been fast enough to catch one.

This pond's surroundings present two horticultural opportunities unavailable elsewhere in the garden. The areas between the big flagstones, especially in the arrival area, are wide enough for

During a benefit for Brandywine Baroque held at Ashland Hollow, this string quartet performed beside the Upper Pond while guests toured the garden.

us to grow plants that enjoy full sun, shrug off occasional foot traffic, and like keeping their roots cool underneath stones.

Mazus reptans, the books say, probably came from the Himalayas. It simply arrived here. No one planted it. I have seen patches of it in lawns in this region where it is not always welcome. Because this plant has broad (one inch across), light-reflecting leaves, it stands out amid fine-textured turfgrass; and thanks to its mat-forming spread (roots grow along the stems) *M. reptans* does not mind being walked on. In May it has purple blue flowers spotted with white, yellow, and purple on their lower lips, really quite charming. Several other plants we tried here have not survived. A notable exception is *Lysimachia japonica* 'Minutissima' (Primrose family), admired solely for its minuscule foliage. It must have flowers, but I confess to never having noticed any. This lysimachia told us that it prefers some shade, by moving itself to a spot where the paving goes under an umbrella pine's lowest limb. Even though *Dodecatheon meadia* cannot tolerate trampling, it seems quite happy here: being bulbous, it dies down after blooming. To take over then, we should really have some mat-former growing with it. Indeed, we should be trying many more things here—especially because this is the only version of "rock gardening" that holds any appeal for me.

The other area with particularly desirable growing conditions— which we have used to great advantage—is the narrow, slightly sloping strip just at pond's edge. In fact, the enormous range of plant possibilities for this limited space has necessitated many trials and utmost discipline in selection and rejection. What makes this area so desirable is its constant moisture. The many plants that love both full sun and moisture for their roots flourish here. Originally there was no masonry at all reinforcing

Mauve-flowered *Dodecatheon jeffreyi* with white *D. meadia* in the background

the pond, so water simply seeped into the banks for the plants to absorb. But by 1996 serious erosion had left the pond misshapen, and many stepping-stones were starting to slide into it. To repair the damage and stave off future problems, we installed the "dry" stone wall inside the pond perimeter, approximately 2 ½ feet high from base to water level. This involved digging a perfectly circular trench and constructing a foundation of heavy rock with smaller, flatter stones near the surface. This wall is invisible from above because the bank overlaps it, gradually sloping right to the water's edge. We were pleased to find that enough water passed through the dry wall to make the bank more moist than it had been before.

The idea of a simple "ring of plants" around the pond edge seemed incompatible with our design. We wanted easy access for close-up viewing of the water surface and its microcosm of frogs and other creatures, but we also planned to frame these views. We have ended up with three clumps of larger plants: one clump associated with the prominent vertical stone (and the stone bench behind it), one to the right of the view from the arrival area, and one to the left of that view.

The first plant to go into this strip, in 1968, was our native marsh marigold (*Caltha palustris*)—not a marigold at all, but a member of the Buttercup family. Although this has thrived, disturbances such as the insertion of trial plants and the building of the underwater wall have decreased the *C. palustris* population. Still, its large, yellow, buttercuplike blossoms in May are most welcome.

Iris ensata var. *spontanea*

In 1972, fellow plantsman and friend Dick Lighty gave me a specimen of *Iris ensata* var. *spontanea*, which he had collected in Korea six years earlier.[7.3] I planted it alongside the vertical stone, starting what we now think of as Clump Number One. Back then, however, I suspect that neither Dick nor I realized how important this plant would become to this part of the garden. When the blossoms first opened, their wonderful electric mauve positively stunned me. At the same moment, I was amazed to notice that our native forget-me-not (*Myosotis scorpioides*) had also taken up residence, partly at pond edge and partly in the water. No one ever planted it (of such dynamics my exuberant gardening friend Kitty May would say, "Well, it just blew in from the field!"). The forget-me-not's color, as you may have guessed, is a lively light blue that elevates the beauty of the iris to fabulous.

Sometime in the next 10 years we planted another iris, *Iris pseudacorus*, to the right of the arrival area at water's edge near some existing *Penisetum alopecuroides* and a *Sedum* 'Herbsfreude' ('Autumn Joy')—the beginning of Clump Number Two. The arresting foliage of this taller (about four feet) iris makes it the most important structural plant at that side of the pond. Its flowers are a friendly yellow with a brownish design painted (by a narrow brush) on the lower petals. The large open structure of the flower qualifies it, I think, as a true fleur de lis. It blooms just as *I. ensata* var. *spontanea* is going off. And it clearly loves this spot, growing both on the bank and down into the water, with heavy discipline every three years or so to halt its advance.

At the base of *I. pseudacorus*, in 1997 we added the tough, round-to-oval foliage of *Caltha palustris* var. *polypetala*, a gift from those intrepid plantsmen Joe Eck and the late Wayne Winterrowd. The large scale of the two irises' leaves relates them to each other, while formal differences in the foliage create a striking contrast.

A remarkably handsome hibiscus, *Hibiscus coccineus*, joined this group in 1987. (Although the plant originated in the coastal swamps of Georgia and Florida, I first saw it growing in dry gravely soil in front of an abandoned gas station partway down the Delmarva Peninsula.) Each year its multiple stems rise from the ground to about five feet, and it produces intriguing red-and-chartreuse blossoms during a long period each summer. The red petals are separated at their bases, allowing the chartreuse calyces to show through. The arrangement and shape of the flower parts, combined with leaves resembling those of "pot" (*Cannabis sativa*), give the whole plant a highly distinctive character.

Clump Number Three, to the left of the view from the arrival area, initially consisted of two plants. I planted one of them, indigenous *Sparganium americanum* (American bur-reed), at Nancy's suggestion. Besides really knowing her native plants, she has an eye for those that ought to be used more in gardens. *S. americanum* did so well that after a couple of years settling in on the bank, it sent runners into the water and down to the pond bottom, which they found very much to their liking. Late one summer, we came back from vacation to discover a third of the pond surface hidden under the bur-reed's attractive dark green leaves. Now that we know where it belongs, we are limiting *S. americanum* to a single pot *in* the pond where it keeps company with the waterlily *Nymphaea* 'Helvola', contrasting nicely with its smaller-than-most waterlily leaves. The blossoms of 'Helvola' are proportional in scale, and a romantic soft yellow.

The other member of Clump Number Three—now the only one on land—is the green-and-white variegated rush *Scirpus schoenoplectus* (syn. *Scirpus tabernaemontana* 'Albescens'), another gift from Joe and Wayne. It now seems as though this was meant to be all along. As the umbrella pines have spread inward and the first two clumps have expanded, this "light touch" of the rush seems just right. The subtle repetition of its many tubular stems—nearly uniform in diameter for their entire 4½-foot length, each green stem etched longitudinally with off-white—would be lost among companion plantings. But for this small space, it is a superb piece of sculpture. It holds its own.

Below: *Hemerocallis* 'Spiderman'

Bottom: *Hibiscus coccineus*

Opposite: The Upper Pond's ceramic frog with (from left) candelabra primroses, purple *Iris ensata* var. *spontanea*, and yellow *I. pseudacorus*

Candelabra primroses

Since the submerged wall began letting more moisture penetrate this planting area, two groups of plants have done especially well here: candelabra primroses and recent lobelia hybrids that have *Lobelia syphilitica* as one parent. The primroses bloom in June; the lobelias, in late August or early September.

Anyone who knew the Quarry Garden at Winterthur during H. F. du Pont's lifetime, or has known it since its restoration under Tom Buchter's direction, appreciates the magic of the candelabra primroses there. Besides having a beautiful structure with well-spaced whorls of flowers on single stems, they exhibit a color combination unequaled, as far as I know, in any other group of plants. The mixture includes just enough lavender and mauve to show off the richness of yellows, coppers, and oranges.

A tangerine variant available back in the time of H. F. du Pont accented the brilliant color design so effectively, despite being unreliably hardy, that H. F. kept some in a greenhouse over winter and plugged them into the garden when spring arrived. In recent years, Joe Eck and Wayne Winterrowd have grown a group of *Primula* x *bulleesiana*, the most important part of the original Winterthur planting, at their Vermont garden, North Hill. The primroses have done very well—in fact, replenishing themselves each year with their own seedlings.

Using seed from that group, White Flower Farm has propagated plants it sells as "North Hill Strain," some of which we purchased in 1997 and planted on either side of the vertical stone. They produced beautiful blossoms but set no seed. After enriching the soil in this area, we bought more plants in 2003 and added Tom Buchter's gift of *P. pulverulenta* the next year. Another gift of more *P.* x *bulleesiana* arrived from him in 2005. This sort of persistence and passion is definitely good for the garden—and good for the gardener as well.

Around the same time, Clump Number One received what may be its finishing touch with the addition of an exceptionally large horsetail reed (*Equisetum hyemale* var. *affine* [syn. *E. hyemale* 'Robustum']). This leafless beauty attempts to keep its black-ringed green hollow stems vertical and orderly, the way the *Scirpus* does. Periodically, however, a stem or two will blow over and young sprouts will occur along the bottom half of the stem, adding to its crazy charm.

Lobelia siphilitica, which is native to this property, puts up stalks of violet-lavender flowers in late August and September. Because this plant is usually one of the few perennials greeting us when we get back from vacation in mid-August, it has always been a favorite of ours. When we learned that the North Carolina

Lobelia 'La Fresco', a Manus hybrid

lobelia expert Thurman Manus was breeding this with other species and cultivars to get new color forms, we knew we should try them. Paul got a "fan mix" of seeds from Park Seed Company in 1995. When we returned from vacation that year, we found a half-whiskey barrel of these lobelias in full bloom in front of the house. In the muggy August heat the colors were exuberantly refreshing: deep red, shocking purple, electric mauve, and all the shades in between.

We were hooked! More seed has been planted every year since then. Some seedlings, we have discovered, are hardier than others. In recent years, Paul has taken to potting the seedlings and bringing them through two winters in the greenhouse before planting them in the garden. This makes it easy to determine which is going to be hardy and which is not.

We have also bought named plants[7.4] and been given some by friends. The following cultivars are *Lobelia* x *speciosa* (*L. cardinalis* x *L. siphilitica*):

'Sparkle Devine'—deep electric purple
'Knee High'—deep violet
'La Fresco'—dusty, muted plum

Planted on the north side of the Upper Pond, this colony gets the most sun light available in any part of that garden area. The result is a breathtaking color display in late summer, even when a typical seasonal drought may be playing havoc with the rest of Ashland Hollow.

Now you can understand how a long season of bloom, an array of good plants responding vigorously to the presence of water, and the intimacy of the umbrella pine grove contribute to making this a favorite part of our entire garden. The cool stone bench is a great place to read, to contemplate the frogs, dragonflies, and current bloom, or to take a nap on a warm summer day.

NOTES

7.1. This bell originally hung in a small belfry atop the one-room schoolhouse between Corner Ketch and Whiteman's Garage on Pleasant Hill Road. It was rescued by my father, William H. Frederick, Sr., and came to me after his death.

7.2. Inserting this "glass box" window in 1991 is the only major change we have made since the house was built. The bay replaced two single-casement windows with a wall segment in between, which interrupted the view from the center of the dining table.

7.3. Richard Lighty traveled to Korea in 1966 on a plant-introduction expedition, as part of a cooperative program of Longwood Gardens (where Dick then worked as a plant breeder) and the United States Department of Agriculture. In Korea for four months during the growing season, he mailed back cuttings, live specimens, and seeds of 450 different plants. Dick has introduced into commerce a number of those finds that performed well in his own Pennsylvania garden, Springwood. *Iris ensata* var. *spontanea* is my favorite, but there are others I admire greatly, including *Aruncus aethusifolius* and *Calamagrostis arundinacea* var. *brachytricha*. When I asked Dick when the iris had been collected, he wrote back: "Friday, 15 July 1966 on the slopes of Mt. Hall, Cheju-do, Korea, and came into the U.S.D.A. Plant Introduction Station at Glendale, MD that same month. It was distributed to me as a single plant, since neither Longwood nor the U.S.D.A. were interested in it." This is an excellent example of the organizational quality of this great plantsman's mind!

7.4. Tony Avent
Plant Delights Nursery, Inc.
9241 Sauls Road, Raleigh, NC 27603
phone 919-772-4794
fax 919-662-0370
office@PlantDelights.com

Henry Greenewalt, *Beech Grove*, 2007. Charcoal on paper, 22 x 26 in. Courtesy of the artist.

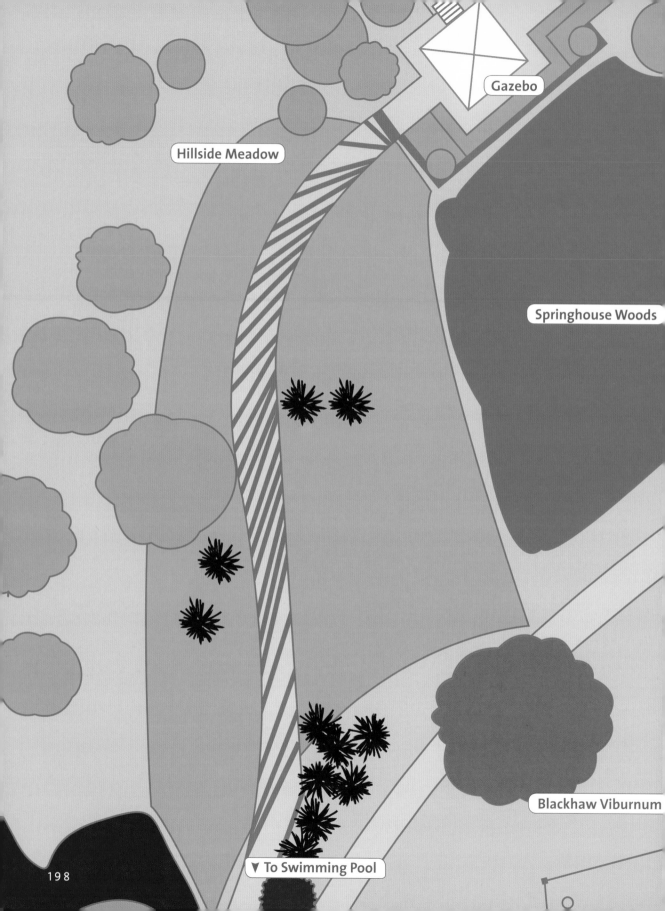

Gazebo

Hillside Meadow

Springhouse Woods

Blackhaw Viburnum

▼ To Swimming Pool

198

8 Vertical March on a Hillside Meadow

Above: Patrick Ross Arnold, *October, Looking North*, 2006. Oil on canvas, 16 x 20 in. The shrub with vivid fall foliage at center is the blackhaw viburnum (*Viburnum prunifolium*) in our meadow.

Opposite: Railroad-tie steps with low risers provide for comfortable walking. Because the timbers fit the natural landform, they give a feeling of security. A drama unfolds as the ascent curves through clumps of large vertical evergreens, and one catches glimpses of the hidden gazebo.

Sentimental Meadow

The year 1976 was a momentous one for the garden. It was the year we closed Millcreek Nursery.[8.1]

On a glorious September day we sold at wholesale auction all of the plants then growing in the fields. For 24 years we had cultivated a selection of ornamental plants primarily for use in our professional design work. And because we had striven to enlarge the palette of plants used in gardens around here, much of our stock was unobtainable at other nurseries in the United States and Canada. I had mentally reserved quite a few of those plants for use in our personal garden. With the nursery closing and the auction impending, it was time to move those plants to Ashland Hollow. A number of them will crop up later in this tale, but I will start with the one that continues to be the most visually significant in our garden: *Taxus* x *media* 'Sentinalis'.

Before discussing *T.* x *media* 'Sentinalis' in detail, I must describe the Hillside Meadow where we planted nine of these sentinel yews. This open ground, between the swimming pool and the barn, is one of the steepest slopes on the property. Just to the east of it, on equally steep terrain uphill from the springhouse, stands a small patch of woods. The sight of meadow and woods together was a big part of the enchantment that swept over Nancy and me when we first saw the property; we resolved then to do as much as possible to keep them as they were.

The meadow was clothed for the winter in marvelous amber broom sedge (*Andropogon virginicus*), which as kids we had known as "poverty grass."

About halfway up the hillside at the edge of the woods, we spotted a well-established domestic pear (*Pyrus communis*) "escape." The next spring, to our delight, its branches were tightly packed with glistening white blossoms.

At the bottom of the meadow was the largest blackhaw viburnum (*Viburnum prunifolium*) either of us had ever seen. Visitors seldom recognize it because it resembles a thickly branched, multitrunk tree, and a tree-form version of this shrub is quite rare.

That pear is still with us and, though the fruits are too hard for humans to eat, we can count on the spectacular blossoms to appear every spring. The viburnum, now 42 feet in spread and very close to 20 feet tall, remains in good health. The several gracefully intertwining trunks splay out into branches weighed down by smaller branches and twigs near their ends. This presumably contributes to the dipping or pendulous effect in the outer third of each branch. Fearful of fractures and breaks caused by accumulated ice and snow, we thin the branches occasionally. The abundance of white blossoms and dark blue fruit varies from year to year.

We had hoped that the meadow's cover of broom sedge would prevail indefinitely, because we had been told that the plant was allelopathic, meaning it would discourage the intrusion of other herbs. This has not been the case. In addition to the expected woody invaders, such as Japanese honeysuckle (*Lonicera japonica* 'Halliana') and Oriental bittersweet (*Celastrus orbiculatus*), the greatest thugs have turned out to be several heavy-duty forms of goldenrod. Today, only a few remnants of broom sedge survive, and the winter picture of dead goldenrods has been sufficiently depressing that we now mow the hillside in the fall rather than in the spring, as had been our practice.

Fortunately, the character of the meadow has also changed for the better, and there are two reasons for the improvement. First, the most thuggish goldenrods seem to be diminishing slowly, and they are being replaced by smaller, less aggressive, more graceful ones. Second, our trial introduction of other meadow flowers has, for the most part, succeeded.

My idea of putting in orange butterfly weed (*Asclepias tuberosa*) was a bust—rodents like the roots. Luckily, several gardening friends looked upon this dry clay hillside as an interesting challenge. In 1979 we received the following recommendations: from Virginia Callaway, the dramatic *Silphium compositum*; from Bill Brumback, the same plant's close relation *S. asteriscus* var. *laevicaule* (syn. *S. dentatum*); from Polly Hill, *Manfreda virginica*; from Tom Buchter, *Liatris scariosa* and *Monarda fistulosa*; and from Hal Bruce, *Helianthus mollis*. These all suited my goal, an alternative to the standard "old field" effect, the look of disused farmland cycling back to nature. Each friend sent seeds or plants, all of which have thrived.

Monarda fistulosa

As Nancy and I had initially envisioned, these plants turn midsummer into a time of great delight. The colors, sounds, and movements of birds, butterflies, and other attractive insects are captivating. I have become especially fond of Hal's "prairie sunflower," *H. mollis*, which, though only 2-to-2½ feet high, is vigorous enough to hold its own and even spread into some of the worst goldenrod areas. It has fuzzy gray green leaves (the botanical description makes me laugh: "densely and softly hairy, scabrous—hispid above, ashy pubescent beneath") and handsome, rich yellow daisylike (disc) flowers. This Hillside Meadow changes some each year, and we enjoy sitting back and watching.

Steps on Contour

From the outset, our long-range planning embraced the upper parts of the hillsides surrounding the Stream Valley as significant parts of the whole garden. It took the installation of four flights of steps to accomplish this aim. We built one flight through the Hillside Meadow in early 1971. It leads from the swimming pool area and (then future) Winter Garden to the Green and White Path and the gazebo (also added later). We had already constructed a prototype for all four sets in 1968: an outdoor stairway connecting the east side of the Studio Garden with the stream valley below, via the archway under the house.

Except for the Statue Steps and those in the Stream Valley Garden, all of our garden steps use railroad ties. Because these eventually rot, we replace a few every year. During our annual vacation in Maine, I look longingly at the slabs of beautiful, everlasting granite lying about in a number of inactive quarries. Had those slabs been left down the road from us in Delaware, we surely would have put them to use at Ashland Hollow.

Most of our paths and steps are 5 feet wide. A few are 6 feet wide. Each tie is set on 6 inches of Type 2B crushed stone. The treads initially have 2 inches of crushed bark on 4 inches of the same crushed stone. All risers are $4\frac{1}{2}$ inches high and all treads measure 18 inches deep or some multiple thereof.

In line with our belief that minimal change is the best way to honor the sculptural beauty of our valley's landforms, we have not built steps by the usual process of cutting and filling. Instead, we have set almost every step on the terrain's existing

Opposite: Timber steps below the Studio Garden, built to the same specifications used throughout Ashland Hollow

contour. This is most easily done by laying out a centerline for the whole set of steps, and then measuring $2\frac{1}{2}$ feet out to either side, at 90-degree angles from the centerline, to determine the steps' outer boundaries, which we mark with strings. Next, in order to draw up a paper plan of the centerline's changing elevation, we drive stakes into the ground at 10-foot intervals along that line and shoot their grades with a transit level on site. After entering these readings on the plan at the same intervals, we can develop a vertical profile. This makes it easy to figure out how many $4\frac{1}{2}$-inch risers are necessary between each pair of 10-foot markers, and accordingly, whether all treads will need to be 18 inches deep or some multiple of that (36 inches, 54 inches, and so on).

The crew installing the railroad ties uses this plan to put a tie in each location indicated on the centerline and then swivel the tie until its ends meet the two boundary strings, at an elevation equal to that on the centerline of the string. This means that very few steps lie at right angles to the centerline, as would be the case with a normal stairway. It also means that the steps hug the extant landforms, negating the need for regrading. Two successive grass ramps lead from the swimming pool area to a landing at the base of the Hillside Meadow. The lower ramp starts near the pool and rises to the elevation of the first Winter Garden path. There, after an approximately 180-degree turn, the upper ramp rises almost parallel to the lower one until it meets the meadow landing.[8.2]

Construction of these ramps enabled us to start the steps to the gazebo site from the western side of the meadow and take them diagonally across its more gradual upper slope. Seen from other parts of the garden, the steps perform the aesthetic function of leading the viewer's eye to the barn on the crest of the hill and the gazebo that now sits just below it.

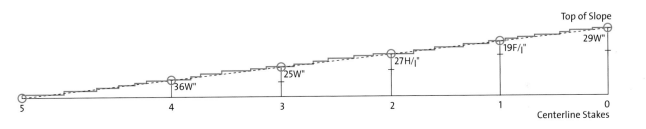

Sample Profile of Timber Steps

We have used diagrams like this, drawn to scale in pencil, to design timber steps for various slopes in the garden.

Top: In this very early shot of the Hillside Meadow, stakes act as placeholders for the future gazebo and surrounding plantings.

Middle: To prevent yew branches from bending outward under the weight of snow, we keep them tied in permanently.

Bottom: The yews at maturity

Dark Green Sentinels

When many plantsmen first visit our garden, they mistake our unusually narrow, dark green *Taxus* x *media* 'Sentinalis' for Irish yew (*T. baccata* 'Fastigiata'), a common cemetery tree in the British Isles. One occasionally sees Irish yews in old graveyards in this part of the United States as well, but they are of borderline winter-hardiness here and quite unhappy with our hot summers. The *T.* x *media* 'Sentinalis' in our hillside meadow do not complain about either condition.

A sharp-eyed nurseryman and plant lover, John Vermeulen, of Neshanic Station, New Jersey, spotted a number of *Taxus* seedlings coming up in an abandoned field at the old Hicks Nurseries (founded in 1853) on Long Island. He was immediately drawn to those with a narrow, fastigiate shape.

In the business of propagating "liners" for sale to wholesale growers, he felt confident that a hardy, heat-tolerant vertical yew would interest his customers. He selected a half-dozen seedlings ranging from narrow to narrower to narrowest, named them, and stuck cuttings of each in his propagating bench. I believe that there were also forms of *T. cuspidata* (Japanese yew) and *T. baccata* (English yew) at Hicks Nurseries, and possibly some *T. canadensis*, as well, which makes them the putative parents of Vermeulen's selections.

We first planted his cultivar 'Sentinalis' (the narrowest form he listed, I believe) at Millcreek Nursery. By the time we were ready to transfer nine of those yews to Ashland Hollow in 1976, the plants ranged in height from four to nine feet, providing a nice opportunity for arranging three varied groups of them along the meadow steps.

I have always felt that plants with a fastigiate form attract the eye more readily than those with a horizontal or weeping habit. For this reason I have never isolated a solitary fastigiate specimen unless I wanted the viewer to focus instantly on that point. Such a composition can be visually irritating. If carefully arranged (occultly balanced)[8.3] in groups, however, slender upright plants can create a strong and attractively contained statement. We clustered five sentinel yews at the bottom of the meadow steps, at the corner of the landing on the right as one starts the ascent. We placed two more yews roughly one-third of the way up the steps on the left, and another pair two-thirds of the way up on the right. Back then, the relative positions of plants of various heights seemed critical to the design. But over time the trees have evened out to almost the same height (16 to 20 feet), and those in each group have essentially grown together. Now it is only the placement of the three groups that matters, and it is all a great success.

As one goes up and down the steps on what is, after all, a precipitous incline, this planting gives a sense of security while simultaneously framing vignettes of the garden below. The hillside is clearly visible from the swimming pool, the driveway, the Vegetable Garden, and parts of the Winter Garden. From each vantage point, the "structured" meadow evokes an intense yet different response.

In 1991, Nancy and I visited the Val d'Orcia, a multifarm valley in Tuscany with a villa at one end that had belonged to the late Iris and Tony Origo. Very soon after the First World War this pioneering couple bought a badly run-down estate, La Foce, and poured energy and money into its rejuvenation and improvement. The Origos restored and enlarged the villa (formerly an inn), and developed a very fine garden with the help of Cecil Pinsent. The view from the house and garden takes in the whole valley. In addition to instituting modern farming practices, the Origos attended to the aesthetic aspect of the scene. The principal road zigzagging up a hillside reminded them of the background landscape scene in a particular Renaissance painting (perhaps more than one painting), which was structured with the dark green verticals of Italian cypress (*Cupressus sempervirens*), a tree even narrower than our sentinel yew. The landscape in the painting is a distinguished one, and so is this artistic touch in the Val d'Orcia. In a small way, our Hillside Meadow planting manifests the same impulse felt by Renaissance painters and the Origos.

It was only a few years later that I became aware of a similar use of verticals in Chris Woods's transformation of the former Adolph Rosengarten estate, Chanticleer, in Wayne, Pennsylvania—a zigzag march of verticals on a meadow hillside teasing the eye of a relatively distant viewer.

An Italian use of verticals similar to ours, at La Foce in the Val d'Orcia, originally laid out by Iris and Tony Origo after the First World War

View Worth a Viewpoint

Of the many good sites for viewing the hillside composition at Ashland Hollow only one is permanently marked. It lies at the lower edge of the Winter Garden's eastern end (distinct from the principal Winter Garden path and its focal point). This heavily planted area offers just the one view out.

Reached by means of an attractive flagstone path, the area takes the form of a circle, 15 feet in diameter, covered with a handsome long-leaved fescue that we leave unmown. The path, roughly 80 feet long, consists of large, irregularly shaped tannish brown stepping-stones found nearby, which touch one another only along the path's axis. [8.4]

Within the fescue circle, each of a set of five sheet-bronze seats—designed and fabricated by the blacksmith-turned-sculptor H. Jack Hemenway in 2005[8.5]—rests on an irregularly shaped stepping-stone from the same batch used in the entrance path. Three seats form a tight group to the right of the path's main axis; the other two sit close together to the left. Each group touches part of the circumference of the circle, and the stones have been cut to meet that curved perimeter. The bronze seats are vertically rectangular with a slight outward camber on all four sides. The three to the right have what look like bronze pillows on top; those to the left do not.

The placement of the bronze seats and their stone bases encourages viewers to look in the direction of the Hillside Meadow, its on-contour steps, and the grandeur of the vertical yews. Close in, the heavy planting of *Taxus* to the northeast blocks out the nursery and the Vegetable Garden. Large deciduous hollies reaching above the yews focus the view to the meadow above the *Taxus* planting. The view is framed to

Opposite: Bronze seats in a circle of fescue focus attention on the steps, the yews, and the barn (for the trajectory of this view, see the two red arrows on plan, page 215).

the right by two *Ilex* 'Harvest Red', and to the left by a cluster consisting of:

Ilex 'Raritan Chief' (one plant)

I. 'Autumn Glow' (two plants)

I. verticillata 'Winter Red' (one)

I. verticillata 'Scarlett O'Hara' (three)

The lowest point of the view centers on the ancient blackhaw viburnum (*Viburnum prunifolium*) with the Hillside Meadow behind it. The timber steps rise across the hillside from left to right, passing between several extraordinarily large and dramatic *Taxus* x *media* 'Sentinalis'. Near the top of the view a broad spreading Yoshino cherry (*Prunus* x *yedoensis*) displays its form handsomely against the distant Conifer Windbreak. The grove of American hollies brackets the view to the left.

Even farther uphill from the cherry tree, a white oak, an orange- twigged *Cornus sanguinea* 'Winter Beauty', and a majestic *Abies firma* stand near the barn, which peeks above them. Off to the right, through the Springhouse Woods, one can just catch a tantalizing glimpse of the two-story gazebo.

Below: Yoshino cherry (*Prunus* x *yedoensis*) in early spring. The blackhaw viburnum below it has not yet flowered or leafed out.

Bottom: The same viburnum (at least 60 years old) in full spring bloom.

View of Hillside Meadow from Winter Garden

215

Looking down from the gazebo onto timber
steps and vertical *Taxus* in the Hillside
Meadow at wildflower time

8.1. For a detailed history see Frederick, William H., Jr. *Millcreek Nursery 1952-1976, A Brief History* (privately published, 2001; available at the University of Delaware's Hugh M. Morris Library).

8.2. The other three sets of steps incorporating hillsides into the Ashland Hollow garden were built at the following locations (listed with dates of completion):
    From Studio Garden to (future)
        Frog statue, 35 steps; January 31, 1971
    From Umbrella Pine Grove to Wisteria
        Lawn, 40 steps; August 21, 1975
    From southern end of Game Lawn to
        (future) Winter Garden, 30 steps;
        October 24, 1993
Specifications for the above matched those described for our first set of steps, constructed from the east side of the Studio Garden to the Stream Valley Garden in 1968.

8.3. For an explanation of this term, see Chapter 3, page 63.

8.4. As yet only partially realized, plans for both sides of the path envision tightly planted beds of small plants carefully selected to delight connoisseurs. Selections are to be made on the basis of strong winter interest and arranged for maximum color and textural contrast. The palette at present includes the following (already doing well in this area):
    Cephalotaxus harringtonia 'Prostrata'
    Cyclamen coum (mauve, purple, and
        deep red forms)
    Elaeagnus pungens 'Maculata'
    Hamamelis x *intermedia* 'Arnold Promise'
    H. x *intermedia* 'Pallida'
    Ilex 'Verboom'
    Kerria japonica 'Golden Guinea'
    Narcissus 'Rijnveldts Early Sensation'
    Pachysandra terminalis 'Green Sheen'
        (repeated from elsewhere in the
        Winter Garden)
    Vinca minor 'Aurea'
    Viola labradorica
    Yucca flaccida 'Golden Sword' (repeating
        another grouping across the circle)

8.5. These were inspired by wooden stools that Nancy and I had admired at the Soho Grand Hotel in New York City. In a conversation with Jack, I bemoaned the fact that those stools would not hold up outdoors in a garden. Jack took this as a challenge. The following winter, one of his stools—fabricated out of sheet bronze—appeared in our breakfast area at Ashland Hollow, for us to take on trial. Nancy and I both loved its appearance. She found the height comfortable. I thought it too low and tossed a pillow on top, which made it just right for me. When Jack came for a visit a while later, he liked my idea of making a "pillow" out of bronze as well. The result: five stools—two without pillows and three with.

8.6. The planting around this viewing area is noteworthy for its strong character. As one enters on the flagstone path, three mature cut-leaf European beech trees provide a stunning background all year.
    Layered plantings fill the space between the beeches and the fescue circle in the following order: red-twig dogwood (*Cornus sericea* 'Bloodgood'; see 8.7, below), *Ilex glabra* (cultivar name unknown; this stays dark green in the winter, is well-dressed to the ground, and has densely spaced leaves), *Yucca flaccida* 'Golden Sword', and *Bergenia* 'Sunningdale'. A trio of specimen paperbark maples (*Acer griseum*) provides structure to the entire surround of this area. The *Taxus* planting to the east, structured with two *Pinus thunbergii* 'Oculis Draconis', has a backdrop of three *Ilex* x *meserveae* 'Mesid' Blue Maid®. A single *Ilex* 'Sparkleberry' stands on axis with the path.

8.7. My original plant was a gift from that superb plantsman Doug Ruhren.

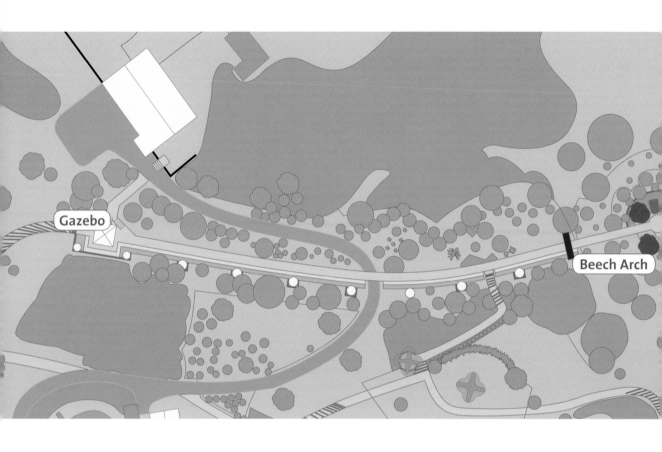

Gazebo

Beech Arch

Above: The Green and White Path, between
the gazebo hilltop and the Beech Arch, was
designed to be seen on summer afternoons,
evenings, and moonlit nights. On the
plan, white dots represent white-flowered
Hibiscus syriacus 'Diana' standards.

Opposite: Stan Sperlak, *Morning on the
Green and White Path*, 2007. Pastel, 12 x 16 in.

9 Green and White Path

Top of the Garden

The head of the Hillside Meadow Steps marks the beginning of what had been a second sod-covered swale for slowing the flow of storm water and, in this case, diverting it past the portion of the south-facing hillside within the garden and beyond the house into the east meadow.[9.1] Anticipating that the surface of this swale might someday double as a path, we made it more than six feet wide.

Sure enough, in 1979 we transformed that strip of land into the Green and White Path (or, to be totally accurate, the Green, White, and Gray Path), a place to be enjoyed on summer afternoons and evenings and by moonlight.

The path forms part of a long narrow area that would be perfectly rectangular if it did not partially follow the hillside's gentle curvature from west to northeast. Because the path also curves as it gradually descends from west to east, it creates an allure that a straight line would lack.

As the highest path in the garden, this provides the visitor many fine views to the west, south, and east. The best of all occurs at its western end, above the Springhouse Woods. The woodland seems to grip the path and fix it securely to the steepest part of the hillside.

Certainly, one of the path's raisons d'être is helping to complete the circuit around the garden. Approached from the Hillside Meadow Steps, the path starts at the gazebo, which we built in 1989 to celebrate the garden's 25th anniversary the following year. For some time we had intended to put a terminating feature at this point, probably a summerhouse or a gazebo. But I was held back (unconsciously, I believe) by a concern about blocking the view for anyone approaching this

Opposite
Top: The gazebo under construction, 1989

Middle: From the landing between the two flights of steps, a grass path climbs to the barn.

Bottom: A view from the barn path to the upper flight of steps with the Spring House woods in the background.

area from the east. In an early morning dream I found myself in the harbor of Rio de Janeiro where several newer waterfront buildings had been constructed on stilts, so that passersby one street inland could look through to the harbor. As I awoke, the connection between the Rio buildings and Ashland Hollow's gazebo hit home. If we mounted our gazebo on legs, we could preserve the ground-level vista straight ahead. After some sketching, I contacted Peter Shepheard in England,[9.2] to get his reaction. He was keen on both the problem and the solution. Besides producing drawings for the beautiful structure now in place,[9.3] he designed a perfectly proportional finial and had it made of lead in England.

The gazebo's elevated platform is accessible by two sets of steps. Seven stone ones leave the Green and White Path at an acute angle (slightly north of west), climbing the hillside until they meet another grassy path. Just to the left, eight wooden steps complete the ascent to the gazebo.

The point of the climb is, of course, the views. To the south, thanks to a cut we made through the Springhouse Woods, one can see to the Orchard on the far hilltop. To the west one gazes down on the delightful pattern of the Hillside Meadow Steps. And to the east, one takes in more of the total Green and White Path than is visible from any vantage point below.

Plantings alongside the walk hide its eastern end, conjuring the illusion that the walk goes on a great deal farther than it actually does. When Geoffrey Jellicoe visited the United States around 1991, and stopped by Ashland Hollow to see the gazebo his countryman and friend Peter Shepheard had designed, he noticed that the Green and White Path aims toward what appears to be a niche cut into the woods on the horizon (some

Overleaf
Left page: Views from the Gazebo include the Hillside Meadow Steps in spring.

Right page, top: The distant hilltop Orchard above the drive, seen from the gazebo through the Springhouse Woods

Right page, bottom right: The evergreen-structured planting to the east

223

distance away in the nature preserve next door to us). Gazing at the woods, he exclaimed, "Isn't it remarkable that this path goes that far!"

In fact, the Green and White Path concludes much nearer to the gazebo with a clipped archway of burgundy-colored European beech (*Fagus sylvatica* 'Riversii').[9.4] Hidden among the beech leaves is the vine *Clematis* x *durandii*. When its deep cobalt blue flowers open (with distinctly angular, widely separated petals), they give the impression that the beech itself has come into bloom. The striking harmony, in both color and shape, of the deep burgundy foliage and the cobalt flowers emphatically signals the transition to the next part of the garden, the Frog Steps.

Above: Catherine Drabkin, *Path*, 2006. Oil on canvas, 15 x 16 in. Courtesy of the artist. The reddish structure (center left) is a pair of Rivers European beech trained over a stainless-steel arch to mark the end of the Green and White Path.

Left: A *Clematis* x *durandii* climbs through the beech branches. The vine's cobalt flowers are stunning when they blossom among the burgundy leaves of the trees.

Above: View from the gazebo at *Cornus kousa* time

The Strong Grip of Minimal Color

Selecting the color theme of green, white, and gray for this path-side garden fulfilled a smoldering ember of a memory that had been with me ever since my first visit to Sissinghurst. It flickered as my mind went through the various alternative color combinations and then burst into a "just right" flame. At Sissinghurst the visitor is treated to the pleasure of the Purple Border as the first item on the circuit. The wonderful brief wave of cool color combinations in that border and in the adjacent Rose Garden are followed by a conflagration of reds, oranges, and yellows in the Cottage Garden. What could be better than that? Vita knew! Next at Sissinghurst, one passes through the long Yew Walk; the plants block out the rest of the garden, and one's eyes are cleansed of that vibrant color experience. Then the design arranges a charming—shall I say polite?—departure by landing one in the midst of a carefully modulated display of green, white, and silver gray! I cannot claim that such adept emotional planning lies behind our take on the same color scheme. I did know that I wanted to experiment and find out which plants could be used in our country and climate to achieve a similar effect—and this spot seemed culturally suitable and free of visual distractions for anyone walking through.

I had also hoped to accomplish this entirely with woody plants, to me synonymous with low maintenance. Subconsciously, I may have anticipated the interplay between this garden and the adjoining Frog Steps area (the next event on *our* circuit), also being planned at that time. A clean, clear palette would certainly enhance the impact of chartreuse and scarlet, one of several surprises the Frog Steps would spring on visitors. Although not, perhaps, polite, this jolt satisfied the Fauvist in me.

My green, white, and gray experiment involved trying out an enormous number of woody plants, about half of which I eventually discarded. The greens, I found, needed to be dark, almost black. The grays could not be cool blue grays; only warm shades would do. And the whites, of course, had to shine and sparkle. I confess that I knuckled under to herbaceous plants, because soft gray lamb's ear (*Stachys byzantina*) could provide an ideal ground-cover color. After that, the floodgates were open, but primarily in the selection of foreground details.[9.5]

Structure

Existing site constrictions dictated the layout. The path could not run straight; it had to bend. It could, however, be adjoined by a strongly articulated spine. This would structure the whole area and give it sorely needed scale. We have met that need with a hedge of clipped *Taxus cuspidata* 'Nana', approximately 27 inches high, on the downhill side of the path, which follows the very slight curve and descending slope of the grass swale. Just behind the hedge, at 42-foot intervals, we planted individual standards of *Hibiscus syriacus* 'Diana', identically trained to a single stem with a ball on top. About 6-to-10 inches of each stem is visible above the hedge, supporting a 50-inch-diameter globe. The curved line of jaunty clipped balls makes a strong statement.

The voids above the hedge and between the trimmed hibiscus become broad windows onto varying green, white, and gray plant "events" and seasonal activities in distant parts of the garden.[9.6] The 15-inch-wide lamb's-ear planting on the path side of the hedge is sharply delineated against the grass of the path by sunken Ryerson steel edging.

Sarah Yeoman, *View from Green and White Path into Rest of Garden (Ashland Hollow)*, 2006. Watercolor, 20 x 25 in.

Background

Near the top of the hill that rises above the Green and White Path, a part of our windbreak planting contains beautiful mature conifers: the dark greens of Nordmann fir (*Abies nordmanniana*) and Japanese fir (*A. firma*) contrast with eastern white pine (*Pinus strobus*), Mexican white pine (*P. ayacahuite*), and Japanese white pine (*P. parviflora* 'Glauca') with its dramatic open, sculptural shapes.

This background sets off the black greens and warm grays of our palette of smaller-scale plants, such as various *Taxus, Chamaecyparis, Juniperus* 'Gray Owl', and several extremely fine *Ilex* cultivars.[9.7]

Establishing the strong spine of the hedge and the *Hibiscus syriacus* 'Diana' topiaries enabled us to make the rest of our design quite informal. For the most part, this relies on either repetitive groupings of a single plant for over-all impact during seasons when the path is primarily intended to be viewed (late June, July, August, and early September), or more detailed planting to be enjoyed up close, regardless of the season.

Opposite: *Paeonia* 'Festiva Maxima' at the top of the stone steps to the gazebo

Major Bloom Seasons (Seven)

These seasonal splashes of white involve the following plants:

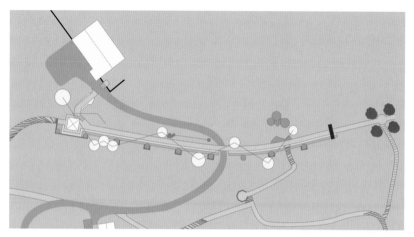

1. Late May, Early June

We have staggered eight Korean dogwood trees (*Cornus kousa* 'Milky Way') from side to side along the full length of the path. Companion plantings include *Crambe cordifolia, Philadelphus* 'Burkwoodii',[9.8] *Allium stipitatum* 'White Giant', *Paeonia* 'Festiva Maxima', and *P.* 'White Ivory'.

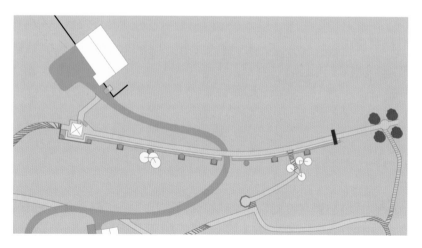

2. Mid-June

Two clusters of *Stewartia koreana*—two trees in one cluster, three in the other—stand on the downhill side of the path, to provide the best view directly into their waxy, white camellia-like flowers.

232

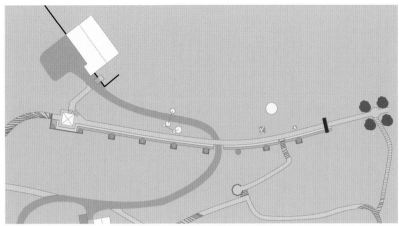

Above: *Lilium* 'Black Dragon'

Opposite
Top left: *Ligustrum quihoui*

Top right:
Lilium 'Black Dragon'

Bottom left: *Vitex agnus-castus* 'Silver Spire'

Bottom right: *Miscanthus sinensis* 'Variegatus'

3. Late June

The shrub *Deutzia ningpoensis* (syn. *D. chuni*) has lead-colored buds and stems and white bells. *Onopordum acanthium* is a dramatically sculptural, silver-foliaged Scotch thistle. One large specimen shrub of *Ligustrum quihoui* is accompanied by *Lilium* 'Black Dragon'.

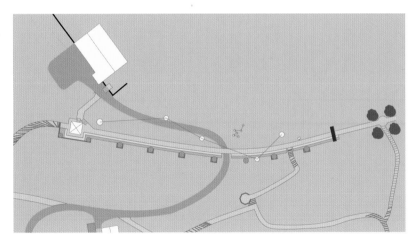

4. Mid-July

We have scattered five individual specimen shrubs of *Vitex agnus-castus* 'Silver Spire' on either side of the path from end to end, accompanied by *Yucca flaccida* (Henry selection) and the diminutive white spires of *Verbascum chaixii* 'Album'.

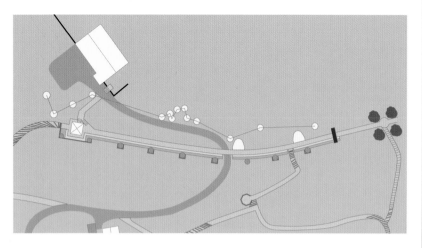

5. Mid-August

Nine *Hydrangea paniculata* 'White Tiara' form background drifts on the uphill side, along with patches of *Liriope muscari* 'Monroe White' as a ground cover.

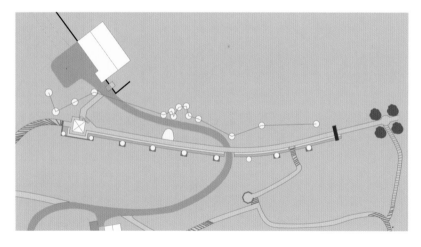

6. Early September

Nine *Hibiscus syriacus* 'Diana' standards bloom at the same time as the hardy white *Begonia grandis* 'Alba'.

Above: *Hydrangea paniculata* 'White Tiara'

Opposite
Top left: *H. paniculata* 'White Tiara'

Top right: *Liriope muscari* 'Monroe White'

Bottom: *Hibiscus syriacus* 'Diana'

235

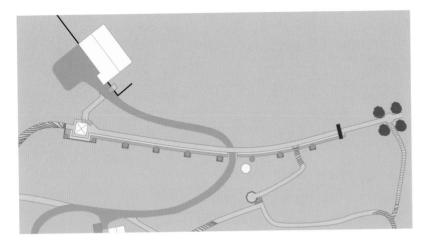

7. Mid- to Late September

One spectacular small tree, *Heptacodium miconioides*, displays its crape-myrtle form, exfoliating bark, and extremely showy racemes of fragrant white flowers.

Tableaux Vivants (Thirteen)

In addition to these enchanting seasonal displays of white flowers, another, more subtle and complex series of smaller seasonal events takes place here. The "windows" between the hibiscus standards on the south side of the path, and beyond the easternmost standard, frame eight distinctly different plant combinations. These depend mostly on shrubs and tall herbaceous plants; ground covers are unimportant because the hedge hides the ground from anyone on the path (see Appendix 2). To the north, a series of five bays of ground cover-based plantings also rewards close inspection (see Appendix 3).

These 13 horticultural events, make a stroll along this path immensely interesting to any plant lover, regardless of age, knowledge, or gardening experience. I liken the rich sequence of visual experiences to the tableaux vivants ("living pictures") that Emma, Lady Hamilton, enacted in Neapolitan drawing rooms,[9.9] or to the stunning series of plantings that Susan Jellicoe created next to a boring piece of architecture at Wexham Springs in England. (Detailed accounts of five significant events in our own garden appear at the end of this chapter.[9.10])

The gazebo's four legs rise from a square bed of beautiful water-worn pebbles enclosed in a border that is four paving bricks wide. The basket-weave pattern of this border consists of two bricks laid parallel to each other, alternating with two more pavers perpendicular to them. We omitted one brick from each inside pair that parallels the pebbles, allowing the pebbles to "flow" into the brick border by the distance of one half-brick. Because of this, the border appears to have teeth that control the pebbles.

A stone retaining wall to the south of the gazebo raises the level of the soil 3½ feet to match that of the Green and White Path farther south. Another stone wall, north of the gazebo, lowers the natural grade to that of the path. As a result, the gazebo sits on a level square of pebbles. The brick border edges three sides of the square; no border is necessary on the north side where the stone wall contains the pebbles.

We worked out this geometry so that the central axis of the Green and White Path coincides with the centerline of the square. The brick pavers are a weathered tan pink and the pebbles are a warm light gray. The area at the top of the wall lacks the low hedge found everywhere else along the south side of the path— a narrow bed of lamb's ear is all that separates visitors from the precipice. We omitted the hedge to give a feeling of spaciousness to the pebbled area and to connect it visually with the upper portions of the neighboring trees in the Springhouse Woods.

The planting in this area presents three separate performances. The first starts any time from late March until late April with double bloodroot (*Sanguinaria canadensis* 'Multiplex') planted in the squares from which two of the hibiscus topiaries rise (equidistant from the two southernmost legs of the gazebo). Each bloodroot emerges from the ground looking like a knuckle or a pebble (only a little larger than those the viewer stands on), and as the spring sun warms it, shiny white double blossoms burst forth, gloriously reflecting the spring light. Being sterile, this double form has exceptionally long-lasting flowers, a desirable trait in formal settings such as these symmetrical squares.

To arrange this area's second plant performance, we have trained white-flowered *Wisteria brachybotrys* 'Shiro-Kapitan' to climb the gazebo leg farthest to the southwest. This wisteria is the earliest to bloom in our garden (April 15) and it has larger florets than our *W. floribunda* cultivars, as well as a distinctive honey scent. The training encourages widely spaced branches with multiple flower heads clustered on each—an inviting picture as one comes up the Hillside Meadow Steps.

The third performance gets under way by the mid-May, when a line of soldiers starts to march single-file through the narrow bed of lamb's ear along the precipice. The troops are stalwart ball-on-a-stick *Allium giganteum*, a white-flowering cultivar instead of the usual lavender. Their attempt to keep us from falling over the wall always brings a smile to my face.

Opposite
Top left: Double bloodroot (*Sanguinaria canadensis* 'Multiplex') as a ground cover

Top right: *S. Canadensis* 'Multiplex' flowers

Bottom left: *Wisteria brachybotrys* 'Shiro-kapitan' (on the gazebo)

Bottom right: *Allium giganteum* 'Mont Blanc' and even taller *A. stipitatum* 'White Giant' on the march

NOTES

9.1. This is similar to, and may have been constructed at the same time (1965-66) as, the path between the Studio Garden and the springhouse.

9.2. Formally trained as an architect, Sir Peter Shepheard, KBE, received informal training in landscape architecture through apprenticeship and self-instruction motivated by his passion for the subject. While living part-time in the United States, he headed the University of Pennsylvania School of Design and served as a consultant at Longwood Gardens.

9.3. This was constructed with care and enthusiasm by our former son-in-law, Curtis Testerman.

9.4. We have trained the beech over a stainless-steel frame, which is a pleasure to see in the wintertime.

9.5. PLANT LIST
Black Greens:
  Abies firma
  Buxus sempervirens (Longwood Resistant)
  Chamaecyparis obtusa 'Breviramea'
  C. obtusa 'Dainty Doll'
  C. obtusa 'Gracilis'
  C. obtusa 'Nana Gracilis'
  Hedera helix '(Subzero) Baltica'
  H. pastuchovii
  Ilex x *aquipernyi* 'San Jose' (Dudley #4)
  I. x *aquipernyi* 'Meschick' Dragon Lady®
  I. crenata 'Helleri'
  I. x *meserveae* 'Mesid' (Blue Maid®)
  I. x *meserveae* 'Conablu' (Blue Prince®)
  I. x *meserveae* 'Conapri' (Blue Princess®)
  I. x *meserveae* 'Mesan' (Blue Stallion®)
  Picea orientalis 'Procumbens'
  Taxus baccata 'Repandens'
  T. cuspidata 'Nana'

Pure Waxy White:
  Allium stipitatum 'White Giant'
  A. giganteum 'Mt. Blanc'
  A. 'Mount Everest'
  Anemone blanda 'White Splendour'
  Baptisia alba
  Begonia grandis 'Alba'
  Chrysanthemum weyrichii 'White Bomb'

Cornus kousa 'Milky Way'
Crambe cordifolia
Deutzia chunii
Dianthus (fragrant white)
Hemerocallis 'Serene Madonna'
Heptacodium miconioides
Hibiscus syriacus 'Diana'
Hydrangea paniculata 'White Tiara'
H. arborescens 'Annabelle'
Lespedeza thunbergii 'White Fountain'
Ligustrum quihoui
Lilium 'Black Dragon' (short form)
L. 'Black Dragon' (tall form)
Liriope muscari 'Monroe White'
Lonicera periclymenum 'Graham Thomas'
Narcissus 'Ara'
Paeonia 'Festiva Maxima'
P. 'White Ivory'
Philadelphus 'Burkwoodii'
Sanguinaria canadensis 'Multiplex'
Silybum marianum 'Adriana' (white-flowered form)
Stewartia koreana
Verbascum chaixii 'Album'
V. 'Snow Maiden'
Vitex agnus-castus 'Silver Spire'
Wisteria brachybotrys 'Shiro-kapitan'
Yucca flaccida (Henry selection) (syn. *Y. smalliana* [Henry selection])

Warm Grays
(including green and white variegations):
  Acanthopanax sieboldianus 'Variegatus'
  Antennaria parlinii subsp. *fallax* (syn. *A. plantaginifolia* var. *ambigens*)
  Ballota acetabulosa
  Cornus alba 'Elegantissima'
  Cynara cardunculus
  Eryngium giganteum
  E. yuccifolium
  Euonymus fortunei 'Emerald Gaiety'
  E. fortunei 'Gracilis'
  Juniperus 'Gray Owl'
  Miscanthus sinensis 'Cabaret'
  M. sinensis 'Morning Light'
  M. sinensis 'Variegata'
  Onopordum acanthium
  Parthenocissus quinquefolia 'Monham' (Star Showers)
  Rubus cockburnianus
  Salix alba 'Regalis'
  S. alba var. *sericea*

S. elaeagnos
Silybum marianum 'Adriana'
Stachys byzantina
Stachys 'Countess Helene von Stein'

9.6. The following horticultural "activities" in other parts of the garden, visible through the "windows" along the Green and White Path, serve as backgrounds to green, white, and gray plantings. Most notable when seen on a walk from west to east, these occur during a longer season than that of the path garden itself.
  a. Oriental hellebores and muscari on Rose Path; March-April
  b. Quince and Cherry Hillside; April
  c. Wisteria and *Amsonia* bonanza; mid-May
  d. Shrub roses; late May-early June
  e. The gold of two *Pseudolarix amabilis* (syn. *P. kaempferi*); late October
  f. Fall color in the Springhouse Woods; early to mid-November

9.7. The latter result from the breeding work of Kathleen Meserve. Her crosses of the tender, dark green English holly, *Ilex aquifolium*, and the very hardy ugly duckling *I. rugosa* have produced totally hardy dark green-leaved plants that are free of winter burn at the top of this cold, windy hill. *I.* x *aquipernyi* 'San Jose' (Dudley #4) is the finest of California-based J. B. Clark's hybrids of *I. aquifolium* x *I. pernyi*.

9.8. *Philadelphus* 'Burkwoodii': "Raised by Burkwood and Skipwith before 1931. Thought to be a hybrid of *P.* 'Etoile Rose' x *P.* 'Virginata' (two of Lemoine's hybrids)." From W. J. Bean, *Trees and Shrubs Hardy in the British Isles*, Vol. 3 (London: John Murray, 1991), 145. The rooted cutting was a gift from Hannah, Viscountess Cranborne, in whose garden we first saw the plant bloom (probably in 1995).

9.9. The best description of these tableaux vivants, or "attitudes," that I know appears in Flora Fraser's excellent *Emma, Lady Hamilton* (New York: Alfred A. Knopf, 1987), 246-247. The beautiful and spirited Lady Hamilton (1761?-1815), wife of the British ambassador to the court of Naples,

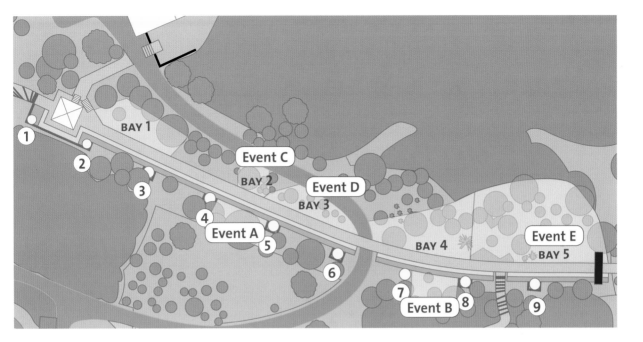

became famous there for entertaining guests by dressing herself (and occasionally others) in neoclassical costume to represent events in Greek mythology. Curtains parted to reveal these depictions on a small stagelike platform (sometimes with scenery) to delighted spectators. I use the expression "tableau vivant" at Ashland Hollow with tongue in cheek, envisioning a beautiful plant or grouping of plants conceived for the entertainment of garden-minded visitors.

9.10. FIVE SIGNIFICANT EVENTS
Event A: Between hibiscus #4 and 5, on the downhill (south) side of the path.

The star of this tableau is *Acanthopanax sieboldianus* 'Variegatus', growing close to the hedge and mounding above it. Slightly downhill and to the west, two handsome *Stewartia koreana* (small trees with nearly horizontal branches) gracefully present camellia-like white blossoms in June. Far enough down the slope for the fine detail of its small, narrow, green-and-white-variegated leaves to be seen clearly from above stands a *Cornus alternifolia* 'Variegata'.

Holding the entire event together are several clumps of medium-height, herbaceous *Miscanthus sinensis* 'Morning Light'. Green-and-white variegation on the

extremely narrow, graceful leaves in fact gives this grass a pronounced gray tone.

The appeal of the dense, somewhat thorny *Acanthopanax* comes from the colors of its little oval leaves. They are technically green and white, but new growth is much more yellow than white. Because this tough plant can put on new growth whenever it receives enough moisture, it may mix yellow with the green and white during various seasons. With all of the other green and white along the path, this performance adds a welcome dash of spice—especially because it is never the same from year to year.

Event B: Between hibiscus #7 and 8.

The plant delight here is a gently weeping, but not lax, June-flowering shrub commonly unavailable in the trade: *Philadelphus* 'Burkwoodii' (see Note 9.8).

Strolling eastward along the path, one passes the dark green of *Buxus sempervirens* (Longwood Resistant), several plants of warm gray *Juniperus* 'Gray Owl', and a cluster of six midsummer lilies, *Lilium philipinense* var. *formosanum*, before reaching the slightly later, spiky blossoms of *Vitex agnus-castus* 'Silver Spire'.

It is just beyond this that the *Philadelphus* holds sway in late May to early June against the broad foliage of *Hydrangea*

arborescens 'Annabelle'. I first saw this *Philadelphus* from an Italianate porch one story above ground level at Cranborne Manor, in Dorset, England, looking down on an ancient walled garden. In a border to the left of the central grass panel, a graceful shrub's white X-shaped flowers popped against its dark green foliage. I kept trying to guess the identity of the shrub, but no name quite fit. After a closer look, I knew it had to be a *Philadelphus*, but a variety quite unlike any I had ever seen. One of those wonderful moments a gardener never forgets! The shrub was, of course, the same plant we now enjoy here, and although not so far below the viewer as my English epiphany was to me, it occupies the same relative position.

Event C: Bay #2, on the uphill (north) side of the path

This is a steep bank shaded by a Korean dogwood, *Cornus kousa* 'Milky Way', with a *Chamaecyparis obtusa* 'Nana Gracilis' on either side at different elevations.

It is the two ground covers around the dogwood trunk, both grown for their gray foliage, that tickle the senses here. The taller of the two, *Ballota acetabulbosa* (horehound, formerly *Marrubium vulgare*) has lusher, gray green leaves and stems. It has surprised me with its persistence through many cold winters. The other ground cover, *Antennaria parlinii* subsup. *fallax* (syn. *Antennaria plantagenifolial* var. *ambigens*) is the thickest and most striking of any pussy-toes I have seen. (This was a gift from Ed Steffek, Jr., at the Sarah P. Duke Gardens. I believe he selected this from the type that ranges from Quebec to Minnesota, and south to Florida and Texas.) Its foliage hugs the ground thickly and tightly. If one of the lead gray-tinged leaves gets rolled back, it reveals an almost white underside.

The *Ballota* stays put; the sheet of *Antenaria parlinii* gradually moves around. It is amid this array that the white-flowered form of hardy begonia (*Begonia grandis* 'Alba') holds sway. This fall bloomer is happy in the shade and puts up with the dryness of the bank. It stands about 18 inches high when in flower. The deep red stems and undersides of the large, fleshy, dark green foliage make it seem even darker. In early fall, pendulous white blooms glow against these dusky leaves and the grays below.

We planted *Rubus cockburnianus* on the hillside above and on the uphill side of a service road that runs along it. In summer, the gray of the *Rubus* foliage filters through the branches and leaves of the Korean dogwood. In winter, its pendulous, white stems make a pleasing pattern behind the dogwood branches. Both seasons provide attractive backgrounds for the ground covers.

Event D: Bay #3

The bank remains steep here. We anchored the top with a woody plant of great beauty—from a group that I normally find ho-hum. This plant is *Deutzia chunii*, a small shrub that blooms in early June. Although the multiflower inflorescences have a typical *Deutzia* form, their buds and stems are a wonderful lead purple. Magic happens when these dark buds crack open and the white of the flower begins to show.

Below this shrub, two biennials cover the balance of the bank: *Onopordum acanthium* and *Silybum marianum*. Both belong to the Aster family, both bear a general resemblance to thistles, and both put forth handsome rosettes of foliage the

first year, and stems that reach impressive heights the second year. We usually have only one or two *Onopordum acanthium* (Scotch thistles). Their large spiny leaves are wonderful shades of silver and gray. The next year, when the stems rise to eight feet, the wings that emerge from them help to give the plant an extremely dramatic and sculptural presence.

The larger number of *Silybum marianum* (St. Mary's milk) have dark green and clear white variegation to their curly-edged spiny leaves. These are smaller than those of *Onopordum* but darker in color, which results in a striking contrast. In the second year, *Silybum* stems top out around five feet with smaller leaves of the same over-all darker cast.

We savor the delicacy of the *Deutzia* performance first. Then come the two contrasting thistle performances, followed (from higher on the bank and beyond the service road) by the late August-to-early September white, conical blooms of *Hydrangea paniculata* 'White Tiara'. The arrangement of two kinds of florets within each cone looks like the work of a jeweler. Diminutive matte white fertile flowers cluster close to the stem. Glistening white, four-petaled sterile flowers, $1^3/_{16}$ to $2^1/_2$ inches across, stand farther away from the stem.

Event E: Bay #5

For someone approaching from the west, this is the largest and deepest bay of all. Except in the foreground, it is largely carpeted with lamb's ear (*Stachys byzantina*), echoing the narrow strip of the same gray-leaved plant alongside the dark green hedge across the grass path. Steps ascending from a lower walk, the Rose Path, roughly align with the center of this bay, on axis with a spectacular member of the Grass family, *Miscanthus sinensis* 'Cabaret'. Its wide green-and-white variegated leaves compose a large, showy clump. Set amid lamb's ear against a U-shaped planting behind, it presents the richest experience on the path.

In the foreground on either side of this clump, plantings of distinctive shapes contain the stunning perennial *Verbascum chaixii* 'Album', *Anemone* x *hybrida* 'Honorine Jobert', and *Allium giganteum*

'White Giant' within a ground cover of *Chrysanthemum weyrichii* 'White Bomb'.

The distant background to this area consists of two silver-leaved willows (*Salix alba* var. *sericea*), eight *Juniperus* 'Gray Owl', six *Taxus baccata* 'Repandens', one *Ilex* x *aquipernyi* 'San Jose' (Dudley #4), and several *Hydrangea paniculata* 'White Tiara'.

Costarring with *Miscanthus sinensis* 'Cabaret', at center rear, *Ligustrum quihoui* (30 feet wide and 15 feet tall) flaunts lovely long spikes of white in July. At its base we planted 37 *Paeonia* 'White Ivory' with waxy white May flowers (on stems far less likely to bend under the weight of a flower than the old-timer *P.* 'Festiva Maxima').

To the right is a nice fat *Cornus kousa* 'Milky Way', underplanted casually with *Liriope muscari* 'Monroe White'. Downhill, Scotch thistle (*Onopordum acanthium*) does an encore from Bay #3.

Finally, three substantial clusters (14 plants in all) of our favorite lily, *Lilium* 'Black Dragon', and one specimen of white-flowered *Vitex agnus-castus* 'Silver Spire ' rise above the lamb's ears. The lilies' shiny white trumpets are borne atop six-foot-tall black stems dressed in dark green leaves. As they arch gracefully downhill, the stems present their blossoms to passersby on the path below.

Opposite: View up the Green and White Path, Bay #5 out of picture to the right

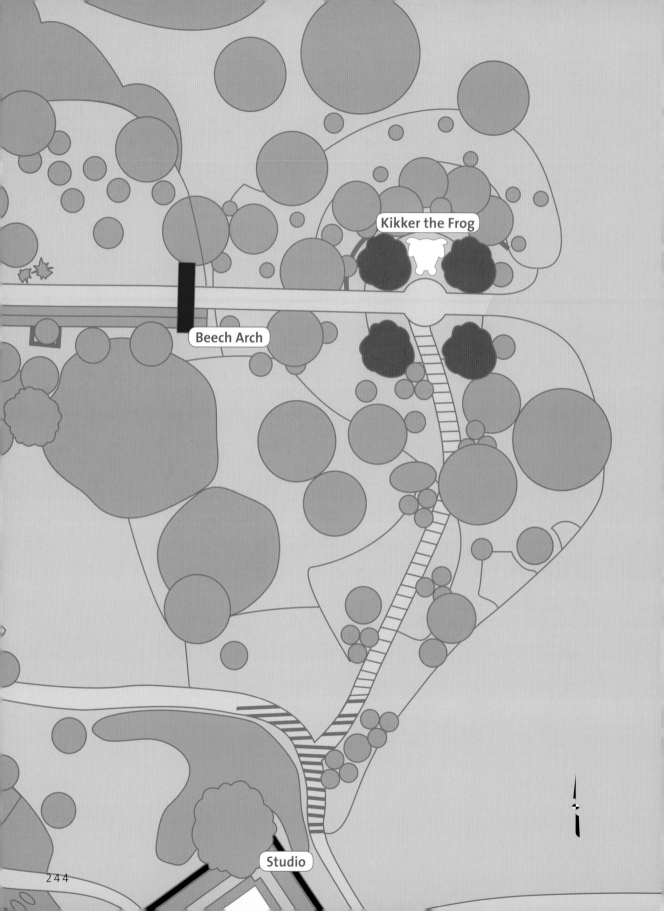

Kikker the Frog

Beech Arch

Studio

244

10 Frog Steps

Kikker the Frog

Three Main Seasons of Interest

Some Special Residents

Winter Anchor

Tragedy and Rebound

Kikker the Frog

The area known as the Frog Steps consists of a grass path running east from the Beech Arch (at the end of the Green and White Path) as well as the railroad-tie steps coming up from the Studio Garden, to the south. Four narrow vertical evergreens, arborvitae, mark the intersection of path and steps.

A majority of visitors probably remember the Ashland Hollow garden primarily as the home of Kikker the Frog. This sculpture—6 feet 8 inches high and 10 feet 6 inches long—is made of cement troweled onto a 3-to-4-inch-thick wire mesh supported internally by a steel frame. Kikker is various shades of green and blue green, except for his eyes. These are gold leaf with black details painted on, providing the ultimate touch of enchantment. New Mexico artist Linda Lee Strong did this marvelous representation of a native American bullfrog after visiting our site and studying photographs of the species. Kikker arrived in 1990 in a large semi-type enclosed truck, packed in a large wooden crate, which was offloaded onto a nursery truck with a rollback bed. Near the present site, the crate was grounded and its top and sides were removed. After footings had been poured, a crane on the grass path lifted Kikker over the two easternmost arborvitae by placing a broad strap under his belly and hoisting him into position. With his head tilted downward and slightly askew, he was a pleading and pathetic sight.

As soon as he came to rest on his footings, however, all was well, and there was much admiration as he looked out over his garden (he *is* the spirit of this stream valley garden). Visitors from the Netherlands, briefly reverting in excitement to their native tongue, kept saying *kikker*, the Dutch word for "frog." This has stuck as the name by which he is affectionately known.

Top: Kikker the Frog, Paul Skibinski (standing), and Bill and Nancy Frederick

Above: Kikker in 1990, still sitting on the bottom of the crate in which he arrived from New Mexico. Bill and Nancy's grandson Ben Testerman was on hand for Kikker's arrival.

Below: After the footings were in place, a large sling was looped under Kikker's belly and this crane lifted him up, over, and around various trees and shrubs to his new home.

Bottom: Kikker's position between the uphill pair of arborvitae at the end of the path hides him from visitors coming eastward through the Beech Arch until this startling view is suddenly revealed.

Nine years after Kikker's arrival, Nancy's ever more enthusiastic campaign to give him a voice succeeded. Gardening friends had a sculptor create a frog orchestra, which plays Mozart as visitors arrive at one end of an allée, and a frog band, which plays Dixieland for people approaching from the other end. We asked the imaginative sound engineer behind those ensembles, John Huntington, to pay Kikker a visit.

Nancy was able to get two good tapes: one of an American bullfrog (*Rana catesbaeana*)[10.1] solo, and one of several voices together in a swamp that includes bullfrogs and a toad. John figured out how to use both tapes, although at his suggestion the solo performance was lowered one octave. We neatly hid two speakers in the two uphill arborvitae on either side of Kikker. The performance is triggered electronically by small garage door openers, which we carry in our pockets.

Kikker sits on the uphill side of the grass path directly opposite the centerline of the steps ascending from the studio, where he can be glimpsed from the driveway through the woods as well as from two or three other locations in the garden. For that reason, visitors to Ashland Hollow often anticipate seeing the frog as we walk them around. They do not usually see him face-to-face, however, until near the end of the tour.

The route we take most often goes from the gazebo eastward on the Green and White Path into Kikker's domain. When visitors first enter through the Beech Arch, the statue is hidden by one of the four vertical evergreens. But as one passes this tree, Kikker suddenly appears, to gasps of surprise and delight. Nancy and I compound these theatrics by pressing the button on the device concealed in our hands. We often pick a hardy soul in the group and suggest that Kikker might say something if patted on the upper lip. We delay pushing the button until that happens. You can imagine the array of responses, but there is almost always a jump of some sort when the frog speaks!

Peak bloom, just as dogwood blossoms drop in May

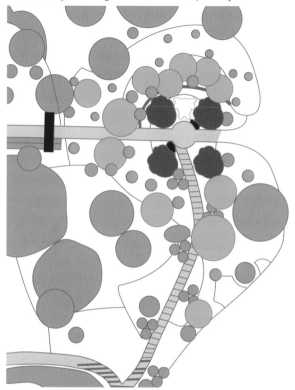

Late June and early July

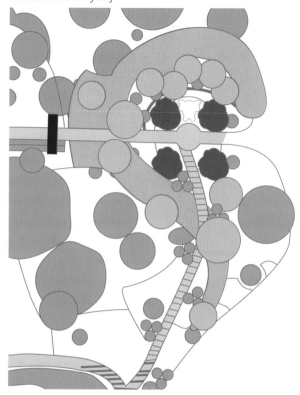

Late September and early October

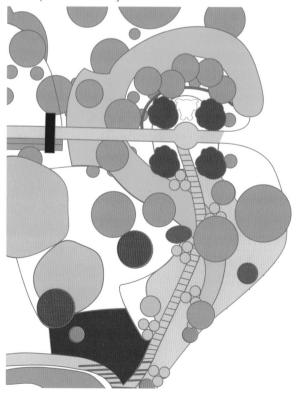

Three Main Seasons of Bloom

Although many parts of this garden have become shadier with age, the Frog Steps remains pretty much in full sun. As a result, it enjoys three very important moments rich with bloom.

The area nearest to Kikker the Frog is enclosed by burgundy foliage (a large display of *Fagus sylvatica* 'Riversii' and, even closer to Kikker, *Berberis thunbergii* forma *atropurpurea* and *B. vulgaris* 'Royal Cloak'). This planting is sensuous in layout, resembling an S running from east to west uphill of the frog, then south and then west to east below the statue, before ending in a small tail that extends south a short distance. The enclosure contains 16 golden variegated dogwoods (*Cornus florida* 'Hohman's Gold'), 20 scarlet orange deciduous azaleas (*Rhododendron* x *gandavense* 'Coccinea Speciosa'),[10.2] and 6 glimmering deep purple Siberian iris (*Iris sibirica* 'Maranatha') within the enclosure.

This group reaches its climax of color just as the dogwoods drop their blossoms. At that time the chartreuse new leaves are emerging, the azaleas are at their scarlet orange peak, and the iris clustered around the lawn in front of the blue green frog are a deep electric purple.

This occurs just after we have been totally jaded by the vibrant display of "evergreen" azaleas in the Stream Valley Garden and while the tree wisterias approach their peak. For me it is a sensational moment.

Discovering things about oneself is an interesting phenom-enon. I had not fully realized how much color mattered to me until 1975, ten years after starting this garden. Nancy and I were in Paris with our daughter Margaretta, then 16, fulfilling part of our promised birthday gift: a visit to various art museums in

Europe. We were inside the Musée du Jeu de Paume, then part of the Louvre and home to its outstanding collection of Postimpressionist paintings. I had seen only a few plates of work by the Fauvist artist Paul Gauguin, when I walked into a room that was solid Gauguin. Stunned, I stood in the center of the room and did a slow 360-degree turn. This was accompanied by total sexual arousal! What a great way to mark a step in self-discovery. I now could understand why it was so important for me to do plantings such as this,[10.3] why I enjoyed H. F. du Pont's color work at Winterthur, and why oil painting with fully saturated colors has become so important to me in recent years.

Opposite
Top Left: *Rhododendron* x *gandavense* 'Coccinea Speciosa' with foliage (behind) of *Cornus florida* 'Hohman's Gold'. Ground cover of *Hemerocallis* 'Spellbinder'

Top Right: Green and gold variegated foliage of *C. florida* 'Hohman's Gold'

Middle Left: Mature specimens of the early-season palette

Middle Right: Azaleas with frog

Bottom: When the planting was young!

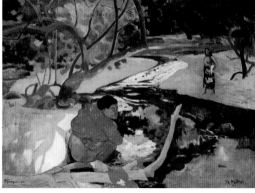

Top: Paul Gauguin, *Tahitian Landscape*, 1891. Minneapolis Institute of Art

Left: Gauguin, *Man with an Axe*, 1891. Private collection

Right: Gauguin, *The Lure of the Exotic*, 1892. Private collection

251

As the foliage on these dogwoods matures, it is part green and part a cheery yellow. This shows to full advantage when the 1,400 apricot *Hemerocallis* 'Spellbinder' (planted as a ground cover outside the azalea planting and following the S-curve) make a stunning display in late June and early July.

The third major display occurs over a fairly long period in the fall on both sides of the steps below the frog statue. The stage set is as follows:

- On the west, moving down the hillside—
  1 specimen Sargent's weeping hemlock
    (*Tsuga canadensis* 'Pendula')
  1 specimen nearly horizontal *Euonymus alatus*
  1 vertical, multistem clumping bamboo (*Fargesia murielae* 'Ems River')
  2 glorious golden larch (*Pseudolarix amabilis* [syn. *P. kaempferi*]) lower than and behind the plants listed above

- On the east, the western grouping is balanced by—
  1 very handsome horizontal specimen of bird's-nest spruce
    (*Picea abies* 'Nidiformis')
  Several clumps of the very narrow-leaved grass *Miscanthus sinensis* 'Gracillimus'

Below this, the steps go through a large sweep of purple-berried beautyberry (*Callicarpa dichotoma*) punctuated with three taller, apricot-fruited plants of *Ilex verticillata* 'Winter Gold'. In addition to the evergreens mentioned, the color scheme so far is deep lavender (beautyberry), apricot (*Ilex*), and yellow (golden larch).

Against this background, the herbaceous display, starting the first week in October, abuts the steps on both sides and flows back among the shrubs.[10.4]

Opposite

Top left: *Hemerocallis* 'Spellbinder'

Top right: Bird's-nest spruce (*Picea abies* 'Nidiformis')

Middle left: *Fargesia murielae* 'Ems River' (*Euonymus alata*, behind)

Middle right: Golden larch (*Pseudolarix amabilis* [syn. *P. kaempferi*])

Bottom left: Sargent's weeping hemlock (*Tsuga canadensis* 'Pendula')

Bottom right: Beautyberry (*Callicarpa dichotoma*)

This area is solidly planted with a ground cover of a selected-seedling Korean chrysanthemum. The single, apricot pink, daisylike flowers with yellow centers provide the ideal color base for the rest of the fall planting.[10.5]

Dominating the picture on either side of the Frog Steps, and rising the highest out of the chrysanthemum ground cover, are numerous 6-to-8-foot plants of the incredible *Aster tataricus*. Its huge domes of violet flowers last into November, and with the lower, mostly earlier chorus of rich colors, end the garden season at Ashland Hollow with a most satisfying cadence.

These three major displays (#1, scarlet orange azalea with the chartreuse foliage of Hohman's golden dogwood; #2, the apricot-flowered *Hemerocallis*; and #3, the violet domes of *Aster tataricus* in a ground cover planting of apricot pink Korean chrysanthemums) are not the only horticultural entertainment, however, in the Frog Steps part of the garden.

Below: The author's *Berries and Asters (from Studio Window)*, 2004. Oil on canvas, 24 in. x 30 in.

Opposite
Top: *Aster tataricus* (violet flowers) against *Euonymus alatus*

Bottom: Korean chrysanthemum (apricot pink) seedling selection along the Frog Steps, across from the purple berries of *Callicarpa dichotoma*

Some Special Residents

The following choice plants are listed in order of seasonal bloom, from spring to fall:

Narcissus 'Small Talk'

Prior to the first true spring display, some delightful teasers appear. The earliest, in mid-March, is *N.* 'Small Talk'. Every aspect of this bulb is like an ordinary yellow trumpet daffodil, such as 'King Alfred', except that it is one-half to one-third the size. It grows in the step treads (near the bottom of the Frog Steps and in the small bank just below the beautyberry). Visitors coming up the steps have a view directly into the flowers' trumpets.

Narcissus 'Small Talk'

Primula x *polyantha* (syn. *P. tomasinii*)

This early-blooming primrose, planted right around Kikker, grows relatively low and produces clusters of rich, soft yellow blossoms. Because the flowers are sterile, *P.* x *polyantha* does not set seed. Clumps expand quickly, however, so it can be turned into a rich ground cover rather easily. My first plants came from Tom Buchter when he lived in this area. With incredibly green fingers, he produced many divisions each year and spread them throughout our community. Tom would have had many gardening friends in any case, but this largesse made him the Johnny Appleseed of primroses!

Tulipa sylvestris

Blooming at the same time as the primrose, in the same location, *T. sylvestris* originated in Europe, North Africa, and Iran. Some question whether this species tulip may also be native to England where it is fairly common. At any rate, it came to North America with early settlers and survives around many

Tulipa sylvestris with *Primula* x *polyantha* (syn. *P.* x *variabilis*)

old farmsteads. It has narrow buds that bend over on very wiry stems. When its lovely bright yellow pointed petals open, the stems seem to stiffen and hold the flowers upright, although they move gracefully in a breeze. It is a most desirable plant. I gave up trying to grow it after a clump with soil from a generous client failed. But subsequently, to my delight, it came into our garden in the soil ball of a *Colutea* x *media* given me by that most charming and generous Solomon of the plant world, Ben Blackburn (then co-owner of Willowwood Arboretum). Seed from this clump caused a good-sized colony to develop nearby. We also raided this colony for successful plantings elsewhere.

Hyacinthoides hispanicus 'Excelsior'

Hyacinthoides hispanica 'Excelsior'

The 'Excelsior' form of Spanish squill overlaps with Display #1. This long-blooming, incredibly beautiful blue-flowered bulb has been subjected to the indignity of four name changes (that I can remember) in my lifetime. I first knew it as *Scilla campanulata*, then *S. hispanica*, and then *Endymion hispanicus*; now it is *Hyacinthoides hispanica*. It grows among the large planting of *Callicarpa dichotoma* at the bottom of the steps. As an annual maintenance practice, we cut the *Callicarpa* to the ground in late winter. This means that spring garden visitors are subjected to the rather unpleasant sight of the stubby stems. Fortunately, we had a brainstorm: plant a mass of Spanish squill to cover the stubs and distract attention until the *Callicarpa* sprouts its new growth. By that time the squill foliage is yellowing and dying down. The *Callicarpa* quickly hides it, and we are all the happier for this arranged marriage.

Hesperis matronalis

There is also a delightful color tease at the time of the first display. A cluster of the perennial/biennial dame's rocket (*H. matronalis*) has established itself on the upper eastern edge of the path. The lilac, light purple, and mauve flowers blend together, making a beautiful pastel cloud. For anyone approaching the Frog Steps area from the west, the cloud does its magic as a moving background to the larger amount of chartreuse and scarlet orange.

Gladiolus communis subsp. *byzantinus*

At almost the same moment, but discretely tucked in at the bottom of the hill near the Spanish squills, bulbous plants of a delicate miniature gladiolus (*G. communis* subsp. *byzantinus*) come into flower. The plants are 12 to 18 inches high; the blossoms, a delicious mauve pink, flower with several of the hardy geraniums. The gladiolus pleases me especially when it is planted with the magenta, black-eyed *Geranium sanguineum*, which blooms in the bulb bed just outside the studio window.

Gladiolus communis subsp. *byzantinus*

Asphodeline lutea

This is one of two more treasures that do their own thing at the upper east corner of the Frog Steps area in early June. A native of Mediterranean shores, *A. lutea* has gray green acutely pointed leaves up to a foot long. The yellow inflorescence takes the form of a spike or spear, and the flowers are fragrant. To my surprise, hardiness does not seem to be a problem here.

Above and near right: *Asphodeline lutea*

Colutea x media

Colutea x *media*

Nearby is the plant of *C.* x *media* (bladder senna) mentioned earlier. This member of the Pea family is a hybrid, probably between *C. arborescens* (native to southern Europe and North Africa) and *C. cruenta*.[10.6] Bladder senna has gray green foliage. Even though short-lived, the flowers are a rare and wonderful bronze yellow. In our climate the shrub dies to the ground each winter, but this does not prevent it from putting on a great show every year.

Hemerocallis 'Autumn Minaret'

After Display #2 showcases the apricot of July-blooming *H.* 'Spellbinder', the elegant long, wiry stems of *H.* 'Autumn Minaret' present delicate, upward-angled pumpkin-colored flowers in late August. This is considerably later than most modern daylilies, making 'Autumn Minaret' of great value to those putting together a garden for that time of year.[10.7]

Hemerocallis 'Autumn Minaret'

Winter Anchors

During the dull days of winter it is the fine narrow vertical Hetz Wintergreen arborvitae and three Golden Girl hollies (*Ilex x meserveae* 'Mesgold' Golden Girl®)[10.8] that anchor Kikker in his acknowledged domain over the valley below. The blue greens of the frog are echoed and contrasted in the bright cadmium green deep (to use the artist's color term) of the arborvitae and the rich deep phthalo green of the Golden Girl hollies. These hollies are especially fine exemplars of Kathleen Meserve's introductions. Dark shiny foliage around and behind the berries beautifully displays their good bright yellow.

Four herbaceous plantings punctuate the grass circle in front of the frog at the four points where the edges of the east and west paths touch the circle. To my delight, these four plantings have come to hold as much interest during the winter as during the rest of the year. The clumps of *Iris sibirica* 'Maranatha' grow at two of these points, diagonally opposite each other. At the other two points are clumps of *Bergenia* 'Sunningdale'. Everything about the iris is narrow in texture, especially the leaves, which in winter are wonderful ambers and whitish tans. By contrast, the bergenias (called pigsqueak by some gardeners) have fat oval leaves, which stay a striking crimson bronze through most of that season. Remnants of *Vinca minor* 'Aureovariegata' remain in the downhill bergenia planting, giving little touches of gold when the sun is out. Patches of *Sedum spurium* 'Bronze Carpet', more black than green, anchor the downhill iris clumps.

Top: *Bergenia* 'Sunningdale'

Above: Golden Girl Holly (*Ilex* x *meserveae* 'Mesgold' Golden Girl®), photograph courtesy Conard Pyle Co.

Opposite: Four tall, narrow Hetz Wintergreen arborvitae mark the top of the Frog Steps where it meets the grass path leading to the Green and White Path.

Tragedy and Rebound

The history of the plantings in this area is worth the brief telling because no other part of the garden at Ashland Hollow has undergone more forced changes since its inception. It has known tragedy, learning experiences, and rewarding success.

In approximately the same location near Kikker where dogwoods (*Cornus florida* 'Hohman's Gold') now grow we originally planted 13 golden chain trees (*Laburnum* x *watereri* 'Vossii'), which by 1981, their fifth year here, had reached a good flowering size. We had effectively combatted their tendency to blow over, because of weak root systems, by means of a unique and relatively inconspicuous system of guying. We looked forward to many years of pleasure from their cheerful pendant blossoms. But this was not to be. Canker had started appearing two years before, and it turned out that our specimens were infected with either *Fusarium latentium* or *Botryosphaeria dothidea*, then uncontrollable diseases.

After considerable deliberation, we removed all of the golden chain trees and ordered *C. florida* 'Hohman's Gold' as replacements. We were intent on maintaining the yellow and scarlet orange color scheme with the Ghent azaleas, and these dogwoods seemed the best bet as far as season and color were concerned. Although fully aware of the anthracnose attacking *C. florida* in our region, we decided to take a chance on 'Hohman's Gold' because the disease occurred almost entirely in older plants and a control had become available.

In 1997 we removed a large planting of *Cotoneaster adpressus* var. *praecox*, halfway down the steps, for two reasons. First, these plants had become serious maintenance problems. Leaves or trash of any kind that blew into them required time-consuming

Paul Hluchan, *Tragedy* and *Comedy* masks. Photograph by the artist

handwork. The same was true of the quack grass whose vigorous stolons worked their way from the adjacent field to the east into the dense growth of these woody plants. Second, the gradual year-by-year increase of shade in the Studio Garden (caused by the increasing size of trees in the stream valley) was severely limiting the palette of herbaceous plants we could grow there. We looked ever more jealously at the sunny area occupied by the cotoneaster. Taking it out enabled us to put in the very, very satisfying *Aster tataricus* and Korean chrysanthemum planting.

One of our most painful decisions centered on the removal in 1999 of the four incense cedars (*Calocedrus decurrens*) that had grown here since 1976, in the spot where the *Thuja occidentalis* 'Hetz Wintergreen' now stand. Among my earliest memories of striking landscape plantings is a grove of incense cedars at Pierre du Pont's Longwood Gardens. Close to Conservatory Road and backed by other, more traditionally shaped conifers (to the north), they grew in the Pinetum. The incense cedar is native from Oregon to northern California where it often grows on dry, well-drained mountainsides. As known in East Coast gardens, it is uniquely beautiful in both color and form, with a notably dramatic narrow, fastigiate habit. Because the top rarely comes to a sharp point, however, and the distribution of foliage gives somewhat lumpy lines to the tree, its form has a soft and aged quality that is utterly charming. The aromatic bright green foliage persists all winter.

If you have ever seen *Calocedrus* growing close to other needle evergreens in an arboretum, you will know that the quality of its foliage is truly distinctive, even when viewed with its many relatives. Unlike most other conifers, it holds its needled branches nearly vertical (always twisted slightly), letting sunlight reach both sides of the needles and making those surfaces uniformly green. The bark is composed of long narrow scales that periodically slough off, revealing an attractive cinnamon-colored underskin.

In instances like this where four plants are arranged in a very architectural fashion, one always runs the risk of having something go wrong with one of the four, thus spoiling the geometry. It happened to us in 1984, after the incense cedars had been here eight years. Cankers appeared on only one tree, but from then on the other three gradually became infected as well. Every year we removed more dead and dying branches.

There were many theories as to the cause. Several fungal diseases were identified and treated regularly. These, however, seemed in the long run to be secondary. In the final analysis, I found it most probable that roots had been damaged in one or more of the extremely cold (Zone 5) winters we had at that time, which our heavy, wet clay soils may have aggravated. As it has turned out, the *Thuja occidentalis* 'Hetz Wintergreen' that replaced the incense cedars have grown quickly and do the job exceptionally well.

Tragedy of another sort struck during the winter of 2000-01. Seven years earlier, in the fall, we had planted 800 plants of a hardy form of *Hedera colchica* 'Dentata' as a ground cover under the 'Hohman's Gold' dogwoods. Paul propagated the ivy from stock grown at the old Skylands estate in northern New Jersey. To our delight, the plants proved totally hardy here and quickly made a dense cover. Its large foliage remained a handsome dark green all winter.

Around the same time, we became enamored with *Helleborus foetidus,* because its chartreuse bracts and flowers are wonderfully effective during the entire winter. To "gild the lily," we cut four or five circular openings in the extensive ivy planting around the frog and filled each one with *H. foetidus.* The juxtaposition of these two plants was stunning; we were very pleased with ourselves. The only maintenance involved keeping the ivy out of the daylilies. This arrangement gave us great pleasure until the spring and summer of 2001, when we realized that most of the dogwoods were dying. Close inspection revealed that all of the dogwoods had been girdled at the base by rodents. The ivy had provided the animals cozy winter quarters where they dined elegantly on dogwood bark and cambium.

This could have been avoided if I had cut the ivy back from the trunks of the dogwoods by as little as 8-to-10 inches. I should have known better, because many years before I had heard a tale about a row of mature specimen ginkgos dying from the same cause. In utter depression we watched as all but one of the original 13 mature dogwoods died slow deaths. This was the final blow to a planting that suffered other problems as well.

Our stand of *Rhododendron* x *gandavense* 'Coccinea Speciosa' had been gradually diminishing. When we first planted them, we had not realized how thin the topsoil was or what heavy clay lay below it. Over time, though, we became aware that most of the water we put on those azaleas during droughts ran downhill, providing no benefit to the azaleas' thirsty roots.

In addition, we confronted significant weed invasions that could be dealt with only by using strong herbicides in slow, painstaking ways; i.e., at a high labor cost. Again, this planting adjoins a farm field. That is a very attractive relationship to look at, but the field was feeding the garden with Canadian thistle and, even worse, quack grass.

We seriously debated eliminating the planting, changing to an entirely different palette, or, alternatively, trying again with the palette we had, which provided such thoroughly successful color combinations and multiseasonal interest.

In the fall of 2002, we removed all dead and dying plants and every *Hedera colchica* 'Dentata', *Helleborus foetidus*, and *Hemerocallis* 'Aten'. All soil was dug out to a depth of 24 inches and replaced with an equal amount of good meadow loam. (We actually made a switch: the poor soil went to the meadow where the good soil came from. Healthy meadow grass will crowd out the undesirable weeds in the garden, and alluvial buildup will rebuild the soil.) We also installed a plastic soil barrier where the bed bordered the field.

We included our *Hemerocallis* 'Aten' in the removal because new, huskier apricot daylilies had come onto the market. After letting the area lie fallow for the spring and summer of 2003, which allowed weeds to appear and be knocked out with herbicide, we did a fall planting of 1,400 *Hemerocallis* 'Spellbinder', a beautiful and vigorous addition that was readily available.

Availability became a problem, however, for the dogwoods (*Cornus florida* 'Hohman's Gold') and the azaleas. We could find neither at any nursery in the United States. The dogwoods had come from Weston Nurseries (west of Boston), which no longer stocked them; the azaleas had come from our own Millcreek

A sea of *Hemerocallis* 'Spellbinder'

Nursery, by then, of course, no longer in business. Fortunately, Harold Neubauer, a truly enthusiastic and talented member of the horticultural community, offered to graft the dogwoods we needed from wood from our surviving trees. The grafts were large enough to be planted at Ashland Hollow in the spring of 2005. Meanwhile our Dutch friend Bill van den Akker found the necessary azalea grafts at a nursery in his country. These arrived here and were planted in the spring of 2004.

We watch more or less patiently. There have had to be a few replacements, but over all, the replanting appears successful. We are taking our time deciding on a ground cover until we are certain that all of the woody plants are off and running. All I can say now is that there will not be any *Hedera colchica* 'Dentata'!

NOTES

10.1. Only the males have voices!

10.2. Its parents were probably *Rhodo-dendron* x *mortieri* (*R. calendulaceum* x *R. periclymenoides*), on the Secret Path behind the Grove of Umbrella Pines, and the Asiatic *R. luteum*.

10.3. Other examples would include the strong memory I have carried for so many years of the color photograph that inspired the color scheme for the Studio Garden (see Chapter 3) and my strong interest in the garden painter Margaret Waterfield. The latter commenced in 1979 when I accidentally came across one of her illustrated books, *Garden Colour*, while browsing in Betty Woodburn's secondhand bookstore, Bookknoll Farm, near New Hope, Pennsylvania.

10.4. Our appetites for color have been stimulated during the summer by the following extremely attractive perennials:
- 3 yellow-flowered hollyhocks (*Alcea rugosa*); June-July
- 3 *Patrinia scabrosifolia* (acid yellow); August-September
- 3 clumps of *Molinia caerulea* subsp. *arundinacea* 'Skyracer', a six-foot grass that for the lower two-thirds of its height is primarily amber yellow stems; September-November

10.5. Korean chrysanthemums are, in my opinion, far more beautiful garden plants than the clipped buns sold as mums in garden centers today. The Korean mums all have daisylike flowers, in a wide range of colors, and very graceful habits that need no trimming. They were quite popular when I was a teenage gardener, in the 1930s and '40s. Their disappearance from popular use is blamed on the fact that they come later in the fall than the clipped muffins. I am told that homeowners are no longer interested in later-flowering plants other than the sheared buns. This is a shame, because Korean mums keep on going, except through the heaviest frost, and therefore extend the gardening season along with *Aster tataricus*.

Barry Yinger says that the Korean mum is a form of *Chrysanthemum zawadskii* (native to Japan, Korea, northern China, Manchuria, Siberia, and the Carpathians). Another source goes further, stating that the group known as Korean chrysanthemums originated as crosses between *C. zawadskii* (syn. *C. coreanum*) and *C.* x *morifolium*, *C. zawadskii* subsp. *latilobum* (syn. *C. rubellum*), and *C. morifolium*. The named cultivars available irregularly in the trade include: *C.* 'Clara Curtis', *C.* 'Pink Procession', and *C.* 'Mary Stoker'. We have an unnamed one from Ryan Gainey that is a very nice pink.

The north section of the Conservatory Garden in New York City's Central Park (at East 110th Street and Fifth Avenue) still has a major display of Korean mums. Beds in the bowl-shaped garden there slope toward the central feature, a glorious piece of sculpture in a circular pond. In spring those beds are solid with a great display of tulips. When the tulips are removed, the same beds are planted with Korean mums started in a greenhouse from seed gathered the prior year. There is a huge range of color, and the resulting "riot" is a very happy one.

10.6. *Hortus III.*

10.7. We have the distinguished 1920s plant breeder A. B. Stout to thank for this.

10.8: Plus one *Ilex* x *meserveae* 'Conablu' (Blue Prince®) for pollination.

Opposite: Kikker, the frog peers down the steps

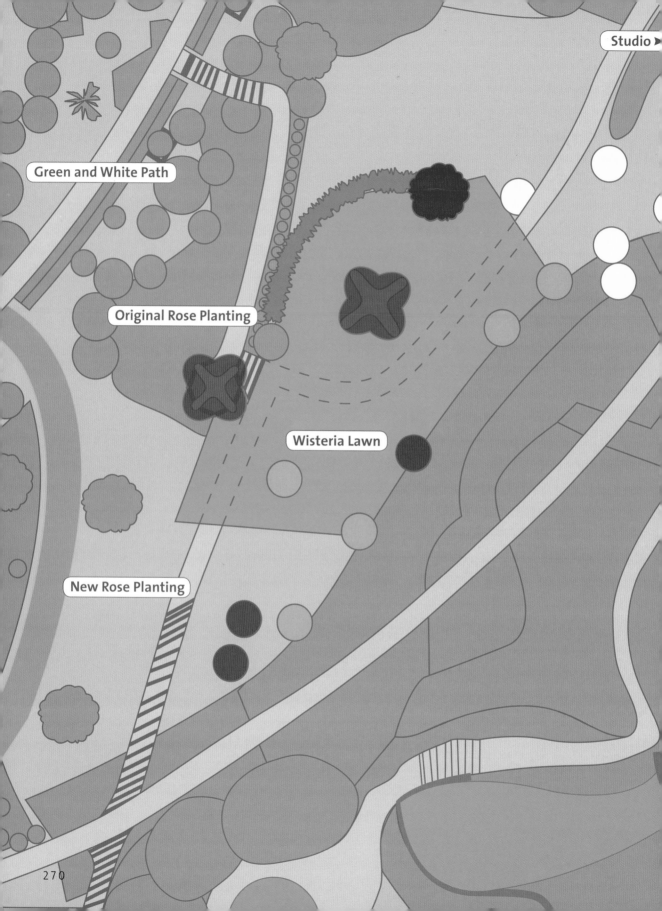

Studio ►

Green and White Path

Original Rose Planting

Wisteria Lawn

New Rose Planting

11 Wisteria Lawn and Rose Path

Opposite: Wisteria Lawn with the 30-foot freestanding conifer-shaped Corten steel frame at right. To the left and overhead (outside photo) is the steel "shade tree." Steps lead up to the Rose Path. The house and studio are downhill.

Above: *Wisteria floribunda* 'Macrobotrys' in training on the "conifer" frame. The vine has subsequently reached the top, completely covering the frame when in leaf.

Tree Wisteria

It is easy to miss and bypass the central part of the south-facing hillside, an area generally defined by the Springhouse Path (and its azaleas) to the south, the service drive to the west, the Green and White Path to the north, and the Frog Steps to the east. This area centers on a bright piece of lawn sloping down toward the Stream Valley Garden, its curious shape defined by the original Rose Path to the north, the two golden larches to the east, the upper part of the Stream Valley azalea planting to the south, and the newer part of the Rose Garden to the west. At the approximate center of the lawn stands a 30-foot-tall Corten steel structure resembling a conifer.

One reaches this area from the Studio Garden by climbing the Frog Steps and veering left at a fork. This leads quickly to a narrow grass path between shrub plantings of beautyberry and *Syringa patula*, which soon connects with the southeastern part of the lawn. Some very sensitive grading[11.1] in the lawn leads one in an ascending curve around the steel "conifer" and across the lawn to the northwest corner where there is a second Corten frame, 12 1/2 feet tall and similar in structure to a midsize shade tree. This frame stands off-center in a level octagonal space enclosed on all but one side by a stone sitting wall.

We installed the steel frames in 1981 as supports for two Japanese wisteria vines (*Wisteria floribunda* 'Macrobotrys') of the type that reputedly produces three-foot-long blossoms in Japan. The flowers on ours never reach that length. The reason for this difference, I am told, is that the Japanese grow such wisteria near bodies of water where the vines can drink all they want. Furthermore, Japanese gardeners feed their plants heavily with phosphorus. Our *W. floribunda* 'Macrobotrys' blossoms, however, do have a characteristic distinctly different from those of our other *W. floribunda* cultivars. The spaces between individual blossoms are greater, so that one actually sees sections of blossom stem through the gaps. This creates the charming effect of drops of water descending vertically.

Farther down the hill are 13 older plants that we started training at Millcreek Nursery around 1964 and moved here two years later. Quite near the top of the Stream Valley Garden azalea planting, and mostly just below the grass path described above, they are trained onto single pipes well anchored in concrete. (For more detail, see pages 96 and 97.) We permanently tie the plants to the pipes and allow them to branch only every 36 inches or so. This spacing displays the blossoms very effectively. (For details of training see pages 353-355.) Most of these plants are staggered informally along the lower part of the lawn area.

From east to west, the colors are white (*Wisteria floribunda* 'Shiro-Noda' [Syn. 'Alba']), pink (*W. floribunda* 'Honbeni' [syn. 'Rosea']), and purple (*W. floribunda* 'Royal Purple'). Most years the wisterias are ascending to their flowering peak just as the azaleas are going by. Only rarely, as in 2005, do both bloom at exactly the same time.

As noted in Chapter 4, this method of training the 13 older plants originated in the Wilmington garden of Mrs. William K. du Pont (1876-1951). She traveled in Japan, although I have been unable to find evidence of such training there. It would appear that the idea originated with Mrs. du Pont.[11.2] I learned of this feat only after her death. At that time, even though the plants were quite old with beautiful large-diameter trunks, mostly hollow, they still flowered heavily each year. It was because of our similar success training the 13 wisterias at Ashland Hollow that we decided to expand the idea into an even grander folly, the vines on the large steel frames.

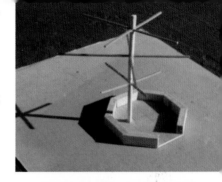

Top: Balsa model of steel frame and stone sitting wall for "shade tree" wisteria

Middle: Steel frame for 30-foot-tall "conifer" wisteria about to be lifted onto concrete footings approximately 6 feet below existing grade

Above: The first frame in place. Work then continued on completing "shade tree" construction and erecting that frame onto its concrete footing.

Opposite: *Wisteria floribunda* 'Macrobotrys', close-up of flowers

Adjacent to the Wisteria Lawn is a planting of 18 *Cotinus coggygria* 'Purple Supreme' (red-leaf smoke bush; see page 356). We grow these for their foliage color, a rich, deep magenta. This tone, which is repeated farther up the hillside by three red-leaf barberries (*Berberis thunbergii* forma *atropurpurea*) in the rose planting, provides a wonderful dense anchor for the colors of both the wisteria and the roses. The small young leaves of the *Cotinus* are the most colorful. To ensure that this new growth occurs every year at wisteria bloom time, we annually cut back the *Cotinus* in late winter to a height of 18-to-24 inches.

The Rose Path, just uphill from the Wisteria Lawn, includes some perennials we planted specifically to bloom with the wisterias. In particular, there is a large planting of *Amsonia hubrichtii*,[11.3] a Missouri native with extremely narrow foliage and star-shaped flowers of an enchanting light blue. At the same time that the old-fashioned pink-flowered bleeding heart (*Dicentra spectabilis*) presents its pendulous blossoms under the wisteria "shade tree," immediately uphill of the *Amsonia,* clumps of *Allium* 'Purple Sensation' flower along the Rose Path.

Top: *Wisteria floribunda* 'Honbeni' (right) and *W. floribunda* 'Shiro-noda' with flowers fully open

Above: The Rose Path, looking west to the "shade tree" frame. (The Wisteria Lawn is five steps down to the left.)

Right: *W. floribunda* 'Shiro-noda' with its glorious white flowers beginning to open

Opposite: *W. floribunda* 'Royal Purple'

278

One of the 13 original tree wisterias trained onto a single galvanized pipe. This is *Wisteria floribunda* 'Royal Purple'. Crimson pygmy barberry in foreground; azaleas in the Stream Valley Garden beyond

279

Rose Path

Five steps up from the Wisteria Lawn (and perpendicular to those steps), the Rose Path is made of stone chips in the color that artists call caput mortuum violet, which nicely weaves together this planting's cool tones. The path runs west to east (roughly parallel with the Green and White Path above it), rising very slightly in that direction. At a right angle to the east end, a dozen steps ascend to meet the Green and White Path.

For anyone approaching from the Studio Garden, and other parts of Ashland Hollow as well, the "shade tree" wisteria frame and its stone sitting wall serve as the landmark for the Rose Path, and there the path begins. To the west of that area is one of three outstanding early-flowering "Higan" cherry trees (*Prunus* x *subhirtella*), which we call "Scott early" because Edith Wilder Scott, founder of the Scott Arboretum, spotted this variation as a seedling. I have yet to find a regular tree-form "Subhirtella" cherry that surpasses it.

Beneath the cherry we have an attractive large, untrimmed specimen of *Taxus cuspidata* 'Nana' (repeated at the path's east end as an eye-stopper). Uphill from this cluster of large woody plants, the handsome multistem seven sons tree (*Heptacodium miconioides*) can be seen when approached from below, its form and nearly white bark silhouetted dramatically against the dark green Conifer Windbreak planting.

Opposite

Top left: *Allium* 'Purple Sensation' with *Amsonia hubrichtii* (a stalwart Missouri native) in the foreground. Its bloom time is an important link between those of wisteria and roses.

Top right: The Rose Path, looking west to the "shade tree" wisteria frame, with the Wisteria Lawn to the left (outside photo)

Bottom left: *Rosa* 'Basye's Purple', *R.* 'Leander' behind *Salvia haematodes* 'Indigo'

Bottom right: The Rose Path looking east. Beyond *R.* 'Lillian Gibson' (left) and *R.* 'Highdownensis' (right), steps lead uphill to the Green and White Walk.

The east end of the Rose Path is anchored by a cluster of three Korean stewartias (*Stewartia koreana*). When seen from downhill, the plantings at either end are visually joined—especially in winter time—by the low, dark green hedge of the Green and White Path in the upper background. We completed this first planting by 1986-87.

Old Shrub Roses: Confessions of an Addict

Sometime before 1980—probably as a result of trips to England in 1960, '70, '73, and '74—I was severely bitten by the bug to collect Old Shrub Roses. Although not normally a collector, I succumbed. There were practical reasons for selecting this group rather than the modern roses more available at that time. Old Shrub Roses are not totally disease resistant, but more so than hybrid teas. All of the Old Shrub Roses that I grow bloom during a short period in early June, an overwhelmingly beautiful display all within two to three weeks. These plants perform best when left to their natural shrub form, not chopped back every year to 18-to-24 inches. The blossoms are meant to be looked at fully open, not as buds. This gives one the chance to observe the many charming differences between their flowers. Some are single; some are double; some are "quartered" (referring to the quadrants into which the petals are arranged when a flower is seen from above); some have a small, bright green dot, or "eye," in the center; and some have green "moss" (thickly spaced green spines) on the sepals and part of the nearby stem.

Many of the flowers are very fragrant. When the roses bloom in this garden, their scents fill the valley. Step out of the Studio Garden door on a warm, still night; walk up the Frog Steps and across the hillside, and you pass through one sort of fragrance after another, becoming totally intoxicated by the time you arrive at the roses themselves. We have come to follow the custom of earlier times: picking a fully opened flower, placing it in the palm of a hand, allowing body warmth to magnify the scent, and sniffing the fragrance while we stroll in the garden.

Learning and Selecting

In an attempt to educate myself about roses, I had trouble finding any book that gave information about the size, habit, and disease susceptibility of each cultivar when it is grown on the East Coast of the United States. There was a lot of information, however, about color and other flower characteristics.

Finally, having to make a list based on descriptions of flowers, I decided to concentrate on very dark colors and very light colors to give contrast. Also, I made fragrance a high priority.

At that time I was enjoying reading various writings of Vita Sackville-West, who for me expresses the gutsy romance of gardens better than any other author. I started with a list of her favorite roses and deleted those that did not fit my color scheme or failed because of an awkward habit, excessive proneness to disease in England, or some other undesirable trait.

The following ended up at the top of my want list (I must admit to being influenced by wonderful names and Vita's seductive descriptions, some of which are quoted here):

Want List of Roses, Plus Dates

1986*   *Rosa* 'Alain Blanchard' (Gallica).[11.4] Mauve and mauve
        blend; petals spotted with lighter colors; fragrant.
        Introduced by Vibert, 1839. One of the roses Vita grouped
        as having "Ancien régime" colors

1983   R. 'Belle de Crécy' (Gallica). Mauve and mauve blends;
        fragrant. Vita: "Such dangerous beauty"; "Ancien régime"

1983   R. 'Cardinal de Richelieu' (Gallica) (Hybrid China). Mauve
        and mauve blend, fragrant. Laffay, 1847. Vita: "Red Indigo,"
        "Ancien régime colors," and again, "Such dangerous
        beauty"

1987   R. 'Mme. Isaac Pereire' (Bourbon). Deep pink, very fragrant.
1990   Garçon, 1881. Vita: "Shaggy Purple." Graham Stuart
1993   Thomas: "Most powerfully fragrant"

1987   R. 'Souvenir du Docteur Jamain' (Hybrid Perpetual). Dark
        red, very fragrant. Lacharme, 1865. Vita: "Dark red, almost
        black...dangerous beauty"

1986   R. 'Tuscany'; aka The Old Velvet Rose (Gallica). Dark
1987   maroon crimson, yellow stamens, fragrant. Unknown,
        1597. Vita: "Crimson velvet...dangerous beauty"

1986   R. 'William Lobb'; aka Old Velvet Moss (Moss). Mauve and
        mauve blend, fragrant. Laffay, 1865. Vita: "Purple and lilac,
        old velvet... dangerous beauty"

Years indicate planting dates at Ashland Hollow.

The want list expanded from this base group, thanks to a variety of influences. Probably the most helpful garden visit occurred in 1980 when Tom Buchter and I went to the Garden of Roses of Legend and Romance at the Ohio Agricultural Research and Development Center, in Wooster, Ohio. Fred K. Buscher, of Ohio State's Cooperative Extension Service, showed us around, and what we found there was a tremendous help in sorting out Old Shrub Roses. The immense number of cultivars was well cared for. Most were in bloom during our two-day stay, June 10 and 11. I added 15 rose names to my list (see Appendix 4), and we were given cuttings of several cultivars, which Tom rooted for me.

Later, because my antennae were out in various directions, the addition of 17 more plants (Appendix 5) lengthened the list to a total of 39 (Appendix 3).

By 1982 our rose beds had been prepared, and we were locating sources for the plants. We found a baby backhoe that gracefully fit into that part of the garden and neatly did the equivalent of what the British call double digging—thoroughly mixing compost and manure two spades deep into existing soil—in much less time than it would have taken three human beings with spades, even if they were willing. We have never regretted this investment.

Back then, fewer nurseries specialized in Old Shrub Roses than do now. Most of those that still exist supplied reasonably husky, field-grown plants, however, unlike the weak, rooted cuttings that many firms send out today. The enjoyment and learning that came with our first rose order have continued year after year ever since.

Favorites

Here, listed by the years when they were introduced into gardens, are some of my all-time favorites among the old roses:

1596 *Rosa centifolia*
Also known as cabbage rose and Provence rose. A lovely, graceful plant, which we keep staked to best display its many medium-pink flowers. The fragrance carries quite a distance.

1746 *R. 'Charles de Mills' (Gallica)*
I cannot omit a synonym for this: 'Bizarre Triumphant'! The elegant dark mauve red flowers are larger than those of *R. centifolia*—just the right size for cupping an open blossom in one's hand to enjoy the extremely fine fragrance.

1753 (possibly as early as 1551) *R. rubiginosa (syn. R. eglanteria)*
Also known as eglantine or sweetbriar rose. Native to Europe and western Asia; naturalized in the United States. A large shrub, 6 feet by 8 feet and larger. Distinguished by bright green leaves that give off an aroma of green apples when crushed

1827 *R. 'Crested Moss'*
Unfortunately, this is no longer known by its more romantic name, 'Chapeau de Napoléon' ("Napoleon's Hat"). "Moss," as noted above, refers to small, thickly bunched spines on the sepals and adjacent part of the stem, which I find curiously attractive. The flowers are fragrant and light pink. A must, in spite of the plant's floppy habit

Top: *Rosa centifolia*

Middle: *R.* 'Charles de Mills' (Gallica)

Above: *R. rubiginosa*

1839   *R. 'Alain Blanchard'* (Gallica)
The blossoms are mauve and a mauve blend with some petals spotted very attractively with lighter colors. Fragrance is part of its great charm.

1847   *R.* 'Cardinal de Richelieu' (Gallica)
The concentration of a rather deep shade of mauve in these small blossoms is most distinctive.

1867   *R.* 'Alice Vena' (Gallica) (Hybrid China)
A very dark purple-to-old-rose color (murrey) is concentrated in medium-size flowers on happy little plants that romp around a bit by stolons.

1867   *R.* 'The Bishop' (Centifolia)
The good-sized rose pink blossoms are "quartered," a pleasing feature for an intensely fragrant rose.

Top: *R.* 'Cardinal de Richelieu' (Gallica)

Middle: *R.* 'Alice Vena' (Hybrid Perpetual)

Above: *R.* 'The Bishop' (Centifolia)

My favorites also include six cultivars introduced after 1900. Most of these are larger shrubs than the earlier group, which makes them very useful for structuring a planting that consists mainly of the older roses. They are also useful in a border comprising other kinds of shrubs. They hold their own very well and often carry the shrub border with their late-May-into-early-June season of bloom. In order of introduction they are:

Top: *Rosa* 'Roseraie de l'Haÿ (Rugosa Hybrid); the most seductive fragrance of them all

Middle: *R. roxburghii* forma *normalis* (burr rose, chestnut rose)

Bottom: *R.* 'Variegata de Bologna' (Bourbon)

1901   *Rosa* 'Roseraie de l'Haÿ' (Rugosa Hybrid)
A graceful medium-sized shrub with deep mauve flowers and the most seductive fragrance of them all. Even the smallest rose collection should not be without this one.

1908   *R. roxburghii* forma *normalis* (Species from China and Japan)
Also known as burr rose or chestnut rose, because of the spiny enclosures in which the seeds are carried; they resemble chestnut burrs. Can eventually reach 15 feet by 15 feet. Its foliage is disease-free and smaller-scale than that of most roses—a perfect background for lovely small single pink blossoms. Attractive rough, partly exfoliating bark is an added bonus.

1909   *R.* 'Variegata di Bologna' (Bourbon)
One of the few very attractive "striped" roses; in this case, white stripes on petals of blended red. Striking!

1926 *R.* 'Sarah Van Fleet' (Rugosa Hybrid, not shown)
This is a large shrub, 10 or more feet high. We stake ours to about
5 feet; above that height, the branches arch outward, floating
the shrub's fragrant light pink blossoms above its neighbors.

1928 *R.* 'Highdownensis' (Shrub, Hybrid *R. moyesii*)
I find this large, rangy shrub to be one of the most exuberant
plants in the garden. It produces long sprays of small, very
modern cadmium red blossoms above the many "Ancien régime"
reds and purples of the old roses. This provides unequaled
visual stimulation by combining such a modern red with totally
different hues.

1938 *R.* 'Lillian Gibson' (Shrub, Hybrid *R. blanda*)
Another large (five-to-six feet high and wide) shrub of good
behavior. The blossoms are medium pink and fragrant.

Top: *R.* `Highdownensis' (Shrub, Hybrid
R. moyesii).

Above: *R.* `Lillian Gibson' (Shrub, hybrid
R. blanda)

Changes

In recent years we have focused on two activities that are still bringing fresh changes into the Rose Path and the adjacent area: color tinkering and expansion.

The tinkering progresses slowly. Great lover of color that I am, the urge to create more sophisticated effects—which takes time—is always present. In this case, I have come to realize that adding even darker roses and more selections in the peach-and-apricot range along the Rose Path would provide a higher degree of pleasure. These colors, however, can be difficult to find in types of roses that also perform well. *Rosa* 'Basye's Purple' (Shrub, Species Cross) produces quite dark single roses in the mauve, murrey purple direction. Fortunately, it seems to like us. *R.* 'Alchymist' (Shrub) and *R.* 'Austea' (aka 'Leander', Shrub), which both lean toward apricot, are still on trial here.

The second change in this area responds to an increasing amount of shade. The trees we initially planted with our original roses at either end of the path—*Prunus* x *subhirtella* "Scott early" and the "shade tree" *Wisteria floribunda* 'Macrobotrys' to the west, and three *Stewartia koreana* to the east—have grown large enough to shade out some of the roses.

To the west of the Rose Path, and west of the *Prunus* x *subhirthella* "Scott early," a fairly steep bank with reasonably good soil benefits from full sun and adequate air circulation. A graded sod path and railroad-tie steps, starting near the stone sitting wall around the tree wisteria, bisect this area on the way to the Secret Path behind the Grove of Japanese Umbrella Pines. We requisitioned this area for more roses and bought replacements for all of the favorites that had been shaded out. These purchases were planted here along with a rose new to the garden, *R.* 'Doorenbos Selection' (Shrub, Hybrid *R. spinosissima*), which we used as a shrub ground cover on the lower part of this slope.

Below: Steps from the Springhouse Path to our new rose planting. The oxeye daisies blew in from the field.

Bottom: *Rosa* 'Doorenbos Selection' (Shrub, Hybrid *R. spinosissima*)

Top: Part of the shrub background for the new rose planting. The plant with pendulous branches and clusters of lavender flowers is *Buddleja alternifolia* selected by nurseryman and landscape contractor Chuck Witman.

Middle: *Rosa roxburghii* forma *normalis*, an ancient specimen

Above: *Sophora davidii*

This hybrid of the Scotch rose is in a class entirely by itself. Two feet high and three feet wide, the densely twiggy plant has the lovely small leaves of *R. spinosissima*. While visiting the Arnold Arboretum's Case Estates in the Boston area, in June 1966, I spotted blossoms of this rose with petals very, very close in color to the foliage of our *Berberis thunbergii* 'Atropurpurea Nana' (syn. 'Crimson Pygmy') at the same time of year. There was more to catch my attention, however: a light yellow disc in the center of each flower producing a most distinguished effect!

Uphill from the graded sod path and its connecting set of steps is a second "Scott early" cherry and our giant plant of *Rosa roxburghii* forma *normalis*. At the time of the new rose planting we added two shrubs nearby. The first of these is a form of the beautiful *Buddleja alternifolia* selected by Chuck Witman.[11.5] Its cascading branch structure, loaded with lavender violet blossoms, brings the eye down to this recent planting of an old favorite rose. We put the second shrub, *Sophora davidii* (syn. *S. viciifolia*), nearer the path because of the subtle detail of its leaves and blossoms. Native to China, this eight-foot member of the Pea family presents its small, very light blue-to-blue gray pealike blossoms against small dark blue green leaves. Viewing this muted harmony offers a restful contrast to the intensity of looking at the wonderful variations in the Old Shrub Roses.

As the path and steps move downward through the new rose planting, *Iris sibirica* 'Ausable River' adds the structure of vertical foliage and the rich color of extremely handsome dark blue flowers. Here and there in the rose planting, farther back from the path and steps, the inflorescences of *Baptisia australis*—spikes of blue, pealike blossoms—effectively contrast with the mounded rosebushes and their blossoms.

Companion Plants

At bloom time on the original Rose Path, some perennials add substance and support to what otherwise would have been nothing but a "collection of roses."

The supporting cast consists of:

Carex elata 'Aurea' (syn. *C. stricta* 'Bowles Golden')
Clumps of narrow, yellow foliage, the color of which holds up well in shade. Found in the Norfolk Broads by British garden writer E. A. Bowles

Euphorbia dulcis 'Chameleon'
Rich purple and marbled green foliage; yellow blossoms flushed with bronze purple. Not a true perennial, it self-sows, with seedlings coming true.

Geranium x *cantabrigiensis* 'Karmina'
Light mauve pink blossoms at rose time. A German introduction

Phlox pilosa subsp. *ozarkana*
A loose habit, somewhat like that of *Phlox divaricata*; lovely old-rose-colored flowers

Top: *Iris sibirica* 'Ausable River'

Above: *Baptisia australis*

The leads in this production are:

Phuopsis stylosa (syn. *Crucianella stylosa*)
Herbaceous (self-seeding annual) ground cover from Iran. Grown for its ground-hugging mats of bright chartreuse needlelike

foliage. I am a great fan of chartreuse as a mixing color: it works with either a cool palette, as here, or a warm one. The flowers (unimportant to me) are a deep rose-colored mix. Plants will spread rapidly if not disciplined, although they are easy to cut back. The sole disadvantage is a skunky, foxy odor noticeable only when the foliage is touched or disturbed.

Salvia haematodes 'Indigo' (syn. *S. praetensis* 'Indigo')
Groupings of *S. haematodes* 'Indigo' grow in three areas along the path: two on the uphill side and one downhill. This gives just the right amount of spiky lavender flowers to provide interesting contrast in color and form to the quantity of roses involved. *S. haematodes* 'Indigo' is a thoroughly hardy workhorse of a plant with dark green foliage. Cut it back immediately after bloom and expect a second flowering.

Above: *Phlox pilosa* subsp. *ozarkana*, used as a ground cover around a shrub rose

Right: *Salvia haematodes* 'Indigo' (syn. *S. praetensis* 'Indigo') in front of *Rosa* 'Highdownensis'

Under the "Shade Tree" Wisteria

From the beginning, it was my intention to make the complex of tree wisteria and sitting wall, at the west end of the path, the richest and most eye-catching part of the planting. I knew that a strong vertical would introduce the best foliage contrast to the many mounds of rose foliage. Again, *Iris sibirica* came to mind immediately. One that flowered in the best light blue would surely be "it." Three or four tries later, I found the solution: *I. sibirica* 'Orville Fay', now situated immediately to the right as one enters the stone sitting-wall enclosure.

In the same area, just uphill of that wall and farther west of the entrance, is the coarse, dramatic, blue green foliage of *Paeonia* 'Gauguin', a gift of Lee Gratwick in 1999.[11.6] This tree peony is one of many excellent hybrids that resulted from the joint plant-breeding efforts of Bill Gratwick (Lee's father) and the artist Nassos Daphnis, at Gratwick's country place south of Rochester, New York. The superb collection of tree peonies already there included the hybrids of Professor A. P. Saunders as well as those of his daughter, Sylvia Saunders. Each spring at bloom time, Nassos Daphnis would leave his painting studio in New York City, come to Bill Gratwick's, and use his artist's eye to make more crosses. Gratwick would then sow the seed and grow the seedlings on to flowering size. The two men would watch each batch of flowering seedlings for several years before selecting any that proved to be different and beautiful, and naming them. I have difficulty describing the color of each selection, because the tones within every flower change daily while it is open.

Perhaps 'Gauguin' can best be visualized by reading this note I made on May 16, 2005: "We have once again been enchanted

Above: *Bletilla striata*

Opposite: *Paeonia* 'Gauguin'

by the color changes each day and especially the way the copper and alizarin tones keep blending [in different amounts and in different ways]."

Tree peonies have such a short bloom period, the blossoms are so evanescent, that whoever sees the first blossoms open here at Ashland Hollow runs to tell the rest of us. It is a great, great moment in our gardening year.

This reminds me of Barry Yinger's story about one of his earliest trips to Japan. While he was refreshing himself in a bar, a regular customer rushed in and announced, "The almond tree down the street is opening its blossoms!" Everyone in the bar stopped talking, got up, and rushed down the street to see it!

Other Seasons

We originally intended the Rose Path to be a one-season destination, worth visiting only when the Japanese wisteria and Old Shrub Roses were in flower. And because these plantings lay in the center of the garden where main paths bypassed them, one could easily ignore the area during the long periods when nothing bloomed there. It has not turned out that way, however, and we have reaped the benefits of a richer garden.

The season of bloom along the Rose Path has been extended for two curious reasons. In the first place, early on I truly disliked the color pink—except when it could be isolated from other colors and kept with its own kind. Therefore, pink and other cool-colored flowers that we found interesting for other reasons ended up on the Rose Path, regardless of when they bloomed! Years of exposure to these plants has produced an unexpected result: both as a gardener and, more recently, a painter, I have come to enjoy the whole spectrum of pinks.

The second reason for extended bloom here is the presence of various spaces that are unsuitable for roses—too small, too shady, and so on—but just right for other plants we think we cannot live without, some of which happen not to flower during rose season.

I have listed all of the non-rose-season plants that grow in this area in Appendices 7 and 8.

Special Homes, Special Plants

The microclimates on the Rose Path's sun-flooded hillside deserve special mention. We have gradually become aware—as gardeners do when they are lucky enough to live in one garden for a long time—of the happiness of four plants that enjoy both the heat and the presence of stone in this area.

Top: *Lespedeza thunbergii* 'Gibraltar'

Above: *Amsonia hubrichtii* in its yellow fall color, behind a seedling selection of Korean chrysanthemums

The segment of the seven-sided sitting wall adjacent to the Wisteria Lawn is home to two of these plants. Against the south-facing, downhill side we have *Dierama pulcherrimum* (angel's fishing rod), from South Africa. This member of the Iris family has extremely long leaves that bend over gracefully when they reach their full length (four feet), all the better to show off tall, wiry, arching stems with pendulous, soft pink, cuplike flowers. The engineering of this plant is such that the blossoms move gracefully in the wind.

Also thriving at the base of the wall is *Acanthus spinosissimus* (sometimes called bear's britches), a native of southeastern Europe. Reference books say next to nothing about it requiring a location like this. However, this is where it thrives at Ashland Hollow. The compound leaves—dark green with lighter green veins and stems—are more spiny and twisted than those of English holly. I know of no foliage with such distinctive elegance! Our foliage clump, which measures 3 feet in diameter and more than 12 inches high, looks especially dramatic against the grays and tans of the fieldstone wall.

Acanthus spinosissimus (bear's britches)

Two more plants of note thrive in the warm and well-drained crushed stone of the path and step treads: *Corydalis sempervirens* and *Indigofera* 'Rose Carpet'. I think of them as friends that disappear every winter and yet always surprise me when they seem suddenly to reappear in bloom the following year.

The *Corydalis* (also known as rock harlequin or Roman wormwood) is a truly North American plant found from Newfoundland to Georgia and west to Minnesota, British Colombia, and Alaska. It is an annual or biennial here. I will catch sight of a few glaucous blue green leaves and then the pale pink flowers with yellow tips to the petals, an unexpected and most successful color combination.

In Asia the *Indigofera* grows as a shrub up to three feet high. Here, the woody roots survive below the crushed stone in winter and then abruptly, it seems, the plant comes to life in summer as a 6-to-10-inch-high mat of foliage covered with attractive pealike flowers of a marvelous rich mauvey rose.

Playing A Trick

An especially noteworthy vine that blooms with our roses is the form of *Wisteria frutescens* that a friend and I found atop the porch of a house on the Edwards Boatyard property near Rock Hall, Maryland. Because this wisteria grew on the roof, the narrow ends of its small, cone-shaped flowers pointed upward (the pink buds open into lavender flowers). We have planted the vine to climb up a stewartia at the east end of the path. This wisteria is not well known, however, so when visitors first spot its blossoms among the stewartia leaves, they usually ask, "What is that tree with the purple conelike flowers?"

Above: Climbing **Wisteria frutescens** blooms amid the foliage of **Stewartia koreana** (upper right). **Rosa** 'Lillian Gibson' (center and left) flowers at the same time.

Left: *Wisteria frutescens*

A Bowl of What?

Obviously, the very short rose season (a mere two to three weeks) is an extremely rich moment for us. By 1995, it became clear that we needed some way of pulling this extravaganza together. The mounded rosebushes covered with fragile, single-color blossoms somehow or other suggested glass balls to me—and that led to a bowl of glass balls. I designed a shallow vessel 29 inches in diameter but only 5 inches deep, with sides tapering acutely to a small base, $2^{1}/_{4}$ inches high. I planned for this to rest on the uphill entry corner of the sitting wall around the "shade tree" wisteria. After I tried unsuccessfully to get the bowl made out of brass, an excellent craftsman suggested using stainless steel. His comment came right after I first discovered how well the texture and color of stainless work in the garden. I agreed.

In an area of southern New Jersey where generations of glassblowers have thrived I found another fine artisan, Melanie Guernsey, who consented to make the colorful balls. Since it was hard to estimate how many balls we would need, Melanie produced 23 for us in 1995. We went back for 46 more the following year, and another 10 in 1997, bringing the total to 79. Tinted pink, aquamarine, blue, peach, or chartreuse, the glass balls were blown to four diameters: $2^{1}/_{4}$ inches, $2^{1}/_{2}$ inches, $3^{1}/_{2}$ inches, and 5 inches.

Drainage holes in the bottom of the bowl enable it to stay out in all kinds of weather from May to September. In wintertime it resides indoors on the low kitchen windowsill. From there we can see the bare twigs of the roses and anticipate the moment in May when we can return Melanie's glorious glass balls to their summer quarters.

Glass balls in a stainless-steel bowl pick up the colors of roses and other blossoms in the garden.

NOTES

11.1. Done by our landscape-architect friend
Andy Durham when he was an intern here.

11.2. Longwood Gardens subsequently
adopted the system with great success
in a garden designed for Longwood by
Thomas Church.

11.3. Found by Mary Henry, this *Amsonia*
flourished (but was not distributed) at
the Henry Foundation until 1979, when a
plant found its way here. My friend Dale
Hendricks, a truly singular plantsman,
collected seed in 1982 and put it on the
U.S. market shortly thereafter.

11.4. After the first rosebush failed because
of too much shade, a second one was
planted in a more favorable location in
1993. We followed the same procedure for
our initial planting of *R.* 'Sarah Van Fleet'.

11.5. Charles J. Witman, a keenly observant
plantsman (and a first-rate landscape
contractor) in York, Pennsylvania.

11.6. The very imaginative "keeper of the
flame" in the tree peony world.

Opposite: Seedling Korean chrysanthemum
and glass balls beneath "shade tree"
Wisteria

Springhouse

Vegetable Garden

12 Delicious Vegetables, Jumping Quince, and Happy Puppies

Opposite: Cherries blossom (shown in pink on plan) throughout the garden at the same time that the Quince Hillside (in lavender) blazes.

The Quince Hillside, framed by two "Scott early" flowering cherries, looking south with the Orchard in the background.

Hidden Valley

The most dominant design feature in the upper part of our valley floor is the strong geometric form of Nancy's Vegetable Garden. This plot stands out because of the large, open, sunny lawn in which it is situated and because the beds' straight lines contrast with the curves of the surrounding hills and plantings. We located the Vegetable Garden at the center of the space I have always thought of as our Hidden Valley. This area lies along a northwest-southeast axis at the upper end of our principal stream valley, which runs east-west. Invisible from the house, the upper valley is enclosed by the western and northwestern parts of the Winter Garden Hillside, the Hillside Meadow, the Springhouse Woods, and the Quince Hillside, all to the north, as well as by the springhouse to the east. To the south, this valley has a narrow opening that allows a full, unobstructed flow of sunlight onto the Vegetable Garden.

Springhouse Woods

The Springhouse Woods was here when we came. Presumably, prior owners left it uncleared as protection for their water supply and because the terrain was, in any case, too steep to farm.

Springhouse Quince Planting

The area occupied by the quince is relatively small. It is located between the Green and White Path and the curve of the back drive; the Springhouse Woods lies to the west. The Quince Hillside came into existence relatively late, 23 years after we moved to Ashland Hollow. This may seem strange, because it occupies a site in the center of the garden and has the significant design advantage of being a steep south-facing incline, tilted in the direction from which a large part of garden "viewing" takes place. The reasons for my delay, I think, were the hillside's poor soil and that area's particular susceptibility to drought. I was attracted to more culturally favorable locations first.

Quince Hillside

Above: With its powerful color, the Quince Hillside pulls together other plants' spring tones.

Opposite: The Springhouse Woods in fall

I have to admit that this planting followed no long-range plan. It was much more of a sudden inspiration. Three "Scott early" cherries essentially surround it: one at the top of the hillside, and two across the back drive, at the west end of the Rose Path (mentioned in Chapter 11) and at the top of the slope in the "new" rose planting.

The idea for a batch of flowering quince comes straight from H. F. du Pont's quince planting at Winterthur. Since first discovering it, I have made an annual pilgrimage there to enjoy the highly successful, bombastic color display.

There must be 12 to 15 different cultivars of flowering quince in that planting with colors ranging from yellow through orange, salmon, pink, rose, and carmine to deep red. Most of these cultivars are hybrids created by the famous nurseryman and plant breeder J. B. Clarke, in San Jose, California. Like John Wister at the Scott Arboretum, H. F. du Pont kept abreast of contemporary plant breeders and eagerly tried their creations.

In the case of the quinces at Winterthur, as with everything there, the arrangement of colors is both subtle and daring. The most important brushstroke of all, however, is the use of several *Viburnum macrocephalum* forma *macrocephalum* as companion plants. At the moment the quinces bloom, the viburnums' large 10-to-12-inch "balls" are a cool chartreuse[12.1] that blends the exuberant variety of colors together and causes the whole planting to dance: another example of H. F. du Pont's design genius. I am sure it was after two or three years of annual visits that the cumulative effect of color on my body and subconscious made me connect the quince and my barren hillside. Since ornamental quinces are not fussy about soil or drought, neither factor prevented their use here.

Wind and repeated late frosts can shatter quince blossoms, but this hillside is warm and protected from north winds. I saw it as a spot to do my own thing with flowering quince (in a much smaller way than Mr. du Pont's).

Top: Several of the author's selections from the Winterthur quince collection. The lightest one is probably *Chaenomeles* x *superba* 'Perfecta'.

Above: *C.* x *superba* 'Perfecta'

Opposite

Top: *C.* x *superba* (Winterthur deep orange)

Middle: *C.* x *superba* (Winterthur #3) with a ground cover of *Phlox* 'Millstream Jupiter'

Bottom: *C.* x *superba* (Winterthur #2); *P.* 'Millstream Jupiter' in background

Part of the revelation that came to me at that time was the design potential of a small but powerful core of color centrally located in the garden (adjoining the springhouse itself). I now perceived the quinces and the three "Scott early" cherries associated with them as the element that would pull together all of the color in the garden in that season—i.e., many other cherries and several areas with large sweeps of naturalized narcissus[12.2]—thereby strengthening their relationship with the springhouse (see plants on plan, page 302).

The quince planting we have now would be much smaller in its color palette, and not nearly so representative of this plant group's breeding possibilities, had we not had Winterthur gardeners' generous assistance. After letting me point out my favorites in their collection, they had my desiderata propagated along with their own.[12.3] Rooted cuttings arrived here in 1984, to be grown on in our nursery, after which we planted most of them on the hillside by 1988. Because the Winterthur cultivars bred by J. B. Clarke had no names, I assigned identifying numbers to them (e.g., "Winterthur #1"). The total gift was as follows, listed with the quantity of each cultivar I requested:

4 *Chaenomeles speciosa* (Winterthur #1)
  Rose-colored; tall; a little leggy
1 *C. speciosa* 'Apple Blossom'
  Light pink; single flowers; tall rounded shrub, dressed to the ground
8 *C.* x *superba* (Winterthur #2)
  Brick red; distinctly spreading habit[12.4]
6 *C.* x *superba* (Winterthur #3)
  Salmon; low, but taller than Winterthur #2
4 *C.* x *superba* (Winterthur orange)
  Deep orange
4 *C.* x *superba* 'Knap Hill Scarlet'
  Red; single-flowered
13 *C.* x *superba* 'Perfecta' (Winterthur #282—*their* number)
  Salmon yellow

To these I was able to add the following charmers later on:

1 *Chaenomeles speciosa* 'Cameo'
   Strong yellowish pink; double flowers;
   ordered from White Flower Farm in 1991

1 *C. speciosa* 'Hollandia'
   Scarlet; introduced before 1956;
   ordered from Fairweather Gardens in 1996

I also added one plant of *Viburnum macrocephalum* forma *macrocephalum*, out of respect for H. F. du Pont's bold stroke. The ground cover in his quince planting is bright green spring lawn. Even if I wanted to, I could not duplicate that on our steep hillside's poor soil. Instead, the ground cover at the top of this slope is viridian green broadleaf *Trachystemon orientalis*; lower down, we carpeted the open space surrounding the quinces with true blue *Phlox* 'Millstream Jupiter'.[12.5]

It is, I think, this blue background[12.6] that causes the paintbox colors of the quince to sing. They sing so gloriously that they can be seen from our driveway across the valley (just before it enters the woods) that is immediately associated with the springhouse. The cheery pink of the three "Scott early" cherries above and to the left of this combination enhances at least part of the quinces' (early) season of bloom. It is a car-stopper.

Later, we scattered clumps of *Narcissus* 'Geranium' (clusters of small white flowers with orange cups at their centers) amid this carpet. They flower at the same moment as the quince, picking up on the orange in the paintbox. This makes the event just as enchanting close up as it is at a distance.

Top: ***Narcissus*** 'Geranium'

Middle: ***N.*** 'Geranium' in front of several quince cultivars

Bottom: ***Phlox*** 'Millstream Jupiter'

Opposite: The blue phlox sets off warm-colored quince near the springhouse.

Above: Nancy's rectilinear Vegetable Garden and its relationship to the two circular Overlooks (bottom right) and the free-form swimming pool (top right)

Opposite: The orderly layout of beds within the Vegetable Garden's fenced enclosure. A solar collector (bottom left) powers the single wire on top of the fence. Climbing groundhogs do not like it!

Hidden Valley Floor

The Vegetable Garden still occupies the level space we graded for it early in the spring of 1966, our first spring at Ashland Hollow and the season when Nancy planted her first vegetables. As I explained in Chapter 4, we graded this area, the Game Lawn, and the nursery at the same time. The back drive runs on contour just below the Vegetable Garden, and downhill from that we added the swimming pool in 1971.

These grade changes have substantially influenced the character of this whole upper part of our valley. In section, the ground floor of the springhouse and the swimming pool with its stone paving mark the lowest level. The next one up is the Game Lawn (which connects to the lower part of the valley by means of the Statue Steps, and to the swimming pool area via wooden steps). On the third level we have the back drive (linked directly to the pool by timber steps). The fourth level, a grass terrace only a few feet higher, contains the Vegetable Garden, and above that is the nursery.

During Nancy's first few years of vegetable gardening here we had the garden plowed every spring, after which she would tend it with a push cultivator throughout the growing season. Around 1971, she converted to hay-mulch gardening after our elder son[12.7] delivered her first ton of mushroom hay. At about the same time, a 24-inch-high chicken-wire fence became necessary to keep out foraging groundhogs.

1983 and All That

The current configuration of the Vegetable Garden dates to 1983. By then we had fewer mouths to feed, reducing the quantity of vegetables needed, and Nancy had read Mel Bartholomew's *Square Foot Gardening*. The book's principal lesson is a more intensive and less backbreaking form of vegetable gardening than standard methods prescribe. Bartholomew limits the size of any bed to 4 feet by 4 feet, making its center easy to reach from all directions. Seeds are to be sown at the final spacing desired for mature plants, not thickly sown and later thinned, although the plants should grow relatively close together.

Our only adjustment to Bartholomew's specifications involved raising the beds 8 ½ inches above ground level. We spaced the 25 beds 18 inches apart and 18 inches from the fence that now surrounds them. Grass paths in the Vegetable Garden are 7 feet wide and sharply edged with steel strips. We keep a mulch of salt hay (no weed seeds) on the areas between beds, between beds and fence, and in all other ground-level parts of the garden except the paths. Under the salt hay, a layer of water-permeable black plastic helps to keep weeds down. The mulch continues under the fence and 5 inches beyond, where it is stopped by another strip of steel edging. This facilitates mowing and trimming around the garden, giving it all a very sharp look from the outside.

Below: An aerial view shows the Vegetable Garden (lower right), the barn (lower left), and the swimming pool (beyond tree trunks in the Springhouse Woods).

Opposite

Top: Instead of standard-gauge chain-link fencing, we used a type with smaller openings that rabbits cannot fit through. At the base of the fence, we mulch on both sides to minimize trimming. On the outside, Ryerson steel edging separates mulch from lawn.

Bottom: Areas between the raised beds and larger ground-level open spaces are mulched with salt hay.

314

The ground-level areas include a 40-by-4-foot strip for pole lima beans, two rows of raspberries (one 21 feet long, the other 30 feet long), a 12-by-15-foot asparagus bed, and spaces for two rhubarb plants and seven tomatoes trained vertically in circular wire cages.

Our son Dixie made metal supports for the two rows of raspberries in 1973, when he was just learning to weld. This was a gift to Nancy, who was suffering from the classic raspberries-all-over-the-place syndrome.

When the leaves are off the raspberries, Dixie's work becomes fully visible. A vertical 4-inch-diameter (outside) pipe, capped at the top, stands at each end of both rows and in the middle of the longer one. Welded onto each of these are two parallel 24-inch-long crosspieces of $2^1/_2$-inch-diameter pipe. The higher crosspiece sits flush with the top of the vertical pipe; the lower is 2 feet below it. Through metal eyes welded to the ends of the crosspieces we run heavy braided wire, which is then pulled taut and fastened at the ends of the rows. To make sure that his creation would not move, Dixie sank every vertical pipe at least 30 inches below ground and poured a large chunk of concrete around it. When we redesigned the Vegetable Garden in 1983, there was no question about changing the location of

the raspberries. The new plan arranged for them to stay exactly where they were.

As part of the '83 redesign we added a new fence, 33 inches high and made of black-coated chain link. A horizontal 1½-inch-diameter (outside) pipe runs even with the top of the fence and ties into posts of identical pipe at the ends of each panel. Support from the horizontal pipe enables the wire panels to extend as far as 8 feet without sagging. This top rail also gives the whole fence an emphatic horizontality, providing a strong visual frame for the diverse sizes and shapes it encloses. Lima beans, probably the Vegetable Garden's tallest denizens, are trained to a 7-foot-high frame of wire and string.

The raised beds have the advantage of letting soil warm up earlier in the spring, which allows us to sow peas and other cool-climate vegetables sooner than other gardeners in our area do. However, the elevation also means that in summertime the beds dry out more easily than they would otherwise. Paul designed and installed a low-pressure watering system. This provides Nancy with one sprinkler head on an 8-inch spike for every bed. Each head connects to a short section of hose attached to a valve (on a buried pipe) for that bed. When necessary, Nancy places the sprinkler at the center of the bed, turns on the valve, and in many cases leaves it on overnight. This supplies the equivalent of an all-night rain on that bed. Irrigation is therefore very efficiently targeted.

All in all, the vegetable garden is not only geometric but, thanks to its curious shape, dramatized by crisp lines against a grass green background. It does catch the eye when seen from higher elevations.

Top: Later summer crops stay lush, thanks to low-pressure sprinklers, one per bed, each with its own on/off control.

Above: Another full-summer view includes the two rows of raspberries with caged tomatoes just beyond.

Overlook

The views into this valley from surrounding hills have a special charm. One spot in particular offers a view so moving that we have made the place an architectural feature.

It came about this way. Sometime after 1983 I was thinking of doing an oil painting of the Springhouse Woods, then ablaze with color. I visually tested compositions from a variety of compass points and elevations. No location enabled me to capture the essential dynamic of these colors until I reached the lower part of the Winter Garden. The view from there, with the Vegetable Garden's geometry in the foreground, turned out to be the sort of composition for which I had been searching.

As I looked out from this vantage point, moreover, I realized that the magic of our small valley would be even more apparent if the elevation from which I was painting could be extended forward another 20 feet or so. I rejected the idea of a wooden deck as out of keeping with the rural, agrarian aesthetic of the rest of the garden. Instead, we built a circular stone retaining and sitting wall, 15 feet in diameter, and filled it with soil up to the desired elevation. Now covered with mown grass, it forms a continuation of the Winter Garden path system.

We determined the circular Overlook's exact location by sighting an axis from the midpoint of the double gates on the west side of the Vegetable Garden and perpendicular to them. This axis, if continued into the Springhouse Woods on the hillside to the north, arrives exactly at the base of a native *Prunus serotina*, the trunk of which dramatically arches out from its neighbors toward the nursery. Inside the Vegetable Garden, we have placed a terra-cotta birdbath on the same axis.

By sheer luck, the axis crosses a lower Winter Garden path at right angles. A large circular paving stone has been set precisely where the axis intersects the centerline of the grass path.

The entrance path to the Overlook (built in 1997), which commences eastward from this point, follows the axis through a narrow break in the sitting wall before joining the mown-grass circle within. The planting has been designed to "pinch in" upon this "path penetration"[12.8] into the valley, clearly separating the year-round Overlook experience from the seasonal one of the Winter Garden.

The view of the "secret" valley starts with the grid of Vegetable Garden beds in the foreground. The eye frequently returns to their geometric stability between farther-ranging explorations into the panoramic view suggested by the curve of the stone wall. Beyond the Vegetable Garden's geometry lies the hillside woodland. The ancient *Viburnum prunifolium* at the base of the hillside meadow partially obscures all but two of the handsome dark green *Taxus* x *media* 'Sentinalis' that rise above it in the background. After the leaves of the hillside forest are totally gone, views of the gazebo appear as well.

To the right of center, the character of this whole area largely hinges on the view down to the springhouse, glimpsed through the heavy, pendulous branches of the weeping European beech. The swimming pool is mostly hidden by the change of grade just beyond the Vegetable Garden and the service road.

Opposite: A view from the Winter Garden Overlook axially aligns with the Vegetable Garden's double gates, cross path, and birdbath. The geometry of that layout gives special strength to this vista into the Hidden Valley.

When a young *Idesia polycarpa* we planted close to the Overlook grows larger and bears ample grape-form clusters of red fruit, it will help frame the views to both left and right. In the distance, beyond the Game Lawn, one sees the bright green of the umbrella pines (*Sciadopitys verticillata*) in their grove around the Upper Pond.

The view, of course, changes with the seasons. Much of what goes on today, such as the growing and harvesting of grapes on the long arbor attached to the springhouse, retains the intense hands-on feeling of 19th-century agriculture. The old building itself evokes memories of springhouses not only supplying clear water for domestic use, but also cooling fresh milk and preserving butter and cheese. Our springhouse also has a massive 32-inch-diameter kettle built into a brick enclosure above a firebox. Here, scraps left over from butchering were no doubt rendered into lard and/or scrapple.

The Vegetable Garden in the foreground is a 21st-century continuation of the farmhouse vegetable garden. Nancy works as hard as any farmer or farmer's wife ever did on the production of delicious fresh vegetables. And of course, there is the timeless drama that starts with planting peas in early April and continues until the last harvesting of root crops in December.

Policies and Problems

It helps to have firm policies about what one will and will not grow. For instance, Nancy does not grow anything specifically for freezing. She freezes only what is not eaten at the gathering time for one meal, on the principle of "Less pressure, less acreage, more fun."

She has tried out all sorts of odd vegetables over the years, settling eventually on "those veggies that grow well and taste good." Examples of discards: blue potatoes, which have a poor taste; spinach, celeriac, salsify, and melons, which don't do well here; yellow beets, which just don't seem like real beets; broccoli, which gets too many worms; and Jerusalem artichokes, which are too invasive.

There have been problems that were in no way related to the "square foot" gardening scheme:

> French sorrel dies out occasionally and has to be replaced. We like it very much, especially for soup.
> Raspberries have given us a hard time with virus. Despite having made a big effort over them, at the moment we are really not sure whether they are disease-free or not.
> One summer we left for a month in Maine, Nancy thinking she had turned off the sprinkler watering our asparagus. A day or two later, the sprinkler was discovered still going, causing a low-lying area in the asparagus patch to die out.

It is now 13 years since Nancy started using the square-foot system. She is very pleased with it because of the ease of maintenance. Part of this, she says, is psychological. You plant or weed one 4-foot-by-4-foot bed; it takes very little time. Encouraged, you decide to go and work on one more, and then one more... You end up doing a half-dozen beds, and walk away with a strong feeling of accomplishment.

Douceur de Vivre

While Nancy is vegetable gardening, leafage surrounds her, except in the direction of the springhouse. She has a charming view of that, mostly of the frame upper story with its six-over-six-pane windows and the top of the grape arbor just below it. The wider part of the Vegetable Garden is also visually connected with the swimming pool. In fact, the vegetable gardener finds it very handy to break up a hot day's work with trips to dunk in the pool. Its sunny, quiet, private location, heavily screened from both the main driveway (uphill) and the house, adds, I believe, to the pleasure of vegetable gardening.

Our Norwich terriers, Plato and Socrates, feel cheated if Nancy does not invite them to come along when she goes to work in the Vegetable Garden. Even on the hottest days, the dogs can be seen settled into a spot shaded by raspberries or pole beans, keeping track of everything Nancy does.

When asked in November 2004 what she wanted for Christmas, she said that it would be nice to have our artist friend Simple make a sheet-steel pig silhouette (painted pink) for the Vegetable Garden. He made two *pigs*. Installed the following spring, these get moved around regularly, "rooting" through the herbage. I am convinced that putting the pig cutouts in the garden has something to do with the mystique of sharing the garden with animals, a pleasure Nancy wants to share with garden visitors who never see her and the puppies at work.

The sight of Nancy in her Vegetable Garden has always given me a great deal of pleasure. She is a scientist by nature. She is a biologist by training. She is a full-blown "mothering" female by instinct. To me, she represents everything that is good, best, and wonderful between human beings and the soil.

Above: Plato

Opposite: Nancy in her Vegetable Garden with Plato, 2009

322

Above: Carticopia—rewarding produce

Above right: Lima beans

Right: Summer bounty

Opposite

Top: Eggplants

Bottom: Jerusalem artichokes

12.1. These eventually turn white as the season progresses into May, making the viburnum useful in very different ways.

12.2. Locations of naturalized *Narcissus*:
Chapter 3—The hillside above the Studio Garden, between the burgundy beeches and the Torreya Grove
Chapter 6—The Orchard
Chapter 15—The east and west sides of the drive as one enters

12.3. Hal Bruce, Winterthur's curator of plants at that time, had asked John Feliciani, Winterthur's propagator, to have all quinces in the group repropagated, for use in the future restoration of the planting. John tells me that volunteers from the Garden Club of Wilmington did the actual propagating.

12.4. The extensive breeding and seedling selection of ornamental flowering quince for our climate has used two species: *Chaenomeles speciosa* and *C. japonica*. Cultivars of *C.* x *superba* are hybrids between these two.

12.5. A selection from the great planting of creeping phlox in the garden of those profound rock gardeners Linc and Timmy Foster.

12.6. We planted the phlox before knowing for certain that all existing grass had been killed. As it happened, surviving grass killed the phlox, making an unattractive-looking mess out of it, and we had to start over. This was a hard lesson, but the result is worth the second round.

12.7. Age 21, operating with a secondhand truck as a Man for All Seasons.

12.8. The planting along the approach to the Overlook through the Winter Garden is rich. We placed the tallest part of the planting in the "pinch" just as one enters the Overlook. To the left are the bright green twigs of *Cytisus scoparius*, through and above which the red berries of *Ilex verticillata* 'Scarlett O'Hara' (part of the total bank planting in that direction) may be enjoyed. To the right another large, heavily fruited *I. verticillata* 'Scarlett O'Hara' stands with the youngest, and one of the most beautiful, of our *Betula nigra* in the background. The adjacent planting includes one *Buxus* 'Green Gem', one *B.* 'Morris Dwarf', and another (unidentified) dwarf boxwood, as well as two *Leucothoë* 'Green Sprite'. Also present is our oldest *Abeliophyllum distichum*. Its buds and recently opened flowers are pink, but with time they turn white. The flowers provide delightful decoration for the plant's scrambling light grayish tan branch structure.

An eye-pleasing ground cover of *Arum italicum* 'Marmoratum' (syn. *A. italicum* 'Pictum') ties the whole planting together. This *Arum* likes our valley. Birds have seeded it into many locations where we had not planned to put it. The variable light gray green markings on the leaves are quite intriguing. We have selected from these colonies and used those with the most interesting markings to make this planting. The foliage remains attractive all winter. Even when snow and ice seem to smash the leaves, they somehow recover, and the effect for the balance of the winter is perfectly satisfactory.

13 Paul I

Paul Arrives

IIn 1985 Paul Skibinski came to work for us as head gardener. Without a doubt, this event was tremendously important to the future success of the garden. It ranks in importance with the earlier gift to us of this incredibly beautiful valley and its spring-fed stream.

Paul, like me, had been interested in gardening since child-hood. At the age of eight he was buying garden plants with his allowance. He was fortunate that his hometown high school in Newark, Delaware, offered good courses in horticulture for grades 10 through 12, which included greenhouse operation and production, landscape design, garden maintenance, and nursery production. One summer he worked as the high school's green-house manager and became familiar with watering, fertilizing, and spraying techniques. In his junior and senior years Paul served as president of the school Horticultural Club.

Paul Andrew Skibinski

He had no trouble gaining admission to Longwood Gardens' two-year Professional Gardener Training Program, from which he graduated in 1980. I doubt that many students in the program started out with the background and passion Paul already had, attributes that enabled him to benefit from Longwood to the fullest extent. At the time of graduation he also passed the exams that earned him a Certificate in North American Horti-culture from the American Association of Botanical Gardens and Arboreta.[13.1] Before coming to Ashland Hollow he had worked for two landscape contractors and on a private estate.

It soon became apparent to us that Paul brought a tremen-dous knowledge of plants, enriched by his diverse experiences with many of them. I imagine that the large palette of woody plants here was one of the things that attracted him. He has a tremendous curiosity about everything in the world around him. Once a subject kindles his interest, he reads about it voraciously and acutely observes anything else that might help him to learn more. This has made his participation in the garden as well as other projects—from constructing our deer fence to dealing with bats in the barn—a tremendous asset. I asked him recently what he liked most about this job. He said, "The multiple opportunities to learn." And when I asked, "What do you like least?" he said, "Not enough time."

Before Paul arrived, Tom Williams had been part of this garden since its inception, 20 years earlier, and he had previously worked for us at Sunset Hills. Tom knew that, because of the extensive growth in size and complexity of the garden at Ashland Hollow, we badly needed more help and greater talent. Nevertheless, gaining Tom's confidence and acceptance proved to be Paul's greatest challenge when he first joined us.

Tom Henry Williams

Tom Henry Williams

Tom was born in 1918 in Waynesboro, Georgia, where his father was a respected farmer. The Williams family later moved around, ending up in St. Petersburg, Florida. There Tom worked for a Mrs. Martin and her sister-in-law, Mrs. Lockerman. It would appear that they had substantial gardens, took Tom under their wings, and taught him to be a good gardener.

In 1943 Tom went into the Army and was assigned to the 679th Ordnance Ammunition Company. By the time of his honorable discharge, three years later, he had advanced in rank to Technician Fifth Grade.[13.2]

Tom told me that his father regularly received a catalog in the mail from B. A. Stroats listing farms for sale. After several years of studying what was available, the elder Mr. Williams spotted a farm he could afford near Marydel, Delaware, and bought it sight unseen. The family moved there by train while Tom was in the Army. The property turned out to be a great disappointment. Large but mostly wooded, it would have required extensive clearing. The rundown house needed a lot of work to become habitable. To make a sad story sadder, Mr. Williams contracted cancer and died.

It was, of course, apparent when Tom returned from the Army that the farm stood no chance of supporting him. He was lucky, though, to get listed with the Unemployment Compensation Office as a gardener willing to live on his employer's property. This came to the attention of Florence Bayard Hilles, the wife of a prominent Wilmington lawyer, who lived on an estate along the Delaware River, south of New Castle, Delaware. An ardent gardener herself, Mrs. Hilles recognized Tom's ability. He went to live on the estate and she continued his education in gardening. I believe he was very happy during his nine years there.

After Mrs. Hillis died, Tom worked for her daughter, Katherine Callery, on a suburban property not far from here, until Mrs. Callery's death. At that point her husband decided to move to an apartment. I had a phone call from Mr. Callery at my office at Millcreek Nursery. He told me what a good gardener Tom was and asked if I knew of an appropriate opening among my clients. I said I might.

That night I told Nancy about the phone call. We were still living at Sunset Hills and had already realized that our part-time postman really could not cover all that needed to be done. Furthermore, because of the increasing size of our family, we would soon need to move to a location where there would be even more responsibilities. It sounded like a lucky break for us.

Tom came to work for Nancy and me in 1963, and continued to do so until his retirement in 1992. Fortunately, he not only loved gardens; he loved kids as well. In fact, there was a childlike grace about him. He was adept at avoiding the complexities of the world. We paid him a small salary but took care of his apartment rent and all utility bills, and we did his income tax forms for him.

Tom was an eccentric and wonderful person. He was physically strong and a hard worker. His clothing was always very colorful. Also, we realized after a while that his black hair was really white hair colored with black shoe polish! We never knew what to expect.

I don't remember Tom ever being sick or saying a word about feeling unwell, except when he got much older and had joint problems and other infirmities.

He never ate lunch. We also came to think that he ate little otherwise. There was never any indication of food in his kitchen except soft drinks, potato chips, and the like.

Paul feels that much of Tom's approach to life came from a Southern Baptist upbringing. There was a lot of mysticism of the Book of Genesis sort. When he killed a snake, he insisted on cutting it into many small pieces.[13.3] He once told us that you should never plant a *Magnolia grandiflora* (the Southern, evergreen magnolia with huge waxy white blooms) outside your bedroom window because the intensely sweet fragrance would kill you during the night!

Paul says that Tom was hostile towards him at first,[13.4] and it was not until Paul's second year as head gardener that Tom agreed to have him organize his work schedule. He recognized Paul's mechanical ability and was happy, we think, to depend on Paul when various breakdowns occurred. The only thing he would not relinquish was sharpening his lawn mower blade. He had some strange ideas about that. He used a power grinder with enthusiasm, and his blade gradually took on a very strange shape. Paul hung it up on the wall as a curiosity after Tom could no longer work.

Much of our relationship (mine and subsequently Paul's) with Tom centered around a pickup truck. We had gotten the truck when Tom first came, in order that, among other necessities, he would have transportation between our place and his apartment in an African American neighborhood of Wilmington. He considered the truck his own and grumbled about any of the rest of us using it. Tom frequently had accidents (probably two a year on average). The strange thing was that it seemed never to be his fault. I say this from the facts I would get from the officer involved. Tom, of course, always blamed the accident on the other driver and would be close to hysteria when he phoned us from the scene. We had him take a course in defensive driving. The number of accidents may have decreased some. But Tom's course definitely gave him more ammunition for describing what other drivers did wrong.

Tom and his/our truck

He lived on the first story of a large row house that had been divided into apartments. Tom's apartment, which took up the whole floor, had two good-sized rooms in addition to the kitchen and bathroom. His biggest pleasure in life seemed to be collecting furniture and decorative objects. Apparently, he acquired these at low prices or free at auctions, yard sales, and from curb sides where residents had stacked things to be picked up as trash. He could always find room in his apartment for another piece of furniture. His collection was so thick, piled one piece on another, that you had to follow a narrow path through the rooms.

Tom was a happy and useful person here for many years. Unfortunately, late in life he suffered from increasing paranoia. This often focused on real or imagined "breaking and entering" at his apartment or perceived hostility from his neighbors. It was all described with great drama. Paul and our secretary, Suzanne Winkler, bore most of the burden of phone calls and other complaints, which got worse after Tom retired.

It was very difficult to get him to retire because that meant he would have to give up the truck. He finally retired in 1992 and died two years later.

When Tom first came with us, he had been paying a weekly amount to someone for "funeral insurance." We managed to convince him that this was a bad deal, and that the money probably wouldn't be there after he died. Instead, we put aside an amount each week into a special account where he could watch the total growing. When he died, there was enough for a cemetery plot and a proper graveside burial service. Unfortunately, our family, Suzanne, and Paul were the only ones who came. Because of his paranoia, Tom had cut all remaining ties with his family, friends, and neighbors.

We cherish the memory of a custom Tom established at a church he attended earlier in his time with us. Every Christmas the church held a party at which Tom played Santa Claus. He asked Nancy to make him a small folding cardboard house with a counter at the front. As Santa, he would sit inside the house and hand out gifts as children came up to the counter. Tom supplied and wrapped each present himself, and this seemed to give him immense pleasure.

Paul pursued the necessary agenda for the garden in spite of any problems resulting from Tom's eccentricities. It was a good example of Paul's patient and kind nature.

The Understaffed Garden

By 1992 Paul and I had both come to realize that the garden was understaffed. Although Tom's retirement undoubtedly exacerbated this shortage, the main cause was the garden's growth in size and complexity. The number of square feet had stayed the same, but the addition of garden spaces and new plantings—resulting from passion and enthusiasm—had gone on.

Three changes have occurred since then:

- In 1992 we committed to having one more full-time employee, an assistant gardener.
- After 2001 we ceased accepting interns.
- In 2002 we started hiring one and sometimes two seasonal workers.

Assistant Gardener

The idea of a second full-time employee involved more than simply replacing Tom. We needed someone who would enjoy working with Paul and learning from his many skills, and who would in a relatively short time be able to manage the garden routine when Paul was away.

Until this time Paul had seldom left the property, even though he was entitled to several weeks of vacation a year. What he called vacation, with only a few exceptions, meant spending the time at his house rather than in the garden.

Finding the right person for the job was not easy. We went through four incumbents and ten years before the happy day in 2003 when Frank Green came to work for us. Frank is a quick learner, works hard, and has a marvelous sense of humor.

Frank Collins Green, Jr.

Summer Interns—30 Years

A major element of the garden's life—nearly 30 years of it, from 1974 to 2001—was devoted to annual summer interns. There were three years when we had two interns; in the other years we had one. (See Appendix 9 for a list of summer interns by year.) These were students enrolled in college-level horticultural and/or landscape architectural programs. We paid them a modest stipend and, if they came from out of town, offered a room without charge and made a very small wage deduction for breakfast, lunch, and dinner.

The idea was that interns would learn about ornamental plants and practice gardening techniques that would make classroom work more meaningful and provide hands-on experience for their résumés. They were expected to learn the Latin names and visual characteristics of ornamental plants (mostly woody) on a set list, and they would be quizzed on those plants two or three times during the summer. Before Paul came, Nancy and I helped interns with the learning process and did the quizzing. Paul took over the teaching with regard to both plants and gardening techniques. He is a superb teacher. I am sure that those who came during the first 17 years of Paul's time here benefitted from an excellent program; they also had to study harder under his tutelage than under ours.

We got to know a number of outstanding people in that group of 30. I have not had time to run them all down, to see what sort of work they are doing now and to hear what they think about the program in hindsight. I do hope to get to this. In a recent discussion with Paul, we agreed that the two interns with the most fragile personalities were those to whom the garden and our time with them had meant the most. One had a major setback later when he was diagnosed as bipolar. After

Summer intern Laurie Mack Warden with Paul, 1991

extreme suffering, with the help of today's medications and hard work, he has found his way back to the real world. He has changed his objective to social work, gone back to school, and completed two years of a four-year program (to date). And he is happiest when volunteering, in his spare time, at a halfway house for young people recovering from drug problems. We received a most touching letter from him at Christmas two years ago, thanking us for his time here. His memories of that summer and a kind of peacefulness he found in the garden, he wrote, have sustained him during some very bad times.

The other former intern is quite brilliant and has gone on to a career in landscape architecture. He is becoming known as a landscape architect with a tremendous knowledge of, and enthusiasm for, ornamental plants—a very rare combination. He occasionally turns up with colleagues in his field to tour them around the garden, trying to convince them of the need for this sort of knowledge.

In 2001 we said goodbye to our last intern. Paul had come to realize that the program put great demands on his time, far exceeding the payback in labor received. As for this effort to deal with understaffing, we agreed that we had done our bit and it was time to stop.

Seasonal Workers

This put us in a good position to try seasonal workers. They would start in mid-April (when weekly lawn mowing begins) and continue until gardening at Ashland Hollow winds down, around the first of December. Interns, of course, could come here only between the ends and beginnings of their college semesters. This meant that they often did not arrive until late May or early June, and usually had to leave in mid- to late August.

Paul and Frank said that they felt special training in horticulture need not be a prerequisite for seasonal employment. More important would be a record of doing and liking outdoor work, proof of sufficient physical strength (to, for example, handle a walk-behind lawn mower on some of our steep hillsides), and evidence of a good work ethic. I agreed but privately wondered if such individuals could be found on a seasonal basis.

We started this system in 2002. By 2006 we had been through a variety of successes and failures. Five different individuals had worked for us seasonally.

Our batting average, and to some extent our luck, improved from 2002 to 2006. Paul and Frank have been able to sharpen their hiring acumen and develop their skills in managing these often less experienced individuals during the hot, muggy part of Delaware's gardening season.

Management Problems and Solutions

From 1997 to 2000 I had been taking courses in drawing and painting, mostly at the Pennsylvania Academy of the Fine Arts. Then, in 2000, I closed Private Gardens Incorporated, my garden design firm, to immerse myself further in the pursuit of art training at the New York Studio School. Except during holidays and vacations, I was in New York City (where I had a small apartment) from Sunday evening through Thursday of each week. This meant that I was at Ashland Hollow only one business day a week. Paul, of course, was completely capable of running the garden without me. We usually found time to meet on Fridays, but I may not have been at my best, because of long hours and exhaustion from my studies in New York.

In addition, because Paul is so capable, I asked him to serve as my representative with any outside contractors doing work on the garden and the house. This, along with the changes under way in our labor force, put a heavy burden on Paul.

My three terms at the New York Studio School would have been impossible without the help I got from Nancy and Paul. I am eternally grateful to them both.

During this time it became clear to me that I had not adequately thought through my approach to operating an "understaffed" garden, or expressed and "sold" it to Paul.[13.5] This had left him feeling completely frustrated, because he was not covering every aspect of the garden in the quality way that is his nature.

We both needed help!

Cosmetics

Before help arrived we did manage to improve one aspect of the larger problem. I'll call this the "orderly progression" versus "unforecastable" cosmetics problem. Paul liked to work on one area of the garden at a time, not moving to another area of Ashland Hollow until he had finished with the first. This is perfectly logical and the most effective use of manpower. I understand this completely.

However, because we have frequent visitors to the garden, especially groups of students and professionals, there are times when the completion of one or two tasks in several areas that a group will pass through makes a tremendous difference aesthetically (e.g., the removal of eyesores such as the seedling walnut coming up in the middle of a large planting of azaleas, or the lavender blossoms on the gray-leaved lamb's ear growing in an area where the color scheme is gray, dark green, and white). Paul suggested that, in planning his schedule, he should set aside a period of time to work on cosmetics each week, and that

I should let him know at our regular Monday afternoon meeting about any items of particular concern to me. This has worked very well.

Planning Ahead

The larger problem has to do with setting priorities and trying to plan ahead, both by season and by year. This is not always easy in a garden. Weather is unpredictable. Storms break trees, and heavy rains cause washouts. Droughts occur, and manpower must be spent on watering. Invading wildlife populations suddenly arise and time must be spent on eliminating crayfish, rabbits, and groundhogs.

Special Projects

Another aspect that affects scheduling is what we call special projects. These are items of long-term benefit to the garden that—even though outside contractors may perform the work—require Paul to devote a certain amount of time to expediting, seeing that specifications are met, and taking precautions against damage to the garden during construction. Examples of such projects include the building of a 10-foot-high electrified deer fence around all 17 acres of garden and the erection of a greenhouse for storing tubbed and potted plants and starting bedding plants each spring.

While I was at the New York Studio School, several nongarden projects on the property needed doing, and I succumbed to the temptation to turn these over to Paul as well. Although he took them on very willingly, the process spread him even thinner in taking care of the garden. I was in need of restraint, and Paul deserved a solution to the over-all problem of setting priorities.

Good Coaching by a Non-Gardener

At this moment a friend told me about Marie McCormack, a management coach. Paul and I are eternally grateful to Marie for the very constructive analysis she has brought to our attempts at setting priorities and organizing schedules. She has helped me to see this as a creative challenge, and has made it an exciting part of our gardening.

As in all successful planning, the most difficult task is facing reality. When we looked at our reality, we found that it is not just a case of thinking of spring, summer, fall, winter. There are five distinct seasons with good reasons for arbitrary starting and ending dates. What's more, the length of these seasons varies from one month to four months.

Dec. 1-31	CHRISTMAS	1 month
Jan. 1 – Apr. 15	WINTER	3½ months
Apr. 15 – June 15	SPRING	2 months
June 15 – Oct. 15	SUMMER	4 months
Oct. 15 – Dec. 1	FALL	1½ months

Adding Christmas as the fifth season was simple reality. Formerly, we had attempted to combine the ending of the fall season within the time when we were always involved with preparations for Christmas. This did not work because December weather is less favorable for outdoor work than we imagined it to be, and because our culture has turned Christmas into much more of a stretched-out and complex celebration than it used to be. Our family is no exception. Preparations for various sorts of homecomings, visitors, and a major annual party require a significant part of our gardeners' time. But if the garden is "closed for the year," these preparations are less burdensome for them, and their personal Christmas lives are less stressed by our needs.

Our gardeners tell me that they now begin the Winter Season refreshed and ready for the important days ahead. The routine seasonal work includes planning for the new gardening year, repairing and buying equipment and supplies, ordering seeds, and propagating tender bedding plants, which include annuals, biennials, and tropicals. This is our time to do the important jobs of performance evaluation and salary reviews.[13.6] It is also when the search is on for one or more seasonal workers.

Our Spring Season starts with regular weekly lawn mowing in mid-April. As everyone knows, spring is the busiest season for gardeners. And it is when they end up feeling the most stressed. After the dull days of winter, it seems as if there is no limit to what can be accomplished. I experienced this same phenomenon in my clients when I was designing and developing gardens. I cannot adequately explain this, but it is as old as time. The sap seems to rise in humans just as it does in trees. We put ourselves under pressure to do more and more, regardless of time constraints and complete knowledge that warmer weather will deplete much of the vigor we feel at first. I saw it drop off in my clients when they started thinking about going to the beach, in mid- to late May. I suddenly realize myself that I am adding more and more to our gardeners' load and find that they give back the enthusiasm: "Sure, we can fit that in." Unless this is managed and controlled, burnout results—which is most undesirable, as four to five months of gardening lie ahead.

We consider mid-June the end of the Spring Season. This is when we complete our first field mowing and trimming. A large proportion of our 17 acres is kept in field grass, and these fields provide an important part of the garden's rural farm atmosphere. We mow and trim them three times a season: mid-June, early August, and mid-September. The mowing is contracted out, but we do the fine trimming.[13.7]

The Summer Season, our longest, lasts four months. It is a time of consistent and frequent routine maintenance, such as mowing, feeding, watering, spraying, and the annual pruning of the 15 tree wisterias. It is when most of our employees, especially those with school-age children, take their vacations. It also can bring the most unpleasant weather of the year. Delaware is hot and muggy in late June, July, and August. Although we carefully schedule vacations to avoid overlap, the absence of even one member of such a small crew means that less work gets accomplished. The season's flip side is that the full beauty of the summer flowers (especially Paul's work with tender plants in the Studio Garden and the Swimming Pool Garden) peaks. The pool is full of children and grandchildren and their friends, and there seems to be unlimited time to enjoy them all.

The Fall Season begins after the last field mowing in mid-October. This season lasts only a month and a half, and we have a lot to do. It is bulb potting and planting time. It is time for cutting back perennials and some shrubs and removing tender plants. Special plants in tubs and pots need to be moved to the greenhouse. It is also time for leaf cleanup. Most important, it is the time to do anything that will make the workload lighter in the spring; i.e., mulching, as well as planting and transplanting woody plants. In an attempt to alleviate the crush, we have recently been trying to shift any chores that do not have to be done in the fall to earlier seasons.

From this framework that Paul and Marie worked out, it is now possible to spot spaces where we can undertake special projects during the upcoming seasons. These projects have included such accomplishments as:

- Redoing the circular edge of the Upper Pond, which had been eroding into the pond and tilting the surrounding stepping-stones in the same direction
- Performing major renovations on a mass planting of 35 *Forsythia* x *intermedia* 'Spring Glory', which had become thoroughly infested with woody seedlings and perennial pokeweed
- Building a custom leaf container for the back of our tractor, to carry vacuumed leaves to our compost pile

A truck rigged for leaf cleanup with vacuum, grinder, and storage box

With all of this information in place, we can rough out weekly sheets for each season, to be completed weekly during the season. Marie was of help in this step as well. For many years, Paul and I have met regularly, usually on Monday afternoons, to plan the week ahead. Monday is ideal for me because it is the first workday after the weekend. As the time when the garden at Ashland Hollow is most peaceful and my schedule the lightest, the weekend offers my best opportunity to plan for the coming week as well as further ahead.

When Paul and I meet, he notes my suggestions, separating the urgent cosmetic work from longer-term needs. He and Frank then complete the schedule for the week and return it to me on Tuesday. This means that each week's schedule really starts on Tuesday and runs through the following Monday. Marie enabled us to see that this was simply facing up to reality, and of no consequence as a break with convention. We also began holding time open on Fridays for cosmetics necessitated by some activity over the coming weekend that we had not known about at the time of our Monday meeting.

This scheme has undergone revisions this year and should always remain flexible. It has accomplished its purpose in putting some restraints on me and relieving a large part of Paul's frustration. I think it has also accomplished something we had not anticipated: it has helped Paul to realize that after I propose a project, I am perfectly content once it is on the schedule, even a month or a year in the future.

The success of the December change last year was quite evident. We are now working on the reduction of spring burnout. Paul joins me in the objective of having each season end with less of a feeling of exhaustion and more of a feeling of accomplishment.

Paul Skibinski, left, with Frank Green, who became his understudy in 2003. After Paul's death, 10 years later, Frank succeeded him as head gardener and superintendent.

13.1. Now the American Public Gardens Association.

13.2. Tom received the following decorations: Good Conduct Medal, Atlantic Pacific Theater Ribbon, Philippine Liberation Ribbon, World War II Victory Ribbon, American Theater Ribbon.

13.3. Snakes were considered evil because it was the serpent that encouraged Eve to eat the apple. Snakes represented the Devil.

13.4. Tom had worked for us two years at Sunset Hills and 20 years at Ashland Hollow before Paul came here.

13.5. The option of adding more full-time, trained gardeners simply did not exist, especially if we were to provide adequately for employees we already had. Available funds were badly needed for other commitments about which we had strong feelings. These included paying for the educations of our grandchildren and supporting the activities of the Delaware Nature Society and Bryn Mawr College.

13.6. A significant incident in Paul's early employment took place in 1988. I had always felt and said that professional gardeners were underpaid and not treated as professionals, and that this had to change. From my experience at Millcreek Nursery, I thought that I knew the market rate for a good professional gardener. In '88 Paul came to me and said that Longwood Gardens had an open job for which he was thinking of applying. Frankly, I was devastated, because Paul was doing such a fine job here.

I gave my usual response: that I never stand in the way of a good employee bettering him- or herself. A couple of days later, Paul came back to me and said, "Mr. Frederick, good gardens depend on continuity of the staff. What you need is someone who will stay with the garden and grow with it." My reply was, "Well yes, I know that, of course." I don't remember exactly what else I said, but the gist of it was, "So why are you leaving? Is something wrong with the pay rate?" My recollection is that he nodded and didn't say much. This, of course, rang all of the right bells. I asked for some time and checked salaries at Winterthur, Longwood, and Mt. Cuba. The first two are public gardens; the last was at that time a private estate that maintained very high horticultural standards. (Mt. Cuba's former owners are now deceased, and the property has become the Mt. Cuba Center for the Study of Piedmont Flora, an excellent research facility and garden open to the public on a limited basis.) To my surprise and chagrin, I learned that I was indeed underpaying Paul, and I took immediate action to remedy the situation. Since then, we have done a survey every year to determine the change in pay scales at the best professionally operated gardens around us. This is of immense help when we conduct annual performance evaluations and salary reviews each February. Paul had made his point very gently, and I appreciated his initiative.

13.7. We use outside contractors both to supplement the work of the garden staff on a regular basis and to carry out one-shot projects.

Regular Contractors

Tree Work and Major Spraying
We hire a reliable arborist for above-ground-level pruning and for tree removal. This work requires special skills and very expensive insurance. We do some of our own spraying in situations where we think we can do this most effectively ourselves.

Field Mowing
Major New Planting and Renovations
These involve supplying and planting a large quantity of new plants or digging and transplanting plants already on the property.
Special-Projects Contractors
Examples of work done include:
• Rebuilding the grape arbor
• Building a grower's greenhouse
• Repairing masonry

14 Paul II

Opposite:
The layered effect of two tree wisterias, seen from the Green and White Path looking downhill toward the studio and house. *Wisteria floribunda* 'Macrobotrys' (foreground) is trained on a shade-tree-shaped Corten steel frame. The more distant, and smaller, tree is one of the older *W. floribunda* 'Shiro-noda'.

Good Craftsmanship

Another way of attempting to describe the excitement and quality that Paul has brought to this garden is to describe his good craftsmanship. This appears in connection with both pruning plants and providing special cultural conditions that enable us to enjoy plants that would not normally thrive here.

A list of important creative work involving pruning follows. I have already mentioned some of the examples in commentary about various parts of the garden. Seeing them all as a group, however, gives an idea of the time Paul devotes to this sort of detail as well as the immense range of possibilities that exists.

Pruning Plants

Above: ***Viburnum macrocephalum*** forma *macrocephalum* trained as a five-cordon espalier

Below: *Hamamelis mollis* 'Pallida' in the early stages of being trained informally around the southeast/southwest corner of the studio (Feb. 15, 1990)

Overleaf: *Elaeagnus pungens* 'Fruitlandii' early in the process of being trained on the Entry Garden wall. For a photograph of the mature plant, see page 59.

Formal Espaliers

Poncirus trifoliata (hardy orange)—Entry Garden. Single stem to 2 feet, then branching to right and left 2 feet, then right angle upwards 4½ feet; then right angle left vertical to the right, and right vertical to the left, meeting in the center. This surrounds a terra-cotta wall grill.

Viburnum macrocephalum forma *macrocephalum*—Studio Garden. Five horizontal branches; single vertical stem, off-center

Informal Espaliers

Elaeagnus pungens 'Fruitlandii'—Entry Garden. Selected interesting branches from its natural habit.

Hibiscus syriacus 'Blue Bird'—Studio Garden, southwest corner of studio. Single stem to 5 feet, then allowed to explode into a "puff" of branches breaking the line of the building corner.

Hamamelis x *intermedia* 'Pallida'—Studio, southeast corner. Natural form. Wraps around corner, starting only 12 inches above the ground.

Elaeagnus pungens 'Maculata'—Studio Garden on southwest-facing, 4½-foot-high retaining wall. It is a special challenge to keep the two-tone golden variegated foliage and eliminate reversions to gray green. The actual shape against the wall must be fluid, changing somewhat each year.

Climbers on Walls and Posts

Schizophragma hydrangeoides 'Moonlight'—Very high, northeast/ southeast wall of house. Clings well to stucco wall until parts of the plant become too heavy and fall off.

Hedera helix 'Buttercup'—Stucco retaining wall on west side of studio. Because wall is only four feet high, parts of this ivy must be cut back to the ground on a regular basis.

Bignonia capreolata—Fieldstone wall of springhouse. Climbs well. Young growth a vigorous light green. Long straight runs vertically are quite dramatic.

B. capreolata 'Tangerine Beauty'—Same as above.

Wisteria brachybotrys 'Shiro-kapitan' (syn. *W. venusta*)—Gazebo. Wraps around one leg. Being trained to have short, widely spaced branches.

Climbers on Walls, Posts, Supported with Trellis, etc.

Lonicera etrusca—Entry Garden. Climbing a vertical "water chain" just outside front-hall glass wall.

Clematis 'Betty Corning' (Viticella Group)—Studio Garden. On an aluminum trellis. Heavy pruning in early spring.

Vitis vinifera 'Purpurea'—Studio Garden. On aluminum trellis going up one side and across the top of west-facing window.

Rosa 'Veilchenblau'—Studio. North-facing wall (as at Sissinghurst). No trellis. Fastened to brass eyes lead-anchored into wall. Graceful hanging branches over north-facing window.

Below: *Clematis* 'Betty Corning' trained on lightweight aluminum woven wire on a wall of the house

Bottom: *Rosa* 'Veilchenblau' (the blue rose) fastened to the studio with heavy cord strung through brass eyes set into the wall with lead anchors

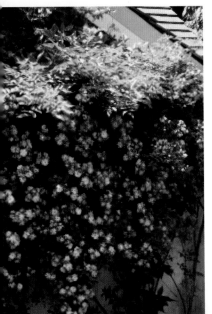

Celastrus scandens—Springhouse. Fastened to 1-by-1-inch mesh chicken wire wrapped around 4- by-4-inch wooden leg of ramp landing.

Climbers on Fences
Wisteria frutescens 'Amethyst Falls'—Swimming pool. Scrambles out over *Berberis thunbergii* 'Atropurpurea Nana'. A few of these branches are allowed to remain.

Lonicera periclymenum var. *serotina* 'Florida' (syn. *L. periclymenum* 'Serotina')—Swimming pool. Not a very graceful habit. Has to be discouraged from becoming a ball!

Climbers in Trees
Wisteria frutescens in *Stewartia koreana*—Rose Path. Seen from both Green and White Path and Rose Path.

Actinidia kolomikta in *Juniperus virginiana*—Upper Pond. Started in 2006.

Lonicera periclymenum 'Graham Thomas' in *Chamaecyparis obtusa* 'Nana Gracilis'—Green and White Path. As with the wisteria, this takes a while to climb without the plant seeking light near the top. I almost forgot we planted it until "suddenly" there were blossoms high in the tree.

Clematis x *durandii* in *Fagus sylvatica* 'Riversii'—Frog Steps Path. The beech is trained on a stainless-steel arch.

Climbers on Grape Arbor

Vitis labrusca 'Concord', 'Golden Muscat', 'Steuben'
Campsis x *tagliabuana* 'Madame Galen'

Wisteria floribunda 'Royal Purple'

Freestanding Vines on Galvanized Pipe and Corten Steel Supports

Wisteria floribunda 'Honbeni' (syn. 'Rosea')
W. floribunda 'Macrobotrys' (syn. 'Multijuga')
W. floribunda 'Royal Purple'
W. floribunda 'Shiro-noda' (syn. 'Alba')

This is one of the most famous displays in the garden. Initial training on the 13 oldest plants required training two or three single stems straight up the side of the pipe, clipping them off at 36 inches until some side branches developed, then repeating this for another 36 inches and yet another. During this time, all vertical stems but the strongest one were eliminated. That one we allowed to go a little farther at the top but not to branch. (For diagram of pipe support, see page 97.) With this basic structure in place, the trunk must be kept strongly fastened to the pipe. This is important, both to prevent the trunk from falling side to side and to prevent the weight of the side branches from causing the trunk to slide downward on the pipe, thus decreasing the 36-inch spacing. We originally used tarred twine wrapped three or four times around the trunk and pipe (with a clove-hitch knot on the pipe). This usually lasted two years. We now use a more durable black plastic linkage called Looplok.

There must be one major pruning a year. This has two objectives: (1) to reduce the length and weight of side branches in order to minimize ice and snow damage, and (2) to encourage heavy bloom. We accomplish the latter by reducing the length of all new growth to the point where only two or three buds are left, a very simple rule of thumb.

354

For a while, we were under the impression that this needed to be done immediately after the flush of new growth had stopped, in late June or July. For scheduling reasons, we have not always been able to do this. We have pruned in August, September, and October—and even early the following spring—and had good enough flower bud set to be happy with the next year's display. We still try for summer pruning.

The quality of the bud set and spring bloom depends much more on the weather. Very dry summers stress wisteria as they do everything else. The event we find most painful to endure is a late spring frost when the flowers are just starting to break. With the number of plants we have, it is beyond our ability to cover them. We just take it on the chin. Such frost damage has not happened since the trees were much younger, but I would be foolish to think, "Never again!"

Woody Plants Cut Back Annually

The following woody plants are cut to the ground early every spring. In our area, these plants fairly regularly sustain winter damage to all or part of their branches. Assessing the degree of damage usually involves waiting until later in the spring to see the results. One can then cut back to where new growth starts. But Paul and I prefer not to have the eyesore of probably dead branches as part of the picture where other, beautiful things are happening. Cutting back the total growth early ensures uniform new growth rather than a somewhat unpleasant half-and-half.

Buddleja davidii 'Potter's Purple'
B. davidii 'Opera' (seedling)
B. davidii 'Black Knight'
B. davidii 'Princeton Purple'
Callicarpa dichotoma
Vitex agnus-castus 'Silver Spire'

Opposite: Ladders in place for pruning the largest tree wisteria, on its conifer-shaped Corten steel frame. We usually do this during the summer, when the plant is in full foliage.

Below: *Cotinus coggygria* 'Purple Supreme' (on the Wisteria Lawn) is cut back early every spring, to produce the most colorful new growth at wisteria time and during the summer.

V. agnus-castus 'Latifolia'
Adina rubella
Pleioblastus viridistriata (syn. *Arundinaria viridistriata*)
Sasa veitchii

Paul has also started a custom I like with the clump of six to eight *Cotinus coggygria* 'Purple Supreme' on the hillside where the tree wisteria are located. He treats them very much the same as the other cut-back shrubs with one exception: he does take the heaviest wood all the way back, but wherever there is younger growth near the ground he leaves some of it. The whole purpose of this exercise is to get larger, fresher "red" leaves as early in the year as possible. We are growing this plant for its foliage color rather than its blossom. The foliage color is a great asset with the rose blossoms as well as with the fall-blooming anemones, chrysanthemums, etc. on this hillside. Leaving the small branches near the ground softens the view of cut ends on the heavy stems before they have resprouted.

Hedges (Woody Shrubs)
Low hedges have frequently served as a structuring tool in my designs. I like them because they suggest the beginning or ending of parts of a garden without completely enclosing one from the rest of the garden or, as in this case, from the agricultural landscape in which the garden sits.

Taxus cuspidata 'Nana'—Green and White Walk. Height: 27 inches. Helps pull together a diverse, mostly informal planting.

Acer palmatum 'West Grove'—Studio Garden. Height: 18 inches. Helps to separate a viewing area from a more intimate area near the door to the house.

The low hedge of *Acer palmatum* 'West Grove' in the Studio Garden

Buxus 'Green Gem'—Studio Garden. Height: 15 inches. Separates a small sitting area strongly linked with the adjoining Stream Valley Garden from the rest of the Studio Garden.

Taxus baccata 'Fowle'—Studio Garden. Height: 18 inches. Helps to create a pause next to the viburnum espalier before the eye moves on to the view of the valley.

Topiaries (Woody Plants Trained as a Ball on a Stick)
Hibiscus syriacus 'Diana'—Green and White Path

Trained Trees
Fagus sylvatica 'Riversii'—Northeast end of Green and White Path. Trained on stainless-steel arch. This is our only example of a large tree being restrained to this degree. One beech was planted on either side of the path. Paul trained them over the stainless steel frame where they meet and interlaced the branches at the top. A plant of *Clematis* x *durandii* was planted with the *Fagus* on the south side. The very unusual blossoms with square-ended petals are a deep cobalt to Prussian blue. Because of the blossoms' harmonious color combination with the burgundy beech leaves, untutored visitors can easily mistake the vine and trees for one plant.

Renovation Pruning
These are just a few examples of Paul putting a positive twist on senescence in a 40-plus-year-old garden:

1. Evergreen Azaleas
Our "evergreen" azaleas were originally planted on five- to six-foot centers. At the time, it was hard to believe that they would ever touch. Now they receive periodic pruning and thinning.

A stainless-steel frame used to train two *Fagus sylvatica* 'Riversii' as an arch

Pruning is necessary to keep them off the paths. And, because they are grouped in multiplant, single-color blocks that interlock on a steep hillside, faster growing cultivars have to be cut back to keep them from blocking the view of slower growing cultivars from the balcony of the house. Some cultivars require thinning to keep up their vigor.

2. *Liriodendron tulipifera*

The tulip poplars (*L. tulipifera*) that provide needed high shade over the azaleas grow too thick with age and cast too much shade. Rather than just remove lower limbs (which is one's first instinct), we have found that it is best to thin these trees at the top every five years or so, removing up to 30 percent of the branches. Taking out lower branches only causes the branches immediately above them to grow downward to protect the trunk from too much light. If this practice is continued, one ends up with a bunch of poles in the azalea planting.

3. *Sciadopitys verticillata*

The danger of breakage from ice and snow in our grove of umbrella pines (*Sciadopitys verticillata*) has always been a great concern. The trees lose a lot of their charm if they have big holes in them. When they were younger, we could knock off freshly fallen snow with long bamboo poles. The pines are much too large for this now. Paul currently has us on a schedule for thinning by branch removal. This allows heavy snow and water accumulation to fall through. We thinned every other plant two years ago. Since then, those in the strongest sunlight have complained. Those in less constant sun are happy. We will continue this process on a regular basis, removing fewer branches from those in the sun.

4. *Euonymus alata* 'Monstrosus'

We allowed a 10-foot spread for a specimen *E. alatus* 'Monstrosa' (we wanted to see it as a piece of sculpture). It spread so far beyond this that it was closing off a path and an important pair of steps. This past spring we bit the bullet and cut the whole plant back to two to three feet from the ground. It was a sorry sight during the height of the spring season. Two months later, it is sprouting and there appears to be hope that we have done the right thing. Paul, of course, was more certain than I that we *had* made the right decision!

5. *Malus* 'Red Jade'

I am very fond of the 'Red Jade' weeping crab apple, not only for its attractive blossoms and fruits, but also for its weeping habit. This requires some special handling for maximum enjoyment. In its younger years, the tree can be so dense that it forms a boring mound. This is easily cured by thinning the branches. A more serious problem exists as it ages and tends to look its most dramatic. The denseness of the upper branches can shade out the lower ones. The lower branches die, leaving a mop of foliage at the top of a crooked pole! Paul goes at this with great vigor, doing what he calls "blowing some holes in the top."

Providing Special Cultural Conditions

Examples are legion of Paul's craftsmanship in providing the special requisites that get a group of beautiful plants to thrive in an atmosphere they might otherwise find uninviting.

1. *Fritillaria persica*

We are very fond of the tall spikes of dusky, eggplant-colored blossoms on *F. persica*. But in our garden, this bulbous plant from Iran tended to die out after one or at most two seasons. Paul has found that sharp drainage and careful positioning of the bulb in the hole can make it quite happy to persist much longer.

Using a posthole digger, he makes a hole 15 to 18 inches deep. He then places 2 inches of No. 2 blasting sand under the bulb and for 2 inches all around the bulb and above it.

The bulb is rather unusual in that the stalk emerges from the center of the bulb rather than the top, and leaves an indentation. Unless the bulb is planted with the indentation down it may fill with water, causing the bulb to rot.

After removing our clay loam from the hole, Paul combines it with more blasting sand, some green sand, and steamed bone meal, and uses this mixture to refill the hole.

Since initiating this practice, we have no longer needed to make annual additions of new bulbs.

Right: *Fritillaria persica*

Opposite: Recommended planting procedure for greatest success and longevity of *F. persica*

360

Fritillaria persica

PLANTING DETAIL

BULB

opening in bulb from stalk

PLANTING ORIENTATION

bulb planting detail

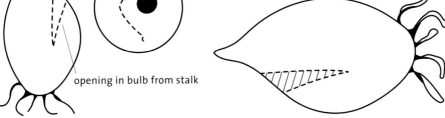

PAUL'S PLANTING METHOD

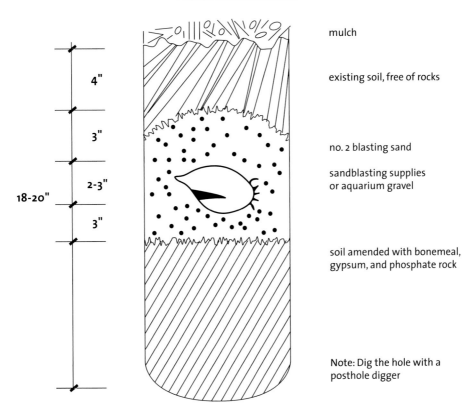

4"

3"

2-3"

3"

18-20"

mulch

existing soil, free of rocks

no. 2 blasting sand

sandblasting supplies
or aquarium gravel

soil amended with bonemeal,
gypsum, and phosphate rock

Note: Dig the hole with a
posthole digger

2. *Verbascum* 'Harkness Hybrid'

Sometime before 1986, while visiting that delightful plantsman Ben Blackburn at Willowwood Arboretum, I noticed an especially vigorous and attractive verbascum in the small formal garden across the drive from the house. Ben gave me seed. He called the plant, which is a biennial, *Verbascum* 'Harkness Hybrid'.[14.1] We have started this in a greenhouse for many years. We plant a group at the diving-board end of the swimming pool just as soon as the second-year plants there have finished blooming and have been removed. Unlike so many other biennials that we value in our garden—

> *Silybum marianum*
> *Onopordum acanthium*
> *Hesperis matronalis*
> *Lunaria annua*

Left: *Verbascum* 'Harkness hybrid', a biennial, stars in the meadowlike planting at the swimming pool.

Below: Every summer, after *V.* 'Harkness hybrid' plants from the prior year have bloomed, they are replaced with new seedlings. The replacements go into pits filled with very gravely soil.

—this plant cannot be counted on to seed itself in situ. This is partly because only 10 percent of the seed will germinate the first year. In three to five years, the rate of seed germination moves up to 80 to 100 percent. Therefore, we start young plants early (late February to early March) in the greenhouse from seed that is several years old.

Verbascums dislike rich soil. Knowing this is Paul's key to success with them. He keeps the seedlings on a very lean regimen until it is time to plant them out in the spaces where those of the current year have finished blooming and been removed, usually in mid-July. The young seedlings are planted in peat pots 4 inches deep and $1\frac{1}{4}$ inches square. A mixture of compost and No. 2 blasting sand is used both for potting and in the 24-inch-deep pits that these plants go into each year. The peat pots provide a way to hold back the verbascum rosettes, keeping them from becoming too lush and rotting.

Paul says that, by contrast, within only two to three weeks of being planted out, they become the large, healthy rosettes that can go through the winter and raise great 8-foot-plus candelabras of yellow blossoms into the June-July air.

3. Candelabra Primroses

The group of hybrid candelabra primroses called *Primula* x *bulleesiana* has immensely intriguing and beautiful color forms. These were initially part of the great planting Henry Francis du Pont did in his Quarry Garden at Winterthur. More recently, they have gained fame for being very happily used by Joe Eck and Wayne Winterrowd in their garden at North Hill. These primroses enjoy rich soil and water's-edge conditions, but their crowns must remain dry. It has taken some doing at Ashland Hollow to find a suitable spot and keep them going. Although

Candelabra primroses prefer having the lower part of their root systems in water, as they do at our Upper Pond.

we have water, the ponds are mostly heavily shaded and have steep sides. The Upper Pond, a perfect circle, is the exception. Our first attempts there met with limited success. Over the years, the edges have been eroding and sliding into the pond. This has meant that plants with crowns set just above water level had changed elevation enough, sliding pond-ward, to diminish and die within two years. Recent renovation of the pond edge has cured this problem, and plants that we planted one, two, and three years ago are now staying with us.

After dramatically modifying our local clay loam with organic matter, we covered the area with fresh sod to prevent the narrow, gently sloped sides from eroding. The primroses were then planted through holes cut into the sod. I initially felt skeptical about the brother/sisterhood of sod and primroses, but so far, they seem as happy as clams.

4. *Dodecatheon*

Many years ago, a friend brought us a shooting star whose "scared rabbit" flowers were a rich, wonderful mauve. This plant lasted only a year, but I have never forgotten it. I believe it must have been *Dodecatheon jeffreyi*, whose range extends from Alaska to Southern California, Idaho, and Montana. We recently decided to try this again, along with *D. meadia*, because its origins—Pennsylvania to southern Wisconsin, and south to Alabama and East Texas—seem a little less foreign. *D. meadia* is slightly taller, and its flowers are pure white.

We decided to try these in three places and let the plants show us their preferences. In each case, we made deep pockets; clay loam was removed, amended with compost and No. 2 blasting sand, and the mixture was returned to the pocket.

Dodecatheon jeffreyi

The first site is the shadiest. It lies on the north side of the steps leading past the upper (double) waterfall to the Upper Pond. *Prunus* x *subhirtella* 'Autumnalis' produces almost complete shade from above. The surviving plants of *D. jeffreyi* have much smaller rosettes of leaves than normal. *D. meadia* is quite robust and puts on better and better shows each year.

The second site is in a pocket amid the stepping-stone paving as one approaches the Upper Pond. When the sun is low, very little sunshine reaches this area. When the sun is overhead, the plants get its full glory. The test here is inconclusive, because the plants have been subject to "lawn mower attack." If we can tame this dragon, there will be more to report.

The third planting is in the soil area just behind the old granite curbstones that make up the Statue Steps. These steps face north, but they get pretty much full sun. Paul feels that this area is the driest, explaining why this is where *D. jeffreyi* performs the best—valuable information, since it is the color form that I find most delightful.

D. meadia seems to be the more easily satisfied, however; and even if it were the only choice, I would still consider it valuable in our garden because of the grace of the flower and the timing of its bloom. Paul's experiment has certainly been a great help.

5. *Thymus* 'Clear Gold'
We have used this thyme as a ground cover for 32 years in what we call the Bulb Window Bed. On the northeast side of the studio, it is just outside the Studio Garden at the top of the four-foot retaining wall. One of the two very large studio windows faces this way. The bed itself sits only 10 feet from the studio window, whose sill is level with the bed. Anything planted

Thymus 'Clear Gold'

within it therefore provides the very important foreground of the view from the window, which consists of the pasture, the Torreya Grove, and the farm landscape beyond.

The story starts with our recognition that this bed, just a little below eye level for someone standing inside the studio, would be the perfect place for a display of diminutive bulbs. We have tried many different sorts, and they have always been a source of great interest, especially at the transition from winter to spring. This sort of bulb is seldom long-lived, but it is not all that expensive to make annual replacements and changes. A few that we consider winners are:

> *Crocus chrysanthus* 'Blue Pearl'
> *C. chrysanthus* 'Prinses Beatrix'
> *Muscari azureum* 'Album' (syn. *Pseudomuscari azureum* 'Alba')
> *Tulipa humilis* 'Violacea' (syn. *T. pulchella* 'Violacea')
> *Gladiolus communis* subsp. *byzantinus*

There are two small shrubs, one at either end, in scale with the miniature landscape they flank:

> *Salix bockii*—little catkins in the fall
> *Cytisus decumbens*—yellow flower in late May

We also have two plants of the small-scale bicolor "plum tart iris" (*Iris graminea*), which has lovely violet-and-deep purple blossoms snuggled into its narrow foliage and rather shyly gives off a fragrance identified by some as that of a freshly baked plum tart. But I digress.

The point of the story is that the bulbs, the major display, are all spring bloomers that go to sleep very soon after they bloom. This means bare earth for the remainder of the gardening season, and hence the need for a ground cover that poses neither a cultural nor an aesthetic threat to the bulbs.

Because the bed receives full sun and we had prepared the soil for the bulbs by adding a lot of gritty material to the clay loam, thyme seemed the perfect plant. I wanted it all to be a single thyme cultivar. Finding one—*Thymus* 'Clear Gold'—whose foliage, when in new growth, is distinctly chartreuse delighted me, since that is such a good background color for a host of other hues. I have not seen *T.* 'Clear Gold' listed since my initial purchase, so when replacements are needed, we repropagate from what we have. This was in place when Paul came, and the job of renovating and keeping this ground cover going fell to him. There has been one major renovation since then.

As many bulbs as possible were saved. Paul amended the soil with stone aggregate from the property and added new propagules. Crushed limestone is put in annually, and fresh propagules are added as necessary. Paul feels that any given plant is good here for only two to three years.

The Greenhouse Syndrome (a Happy Landing)

I am unusual among gardeners, I believe, in that I have always avoided having a greenhouse. This is probably because, in the course of my career visiting clients' gardens, the greenhouses I saw being used as workplaces were more often than not a mess. During the gardening season a greenhouse is often "allowed to go" while higher-priority things are attended to. Also, during some times of the year—especially the winter and early spring—gardeners neglect early spring priorities outdoors because there are things unnecessarily classified as urgent that need doing in the greenhouse. The fact that, on cool or damp

Our 23-by-65-foot stainless-framed greenhouse is covered with sheets of ladder-extruded polycarbonate.

days, the greenhouse is more comfortable than the open air is often overlooked as the real reason for being inside! There are two obvious reasons for having a greenhouse:

1. To grow one's own tender bedding plants
2. To be able to store tender plants (in pots and tubs) that will continue to be used from year to year

For many years I was able to avoid having a greenhouse. When Paul first came, we were trying to have outside contractors fill our bedding-plant needs, and we were renting space at a nearby commercial greenhouse to store plants being carried over to another season.

It was soon apparent that Paul's and my own curiosity were sufficiently rampant that we could not buy all of the different and interesting bedding plants we felt we should try. They were simply not available.

We next attempted to have what we wanted "contract grown." For at least three years we dealt with three different people, supplying them the seed for most hard-to-find items. Our order was never big and important enough (by their standards) to receive the amount of attention needed for them to do a good job.

Finally, in the late 1980s, we decided to rent space at the same commercial greenhouse where our plants were stored and grow the tender bedding plants and tropicals ourselves.

This was never a perfect relationship. However, Paul and his helpers did a good job in the face of adversity. This was our system for approximately 20 years!

In the spring of 2006 the ax fell. The commercial greenhouse went out of business, and there were no alternatives close by.

Wintertime activities inside the greenhouse, above, keep our front hall full of color. This is also where we start a high percentage of summer bedding plants, and where we carry tender tubbed and potted plants through the winter.

After considerable soul-searching—and trying out the feel of doing without most of our tubbed and potted plants, and converting from annuals to perennials in the two places where bedding plants have played such an important part—we built a 23-by-65-foot greenhouse here on the property.

This means that we will be able to enjoy Paul's incredible craftsmanship as a "grower" for a while longer. In addition, we eliminated the previous cost of travel time, and we now have complete control over our production.

Appendix 10 lists the bedding plants for 2006. Appendix 11 lists the tubbed and potted plants we enjoyed in various parts of the garden that year, especially on the swimming pool terrace.

I think we have "done it right." The greenhouse has no masonry footings; its galvanized steel crossbeams are set into galvanized steel sleeves sunk 18 inches into the ground. We covered the frame with sheets of ladder-extruded polycarbonate, which provides good light transmission, good insulation, and maximum durability. The "floor" is a drop cloth of UV-stabilized polypropylene laid over eight inches of crushed stone. Paul has built benches for some items, and other things will reside in tubs and pots on the floor. There are two propane heaters (one could provide enough heat if the other one went off). There is no ridge ventilation. Instead, we put two fans at one end and a louver at the other. There is one door.

Most important, we have invested in a propane generator that practices weekly, automatically, and has a good transfer switch, so that it comes on the moment the power goes off. Paul and I went to see larger houses of the same sort west of Emmaus, Pennsylvania, that belonged to an Amish grower who produced bedding plants of excellent quality.

"The Biggest Problem"

Recently, I asked Paul what he considered the biggest problems he faces with the garden. The answer that stands out is "The lack of suburbia around us." At first one is shocked that this would in any way be a problem. In suburbia, however, all of one's neighbors are busy combatting noxious weeds. No one is combatting noxious weeds in the farm fields and forest edges that surround Ashland Hollow!

Japanese honeysuckle (*Lonicera japonica*) and Oriental bittersweet (*Celastrus orbiculatus*) are the worst of the woody weeds. Canadian thistle (*Cirsium arvense*), quack grass (*Agropyron repens*), and pokeweed (*Phytolacca americana*) are the worst of the herbaceous ones. In addition, woody tree seedlings such as American walnut (*Juglans nigra*) and choke cherry (*Prunus serotina*) love to pop up in the middle of woody shrubs.

Japanese honeysuckle can be controlled by close mowing for a season, if it is in a location where this is practical. Pokeweed can be eliminated, if one has only a plant or two, by very time-consuming digging that takes immense care to extract every single piece of the big fleshy root, which goes quite deep. All the other weeds require the use of herbicides. Paul has worked diligently with these and now knows as much about the subject as anyone I know. None of his successes have come easily. Most procedures require more than one spraying, and several take more than a year's work. The biggest part of the challenge has been killing the invaders without killing the treasured ornamentals they like to invade.

Paul also suffers as much as the plants whenever we have a drought, especially a prolonged one. This is because he knows better than any of us not only the short-term setbacks for many different plants but also the multiyear effects on some of the woodies. Plants weakened by drought lack adequate defenses to handle insect and disease attacks when they come along.

One could get pretty gloomy about all of this, especially if one is an American who compares gardening here with gardening in England. A friend who has gardened in both countries says that there are many fewer weeds, insects, and plant diseases in England than here. In fact, he says, a garden here would require twice as large a crew to care for it as an identical English garden would. I think this ought to make us cherish our gardens all the more when they are successful. Certainly, the challenges we face have not slowed Paul down.

Favorite Spots

Paul's favorite parts of this garden are the Upper Pond and the Studio Garden. This is because of the opportunities each provides for using herbaceous plants. The former offers water's-edge planting conditions; the latter presents the challenge of increasing shade. Paul particularly likes the fact that the Studio Garden is the hub for the rest of our entire garden. From either of two exits one can reach any other part of the garden by a relatively short route.

Paul's favorite time of the year at Ashland Hollow is the fall (September to December). He loves the transition as leaf coverage falls away, revealing the landforms and the structure of the garden. I second the motion!

Visitors

We all enjoy having visitors to the garden. The worst that can happen is when they do not react at all. Almost as bad are those who go around saying nothing until they come to a part of the garden that has frequently been photographed and published.

Suddenly they become excited and say, "There it is, there it is, just like the picture in...!"

Another unfavorite is the visitor who keeps asking, "What's that?" and then, "What's that?"—when you know perfectly well that he or she is not registering a word you say. My solution, depending on my patience on any given day, is to announce, "I will not answer any more questions until you take out a piece of paper and a pencil and write these names down." I have never known this to fail.

The majority of visitors are truly a great pleasure, and we invariably learn as much from them as they do from us. Paul summed it all up when he said, "I like the ones who really get it."

I asked him if any particular garden visit stood out as a wonderful memory. He mentioned a visit from the American Public Gardens Association. Then a twinkle came into his eyes and he said the name of a landscape architect from the West Coast whose friendship I cherish and with whom I share similar taste and enthusiasms in gardens. When I first met her (elsewhere), I had said that I seldom got turned on by pink. One of her earliest visits to Ashland Hollow occurred when both Nancy and I had to be away. Paul went around with my friend, enjoying every minute of it. When they came to the Rose Path she said, "For someone who doesn't like the color pink, there's a lot of fuckin' pink in this garden." Although this incident had occurred six or seven years before, it still rested, with delight, in Paul's memory when he quoted it to me a few days ago! It is so much in character that I am sure his recollection is accurate.

The Future

During that same conversation, Paul and I talked about the future of this garden we have both come to love so much. I asked him what he hoped for in the next ten years. His response was, "Developing a really good garden crew." With what we have both learned from the past, this seems very likely to happen.

I then reminded him of something he had said, and which I had noted in my journal, seven years before: "Caring for this garden is like riding a dragon. It is a very sensual relationship." Upon further questioning at a later date, Paul explained that, "According to Tibetan Buddhism, the dragon—mystical and ultimately wise—embodies strength, wisdom, and the divine power of transformation. A flirtatious wag of the dragon's tail can send us reeling, when to the dragon it is a simple gesture." As you ride you gain wisdom, or you are swallowed whole. Either way, it is a transforming experience.

It is true to character that Paul has absorbed this mystical story into his dedicated nurturing of this garden. He has essentially turned it into a love song.

As I meditated on this, I was brought up short by memories of the many times I had been enjoying a creative moment when the beautiful angels who hang over my shoulder tried to put in their two cents. This always turned out to be frivolous and without substance, and it detracted from the strength I drew from the landforms, the vegetation, and my own steaming teapot of color relationships!

Friends had been floating various titles for this book past me, but it was at this moment that Steve Hutton's *Wrestling with Angels and Singing with Dragons* clicked into place to stay.

The Beech Arch
(*Fagus sylvatica*
'Riversii') in summer

NOTE

14.1. Pat Christopher, who has done considerable work with verbascums, suggested
this parentage: *Verbascum olympicum*
(syn. *V. longifolium* var. *pannosum*, from
southern Europe) x *V. densiflorum* (syn.
V. thanpsiforme, Europe).

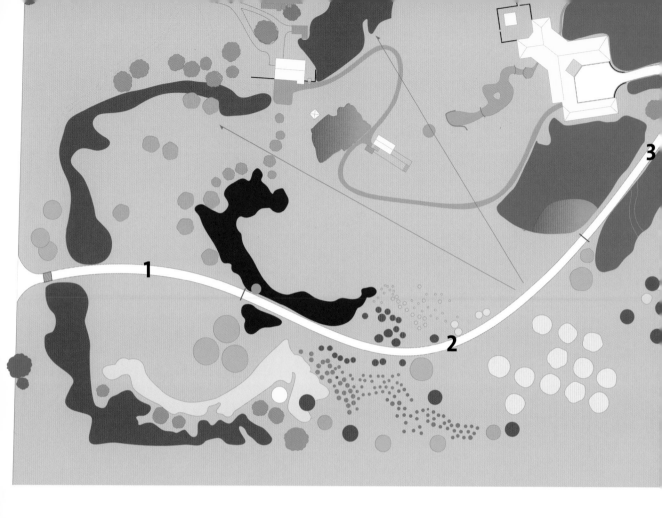

Above: As the numbers indicate, I have
divided my discussion of this area into
three parts.

Opposite: An aerial view of the first two
parts of the drive, before it enters the woods

15 Along the Drive

A Garden Experience by Car

The driveway leading from the public country road to our house at Ashland Hollow is just a little over a third of a mile long. It drops in elevation by 64 feet as it descends into the valley. The drive was designed by Doug Buck, along with the very successful house plans he did with his partner, Ted Fletcher, in 1964. I have always felt that the drive made a beautiful fit to the landforms of our valley. I have enjoyed every trip in and out.

Part of my exercise routine for many years has been two miles of fast walking every other day. For a long time, I did this on Ashland Clinton School Road. But because commuter traffic has recently become heavier, I have changed to walking three round-trip laps on our driveway. This has given me an even greater appreciation of the plantings on either side during every season. Although the plantings were designed to be seen from a moving car, I find this route equally fulfilling on foot. The design can best be explained, I think, as an experience in three parts.

The first part begins with a gradual descent just after leaving the public road, crossing the cattle grate and passing through the Conifer Windbreak. It continues through an open field, which acts as a sort of decompression chamber, and then tightens down at a low point at the start of the Holly Grove.

The middle third has essentially no grade change. It was cut through a small ridge in order to achieve this. That one cut causes the landform to "pinch in" from the west side of the drive, giving a feeling of anchorage to the whole scheme. It also causes one to sense that he or she has left a more public area behind and is now becoming part of a new, exciting experience.

The third part is a steep descent through the woods, causing brakes to be applied as the driver recognizes a sharp curve ahead and begins to glimpse the house and its arrival courtyard below.

Top: A view from the Orchard north toward Ashland Road

Above: Looking south from Ashland Road through the stone gateposts and the wooden gates

378

Before discussing the planting character of each of these parts, one needs to understand the significance of the following three events in providing definition to the whole area:

- The planting (in 1967) of the Conifer Windbreak (see pages 122-126), which encloses the first third of the drive to the north, the west, and partly to the east, and then ends partway into the middle section
- The planting of the Orchard (1969) on its knoll to the south (see pages 134-138), which brings a strong country character to the middle section
- The planting of American hollies (1971, 1976) in the middle section mostly to the east (see page 441), which separates the driveway from the Winter Garden. This extensive curvilinear Holly Grove has "arms" reaching southwest across the drive as well as northeast where the spacing of trees increases dramatically.

We started the entire first two-thirds of the driveway planting after moving here in 1965. The structuring relies on the evergreen character of the Conifers Windbreak Planting, the Holly Grove, and two groupings of American red cedars (*Juniperus virginiana*), as well as on the following large deciduous trees (listed in the order in which they are seen on the way in from Ashland Clinton School Road) in the quantities noted:

Shagbark hickory (*Carya ovata*) (3)

White oak (*Quercus alba*) (3)

Ginkgo biloba, staminate (1)

Kentucky coffee tree (*Gymnocladus dioicus*) (1)

Black walnut (*Juglans nigra)* (1)

Black locust, chartreuse foliage form
  (*Robinia pseudoacacia* 'Dean Rossman') (1)

Red oak (*Quercus rubra*) (2)

Within this structure, important plantings of smaller trees and shrubs provide significant seasonal interest:

- Flowering cherries (cultivars and seedling variants of *Prunus avium, P. sargentii, P. serrulata,* and *P.* x *subhirtella*)
- Forsythia (*Forsythia* x *intermedia* 'Spring Glory' and *F. suspensa*)
- French hybrid lilacs (*Syringa vulgaris* cultivars)
- Winged euonymus (*Euonymus alatus*)

Above: *Carya ovata* (shagbark hickory)

Opposite: The shaggy, exfoliating bark of *C. ovata* gives this hickory its common name.

Below: Our staminate *Ginkgo biloba* in fall foliage

Decompression (First Third of Drive)

While entering the first section of the drive, but before crossing the cattle grate, one sees three specimen shagbark hickory trees (*Carya ovata*) to the left. Years ago at Millcreek Nursery, when we were continually revising our plant palette, Nancy—who seldom voiced opinions on this subject—expressed a passion for shagbark hickory, the most beautiful native nut tree. Its elegant, slightly narrowed, upright form is distinctive. And when its long, vertical strips of exfoliating bark are washed in winter light, they have moments of pink, lavender, and pastel green as part of their basic gray. Nancy and I brought in seedlings, realizing that it would be a few years before they reached maturity as landscape plants. In 1971 we planted three of them here, to be the first trees one sees upon entering our garden.

Beyond the cattle grate, one's eyes go immediately to the right, to three fine specimens of white oak (*Quercus alba*) planted in 1966. We have allowed them to retain their lower branches, some of which even touch the ground.

To the east of the drive in this area is a staminate (male, nonfruit-producing) form of *Ginkgo biloba* (1983). It stands among the American hollies where that grove first touches the drive. Thanks to this tree's widely fastigiate character, minor pruning encourages good neighboring with the hollies. The ginkgo is, of course, highly valued for its clear yellow fall foliage. I have always loved the moment of ginkgos' leaf drop because it happens so quickly. One day you have a totally yellow tree; a couple of days later you have stark naked branches with a perfect circle of yellow leaves below. The latter sight is especially dramatic at Ashland Hollow because the yellow lies mostly on the near-black driveway.

Roberto Burle Marx visited us one year at forsythia season. After seeing three or four of these shrubs in the garden at one house we passed, a lone forsythia in another, five in another, he said, "This is such a wonderful plant. Why don't homeowners join together to make larger plantings for bolder effect?" We had the opportunity to do this on the western side of our driveway, just in front of the Conifer Windbreak. In 1979 we planted more than 100 *Forsythia* x *intermedia* 'Spring Glory'. Moving from north to south, the planting follows the curve of the windbreak and then thickens as its own front curve advances toward the point where we "pinched" the driveway by cutting it through the existing landforms. At that same point, the forsythia planting turns back to the west and concludes there, overlapping the last conifers just behind the first part of our lilac planting.

At "forsythia time" the immense scale of this display is stunning. The gazebo offers one of the best viewpoints. Seen from there through the bare branches of intervening trees, the yellow brushstroke is immensely striking as it emphasizes the landform that it follows.

In addition to the forsythia feature, this area presents another spring extravaganza of Asiatic plants: the flowering cherry display. Five *Prunus* x *yedoensis* (Yoshino cherry), here since 1989, make up the major part of this planting. A hybrid between *P. serrulata* and *P.* x *subhirtella*, this wide, spreading tree is reliably loaded with beautiful light pink blossoms every year. These quickly change to a long-lasting white as the forsythia is finishing.

I had originally looked forward to finding a really good white cherry that would bloom at the same time (midseason). There was great hope that "The Great White Cherry" (*Prunus serrulata* 'Taihaku', planted here in 1980-83), which gets an incredibly

Opposite

Top: *Forsythia* x *intermedia* 'Spring Glory' glows behind white oaks, as seen from the drive when entering.

Bottom: The forsythia with two of the three Swiss stone pines (*Pinus cembra*) in the foreground

good review in Collingwood Ingram's famous book on cherries, would fill the bill.[15.1] I was able to obtain three plants that Princeton Nurseries had propagated from a Scott Arboretum tree. Unfortunately, these had a problem no horticulturist seems ever to have heard of. For many years they set what looked like fat blossom buds, but each spring, what should have been white petals turned out to be nothing more than green leaves. We took two trees out and left one, to see if it might change with age. Around 2001 it did produce a few true blossoms: nearly single, white, and larger than any flowering-cherry blossom I have ever seen—and then there was nothing more until 2006, when the whole tree was covered with bloom. However, it was not at all what I had hoped for. The plant had already leafed out enough by then to hide a fair percentage of the blossoms. Also, the bronzy new growth that Ingram considered such a significant feature seemed to me a distraction.

At cherry blossom time a few years back, I happened to be at Longwood Gardens where I saw a cherry in bloom that I wish I had known about earlier. It was broadly spreading and laden with nearly double, pure white flowers that had very little competition from the leaves. That tree is *P. serrulata* 'Ojochin'.[15.2] I have yet to find out if it is "in the trade." It certainly should be.

I had more bad luck with *P. sargentii* (first planted here in 1977). Two huge old specimens, which are very broadly spreading, have been left to themselves on a grassy bank at Winterthur. Early in the season, they are loaded with lush pink blossoms. Several nurseries listed *P. sargentii*, and I assumed that their stock would be the same as those trees at Winterthur. Not so! The one I got first was columnar, which the nurseryman apparently took to be this cherry's characteristic form. The second tree I bought, from another source, was a much fatter

Below: *Prunus serrulata* 'Ojochin' (photograph courtesy the Brooklyn Botanic Garden)

Opposite
Top: Yoshino cherry (*P.* x *yedoensis*) (two trees at left rear, one tree on extreme right). In front: *P.* x *subhirtella* 'Rosy Cloud', a deeper pink hybrid

Bottom: The white-flowered trees behind the gazebo are *P. subhirtella* "Scott early," pink in their earlier stages and the first cherries to bloom in our garden.

vertical, which I kept hoping might spread more with age. Its form still does not remotely resemble that of my Winterthur inspiration.

Prunus sargentii is, of course, a true species. I now understand that it has most likely been propagated by seed for many years, probably resulting in a variety of forms. This would account for my disappointments. I should have gotten some enterprising nurseryman to propagate plants asexually from the Winterthur tree. Ours, although dissimilar in form, does have similar flowers and that in itself is a joy.

As for earlier-blooming cherries, I was eager to find a cultivar of *P.* x *subhirtella* with flowers as early and successful as those produced by *P.* x *subhirtella* 'Pendula'. I found exactly what I wanted at the Scott Arboretum in 1980. This was a *Prunus* x *subhirtella* seedling that Mrs. Scott herself had chosen for its spreading shape and excellent blossoms. Tom Buchter very kindly propagated this cherry for us, and the tree now thrives in three different parts of Ashland Hollow, including the driveway planting (where we have one specimen).

We also have another *P.* x *subhirtella* cultivar, 'Rosy Cloud' (planted in 1983), which is a deeper pink. It grows more slowly than Mrs. Scott's selection and will never reach its size. I find ours quite satisfactory, however, and I hope that other plantsmen will work at finding good forms of the early cherries.

Studying the cherry planting in our garden, now in its maturity, I was struck by the desirability of having one more light pink *P.* x *yedoensis* in the next (second) section of the driveway planting, to the extreme right just before the Orchard. This tree is now getting old enough to tease a driver's eye from the big splash back to that location.

Another addition to our group of cherries has not been Asiatic, but Western: the double form of the European bird cherry (*P. avium* 'Plena', planted here in 1988), which is pure white and quite showy, even though there are already leaves on the tree when it blooms. As with many double-flowered plants, the blossoms are long-lasting. This cherry's flowering time overlaps the end of forsythia bloom. Our *P. avium* 'Plena' stands in the thickest part of the forsythia planting where it sweeps down close to the west side of the driveway.

We have also made several efforts at naturalizing bulbs in the first third of the drive experience, and this process continues. After a few years under the white oaks, our *Narcissus* 'Red Shadow' showed signs of declining. But we had already come to

Above: *Prunus avium* 'Plena'

Opposite
Top: *Narcissus* 'Ara' under one of the white oaks with *Forsythia* x *intermedia* 'Spring Glory' as background

Second from top: *N.* 'Ara'

Second from bottom: *N.* 'Spellbinder' under a Yoshino cherry with a Tanyosho pine (left)

Bottom: *N.* 'Spellbinder'

feel that a larger-flowered cultivar with a white perianth would, in any case, be better aesthetically.

When naturalizing bulbs in this area, we have had to consider three factors:

- We prefer white-flowered varieties in combination with their blooming partner, the forsythia planting.
- The elevation of the landform on which the white oaks sit is close to the eye level of motorists entering the drive. It is too high for departing motorists to enjoy.
- The *Narcissus* blossoms on this knoll all face south, 180 degrees away from incoming traffic—our primary audience for the bulbs. This is not a problem so long as the flowers' perianths are white. And since no one sees the trumpet (or cup) in any case, the color of the front of the flower does not really matter.

We tried all-white N. 'Thalia' in 2001 but found that cultivar too frail and diminutive for planting in the midst of field grass. Since a 2005 trial of the relatively new N. 'Ara'—a bolder, more vigorous bicolor pink with a white perianth—we have felt that this is "our plant." We will keep on planting whatever we can get each year, as more bulbs become available.

On the east side of the drive—partly into, partly just in front of—the planting of Tanyosho pines (*Pinus densiflora* 'Umbracu-lifera'), we continue to work on another *Narcissus* planting. Here the flowers face departing motorists but cannot be seen from cars coming in the drive. This makes selection a little easier. We originally planted (in 1971) the very fine, very old N. 'Fortune'. But because this cultivar diminished (and became commercially unavailable), we tried planting (1977) a few bulbs of N. 'Moon-mist' that we already had elsewhere. This is a beautiful pale yellow, a good early spring color. However, we have had to give up on *Narcissus* 'Moonmist', because the color failed to meet our expectations for carrying the necessary distance (and, in any event, it too is no longer available). Since 2006 we have been working with the readily available *N.* 'Spellbinder', and hoping that we have at last found the best answer.

On the Level (Middle Section of Drive)

The second segment of the drive is truly a part of the garden, and one of the most dramatic parts at that. It is also a teaser for many other areas. The start of the midsection is announced by the sensations of entering the American Holly Grove and feeling the pinch of its associated landforms and plantings.

This part of the Holly Grove presses tight against the drive on the east. The vast swing of *Forsythia* x *intermedia* 'Spring Glory' comes close to the drive on the west, though not quite as close as the beginning of the lilac planting and the adjacent sweep of *Euonymus alatus* on the roadside bank.

Dead ahead is the Orchard with its utilitarian geometry reminding one of this garden's agricultural origins. Four dark olive green native red cedars (*Juniperus virginiana*) on the left repeat this country feeling. They in turn are echoed by four more red cedars on a high knoll behind and to the east of the Orchard. The lack of grade change in this section also speaks up, saying, "Attention! Slow down and look on both sides!"

In the background, on the west side, the Conifer Windbreak ends with the very wide spacing of four exceptionally hardy and beautiful forms of cedar of Lebanon (*Cedrus libani* subsp. *stenocoma*). These finger out towards the orchard along with the young Yoshino cherry. Two red oaks (*Quercus rubra*), planted in 1975, stand closer together in the background.

Top: Firmament lilac (*Syringa vulgaris* 'Firmament')

Above: Edward J. Gardner lilac (*S. vulgaris* 'Edward J. Gardner')

Opposite: Ludwig Spaeth lilac (syn. *S. vulgaris* 'Ludwig Spaeth')

The lilac planting in front of the large trees on the west, and downhill from the drive on the east, comprises three cultivars in harmonizing colors:

On the west:

Syringa vulgaris 'Ludwig Spaeth'; about 40 plants;
   a rich, vibrant purple

S. vulgaris 'Firmament'; about 50 plants;
   as close to cerulean blue as one gets with lilac cultivars

On the east:

S. vulgaris 'Edward J. Gardner'; about 35 plants;
   a true light pink

Lilacs enjoy being cool to cold, and they withstand wind very well. In Denmark they are used as hedgerow plantings, to break the force of the wind across farm fields. I had been thoroughly indoctrinated with the beauty of French hybrid lilacs when I worked at the Scott Arboretum as a student. Creating this high-impact planting, to be seen daily from the car, was certainly a dream come true. We learned three things in the course of doing the planting:

- There must not be a big market for French hybrid lilacs. We had a devil of a time finding the particular cultivars we wanted. In two cases we had to wait two years for them to be custom-propagated. It took us 10 years to complete this planting.
- We already knew that it was highly desirable to have lilacs grown on their own roots. Past practice had called for grafting the lilac onto privet (*Ligustrum*) understock. The privet was supposed to die, and the lilac roots to take over. Often, however, the privet took over instead. I was under

the impression that rooting cuttings had become the preferred propagation method. But I could find none of our three cultivars cutting-grown. I *did* find lilacs grafted on ash (*Fraxinus*). Although I felt no confidence in the latter system, it was the only way we could get what we wanted.

Happily, there has been no problem with ash surviving and taking over the lilac. It has done exactly what it was supposed to do. Flowering has been heavy and the color combinations are extremely celebrative.

- We suffered some losses in the plantings in front of the Conifer Windbreak and across the drive. Individual plants dried out much faster than they should have. Paul's keen eye soon began to see a pattern. In this one area he observed a rock ledge beneath the plants preventing them from getting as much water as their neighbors. There is also an excessive accumulation of dead wood and a lack of renewal sprouts from the bases of the plants—problems yet to be solved.

I must pause to relate a curious tale about a viburnum. During a visit in 1983 to our friends Ben Blackburn and Russell Myers at the Willowwood Arboretum, I greatly admired the lovely chartreuse spring foliage on *Viburnum opulus* 'Aureum'. Two years later, Ben very generously sent a propagule from that viburnum. Suddenly falling in love with a plant such as this can be a problem in a sensitively designed garden. Rather than pop it in some place where its bright color would scream, "Look at me! Look at me!" I got a hold of myself and put it in the small nursery we keep for just such problems.

Every spring for 14 years I would look at this glorious foliage and fail to find an appropriate location for it. The plant was so attractive, however, that I could never bring myself to eliminate

We use the chartreuse foliage of *Viburnum opulus* 'Aureum' (background) as a companion for the flowers of these lilacs.

it from further consideration. The answer finally came when I realized that my stumbling block had been always visualizing only *one* plant. But if I could think of a way to plant a much larger number, this viburnum would be most useful as a color element. Suddenly, the fact that the color of its foliage peaked just as the lilacs reached their peak of flower color told me that this was where a large planting of the viburnum belonged.[15.3]

My original theory positioned the chartreuse viburnum foliage in back of the 'Firmament' and 'Ludwig Spaeth' lilacs on the west side of the driveway, "pushing" this wonderful rich color combination toward the viewer in a moving car. Now that the first viburnum propagules have begun to mature, however, we have modified that theory and are moving some plants forward among the lilacs, which looks even better. This is turning into a unique success, and I feel rewarded for waiting to bring about such a harmonious plant marriage.

We have used none of the viburnums on the east side of the drive with *Syringa vulgaris* 'Edward J. Gardner'. The pink of this

Above: *Euonymus alatus* in fall color

Below: A view from the driveway to the northwest, just before entering the woods. The flagpole is part of the arbor at the swimming pool. Also visible are the roofs of the springhouse and (upper left in the Springhouse Woods) the gazebo.

Opposite: On the next knoll beyond the lilacs, naturalized *Narcissus* drift throughout the Orchard (see Chapter 6).

lovely cultivar is not strong enough to handle the lively yellow green of the viburnum.

Where the driveway cuts through the small ridge at the beginning of this section of the drive, steep banks flank it on both sides. We filled the need for a tough yet highly ornamental shrub by planting *Euonymus alatus* and *E. alatus* 'Monstrosus'.[15.4] A staggered arrangement and wide spacing ensure that these plants will barely touch one another at maturity. Already, their wonderful horizontal branching habit, winged bark, and luscious fall color count as great assets.

The forsythia story initiated in a big way in the first section of driveway planting reaches its conclusion here. In 1979 we planted four light yellow *Forsythia suspensa* with the four *Juniperus virginiana* on the knoll behind the orchard. When leaves are off the trees in wintertime, this knoll is visible all the way from the end of the drive. We intended the red cedars to tease one's eye in from that distant approach. The forsythia does the same by repeating the yellow of the larger planting nearer the entrance. As both plantings matured, they began to seem uncomfortably far apart, and so we recently added a second grouping of *F. suspensa* on the east side of the drive, just where the lilac planting there ends.

On past the euonymus, on the southwest side of the drive, we planted a Kentucky coffee tree (*Gymnocladus dioicus*) in 1985. The vase shape of its strong muscular trunk and branches does a good job of framing the inviting view of the driveway as it disappears into the woods ahead.

Just after this, however, on the northwest side of the drive, comes an unexpected twist—a delightful one. The containment of the driveway now seems to spring open with a glorious view out over a major part of the garden in the valley below. Until this

point, any view out has been blocked by the extensive planting of American hollies (between the drive and the Winter Garden). The enchanting center of the valley view comprises the springhouse, the grape arbor, and the American flag flying determinedly from a pole attached to the arbor. One sees the Conifer Windbreak coming from the barn around to the east, the Corten steel frames for the two giant tree wisterias, and layer upon layer of other planting doing a great variety of things during the course of the year. First-time visitors stop to take it all in!

Downhill and Through the Woods (Final Third of Drive)

The entrance to the woods, the third stretch of driveway landscape, is framed on the south side by a native black walnut (*Juglans nigra*), which was here when we came; some smooth sumac (*Rhus glabra*); and a young black locust.[15.5] The locust is a charming cultivar found by, and named for, a friend: 'Dean Rossman'. Its quite beautiful chartreuse foliage adds special interest to the darkness of the forest behind it. It also picks up the chartreuse in the foliage of *Rubus cockburnianus* 'Aureus' planted on either side of the Winter Garden door (at woods' edge, just below the drive to the north).

We have done very little new planting along this part of the drive where one plunges into the woods. It has been more a case of tree and shrub removal here, because of death, incurable disease, or our wish to reveal and encourage existing desirable plants.

Several mature sour gum trees (*Nyssa sylvatica*) and a number of maturing sassafras grow to the north at woods' edge. Both the sour gums and the sassafras have responded to our clearing around them by growing larger, and they give us a fine fall glow of scarlet and orange yellow foliage, respectively.

The view as the driveway enters woods. These evergreens are our native red cedar (*Juniperus virginiana*).

Coming down the drive in May, one sees this sculptural specimen of native white dogwood (*Cornus florida*) straight ahead.

On each side of the drive shortly after entering the woods we have had to remove a large oak stricken by a disease, prevalent here, called scorch:

- On the right, a badly infested single-trunk tree
- On the left, a double-trunk tree with one trunk completely dead and the other showing infected foliage.

From here on, the woods is quite lovely and dense. By selective thinning, we have encouraged the growth of existing young beech trees whose dense horizontal branches are so attractive during the winter, especially when covered with snow.[15.6]

In early May, the view down the drive in this area features a solitary native American dogwood (*Cornus florida*). This single-trunk tree stands partway up the steep right-hand bank of the drive, which makes a tight curve to the left to enter the courtyard in front of the house. The base of the dogwood trunk leans out from the bank at an angle of perhaps 60 degrees and then suddenly goes straight upward. It is only on this vertical part that branching occurs: the typical dogwood slightly-above-horizontal, sympodial branching habit. I know not what caused the initial angled jut of the trunk—an ice storm, a fallen branch holding the trunk down until its tilt was permanent? Surely, the vertical growth reflects an attempt to reach for sunlight. Early in our days at Ashland Hollow we spotted a few blossoms on the tree and noticed how sculptural the trunk was, which led to more clearing so that we could see it better. This must have been after the large black oak across the drive came down and more light filtered through.

The lost tree had suffered from another disease afflicting many black oaks all through our woodland. After enjoying its majesty for a good many years, we had it taken down because of the danger of deadwood falling on cars in the driveway. The oak was such a giant that it had shaded out much of the small tree and shrub growth below. Its removal improved visibility for drivers going in both directions, letting them see each other more clearly and giving them interesting views of the house. We took out most remaining lower growth, except for an attractive sassafras, a large *Viburnum prunifolium*, and a few existing native red cedars (*Juniperus virginiana*).

Several more red cedars persist on both sides of the woodland part of the drive wherever there is enough light (farther up the hill). In this now open area we found that our native columbine (*Aquilegia canadensis*) did well. On several occasions we grew columbine from seed and planted seedlings there by the hundreds.

When we first got here, another tree in that same area, and close to one end of the garage, was nearly dead. My mother, who somewhat enjoyed being a prophet of doom (or perhaps I should call her a practical and experienced "country" woman), announced early on that we should get rid of this tree because it would fall on the garage. We said, "No, we want to keep it, because it will attract woodpeckers." But we never had a chance to attract many woodpeckers, because within a year the tree did fall on the garage! Our penalty for not listening to my mother was an extremely large and inconvenient bill for hoisting the tree off the garage and repairing a big hole in its tile roof.

At the upper part of the bend in the drive, on the south side, we discovered three natives of great interest:

- Three or four plants of our beautiful native azalea (*Rhododendron periclymenoides* [syn. *R. nudiflorum*]) were in bloom when we first sighted them. While clearing around them we found azalea seedlings, which have subsequently bloomed. They display a nice color range, from dark pinks (some on the muddy side) to beautiful clear medium pinks

Top: Native azaleas (*Rhododendron periclymenoides* [syn. *R. nudiflorum*]) were here when we arrived.

Middle: More *R. periclymenoides* (Pinxterbloom azaleas). The bloom on new seedlings varies from deep to very light pink.

Above: Across from the azaleas, our native columbine (*Aquilegia canadensis*) flourishes in the peninsula rounded by the drive as it descends to the house.

and a few quite light ones. We still clear more space each year, and as the happy parents keep seeding, the size of the colony continues to grow.

- In back of these azaleas we found a large sour gum (*Nyssa sylvatica*). Aged and infirm, it eventually came down. A number of its seedlings lived on nearby. We have cleared around the youngsters somewhat, and they have flourished and competed among themselves. The survivors become more of an asset every year.
- On the same bank with the azaleas, I found and fell in love with *Symphyotrichum cordifolium* (syn. *Aster cordifolius*) and its bloom-mate the unbranched goldenrod (*Solidago caesia*).

This north-facing bank receives no direct sunlight and it has stony soil of doubtful fertility. When Tom Williams regularly weeded the bank once a year, the asters and goldenrods put on a wondrous display.[15.7] But now that we are unable to give them that attention, they are thinning out. I hope that the colony we have planted in the less competitive area of the Torreya Grove will take their place.

As long as we can keep down taller growth, fall-blooming *Aster cordifolius* thrives on the same shady, dry bank as the azaleas.

A recent discovery, just across the drive from the original area, is a young plant of *Cornus alternifolia*, which much larger seedlings of forest trees had hemmed in (we removed them). In the same area, the aforementioned sassafras tree died and left us a young colony, which we will keep down to a grove of six or seven plants. This means that the stretch of driveway just uphill from the big bend now has a vista—framed by the *Cornus* on one side and the Sassafras Grove on the other—to our Entrance Garden and front door.

By the same token, the front door and Entrance Garden now give us a good view of cars heading out the drive. We very much enjoy waving our departing visitors off from that vantage point.

NOTES

15.1. Collingwood Ingram, *Ornamental Cherries* (London: Country Life; New York: Charles Scribner's Sons, 1948).

15.2. A year later I discovered that it is light pink when it first opens, but quickly fades to the exuberant white I first saw.

15.3. We started planting the viburnums with the lilacs in 1999.

15.4. These were preceded (in 1975) by another horizontal brancher, *Crataegus crus-galli*, which turned out to be extremely susceptible to cedar apple rust. The situation was very much aggravated by the presence of a clump of three *Juniperus virginiana* just across the drive from the *Crataegus*. Complete control was impossible, even with a very expensive spray program.

15.5. According to notes from a conversation with Dean Rossman in the studio at Ashland Hollow on December 24, 2007, *Robinia pseudoacacia* 'Dean Rossman' came from chance seedlings found by Dean in the garden of Thelma (Mrs. James) Grad in Great Neck, N.Y., in 1982 or '83. These were potted and the pots were sunk in ground in Mrs. Grad's vegetable garden over the winter. One survived, and from this Dean propagated plants that he has distributed to 18 gardens. This black locust is registered with the International Cultivar Registration Authority for Unassigned Woody Genera at the Brooklyn Botanic Garden. Contact: Gerry Moore, Ph.D., Director, Department of Science, Brooklyn Botanic Garden, 1000 Washington Avenue, Brooklyn, NY 11225-1009.

15.6: Whenever this part of the forest has seemed too thin, we have added more seedling beech (*Fagus grandifolia*).

15.7. After one of these years of heavy weeding, Nancy also found a sudden appearance of great numbers of *Hepatica americana*, in shades from deep blue to white. They slowly disappeared over the next 10 years, as honeysuckle and other competitors returned.

Opposite: A view from the Orchard of the driveway "going out" (areas 2 and 1 on plan, page 376).

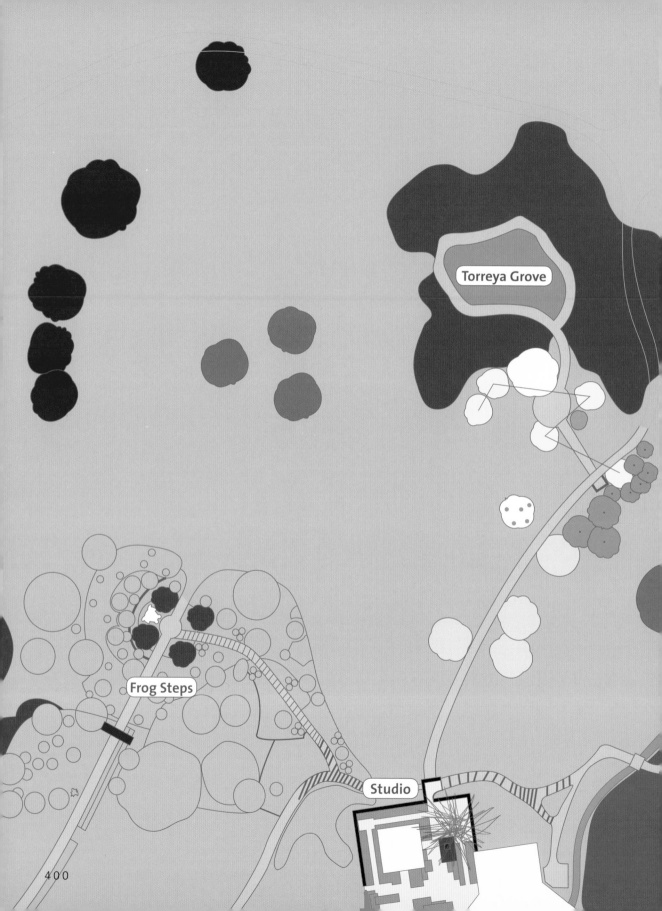

Torreya Grove

Frog Steps

Studio

16 Torreya Grove

As It Has Turned Out

Tragedy, Discouragement, and Starting Over

Trial #1: Woody Shrubs as Ground Cover

Trial #2: Camellias (Hope Springs Eternal)

A Low-Maintenance, High-Excitement Plan for the Future

As It Has Turned Out

In Paul's earliest years here, although the personalities of many parts of the garden were pretty well fixed, a lot of challenge and adventure still lay ahead for a young man eager to learn, eager to make a difference. This was especially true with regard to our growing deer problem and the convulsions of the Torreya Grove.

The Torreya Grove is now one of the most horticulturally interesting parts of the garden. A grass path leads from the east side of the Studio Garden, curving gently to the south, to a stone overlook-sitting wall. The view from there to the left takes in the pasture of Burrows Run Valley below and an intriguing icon of male virility adapted from early Greek and Roman history. This figure stands in the woods directly in front of the overlook, on the far side of the small stream.

In spite of the distance between the grove and the Studio Garden, they feel closely linked, for two reasons: first, the elevation of the path is almost even with that of the Studio Garden; and second, in addition to its attraction as a place to enjoy the views, the grove is also, like the Studio Garden, a place to enjoy horticultural treasures (in the grove, mostly woody).

With one's back to the overlook, one sees a grass path "axing" dead ahead (and on a rise) on a large, venerable *Magnolia denudata* (Yulan magnolia) with a mowed grass circle in the foreground at its feet. From this circle, the path then angles off to the northeast, disappearing into an evergreen grove of Japanese torreya (*Torreya nucifera*), Virginia pine (*Pinus virginiana*), and Asiatic spice bush (*Lindera angustifolia*). The path makes a closed circuit around an open patch of meadow in the center of the grove and returns to the starting point.

This area has its strongest "blossom moment" in early April, when the clusters of rich yellow flowers on six *Cornus officinalis* 'Kintoki' open—closely followed by, and overlapping with, the waxy white blossoms of the *M. denudata*.

Opposite

Top left: A young *Torreya nucifera* in winter with all of its side branches still intact

Top right: The grove is composed of two conifers. This is the beautiful dark green foliage of *T. nucifera*. Its needles are stiff and pointed. The small greenish gray fruits can be seen upper center.

Middle left: *Pinus virginiana*, the temporary partner of the torreyas, is a fast-growing, short-lived pine that tolerates poor soil. We planted it as a wind protector until the torreyas got established. The *P. virginiana*, which have completed their job successfully, are now dying out.

Middle right: The waxy white flowers of Yulan magnolia (*Magnolia denudata*)

Bottom: *M. denudata* with *Cornus officinalis* 'Kintoki' on both sides

403

404

Opposite
Top left: Beyond an early yellow-flowered dogwood (*Cornus officinalis* 'Kintoki'), stone sitting walls define an overlook to the valley.

Top right: Blossoms on *C. officinalis* Kintoki'. The Japanese arrange such branches as cut flowers.

Middle: The Torreya Grove as seen from the studio. The yellow trees are *C. officinalis* 'Kintoki' with opening buds.

Bottom left: From the overlook in the Torreya Grove there is a good view of Priapus in profile in the valley below. For a close look see Chapter 17, page 437.

Bottom right: The structure of a torreya in the center of the grove

The background for this spectacle (every bit as enjoyable from inside our living room, our bedroom, and Nancy's studio as it is close up) is the evergreen grove. We planted the Japanese torreyas in 1976. In Japan, *Torreya nucifera* is a forest tree (to 75 feet) whose small nuts are considered a delicacy when roasted. Because it is a member of the same family, *Taxaceae*, to which *Taxus* belongs, when many observers see *Torreya nucifera* as a small plant, they think it is simply one more yew. However, in addition to being larger at maturity and more treelike than *Taxus*, it has thicker, stiffer needles with sharp points. We grew our torreyas at Millcreek Nursery from cuttings taken from harshly trimmed plants in a hedgerow that had once been part of Bill Phelps's Guyencourt Nursery.[16.1]

Tragedy, Discouragement, and Starting Over

Our original idea was to have a display of white magnolias (*Magnolia denudata*) and cool yellow winter hazels (*Corylopsis*), for which the torreyas would provide a good dark green background. We planted the first *M. denudata* in 1972.

As far as I can tell from the records, we started with five or six *Corylopsis glabrescens* (which Donald Wyman, in his book *Shrubs and Vines for American Gardens*, calls the hardiest of the group) in 1975-76, followed in 1980 by two *C. sinensis* var. *calvescens* (syn. *C. platypetala*), one of several winter hazels that do very well at Winterthur, just three miles away as the crow flies.

We gradually became aware of what a difficult site ours was. Back in its farm days there had been more erosion than we realized, leaving a scant layer of topsoil. Also, this ground lay wide open to cold winter winds.

The winters, and perhaps the soil as well, were too much for the *Corylopsis* and magnolias. Our *Corylopsis* buds very often froze, and we had blossoms only a few years. The magnolias fared a little better, but with one exception, they never thrived.

In January 1984 the temperatures dipped quite low for a prolonged period. For several mornings our thermometer read -10°F, and a client a few miles away (near the Brandywine River) had -14°F. End of story. We had no *Corylopsis*.[16.2] We do still have the one excellent and faithful *M. denudata*, and it has become an important part of our lives today.

That winter the *Torreya nucifera* were bronzed enough to look extremely unhappy. The following year, when Paul came, he remembers cleaning up dead wood and mulching the torreyas. In 1986 the *Pinus virginiana*, which we knew could handle the wind, low temperatures, and poor soil conditions, were planted among them. Their light shade and wind-softening presence played a major role in getting the torreyas going.

Even before the hard winter of 1983-84, most likely because of the poor performance of our *Corylopsis*, we had started plants of *Cornus officinalis* 'Kintoki' in the nursery. At the time (1982), this tree was unknown and unavailable in the United States. Barry Yinger[16.3] recommended it for its heavy flowering: the clusters of yellow blossoms emerge closer together on the stem than those on other *C. officinalis*. We learned that the Japanese had selected this cultivar for use in their cut-flower industry. By contrast with *C. mas*, *C. officinalis* already ranked high on my "desirable" list because of winter interest in its attractive exfoliating bark. This has very successfully altered the original plans for *Corylopsis* with *Magnolia denudata*.

The winter of '83-'84 started us thinking about other woody plants that could survive in this difficult area.

The upper half of this photograph gives a good look at the structure common to *Pinus virginiana*.

Seasonal Gaps

This rethinking of the planting design made us realize that we had a small gap in seasonal interest in May, as well as much larger gaps in the fall and, to some extent, the winter.

In mid-spring we now have a chance to enjoy a favorite plant of Henry Francis du Pont that has also become a favorite of mine: *Malus halliana* 'Parkmanii'.[16.4] This charmer is so special because of the long stem on each flower. These stems join together in clusters at the branch ends. The clusters of pendant blossoms start with red buds (cadmium red medium on my paint palette) opening to truly beautiful rose-colored flowers (Romney rose cut with white).

We also lost five *Betula platyphylla* var. *japonica*, which had been positioned as structural elements along the approach path from the studio. Because these birches had serious problems with leaf miner, we suspect that they were weakened already by some unknown cause, in addition to suffering the adversities of temperature, soil, and moisture.

In 1986 we planted four *Ginkgo biloba*, not just for fall interest, but also because they were famously tough enough to with-stand horrific city conditions and, as far as we knew, disease

Left: *Malus halliana* 'Parkmanii'

Above: Charming long-stemmed buds and blossoms on *M. halliana* 'Parkmanii'

free. To our shock and amazement, after the ginkgos seemed to take hold and behave as expected, we saw branches starting to die back from the tips. This disease was never identified, even though there had been similar reports from elsewhere. Our brilliant and faithful plant pathologist friend, Bob Mulrooney, did his best, but we lost the battle! The ginkgos were removed sometime prior to 1998. In that year we added four *Liquidambar styaciflua* 'Corky' in their place, roughly the same place where *Betula* had become the first failure. The *Liquidambar* provide significant interest in both fall and winter. Their starlike fall

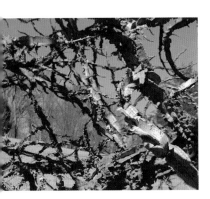

Right: Heavily winged branches of 'Corky' sweet gum (*Liquidambar styraciflua* 'Corky')

Above: After *L. styraciflua* 'Corky' sheds its star-shaped leaves, a source of outstanding fall color, winter sunlight brings out the texture of its ridged bark.

foliage is bright yellow, orange, red, and green—all at the same time. The branches are incredibly ridged and of an alluring texture in the winter light.

Given all of the losses Paul and I had to face,[16.5] it is no wonder that we felt disenchanted with this area and seldom took visitors here. One can view all of these convulsions, I think, as the writhing of Paul's dragon,[16.6] to be dealt with patiently and philosophically as part of the sensuous experience.

Persimmons: A Lesson in Soil and Moisture Requirements

Bearing in mind how glorious the fruit display can be on mature trees, we established a grove of native persimmon (*Diospyros virginiana*) around the Overlook in 1986. Their fine upper branches and twigs are starting to take on characteristically unpredictable changes of direction. This feature is quite beautiful etched against fall and winter skies.

We selected five cultivars[16.7] for their fruit quality. Over the intervening 25 years we have occasionally seen a fruit or two, but nothing like the glorious fruit display along the shore of Chesapeake Bay. The supposition is that a moister soil would cure our problem. However, the persimmons' branching habit earns their aesthetic keep.

A 19th-Century Agricultural Plant

The hedge apple or Osage orange (*Maclura pomifera*), presented in Chapter 2 as part of our Delaware countryside, is a Midwestern native that tolerates a wide variety of growing conditions. Many farm hedgerows in our area contain this plant. The seedlings sold as "living fence" were supposed to be planted close together (12 to 18 inches apart) and, ideally, trained to the desired height by a horticultural process known as in-arching. This involves allowing each sapling to grow a little longer than needed and then bending it over among its neighbors and pegging down the "arch." This causes thick upward sprouting from the bend, making the future hedge especially dense. I doubt that many farmers around here had the time to do this.

A cattle-proof hedge of Osage orange (*Maclura pomifera*) at Winterthur, along Route 52 near Wilmington, Delaware

This method of fencing was employed on a portion of the Winterthur farm near Wilmington, bordering a main road heading westward from the city. Within my lifetime, however, after various invaders infested the fence, it was totally removed. New seedlings were planted and trained according to the in-arching system. Annual trimming has kept it very dense, approximately 12 inches wide, and at agricultural fence height. It would surely do a good job of containing farm animals.

Other farmers simply allowed the saplings to grow into trees, then cut them off at a desirable fence height and strung wire (sometimes barbed wire) between them.

My own interest in the plant focuses on its large fruit, usually about six inches in diameter. A marvelously cheerful apple green/chartreuse, it has a wonderful corrugated surface unlike anything I know—except, perhaps, a sculptor's version of tightly curled hair. In my mind I pictured a tree uphill of the Torreya Grove Path that would drop its fruit on the darker green grass. The fantasy then included a notion of the fruit rolling down to the path where visitors could more readily enjoy it.[16.8]

It was easy to enlist Paul's support in this. He found a nearby Osage orange tree that bore heavily each year and was also thornless. A cutting from this tree was successfully propagated, potted, and grown to planting size. It was then planted uphill from the path. Five falls ago we had our first fruit rolling down the slope to the path! What more could you ask for in the way of decorative fall fruit?[16.9]

This area has been the site of two horticultural trials: the first, now concluded, and the second, still under way.

Untrimmed *Maclura* makes a fair-sized tree. Examples live in many farm hedge-rows here where the farmers did not prune them. The female trees are loaded with large fruits (mostly a little bigger than oranges) whose corrugated outer layer is apple green. These are locally known as hedge apples or monkey balls. We have placed one of these trees on a bank above the Torreya Grove Path. When ripe, fruits fall off the tree and roll downhill.

Trial #1 – Woody Shrubs as Ground Cover

Along with the other "tough guys" planting in 1986-87, we installed a trial area to test the effectiveness of shrubs as ground covers.[16.10] This consisted of a 15-to-18-foot-wide strip along the downhill side of the path to the Torreya Grove. From the Studio Garden it read as a continuation of the on-contour farm hedgerow that incorporated the Overlook. After preparing the existing soil with the usual peat moss and fertilizer additives a landscape contractor would use, we planted significant numbers of the following shrubs:

Comptonia peregrina

Cornus racemosa

Rhus aromatica 'Gro-Low'

Stephanandra incisa 'Crispa'

Taxus cuspidata (a horizontally spreading
    Weston Nursery cultivar)

Xanthorhiza simplicissima

This became an even more rigorous test than I originally may have intended. Not only were the trial plants in a daunting location with field grass on one side, they also got limited care from our gardening staff. This was a time when our understaffing collided head-on with my ambitions. I now believe that this was a good addition to the test.

Paul and I agree that we can recommend two of the groundcover shrubs: *Cornus racemosa* and *Stephanandra incisa* 'Crispa'. This is a 33-percent return, which I feel made the whole thing worthwhile. I also feel that without competition from the adjacent field's quack grass, the *Xanthorhiza* would have proven quite a viable tough-soil, tough-winter ground cover.

Trial #2: Camellias (Hope Springs Eternal)

Moving around the Torreya Grove's circuit path to the starting point, a glimpse of the big Yulan magnolia's gray trunk, one passes through a place darkened by a torreya on either side of the path. A little closer to the magnolia, in a very sheltered spot with more light, we have been trying plants of *Camellia japonica* 'Winter's Fire'. Their dark green foliage and deep red flowers would be great assets. The fact that all our winters seem to be milder now, and that all the other mature plants in this part of the garden divert winter winds and block early morning sunlight, makes me hopeful.

This test planting gained considerable interest from an unanticipated gift in the spring of 2007: a mature, 7 1/2-foot-tall *C.* x *williamsii* 'Aïda'.[16.11] The result of a cross between a *C. japonica* cultivar and a *C. saluenensis* cultivar, this is the only camellia from Longwood trials that survived two extremely severe winters in the mid-1970s. It has beautiful narrow, glossy dark green leaves and double pink flowers.[16.12]

Camellia x *williamsii* 'Aïda'

Torreya Becomes a Winner

Slowly, as the 1986 plantings and those that survived the winter of 1983-84 matured, my enthusiasm returned. The Torreya Grove became mysteriously beautiful, and after lower branches on the *Pinus virginiana* were removed to favor the torreyas, I found that I enjoyed walking through the grove at all times of the year.

In 1977, before that hateful winter, we had planted *Lindera angustifolia*, which retain their foliage all winter. Dick Lighty gave me our original plant that year.[16.13] As seedlings from its briefly held, shiny black fruit come up, we have moved them to some of the grove's outer edges. Because they are branched to the ground, they help to define the space inside. The winter foliage of the *Lindera* is superficially paper-bag colored, but in different lights it shimmers pink, mauve, lavender, peach, and bronze.

The circuit path around the inner edge of the grove provides a gardenesque feeling. One enters this path just after passing the large, faithful *Magnolia denudata*. As the fork to the left goes uphill, it is stopped by a planting of three *Prunus laurocerasus* 'Otto Luyken' and then turns to the right and back to "go."

Looking to the right in the course of this progression, one gets a changing view of the meadowlike open space in the middle of the grove. Off center is a single plant of *Lindera angustifolia*. At the lower end of the meadow a violet-painted bench (its color suggested by one hue of the *Lindera leaves*) sits beneath a tall hanging wooden box with neon tubes inside. Their light glows through piercings in two copper sides of the box. This was created by our incredibly talented and lovable friend Simple.[16.14]

The central meadow is where we are trying to establish *Symphyotrichum cordifolium* (syn. *Aster cordifolius*). This native has become a favorite of mine because it likes some shade, tolerates drought and poor soil, is the last of our native asters to bloom in the fall, and produces clusters of small violet flowers. We have a number of seedlings established.

There are, of course, unknowns.

Above: *Lindera angustifolia* in fall fruit

Opposite

Top left: The summer green foliage of *L. angustifolia* turns paper-bag color in the fall and remains on the plant all winter, when seasonal light brings out pink and lavender tones.

Top right: The violet bench and its torreya trunks face a small hidden meadow.

Bottom left: Above the bench hangs a virtual box of neon light (designed and built by the garden artist Simple), which illuminates the intriguing patterns of the pierced copper sides.

Bottom right: *Aster cordifolius*

415

A Low-Maintenance, High-Excitement Plan for the Future

We are committed by necessity to keeping this whole area low-maintenance. Until recently the only upkeep involved:

1. Field mowing and trimming on the regular field-mowing schedule for all of Ashland Hollow
2. Mowing the circuit path around the meadow and through the grove to coincide with every-other-week lawn mowing
3. Once-a-year hand weeding around the asters

Our hardscape additions are 48$\frac{1}{2}$-inch-long bronze stakes, which project 35 inches above soil level (after insertion into the ground) and weather to near-black. A nickel-plated brass ball, 1$\frac{1}{4}$ inches in diameter, tops each stake—just above the field grass at its highest, in June. The balls subtly guide visitors walking the circuit path, as well as the biweekly lawn mowers cutting the path and the tractor operators mowing the field grass just outside it three times a year. The stakes mark only the one side of the path where it meets the meadow.

Defining the carefully studied meadow shape and the path layout through the torreyas is essential to the design. Aesthetically, the light-reflecting nickel-plated brass balls say "garden" in a very low-key way. In the winter, when interest depends on the paper-bag color of the *Lindera angustifolia* with their highlights of lavender, peach, and bronze, the metal balls will, I believe, be an even more important structuring device and add an unobtrusive sparkle to the scene.

A series of bronze stakes topped by nickel-plated brass balls delineates the path that defines the meadow.

Even assuming that the asters will prosper, I feel that this fall "aster meadow" needs a strong year-round focal point, or at least one that will be of interest in a different season.

A final decision about a central feature for the meadow area—in place of the single *Lindera* now performing this function—is still in the making. We are giving serious consideration to three multistem *Cercis chinensis*. The wonderful clusters of clear mauve blossoms that line the stems of this plant occur at the same time, late April, when the *Lindera* here provide their chartreuse blossoms.

The sequence of dropping leaves and opening flowers on the *Lindera* is subtle, but it gives great delight to those who notice it. Leaves drop first at the ends of the branches. Flower clusters open just after each group of leaves falls in sequence, from the tip of the stem into the heart of the plant.

It seems reasonable to assume that the shocking mauve of the *Cercis* blossoms will attract visitors' eyes here—and that the contrast of this mauve with the chartreuse of the *Lindera* will call special attention to the latter's small but intriguing drama of leaf drop and blossom opening.

Top: Blossoms of **Cercis chinensis**

Above: *Lindera angustifolia* in flower

16.1. Founded in 1923, Guyencourt Nursery was the earliest small rare-plants nursery in this area. Its greatest period of activity was 1929-35, when Guy Nearing worked there. Nearing later became well known as a rhododendron breeder. During his time at Guyencourt he invented and patented the Nearing Frame for growing rhododendrons from cuttings. Bill Phelps, the nursery's founder and a passionate plant lover, later converted the property into a small arboretum. Only minor vestiges remain now.

16.2. To this day, I have persisted in trying to find a place at Ashland Hollow where *Corylopsis* will thrive. It is a truly beautiful early spring bloomer. For a long time I thought the east-facing hillside of the Winter Garden might do. *Corylopsis* 'Winterthur', *C. sinensis*, and *C. glabrescens* were all tried without success. At the moment, we have Longwood's new introduction *C.* 'Longwood Chimes' in the garden. This blooms 10 days later than most *Corylopsis*, and the introducers feel it has greater hardiness. I am hopeful because it has now come through two winters unscathed. Its location near the Frog is protected from all winter wind and sits high enough not to act as a frost pocket.

16.3. Barry was able to get us plants from Japan, which were brought in as a favor by Brookside Gardens, a first-rate small public garden in Wheaton, Maryland. Its director at that time was the top-notch plantsman Carl Hahn. He was regularly assembling a collection of new ornamental plants from all over the world.

16.4. We planted four more of these to form a square through which the drive to the farmhouse passes.

16.5. To summarize, our planting, removing, and replanting covered a period of 26 years, from 1972 to 1998:

1972
  Magnolia denudatea (all died except 1; no replacements made)
1975-76, 1980
  Corylopsis glabrescens
1976
  Torreya nucifera (all survived and are doing well)
Year unrecorded
  Betula platyphylla var. *japonica*
1982
  Cornus officinalis 'Kintoki' (replaced all *Corylopsis*)
1983-84
  Winter of -10° F
1986
  Pinus virginiana (planted as protection for *Torreya*)
1986
  Ginkgo biloba (to replace the *Betula*)

16.6. For more about the dragon, see page 373.

16.7. These five cultivars of *Diospyros virginiana* are 'Early Golden', 'John Rick', 'Killen', 'Meader', and 'Morris Burton'.

16.8. There are still enough plants along country roads in this area to produce such showers of this amazing-looking fruit that cars are forced to drive over Osage oranges, spoiling their beauty.

16.9. Adding small numbers of the following six plants in recent years has greatly enhanced winter interest:
  1. *Crataegus viridis* 'Winter King' (3 plants)
     Most years heavily laden with clusters of matte red berries.
  2. *Euonymus sachalinensis* (3)
     More important for foliage than berries. In good years, its foliage is a blazing scarlet.
  3. *E. sachalinensis* (1)
     Orange berries cluster under bright pink caps, and these "arrangements" hang from the branches on long stems. To appreciate the fine detail, and because fruiting occurs when some green leaves still remain in place, this display is best viewed close up. We moved ours close to the path for maximum enjoyment.
  4. *Rhus glabra* (6)
     To the uninitiated, like myself, this plant looks exactly like staghorn sumac (*R. typhina*). In an "old" field west of our driveway on Ashland Clinton School Road we spotted a clump of what I took to be staghorn sumac. The strong-red foliage was especially long-lasting, and the clusters of pyramidal, muted orangey red berries looked attractive as well. Paul decided the plant was *R. glabra*, not *R. typhina*, and he agreed that we should introduce it into this part of the garden where we were building fall interest.
  5. *Corylus colurna* (1)
     While our Turkish filbert (*C. colurna*) has matured, it has maintained its youthful pyramidal shape and at the same time developed this tree's characteristically beautiful trunk. Streams of small bark platelets—in tan shades from near white to dark brown—run mostly in vertical, slightly meandering directions. The play of winter light on their surface produces mesmerizing results.
  6. *Ilex opaca* 'Villanova' (1)
     This single, yellow-fruited American holly, named and given to us by Mary Louisa "Polly" Butcher Hill (1907-2007) an outstanding plantswoman, who created the Polly Hill Arboretum on Martha's Vineyard. Her holly is beginning to yield good crops of excellent yellow berries. The particular hue of yellow—a little in

the cool green direction—travels well visually and makes it more desirable than any other yellow-berried American holly I know.

16.10. The subject greatly interested me, and it plays a part in the appendices of my book *The Exuberant Garden and the Controlling Hand* (Boston: Little Brown & Co., 1992).

16.11. This was a gift from Longwood Gardens, Inc., on the occasion of my retirement from the Board of Trustees after 36 years of service.

16.12. The following information came with the gift: "'Aïda' was grown from seed resulting from a cross between *Camellia japonica* 'Ville de Nantes' and *C. saluenensis* 'Dogrose' performed by Dr. Clifford Parks, then at Descanso Gardens in California, prior to 1968. In the 1960s Longwood Gardens received a large number of hybrids developed by Dr. Parks, which were then included in the Hardy Camellia Trials. 'Aïda' was selected by Dr. Robert Armstrong of Longwood Gardens in 1974 and accessioned that year under Longwood's number 19740268. Being an avid opera lover, Dr. Armstrong named this cultivar after Guiseppe Verdi's opera *Aïda*. Dr. Armstrong published this name in *Acta Horticulturae* 63:101-107 in 1976. According to Dr. Armstrong, 'Aïda' was the only camellia from Longwood trials that survived two extremely severe winters in the mid-1970s. 'Aïda' has glossy, narrow, elliptic leaves. It is very floriferous. Flowers are double, rose form, with 20-25 petals, exposing, when fully open, a few stamens and 1 to 3 small, cupped and curled petals in the center. The petals are soft pink, shaded, and veined darker pink basally."

16.13. See page 197, note 7.3.

16.14. www.simplegardenart.com.

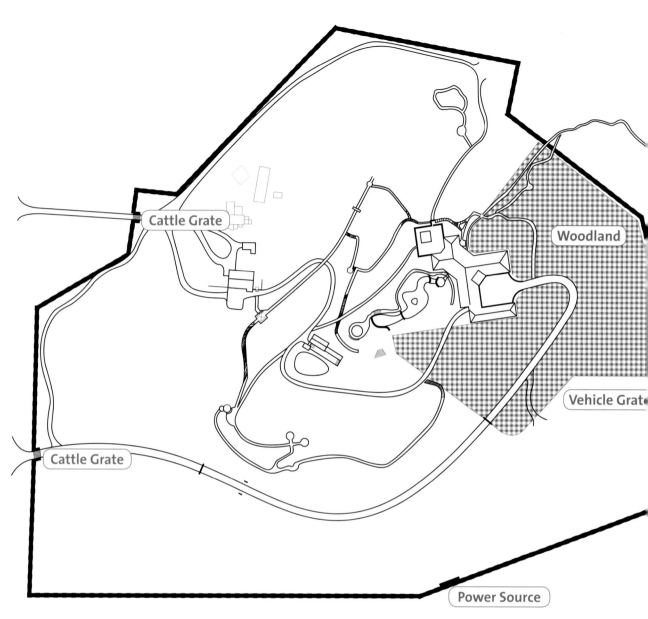

Cattle Grate

Woodland

Cattle Grate

Vehicle Grate

Power Source

The darkest line indicates the 10-foot-
high electrified deer fence enclosing
the 17-acre garden.

17 Deer Fence and Priapus Path

Deer Fence

By 1995 the ubiquitous problem of an exploding population of white-tailed deer had become so difficult for us that we could no longer overlook it. The combination of our 17-acre garden and the 400 acres of farmland in the adjoining preserve had turned into a magnet for the local herd, which multiplied annually. As surrounding land was developed into suburbia, the deer found their haven in this open space. Damage to the garden started innocently enough with antler rubbing on conifers at the periphery of Ashland Hollow each fall. The deer got bolder, however, as the pressure of numbers increased, and they browsed farther and farther into the interior of the garden. One morning in 1985, I looked out of our dressing-room doors into the Studio Garden and saw a buck feasting on our tulips.

We had no choice. For several years we had had a team of dedicated hunters, on our land as well as in the preserve, regularly taking significant numbers of deer off both properties. In 1984, I remember, they removed 35 deer, and yet at the end of hunting season, the hunters said, the herd was no smaller than it had been at the beginning.

After reading everything we could on the subject of deer fences, Paul and I picked three options to see in place on the following properties:

- Bowman's Hill Wildflower Preserve—east of New Hope, Pennsylvania, on the south side of the Delaware River
- The Leonard J. Buck Garden—near Morristown, New Jersey; a formerly private garden now open to the public
- Stonecrop Garden—near Cold Spring, New York; formerly a private garden, now a school for professional gardeners

Our research resulted in the following specifications:[17.1]

1. We would enclose 17 acres, comprising everything we considered "garden."

2. The fence would be 10 feet high with high-tensile wire stretched at 12-inch intervals between poles approximately 60 feet apart.

3. The bottom wire and alternating wires above it would be electrified. Because the in-between wires would ground wires, a deer contacting both an electrified wire and a ground wire would receive an unpleasant shock; but birds sitting on wires would not be grounded, and would therefore stay unharmed. Power would be run from the house to one point in the system on our western boundary. (Although the fence can currently deliver a maximum of 9,000 volts, it regularly runs at 8,400 volts.)

4. Because two driveways serve two separate dwellings on the property, we would put a cattle grate at the point where each drive intersects the deer fence, and thus eliminate the need for heavy gates.

5. Two pedestrian gates would connect our property to the preserve, allowing us to continue our walks around the preserve to observe wild flora and fauna.

6. There would be a wider tractor gate on the side of the property away from Ashland Clinton School Road, to facilitate maintenance in areas outside the fence, such as routine mowing and fence repairs (in the woods, wind and ice storms occasionally bring down trees and/or branches onto the tensile wires).

"Driven" posts (tapering to the smallest diameter at the bottom) support the deer fence's high-tensile wires, which run roughly 12 inches apart.

The contractor installing the fence used 14-foot yellow-pine posts. These were driven four feet into the ground by a modified "high lift" hydraulic post driver.

Two aspects of this installation look odd but work well:
- The narrower end of the tapered round post goes into the ground, so the wider end is at the top, in accordance with the "driven post" system. These posts go in more easily than conventional ones, and they are much more stable.
- Each post (and, of course, the whole fence) stands at right angles to the ground, no matter how steep the slope, unlike posts inserted into holes dug on a slope. The latter are plumb, not at right angles to the ground.

An electrical engineer and a surveyor helped with the planning and staking out. Clearing in grown-up areas of the farm required assistance from our field-mowing farmer and our arborist. The general contractor and subcontractor for the fence both had experience in cattle fencing. Another local contractor installed the reinforced-concrete cattle grates. This entire operation was complex and expensive, and Paul was a tremendous help in bringing it all about.

The good news is that, in almost 20 years of operation, the fence has given us no serious cause for complaint. Deer are seldom tempted to try to come through it, and this occurs only when the power goes off, letting them slip between two of the lower wires without being zapped. They know when the power is off! A cattleman from the Midwest told me that deer can smell the electricity. The fence is now on our generator, so it stays electrified during power outages.

Still, the fence can short out if field grass touches the bottom wire or a tree limb falls on it. And we occasionally turn it off when repairing the fence or mowing close by. It is at these times that a few attentive deer come in for a visit.

I am always surprised that they do not try to leap over the cattle grates, which are only 15 feet across, a distance well within deer's jumping capacity. Again, a cattleman told us that they dislike jumping from hard surface to hard surface—in this case, the bituminous paving of the driveway.

The post driver installing 14-foot fenceposts.

Relocating the Path to the Meadow

Just below the east balcony of our house, the stream that feeds the ponds to the west emerges from the arched open space under the Big Room. The stream heads determinedly straight down into the meadow and eventually flows into the larger Burrows Run. For quite a way before reaching there, however, the stream defines our woods to its south and a tongue of the lower meadow to its north. Until the advent of the deer fence, a mown path used to go from the bottom of the Studio Steps (the *Helleborus niger* area) across this meadow and on into the larger meadow below. This was our primary route into the preserve.

Next to the stream the tongue of meadow is nearly level, but only for a width of 30 or 40 feet. At that point it rises steeply to the north, soon meeting the shrub plantings of the Torreya Grove Path.

This double-trunked walnut tree frames the view of Burrows Run Meadow from the studio terrace. Our path to the meadow, which used to pass between the walnut and the woods, now lies within the woods.

Viewed from the studio terrace, the narrow tongue of meadow grass leads the eye under the branches of an exceptionally double-trunked and handsome vase-shaped black walnut tree (*Juglans nigra*) and then on to the extremely beautiful lower meadow. This includes the plain of meadow grass, streamside black willows, and enchanting native sycamores (*Platanus occidentalis*). These rise out of the plain in noble clumps. Their trunks, variegated in tones of greenish white, tan, and dark brown, provide our best native winter interest.

The plan for the deer fence brought it at right angles to the centerline of this view, at a point beyond the walnut and just where our woodland ends and the big valley opens up. If the grass path remained, we would need a gate for it through the deer fence, which would mean setting four extra posts—two on each side of the gate—in the middle of the view. Without a

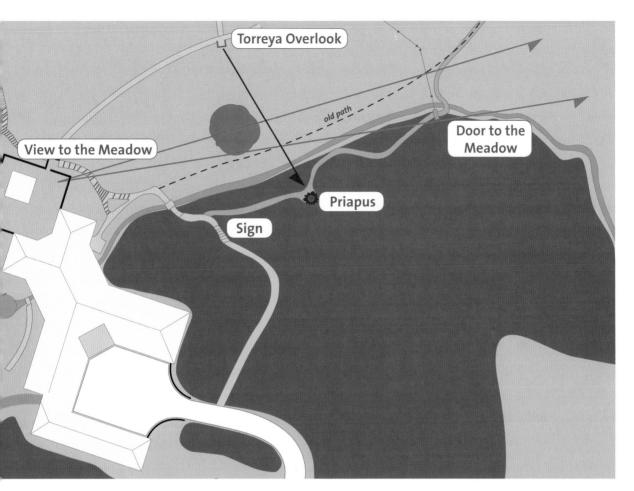

Red lines indicate the view through the deer fence (black line) to the meadow. The path through the woods (gray) features the sculpture of Priapus and an ornamental door into the meadow.

gate, of course, no posts would intrude on the view. In this area the fence wires span a distance of 97 feet, and the posts at both ends are hidden (to the north by shrubs and trees in the Torreya Grove, and to the south by the woods). From the terrace the 10 widely spaced wires are virtually invisible, merging into the meadow grass on either side.

If we moved the path out of the meadow tongue and into the woods on the south side of the stream, the view would remain as it had been for so long.

It was an easy decision to move the path into the woods and leave the view open. The new location was an area I had explored many times, invariably admiring its beauty and enjoying the sound of the stream as it flowed over a tiny waterfall. It presented both a wonderful opportunity and some interesting challenges.

The route to the meadow now crosses the small stone bridge over our stream and, on the left, skirts a pair of woodland giants: a white oak and an American beech (so close together that the distance from one trunk center to the other measures only 5 feet 4 inches). I presume that they thrive so well because their roots are right in the stream and the soil below it. Their branches intertwine in a most sensual embrace! Just beyond them, the meadow path diverges from the path to the front courtyard and makes a left turn, opposite a delightful clump of native ramps (*Allium tricoccum*).

The path curves slightly and descends gradually through the woods, passing an almost level spot where the woods is open to the sky (we removed a huge decrepit sour gum there). Approximately 120 feet past this clearing, the curves in the path tighten as it wends its way downhill between several more closely spaced large trunks before meeting a roofed doorway, reminiscent of a lych-gate, which opens onto the path through the meadow beyond.

Top: Seen from the meadow, looking towards the Priapus Path, the lych-gatelike door features two sinister yellow cutouts of birds just taking off.

Above: There are actually two openings: a pedestrian door within a larger Gravely tractor door.

A Sinister Door

Designed and built for us by Henry Loustau in 1995, the 6-foot-high, 4-foot-wide door is made of vertical boards with pointed tops, like large pickets, spaced about $\frac{1}{2}$ inch apart. The door opens wide enough to let our Gravely tractor drive through for work in the meadow. Set within that door, however, is a smaller one, 54 inches high and 23 inches wide, which people on foot generally use. This added complexity is part of the charm. The ridge of the moss-covered cedar-shake roof runs parallel with the line of the door and the fence on either side of it.

Two round posts flanking the door continue through and above the roof for another 8 inches. A 10-inch-long dowel rising from each post supports a cutout of a bird in flight. The character of these winged silhouettes has a lot to do with the character of the door.

Small holes in the shingled roof gables are the only signs of four built-in birdhouses, two at each end. They are very popular with chickadees. The door is stained brown; the bird cutouts and the roof soffit are butter yellow.

Approaching the door from the meadow and seeing it against the large panorama of our woods, one at first feels welcomed. But as one comes closer, and senses the fear expressed in the flight of the cutout birds, the whole structure takes on an intriguingly sinister quality.

A Greek and Roman God with Authority

Another feature that determines the character of this whole area, and lends its name to the path, is a human-sized statue of the ancient god Priapus. This sculpture was also designed and made for us by Henry Loustau, in 1996.

Four years earlier, my late brother-in-law, who taught classics and archaeology at Berkeley and headed an archaeological dig in Turkey every summer, followed up one of his regular visits here with a letter (dated 10/30/92) of considerable significance to the garden. After some very kind words about Ashland Hollow, he wrote, "What your garden lacks, however, and what no self-respecting Roman garden would be without (I'm doing a 'Pompeii' course again)—is an image of Priapus, god of fertility and garden guardian. (You never know when such protection might be needed!)" I had read a little about Priapus before and understood his importance in matters of fertility. But I had not understood the extent to which he became an important feature of gardens, especially in Roman times. I was charmed by the lighthearted humor that had come to be associated with his principal attribute, an erect and oversized phallus.

My brother-in-law supported his suggestion with excellent scholarly reading material, which made the idea extremely appealing. I also found this in the *Oxford English Dictionary*:

1. The Greek and Roman god of procreation; hence also, of gardens, vineyards, etc. (in which his statues were placed)....
2. A statue or image of the god Priapus; often placed in gardens to protect them from depredators or as a scarecrow.

Priapus in profile with *Rhododendron* 'Azura' beyond the ferns

Henry Loustau's version of Priapus meets, and in some ways exceeds, the specifications my brother-in-law sent me:

> They [Priapus figures] were very simple—just a wooden post, the top carved in the form of the god's head — bearded. (I imagine something like Sir Geoffrey Keynes' 'Job' gatepost (cf. Gates of Memory picture opposite p. 255.) At about groin level on the post, drill a good size (!!) hole, and socket in a huge wooden phallus, and paint it bright RED (actually barn red probably would be most authentic). The phallus should be QUITE LONG!— they were detachable and used as CLUBS to ward off thieves! The images also served as scarecrows!

Henry's sculptural elaboration has the body plain from the buttocks down. However, in addition to a good head of hair, his Priapus has quite distinctive features: eyes, eyebrows, nose, and mouth. The absence of a beard makes him more youthful than Classical prototypes. The conventional lack of arms actually enhances the impression of a thick chest and strong shoulders, because the abrupt cuts where the upper arms should be are quite large. It is as though, while fashioning Priapus out of a rectangular cross-sectioned hunk of timber, the craftsman suddenly came to the end of the wooden block.

In ancient times, a Priapus statue's removable phallus was intended for use as a club to deal with intruders.

The overall figure, which stands 6 feet 4 inches tall, leans forward in a curve (there is a concavity to the entire back of the statue). This gives a feeling of forward movement, a distinct thrusting motion. The torso tapers from the chest to a narrower cross-section at the waist. Although small, the buttocks are sensually rounded and help to make the phallus, by contrast, seem larger. Testicles are attached to the trunk in the appropriate place, just below the phallus.

The phallus, which measures 18 inches long and 1¼ inches in diameter, sports a significant *glans penis* (head). It also has an upward curve to it, which adds to the portrayal of erection. Indeed detachable, it personifies the desired feeling of a club. A "key" cut into the phallus matches a small raised area in the cavity that receives it, so that the phallus can be reinserted only with the curve upward. The god's body, crafted from a block of laminated mahogany, slips into a concrete foundation that keeps it quite stable. The mahogany is stained a rich dark brown with a shiny finish. The phallus is authentically red!

We placed Priapus in the open, nearly level area of the woods. For people walking toward the meadow from the house, the figure stands to the right of the path where he is first seen in profile as one rounds a bend. From the point where the Priapus Path leaves the path to the courtyard, however, he is invisible when the woods are in leaf, even though he is only 100 feet away. To prepare visitors for what is to come, a sign on a post to the right of the path (near its beginning) reads:

> This path leads to the garden gate into the Burrows Run Meadow. En route it passes a contemporary statue of the ancient deity Priapus.
>
> In a broad sense Priapus was the Greek and Roman god of fertility and procreation. This was interpreted to mean that he was specifically the god of gardens and vineyards where his statue was placed. It was thought that the presence of Priapus protected the garden from depredators and he was used as a scarecrow.
>
> These statues, often rudimentary, had one thing in common: a huge, long wooden phallus which was painted red. The phallus was detachable and could be used as a club to ward off thieves. Hence the placement of the statue near the garden gate.

Planting Challenge

The planting along the Priapus Path is predominantly native. Evergreen Christmas ferns (*Polystichum acrostichoides*) ring the figure's base. New York ferns (*Thelypteris novaboracensis*) thrive happily in much of the open space from there out. We have given these some mild structuring with the addition of a few clumps of ostrich fern (*Matteuccia struthiopteris* [syn. *M. pensylvanica*]). Spicebush (*Lindera benzoin*) and *Viburnum acerifolium* predominate in the shrub layer.

In an effort to add a little seasonal color, we are attempting to grow additional shrubs that produce red and dark purple flowers or berries, to harmonize with Priapus's rich dark brown. Because of the deep shade on the north side of the woods and the heavy clay soil, our success has been limited.

Shrubs

Hamamelis vernalis 'Red Imp'
    A limited number of rusty red blossoms
Ilex verticillata 'Scarlett O'Hara' and 'Rhett Butler'
    An abundance of small, shiny red berries, visible from great distances because the red contains a small amount of orange
Ilex 'Sparkleberry'
    Small, shiny red berries
Rhododendron prunifolium
    A limited number of red flowers in early summer
R. 'Zorro'
    A few deep purple trusses even in deep shade

For pre-woods-foliage time (i.e., early spring), we are having success with woodland primroses such as:
Primula elatior
P. vulgaris
P. abchasia

For midsummer, we have hoped to add some coarser herbaceous foliage texture, to contrast with the large sweeps of fine fern foliage. So far this has met with very limited success:

Astilboides tabularis—has died.

Diphylleia cymosa—a small percentage have survived.

Rodgersia pinnata—a small percentage have survived.

Iris pseudacorus (large-flowered form)—the foliage has done well, but the plant has yet to bloom.

Carex pendula—is an unqualified success!

Sasa veitchii—(across the stream where it gets more light) is a great success, especially in its winter variegation.

No doubt, as elsewhere in the making of the garden, the plants themselves will tell us what we should feature, and what we should delete, to give Priapus a happy setting.

There is a splendid view of Priapus and his woodland setting from the stone overlook on the Torreya Grove Path on the hillside above. Especially when the woods is clothed with leaves, one's initial glimpse of Priapus is startling.

Some first-time visitors to the garden come because they have heard about the house built across a stream. Others come because they have seen photographs of the Statue Steps; yet others, because they have heard about the Frog; and a few, because they have heard about Priapus. One might conclude by saying that there is something here for everyone—even someone who is not interested in gardens!

Sasa veitchii in early winter. The leaves of this two-to-three-foot-high bamboo gradually change from green to nearly all white, due to spreading desiccation during our winters (see page 405).

17.1. Some people thought we were overdoing it, as far as fence height and electrification were concerned. But we wanted to take a surefire course from the outset. We did not want to have to go back later for a heavy-duty upgrade.

The sculptor Henry Loustau's rendition of the god Priapus

437

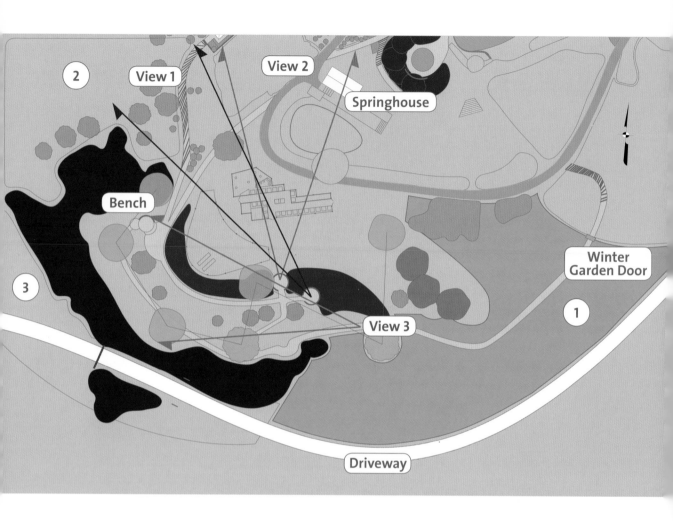

The main area of the Winter Garden (3) is a remnant of the original farm meadow; one crosses an undisturbed part of the original meadow (1) to enter the Winter Garden proper. Upon leaving that garden, one is in the Hillside Meadow (2; see Chapter 8).

18 Winter Garden

Tri-meadow Theme

The long hillside on which we located the Winter Garden curves just downhill from the driveway before entering the woods, and it has a multidirectional orientation. Its southernmost part faces north, the middle (the site of the Winter Garden) faces east, and the northernmost part faces south. The bottom of the hillside is demarcated by the service road, which follows roughly the same contour as the driveway at the top. Encompassing a very large area, this hillside forms the upper limit of the main stream valley. The hillside's northern and western parts both enclose and serve as an intimate backdrop to the hidden valley containing the Vegetable Garden and the swimming pool.[18.1]

Originally, the hillside was all meadow/hayfield, defined at either end by well-established woodland. We have divided it into three parts, and "meadow" remains the theme. All three parts are strongly related in terms of winter interest, but the central portion is the concentrated Winter Garden. Its east-facing orientation is ideal for most winter blossoms.

We have left the southernmost part of the hillside in its hayfield mode, to preserve the view from below to the orchard on the hilltop beyond. Although the northernmost part is still meadow, as described in Chapter 8, it has taken on a rather sophisticated discipline. Early on, when thoughts of a central Winter Garden began, we decided that its main feature should continue to be a meadow capable of exciting visitors with winter color, in both the field grass and the surround.

The real impetus for the Winter Garden idea came about as the demands of the nursery/landscape business left me less and less time to enjoy my own garden. It gradually dawned on me that winter was when my clients were quiescent and I had the most time to savor my own creation. Soon I started walking the area with a garden in mind, and a plan and a plant list taking shape. This realization about my seasonal schedule also helped us achieve our early objective of having interest in the garden every month of the year.

Hollies and Birches

By the time we developed a planting plan and started planting accordingly, we had already done two major plantings in this area. In 1971 and 1976 we had put 67 American hollies (*Ilex opaca*) close to the driveway and spreading out to the north and east where the planting met the Hillside Meadow. Our practical purpose had been to block views of cars from the garden and provide privacy for the swimming pool. But this also gave me a chance to experiment with 14 different cultivars of American holly selected for garden use from native stands on the coastal plain of the mid-Atlantic states (see Appendix 12).

In addition, seven river birch (*Betula nigra*), grown from seed in our nursery, had been planted on the garden side of the hollies to enhance the winter view from the house. While foliage is on the trees it encloses the vista from the house, focusing attention on the Stream Valley Garden; but after the leaves fall, our sight line extends through the naked tree branches until it lands directly against this hillside. The predominantly light shades of tan, pink, violet, and rust in the bark on these multi-stem birch clumps show up beautifully against the background of shiny, waxy green American holly leaves.

Without a doubt, this aesthetically pleasing planting strongly influenced our selection of this site for the Winter Garden. Besides acting as all-season visual screens, the hollies effectively break the sweep of winter's blasting northwest wind. And the zigzag formation of birches supplied a ready-to-begin planting structure for a winter garden.

Below: American holly (*Ilex opaca*)

Bottom: River birch (*Betula nigra*)

Contoured Spine and a Stone Bench

Our first task was organizing pedestrian access to this area, which is roughly halfway between the level of the swimming pool and that of the Green and White Path. Because I did not want visitors to miss the experience of passing through all three sections of the hillside—with a surprise in the center—I settled on one long (650-foot) path, roughly on contour, that starts at the southernmost end and stops at an important stone bench located at a sensual crease in the landform close to the beginning of the Hillside Meadow.

One enters through a colorful, freestanding ornamental wooden door labeled "Winter," which Henry Loustau designed and built. This is approached from the Game Lawn and service road below by means of 30 timber steps through the woods.

To leave the garden at its stone-bench end, one can choose either the down ramp or the up ramp of the Hillside Meadow. (During the winter months we now close-mow that meadow, giving its landforms a special beauty.) Both ramps lead into other parts of the garden. [18.2]

Above: Steps lead uphill through woods to the "door into winter." Across its threshold, one steps down onto a close-mown path through the original meadow and into the Winter Garden.

Below: The upper path's main objective is guiding visitors to the far end of the Winter Garden Meadow and the stone bench and terraces. From there one gets an excellent view back across sweeps of diminutive bulbs and very early-blooming witch hazels.

Planting Design: Native vs. Alien

The planting design is quite casual. I believe I was unconsciously influenced by the "old field" meadow I had seen south of here a few years earlier. Although that mental picture was still clearly a view of meadow grasses, some dogwoods, hawthorns, and viburnums had wandered in. Within our own meadow, a few of the surrounding witch hazels, several yellow-twig dogwoods, and a catkin willow—all represented in greater numbers near the outer edge—interrupt the open space.

The plant palette here takes inspiration from the most ornamental of what one sees in our native fields and woods. There is also a robust injection of alien beauties that feed our souls during the most trying days of mid-Atlantic winters.

Among the significant natives are:
Cornus sericea 'Flaviramea'

Ilex verticillata 'Scarlett O'Hara'
(seven other cultivars; see Appendix 13)

In the category of welcome aliens we have, or have had until very recently:

Abeliophyllum distichum

Acer griseum

Arum italicum 'Marmoratum'

Buxus 'Green Gem'
Cephalotaxus harringtonia 'Prostrata'
Cytisus scoparius cultivars
Helleborus foetidus

Fagus sylvatica 'Laciniata'

Lonicera fragrantissima

Jasminum nudiflorum

Pachysandra terminalis 'Green Sheen'
Parrotia persica
Poncirus trifoliata 'Flying Dragon'

Kerria japonica

Rhododendron mucronulatum 'Cornell Pink'
Taxus baccata 'Repandens'
Yucca flaccida 'Golden Sword'

Three additional groups of plants, discussed in detail below, deserve special attention:

Catkin willows

Asiatic witch hazels

Winter-flowering bulbs

Their predominant flower colors fall within the yellow and white range, which works well with the many dark greens and the subtleties of bark in shades of gray, silver, pale green, dark green, pink, violet, and tan. Early in the season, berries provide red accents. Later in the season, blue, violet, and mauve appear, and at the very end, there is a strong accent of pink. Developing this palette, which now sustains us so exuberantly, has been a great adventure.

The search for winter-flowering shrubs and trees took Nancy and me across the Atlantic Ocean on two occasions. In 1973 our travel led to a private arboretum in Belgium; in 1982, to a fortnightly show of the Royal Horticultural Society in London and to Kew Gardens, just beyond.

Bringing Together the Catkin Willows

At an earlier date I had had the good fortune to meet (and subsequently came to admire and love) Ben Blackburn, life tenant and director of the Willowwood Arboretum in northern New Jersey. His enrichment of a prior generation's great planting had been the addition of an important collection of willows. My first of many visits there had occurred during the winter of 1977. I was impressed by the extraordinary variety of twig color in the willow collection, but even more by those willows that bore significant winter catkins.

Salix acutifolia 'Longifolia'

Thanks to another outstanding plantsman and talented propagator, Tom Buchter, *Salix acutifolia* 'Longifolia' eventually reached our garden from Willowwood. It is the earliest willow to show its catkins for us, reliably appearing just before Christmas. The short, fat, nearly white catkins are held on fine twigs above one's head. Even the slightest breeze causes them to move, and when they do, they sparkle in even the smallest amount of winter sunlight.

A Fortnightly Show and "Down to Kew"

Our trip to London in 1982 helped me to realize the full potential of catkin willows. At the RHS fortnightly show in February, it was a revelation to see so many wonderful plants from British gardens in bloom. Most, however, were things we knew could not stand our low winter temperatures.

While entering the Royal Horticultural hall, we were lucky enough to meet Roy Lancaster, an ardent plant explorer and a superb plantsman, and have him take us in hand. He led us quickly to a display of willows in catkin that had been entered by a delightful lady exhibitor (whose name I cannot remember). The important thing for us was that here were things we probably *could* grow in Delaware.

I remember especially *Salix* x *rubra* 'Eugenei'. This has the longest, narrowest catkins of any willow we have grown. The plants themselves are multistem and tall and narrow with slender branches clustered closely together in a manner reminiscent of bamboo. The long, narrow, silvery catkins, which hug the stems, are especially well displayed when a breeze moving the stems causes a great shimmering to take place.

It was here, I believe, that we met another great British plantsman (who has also become a wonderful friend), John

Simmons. It must have been the very next day that we went down to Kew Gardens where John was then the director of horticulture. He showed us a fascinating, beautifully cared for, and lively botanic garden. The plant we admired the most at that moment was *Salix aegyptiaca*. This grows to be a medium-size tree with large catkins, which open flowers that give off an intoxicating fragrance of gardenia. The plant eventually found its way to Ashland Hollow.

We have grown all of the catkin willows on the following list at one time or another. The dates in parentheses record when we planted them in the Winter Garden.[18.3] Asterisks indicate those that now survive.

Salix acutifolia 'Longifolia' (1983)

S. aegyptiaca (1992)

S. bockii (1999)

S. chaenomeloides (1986)

S. daphnoides (1986)

S. daphnoides 'Aglaia' (1982-85)

Salix gracilistyla (1981)

S. gracilistyla 'Melanostachys' (1981)

S. humilis var. *tristis* (syn. var. *microphylla*) (1981)
S. repens var. *arenaria* (syn. var. *argentea*) (1961, 1987)
S. x *rubra* 'Eugenei' (1986)

As for the high mortality rate, we knew from the beginning that willows were short-lived. I do feel, however, that poor siting (lack of moisture and increasing shade at Ashland Hollow) have contributed to this sad record.

Catkin willows are such an asset to any winter garden that I hope to try several of these again, especially in a newly available sunny area and another, moister spot. I will make a special effort to regrow my favorite, *S. acutifolia* 'Longifolia'.

Asiatic Witch Hazels

Our experience with Asiatic witch hazels is unique in the history of this garden. In the case of most other plantings here, the palette has been dominated by plants currently, or previously, in commerce in the United States. The Asiatic witch hazels are a different matter.

I first saw members of this genus during my undergraduate years at Swarthmore (1944-48). A group of Korean soldiers took part in an R.O.T.C. unit then, and as I recall, their presence was commemorated by the construction of a handsome set of steps leading down from the plaza in front of Wharton Hall (a dormitory I lived in during the latter part of my time at the college) to the tennis courts.

On either side of these steps was a pair of *Hamamelis mollis* (Chinese witch hazel), heavily covered each winter with twisty-petaled, medium yellow blossoms. Also, a screen planting around the old kitchen wing of Parrish Hall contained several plants of *H. japonica* (Japanese witch hazel) and, I believe, its cultivar 'Flavopurpurascens'. The *H. japonica* were not nearly as pleasing, mostly because they held onto their leaves during the winter, impeding one's view of the butter yellow flowers.

Twenty-two years later, I found *H.* x *intermedia* 'Pallida'[18.4] commercially and espaliered it around the corner of the studio nearest our house. It produces warm yellow flowers abundantly through January and February.

Two years after 'Pallida' arrived, Bill Flemer, the president of Princeton Nurseries and a very knowledgeable and discriminating plantsman, gave me a plant of *H.* x *intermedia* 'Feuerzauber' (syn. 'Fire Charm' or 'Magic Fire').[18.5] It was the first witch hazel

The first winter-flowering witch hazel in our garden was *Hamamelis* x *intermedia* 'Pallida', which we trained around a corner of the studio.

planted in the Winter Garden, and I still consider it one of our best. The flowers are smaller than those on most other cultivars here, but lots of them reliably cover the branches every year. *Hamamelis* x *intermedia* 'Feuerzauber', a beautiful copper red and fragrant, is often the first witch hazel to open here.

Drama at Kalmthout

It must have been around this time that we heard or read about a family in Belgium named De Belder that had been breeding witch hazels and still grew several different color forms unlike any seen before.

Mrs. De Belder and her two grown sons, the story went, lived in a house on part of an old nursery. One son, Robert, the head of the diamond business founded by his late father, had married a horticulture student from Yugoslavia (as it still was then) named Jelena Kovacic. The charming account of their courtship that I was told is worth repeating.

When Jelena graduated with distinction in Slovenia, her school awarded the aspiring horticulturist a trip through Europe and England to visit gardens and nurseries, and also work in the latter. High on Jelena's own list of places to see was Kalmthout, the De Belder's well-known arboretum.

It seems that when she finally reached Belgium, found the right house, and rang the bell, a man in shirtsleeves opened the door. Jelena explained that she had come to see the garden and asked if Mr. Robert De Belder was at home. "No," the man said, "Mr. De Belder is not at home, but I will be glad to take you around the garden." This he did. When she was about to leave, the young traveler thanked him and asked if she might stop by again on the way back from England, in hopes of meeting Mr. De Belder. Her guide said yes, and she continued her trip.

Following her tour of English gardens, she indeed returned to Kalmthout. But this time Mrs. De Belder answered the doorbell. Once again, Jelena asked if Robert De Belder was available; she so hoped to meet him before departing for Yugoslavia. Mrs. De Belder replied that her son, unfortunately, was not at home, but the young lady was mistaken: the man who had shown her around the family garden was in fact Robert himself. Jelena went on her way, expecting never to see anything of the De Belders again.

Robert, though, had been smitten with this wonderfully enthusiastic lady who shared his interest in gardening. He pursued Jelena to Yugoslavia, proposed marriage, was accepted, and in exchange for paying the Tito regime the cost of her education, received permission to bring the bride-to-be back to Belgium. Diane Adriaenssen's recent book[18.6] about the couple reveals the apocryphal nature of this tale and tells the true story, which is only slightly less charming.

There are many other wonderful stories about the De Belders, because of their hospitality to the international horticultural world, the development of their celebrated arboretum, and their custom of taking on international student interns.

Another February Trip: Robert and Jelena De Belder, Passion, and a Great Eye for Plants

In 1973 it seemed essential to Nancy and me that we go to see the witch hazels we had heard so much about. I wrote to the De Belders and received a cordial reply from Jelena suggesting that we come for lunch on February 19, at the peak of the witch-hazel bloom season. Our garden-visiting friends Jerry and Shirley Eaton went with us. After spending the night in Antwerp, we arrived at the De Belders' and pressed the doorbell (now famous, in our minds, because of the courtship saga). The maid who came to the door spoke only French. But when Nancy, who speaks some French, explained about our appointment, the maid became agitated. She was obviously distressed because *Madame* had gone with the farmer to kill pigs and would not be back before lunchtime... "There is no way of reaching her." We said we would go around the garden on our own and be glad to see *Madame* at midday. Obviously, she had forgotten our appointment.

The timing for the visit, however, was perfect. The witch hazels were in full bloom. Many of the plants were enormous, 15 feet or more in spread. The temperature hovered around 35-40°F, and due to a low cloud ceiling with steady drizzle, the light was dramatic and the sparkle of moisture on the blossoms, unforgettable.

Jelena did appear at noon, terribly embarrassed about forgetting our rendezvous and looking a bit like someone who had been "killing pigs." We were cold and damp. She was warm and wonderful, swept us off to a nearby restaurant for lunch, and answered all of our questions with the same enthusiasm that had won Robert's heart. She then took us to Hemelrijk, their new property near the Dutch border, where they were planning to establish an arboretum and convert an attractive barn into a major horticultural library.

When Jelena learned the time of our flight back to London, she said, "Robert will be on that flight also! You must look for him at the airport and introduce yourselves." She described her husband and added, "There will be another man with him." This was the last time we saw Jelena. We corresponded with her for a while afterward, but the language difference made this difficult. She hoped to come for a visit here, but that never occurred.

We did find Robert at the airport and had a lively discussion with him about the witch hazels. He explained that some of those we had seen were seedlings saved by Antoine Kort, the nurseryman who had previously owned the De Belder property—seedlings still there when Robert and his brother bought the place.[18.7]

They had consciously duplicated what Robert hypothesized had occurred in Kort's time: the mating of *Hamamelis mollis*

Opposite

Top left: *Hamamelis* x *intermedia* 'Jelena' (front) and *H.* x *intermedia* 'Luna' (rear)

Top right: Blossoms of *H.* x *intermedia* 'Jelena'

Bottom left: *H.* x *intermedia* 'Fire Charm'

Bottom right: *H.* x *intermedia* 'Luna' (far left); *H.* x *intermedia* 'Pallida' (center left); *H.* x *intermedia* 'Primavera' (right)

455

and *H. japonica* 'Flavo-purpurascens'. The resulting seedlings exhibited the same marvelous color range, including orange. The pieces of the puzzle now fell into place.

Curiously, the man standing with Robert did not participate in the discussion, and when it came time to board the plane, he vanished. But as soon as we stepped off the plane in London, a different man appeared and took his place. It was then that we noticed the narrow black briefcase Robert carried, and a bell rang: diamonds! Robert offered us a ride to our hotel, which we accepted, and that was the last we ever saw of him.

Nancy and I followed reports of the development of Hemelrijk (with design work by Russell Page), Robert's election as a vice president of the RHS, the De Belders' financial reverses in the diamond trade, the sale of a major part of the great library Robert had assembled, his death in 1995, and later the sad news that Jelena had drowned while swimming in the surf on a vacation in Croatia. The book about her and Robert gives a full portrait of a very generous couple.

But back to 1973... Inspired by our stimulating visit to Belgium, we returned home and waited impatiently for De Belder cultivars to become commercially available in the United States. Here is the order in which Ashland Hollow's witch hazels eventually arrived:

1976	*Hamamelis* x *intermedia* 'Jelena'
1977	*H.* x *intermedia* 'Arnold Promise'
	(This was introduced in 1963 by the Arnold Arboretum. It is a selection from the typical plants of *H.* x *intermedia* raised there.)
	H. x *intermedia* 'Luna'
1979	*H.* x *intermedia* 'Diane'
1982-83	*H.* x *intermedia* 'Primavera'

Opposite

Top left: *Hamamelis* x *intermedia* 'Luna'

Top right: *H.* x *intermedia* 'Pallida'

Bottom: *Cyclamen coum*, which grows under, and flowers with, our *H.* x *intermedia* 'Pallida'

These were all of such high quality that we added more of each cultivar up through 1993 (see Appendix 15).

Since then, more De Belder witch hazels have come onto the market, as have other cultivars from New Zealand and Japan. In casual observations, however, I have not found any that surpass the palette listed above.

We arranged the early plantings in such a way that the dark-flowered witch hazels, such as *Hamamelis* x *intermedia* 'Diane' and *H.* x *intermedia* 'Jelena', would be seen against the lighter yellows when viewed from the stone bench. From season to season, this has worked well. Our subsequent additions have been mostly the yellow shades.

Frankly, I feel that these "intermedia" witch hazels are one of the two greatest contributions to gardens in the mid-Atlantic United States during my lifetime.[18.8] We owe a great debt to the De Belders for their passion, high standards, perseverance, and generosity.

The Burning Bush

I have had one incredible mystical (if you like) experience with winter light on the copper red blossoms of *H.* x *intermedia* 'Diane'. Late one afternoon, I stood on the stone terrace watching a spectacular display to the south. As the sun moved westward and sank close to the horizon, a narrow ray of intense light came between two of the American hollies (to the west), landing directly on our large original plant of 'Diane', which it hit at a roughly 90° angle to my line of sight. At first the colors of the flowers were simply enhanced. But suddenly the framework and details of the plant's structure and flowers vanished, and what remained was a ball of fire! I could not remove my eyes from it.

Above: *Hamamelis* x *intermedia* 'Diane'

Opposite: My "burning bush," *H.* x *intermedia* 'Diane' (upper right), behind a yellow carpet of winter aconite (*Eranthis hyemalis*)

It seemed as if we were fused together and that the fire blazed as long as five minutes. Although I doubt it really lasted that long, it was long enough for the rest of my world to disappear; I was totally consumed by the burning bush. What a tribute to the surreal quality of light and flowers!

Diminutive Bulbs

The meadow that forms the centerpiece of the Winter Garden is mowed only three times a year. Its longer grass and casual country appearance are the backdrop for the various shorter seasons of willow catkins and the very long season of witch-hazel bloom. It is also home to several thousand diminutive early-blooming bulbs and an increasing number of plants of our earliest blooming perennial, *Adonis amurensis* 'Fukujukai'.

These little beauties occur in the sequence laid out below, although one must bear in mind that part of this drama—and of its players' charm—is that they overlap with one another. They may overlap more during a short, compressed spring, and less when the season is lazy and slow-moving, because each bulb has a longer bloom period. Then again, in some years part of the spring may be compressed and part not, causing a different drama. This is all part of the excitement of spring!

Taking such unpredictable entrances and exits into account, here is the sequence of bloom in the Winter Garden meadow:

Eranthis hyemalis (winter aconite)

Adonis amurensis 'Fukujukai'
   A bulb companion and our earliest perennial (a member of the Buttercup family)

Galanthus elwesii (snowdrop)
   Exception: a few late autumn bloomers known as spring ephemerals

Crocus tommasinianus 'Whitewell Purple'
   Selected seedling from a Yugoslavian native

Galanthus nivalis 'Flore Pleno'
   A double snowdrop

Below: *Eranthis hyemalis* (winter aconite)

Bottom: A mouse's-eye view of the *E. hyemalis* planting

Scilla siberica

Eranthis x tubergenii 'Guinea Gold'
   A later-blooming hybrid winter aconite

Chionodoxa luciliae 'Alba'
   White form of glory of the snow

Narcissus 'Henry Irving'

N. obvallaris (Tenby daffodil)

Adonis amurensis 'Fukujukai' enjoys a very long season of bloom. This gives it an interesting relationship with *Eranthis hyemalis* (winter aconite), which flowers at the same general time but has a shorter bloom period.

Because of their extremely early bloom, both plants should be grown more than they are. Unfortunately, winter aconite has been available only as dry bulbs in the fall. Even though instructions say to "soak them in warm water overnight" before planting, this seldom succeeds at getting the bulbs started, and so frustrated purchasers stop trying. But if these bulbs were sold in soil in the spring, while they are growing, the buyer would have total success. When I had had one of the usual bad experiences, Gertrude Wister gave me a shovelful of these bulbs after they had bloomed but while they were still in foliage. I planted the fat, firm bulbs right away. They flowered beautifully the following spring and immediately began to seed themselves around the meadow. We now have several thousand!

A. amurensis is not well known because, having sterile blossoms, it does not set seed. One can, however, propagate this perennial by division after it dies down.

Below: A view across the meadow at winter-aconite (*Eranthis hyemalis*) time

Bottom: The *Eranthis* continue flowering as snowdrops (*Galanthus elwesii*; white in foreground) and *Adonis amurensis* 'Fukujukai' (background) begin their show.

Before we imported our *Adonis* from Japan, I knew the plant only from one garden, Winterthur, where it forms part of the famous planting called the March Bank. As far as I know, those plants have never been propagated by seed, but they have thrived and the clumps are now enormous in size. In Japan, *Adonis* grow exceedingly well. They are very popular and there are quite a few selected cultivars. Frequently used for pot culture, they often appear in the collections of choice potted plants that the Japanese display on small racks on the sidewalks in front of their homes.

It is from Japan that our long-time friend the sharp-eyed international plantsman Barry Yinger—with the help of another great plantsman and most generous friend, Roy Klehm—imported for us an order of *A. amurensis* 'Fukujukai' [18.9] in the fall of 1989. These have thrived and, thanks to several "dividings," their number has increased at least threefold.

Because *Adonis* belongs to the Buttercup family (*Ranunculaceae*), it makes its spring debut as a round green ball visible just at soil level. This is what we watch for carefully as our first major sign of the season. With any warmth at all, the green ball will start to crack open, showing a glint of butter yellow. This becomes a semidouble yellow blossom, still right at soil level, with petals that sparkle in the early spring sunlight. I always feel as though we have been presented with a great gift.

A fascinating progression follows the initial opening, as the stem pushes upward and the flower rises from the ground. Eventually 15 to 18 inches tall, the stem is covered with a most unusual and attractive fernlike foliage. Out of this more blossoms appear, often slightly smaller than the initial flowers but quite showy in other ways. This developmental process takes a long time, often 20 to 30 days.

Top: *Galanthus elwesii* (snowdrops)

Above: *Crocus tommasinianus* 'Whitewell Purple'

Although the winter aconites usually start blooming first, they tend to stop long before the *Adonis* have completed their display. When paired, they make an unbeatable combination! The aconite is a greener yellow than the *Adonis*. For at least the latter part of their dance together, the *Adonis* is taller and forms a clump with the aconite, a seeder, densely scattered around it.

This pas de deux can begin as early as the first two weeks of January or as late as mid-March, depending on the year. The big show of *Galanthus elwesii* (snowdrop), teardrop-shaped white bells, comes very soon thereafter. The whole performance commences with the *Adonis*-aconite duo and lasts just about as long as the aconites.

As I noted earlier, *Crocus tommasinianus* with its violet blossoms, silver on the outside, has been a stalwart friend in the Beech Grove. We selected a cultivar, 'Whitewell Purple', for the Winter Garden. It is now well established and spreading, though more slowly than the species in the grove, owing to the heavy turf here. We chose this cultivar because its violet color is deeper and similar to that of some cyclamens. The fact that this cultivar varies slightly in the depth of its tones makes it especially attractive next to the oranges and reds in some of the witch hazels; the violet hue is also minimally present in the river-birch bark. We can usually count on these bulbs to start their season in sync with the appearance of ferny foliage on the *Adonis*.

Two important bulbs—the double snowdrop (*Galanthus nivalis* 'Flore Pleno') and the hybrid form of aconite, *Eranthis* x *tubergenii* 'Guinea Gold'[18.10]—are sterile, like the *Adonis*. They do not set seed, but their clumps expand nicely each year. Both start to bloom almost simultaneously, about ten days after *Eranthis hyemalis* stops flowering in late March.

Top: *Eranthis* x *tubergenii* 'Guinea Gold'

Above: *Galanthus nivalis* 'Flore Pleno'

The bloom on the double snowdrop lasts longer than that on its close relative *Galanthus elwesii*, probably because it is both double and sterile. By the same token, the bloom on *Eranthis* x *tubergenii* 'Guinea Gold' outlasts that on *E. hyemalis*, probably because of its sterility. We have small quantities of both bulbs. If we had the time to divide the clumps, we could undoubtedly have more. Instead, we treat them as treasures.

I have never been particularly fond of double flowers. Thanks to the double snowdrop's diminutive size and considerable distance from the eye of a standing viewer, it does not look noticeably double, only extra fresh and a richer-than-usual white. The 'Guinea Gold' aconite's flower is much fuller of petals (though not fully double) than that of *Eranthis hyemalis*, probably a little broader, and its vibrant yellow glistens, rather like the earliest *Adonis* blossoms.

Not until early April does the final meadow display start. By then the magical starlike white blossoms of *Chionodoxa luciliae* 'Alba' are ubiquitous, and the meadow grass in which they grow has turned bright spring green.[18.11]

While the meadow features these bulbs, it is essentially surrounded by the blue of *Scilla siberica*, in patches and drifts that express its preference for some spots over others. At the same moment, four shrubs perform in harmony with these late bulbs; together, they put on a splendid show, creating a grand finale to the Winter Garden's season.

The latest-blooming catkin willow (*Salix gracilistyla*) stands near the middle of the meadow. As it matures it produces its long, handsome, slightly curling gray catkins. Just above the

Opposite
Top left: *Chionodoxa luciliae* 'Alba' blooms just as the grass turns bright green at winter's end.

Top right: A close-up of *C. luciliae* 'Alba'

Bottom: *Rhododendron mucronulatum* 'Cornell Pink'

465

meadow, the long irregular drift of yellow-twig dogwood (*Cornus sericea* 'Flaviramea') is now at its brightest.[18.12] Three plants of the leafless, open-branched, clear pink Korean rhododendron (*Rhododendron mucronulatum* 'Cornell Pink') flower high at the south end of the meadow, still within the blue *Scilla* surround. Coming from the south into the garden and looking through these beauties, one sees yet another shrub, *Abeliophyllum distichum*, with its charming fragrant white flowers (opening from pale pink buds distributed along very light tan stems) and the meadow of sparkling white *Chionodoxa luciliae* 'Alba'. Now the Winter Garden comes to rest, as the flowering cherries call us out into the other areas of the Ashland Hollow garden for the visual riches of the season to come.

Ophelia Selection

From this grand, long-season display, an intimate picture of equal duration has been created in the area of the stone bench. Essentially, a few of each of most of the bulbs described above have been brought together with small amounts of other charmers that might be lost in the meadow grass. Behind the bench in the bottom third of the bank planting and in pockets left in the stone paving in front of the bench we find what we have chosen to call the Ophelia Selection:

> *Anemone blanda*
> *Crocus ancyrensis* 'Golden Bunch'
> *C. sieberi* 'Firefly'
> *C. tommasinianus* 'Whitewell Purple'
> *Eranthis* x *tubergenii* 'Guinea Gold'
> *Galanthus nivalis* 'Flore Pleno'
> *Iris* 'George'

I. 'Cantab'

I. 'Harmony'

I. histrioides 'Major'

Narcissus 'Henry Irving'

N. 'Hunter's Moon'

N. 'Small Talk'

N. obvallaris—the early Tenby daffodil

Scilla siberica (Winterthur Selection)—
    deeper blue than the type

This rich mix of tiny flowers in small quantities has always reminded us of Sir John Everett Millais' amazing painting of the dead Ophelia floating on her back in a stream whose surface is strewn with just such a mix of diminutive blossoms. And then we laugh, because we have been told that Millais had his model float in a bathtub of warm water while he painted her, a comforting thought in a winter garden.

Overleaf
Left page
Ophelia Selection—behind the stone bench
Top left: Anemone blanda
Top right: Iris 'Cantab'
Bottom left: I. 'Harmony'
Bottom right: Narcissus 'Small Talk'

Right page:
Ophelia Selection—in pockets of the stone terrace
Top left: Crocus ancyrensis 'Golden Bunch'
Top right: Iris histroides 'Major'
Bottom: Scilla siberica (Winterthur Selection)

18.1. Because we had originally thought of this hillside as a summer-blooming backdrop for the swimming pool, we planted it at first with an extensive grove of golden rain trees (*Koelreuteria paniculata*). Our expectation was that late June and early July would feature a great froth of yellow pyramids against dark green compound leaves! Alas, the trees sulked, complained, filled up with deadwood, and never prospered. They yearned for gravelly soil such as one finds along I-95 highway banks near Baltimore where they have seeded in without the help of human hands. Ours said, "No, thank you," to our heavy clay loam. Finally, we had to give up.

18.2. Initially, foot traffic flowed in the opposite direction. It soon became apparent, however, that walking from north to south put visitors in the awkward position of looking at winter flowers with the sun in their eyes and the blossoms facing away from them. Now that the direction has been reversed, light shines on the flower from behind the observer.

18.3. For a chronological listing and sources, see Appendix 14.

18.4. This cultivar, I learned much later, had been raised in the garden of the RHS from seed that, according to the records, came from a neglected nursery in the Netherlands. Robert De Belder suggested that this may in fact have been the former Kort nursery at Kalmthout, which is quite near the Dutch frontier.

18.5. Raised in Germany by Messrs. Hesse of Weener, this was said to be an improvement on 'Ruby Glow', an older cultivar bred at Kalmthout by Kort in 1933 and originally distributed as *Hamamelis japonica* var. *flavopurpurascens* 'Superba'. It would appear to be a cross between *H. mollis* and *H. japonica* or some form thereof.

18.6. Diane Adriaenssens, *Jelena and Robert De Belder: Generous as Nature Herself* (Brussels: Laconti, 2005). Originally published in French, the book is now available in an English translation.

18.7. See W. J. Bean, *Trees and Shrubs Hardy in the British Isles*, 8th ed. rev., vol. 2 (London: John Murray, 1989), 316. When we saw Robert De Belder in 1973, it was quite clear that there were crosses between *Hamamelis mollis* and *H. japonica* 'Flavopurpurascens'.

18.8. The Meserve hybrid hollies are the other contribution.

18.9. With these came samples of several other cultivars. None of them, in my limited experience, is as beautiful and vigorous as 'Fukujukai'.

18.10. The plant is not as well-known as *Eranthis hyemalis* because of its sterility (*E. × tubergenii* does not seed itself around). It can be reproduced only by dividing small bulbs off the expanding clump from the mother bulb. Bloom commences 10 days to a week after *E. hyemalis* finishes blooming. The flower is semidouble and a richer yellow than that of *E. hyemalis*. It is extremely attractive on its own; here, it shows particularly well against the dark green of *Buxus* 'Green Gem'. *E. × tubergenii* always reminds me of my Swarthmore mentor Gertrude Smith, who pointed out its merits to me and gave me my "starter" bulbs.

18.11. They are joined in small number by the antique daffodil *Narcissus* 'Henry Irving'. A small yellow trumpet *Narcissus*, it looks a lot like the Tenby daffodil (*N. obvallaris*). We found 'Henry Irving' growing around the old farmhouse we lived in at Sunset Hills. Art Tucker of Delaware College, in Dover, Delaware, later identified it for us.

18.12. Among the yellow-twig dogwoods, the double snowdrops (*Galanthus nivalis* 'Flore Pleno') have finished their run, and a few clumps of the distinctly nonaggressive spring snowflake (*Leucojum vernum*) are showing their convex white with a drop of yellow at the edge of the flower on each dividing line.

Pages 470–471
John Everett Millais, Ophelia, 1852. Oil on canvas, 30 × 44 in. Tate Britain, London.

The many varieties of flowers floating with Ophelia has inspired me to make a collection of similar diminutive winter flowers behind the stone bench.

A Afterword

By Charles A. Birnbaum, FASLA, FAAR

The introduction to Susan and Geoffrey Jellicoe's *Modern Private Gardens* (1968), a much-referenced garden survey that sits dog-eared in Bill Frederick's library, concludes, "If we visit a gallery of modern painting anywhere in the world—London, Tokyo, New York, or Rio de Janeiro—we find that behind the visual and literary associations belonging to that particular part of the world, there lies an abstract art that is universal in its appeal. So it is with gardens. Just as the mind is responding, in abstract art, to shapes which it appears to seek and often crave, so it responds to shapes in landscapes... Like a painter, a designer of a garden may be unable to explain how he has groped his way to the result..."

In a recent conversation, Bill told me that the Jellicoes' book had influenced his own design enormously. I recalled an earlier visit with Bill and his wife, Nancy, in the spring of 2006, when Ashland Hollow's azaleas and wisteria were at their explosive peak of color. The tour began inside the Fredericks' living room, where a wonderful painting by Roberto Burle Marx demands attention with its bold use of color and flowing curvilinear forms. Little did I realize then that the painting offered more than a preview of the landscape outdoors. Now, thanks to the publication of *Wrestling with Angels and Singing with Dragons*, along with other authors' reappraisals of Burle Marx, we can unlock and critique the motivations, inspirations, experiences, and creative encounters—both conscious and subconscious— that have collectively shaped Bill's approach and philosophy as a designer. In his garden we can revel in a richly articulated and illustrative personal narrative spanning an unrivaled 50-year continuum of creativity and exploration.

My 2006 visit was part of a two-day excursion in Wilmington, Delaware, and other parts of the Brandywine Valley, an area where celebrated garden owners wear multiple hats, often serving as patrons, designers, master planners, horticulturists, and stewards. This tradition began with the du Ponts' significant garden and estate designs, mostly in the Beaux Arts and/or Picturesque style at Gibraltar, Nemours, Hagley, Winterthur, and Longwood Gardens—and continues today with Elise du Pont's Patterns, a garden that includes the last private residential design by Dan Kiley.

Like Henry Francis du Pont and his creative collaborators at Winterthur, Bill and Nancy Frederick share a quest for "strong bones, innovative design, and horticulturally rich" solutions. It is worth noting, in terms of regional garden heritage, that du Pont opened his house to the public in 1951, the same year the Fredericks were married and entered Cornell University. If H. F. du Pont had epitomized American decorative arts in the home and its grounds during the first half of the 20th century, Bill Frederick would subsequently import the emerging Modernist garden design movement from Europe, Scandinavia, and California to the Brandywine Valley, where he naturalized it with a sure hand. The international group Bill that refers to as Modernism's "bubbling cauldron" of talent included Conrad Hammerman and Peter Shepheard, who both contributed to the design of Ashland Hollow, as well as Thomas Church, Geoffrey Jellicoe, Roberto Burle Marx, and Mien Ruys. All but Ruys visited the Fredericks in Delaware, though Bill and Nancy visited her at home in the Netherlands, as they did Burle Marx at his country place in Brazil.

It is no accident that all of these designers are represented in Shepheard's book *Modern Gardens* (1953) or that Bill Frederick took up the author's cause. Just as Dan Kiley, Lawrence Halprin, and Garrett Eckbo promoted of Christopher Tunnard's *Gardens in the Modern Landscape* (1938), Bill became an advocate for this new wave of thinking. Shepheard wrote, "In the last few years the gardens of the painter-gardener Burle Marx ... have made a revolution in Brazil. What there was of a landscape tradition in Brazil, in spite of its tropical climate, was European, and has produced little other than sterile symmetrical layouts, making little or no use of the country's flora and taking no account of the need for shade-giving trees. Burle Marx's gardens...show a fierce reaction against all symmetry and rectangularity; they are full of sinuous curves, bold and aggressive on plan...." He goes on, "But Burle Marx's most important lesson for Brazil has been the one William Robinson and Gertrude Jekyll preached in England—the paramount value of plants native to the country."

While Ashland Hollow displays the clear influence of Shepheard and the Jellicoes, it also embodies a very personal sensibility. It exemplifies an artist at work in the garden, and it manifests Bill Frederick's study of the connection between painting and horticulture. A landscape architect and a preeminent horticulturist, Bill is also a painter who explores the expressionistic use of color in representations of the figure and landscapes on canvas, in many ways similar to artwork by Burle Marx. Bill has been influenced by his long fascination with Fauvist painting in the early 20th century; Ashland Hollow is testimony to decades of experimentation with color in the garden. This shows a courageous spirit and exacting discrimination, and it also achieves Bill's personal quest for "something of interest going on in the garden every month of the year."

Wrestling with Angels comfortably places Bill's work in the bubbling cauldron of modern garden design, as is clearly evidenced by his sweeping, biomorphic water features and planting beds, bold hardscape geometry drawn from Bauhaus principles, and strikingly expansive applications of color. Even so, the garden's ever-changing horticultural features and events lie lightly on the land. The sophistication, richness, and complexity of Bill's planting goes beyond the comparatively simple planting plans laid out in Modernist primers such as Thomas Church's *Your Private World: A Study of Intimate Gardens* (1968), whose chapter headings include "Plant It Away," "Plant to Screen Your Window," and "Don't Spare That Tree."

Bill recounts that a lecture his fellow Cornell landscape architecture student Conrad Hammerman devoted to *his* mentor, Burle Marx, back in 1951, was "a real eye-opener to me [and] in many ways the beginning of my search for an appropriate approach to contemporary garden design in our part of the world." *Wrestling with Angels* not only documents how—time and again, over five decades—this challenge has been met successfully. It also serves as a permanent record of a garden that has no equal.

Charles A. Birnbaum, FASLA, FAAR, is the founder and president of The Cultural Landscape Foundation in Washington, D.C.; www.tclf.org.

B Acknowledgements

I am extremely grateful to many people for their contributions to the making of this book.

I want to recognize particularly the following, who gave important assistance at crucial moments in the process: Tom Buchter, Rick Darke, Mac Griswold, Penny Hobhouse, Steve Hutton, Doug Reed, John Sales, Elena Sisti.

Christine Agular provided much needed counsel on nomenclature. Suzanne Maguire, supposedly retired, took on what must have seemed endless typing with admirable cheer and speed. Leslie Morrison gamely put up with the mess I caused in her office and served as an extraordinary coordinator, computer advocate, and teacher.

The late Paul Skibinski our head gardener for 28 years, shot a majority of the digital photographs and skillfully scanned my numerous 35 mm slides. This was Paul's first experience as photo manager, and the job turned out to have moments so burdensome (and remote from gardening) that a less resolute person would have quit.

Brandon Kaufman excelled as this book's gifted young graphic designer. He was succeeded by Diane Lemonides, who completed his endeavor and brilliantly managed the production of this volume. Doug Brenner tolerated my shortcomings and did such sensitive and creative editing that it must be called beautiful.

My wife, Nancy, was not only a most helpful reader, but also the usual steadying rock when various reversals, changes of mind, and other shifts in the book-writing weather occurred.

Heartfelt thanks to them all.

C Photographic Credits

All photographs by the author or his wife, Nancy G. Frederick, other than those listed below.

Rick Darke
page 36 (middle), 53 (bottom), 108, 121, 130 (bottom right), 130 (bottom left), 145 (bottom), 153 (middle), 158 (top), 225, 232 (bottom right), 252 (bottom right), 387 (top), 391, 396 (middle). Also aerial shots: pages 151 (top), 314, 377

Jim Graham
page 29, 36 (bottom), 110 (top), 186, 254 (top), 300, 307 (top), 322, 323

Frank Green
page 36 (top)

Crawford H. Greenewalt
page 179

Dick Keane
page 105, 109

Andrew Lawson
page 246 (top)

Paul Skibinski
page 50 (top), 50 (bottom), 51 (top), 51 (middle), 53 (top), 54 (top), 54 (middle-bottom), 54 (bottom), 56 (top), 59, 62 (top), 62 (bottom), 64 (middle), 65 (top right), 66 (top), 66 (bottom), 67 (middle), 70 (top), 71 (top), 71 (bottom), 73, 77 (top), 77 (bottom), 78, 82 (top), 82 (middle), 82 (bottom), 83 (middle-right), 83 (middle-left), 83 (bottom), 84(middle), 84 (bottom), 86 (top), 86 (middle), 93, 94, 103, 107, 117, 125, 130 (top left), 130 (top right), 131 (bottom left), 136, 138 (top), 138 (middle), 138 (bottom), 139 (middle), 139 (bottom), 140 (middle), 140 (bottom), 143 (top), 143 (bottom left), 144 (top right), 144 (bottom left), 145 (top left), 145 (top right), 149, 151 (bottom), 152 (top), 152 (bottom), 155 (top left), 155 (top right), 155 (middle left), 155 (middle right), 155 (bottom left), 155 (bottom right), 157 (right), 158 (middle), 158 (bottom), 159 (top), 159 (middle top), 159 (middle bottom), 159 (bottom), 160, 161, 162, 164, 166, 167, 168, 171, 173, 176 (bottom), 177 (bottom right), 177 (bottom left), 178, 180 (top), 180 (bottom),181 (top), 181 (bottom), 182 (top),183 (bottom left), 188, 189, 191, 192, 193, 194, 200, 203, 205, 212, 214, 222, 223 (top), 223 (bottom), 224 (bottom left), 225, 229, 231 (top left), 231 (middle left), 231 (top right), 231 (middle right), page 231 (bottom right), 234, 239 (top left), 239 (top right), 239 (bottom left), 239 (bottom right), 243, 251 (top left), 251 (top right), 251 (middle left), 252 (top right), 252 (top left), 252 (middle left), 252 (bottom left), page 254 (top), 256, 257, 261, 267, 269, 272, 273, 274, 276, 277 (bottom right), 278, 281 (top left), 281 (top right), 281 (bottom left), 290 (top), 290 (bottom), 294, 295, 296 (bottom), 298 (top right), 299, 304-5, 308 (top), 308 (middle), 309 (top), 309 (middle), 309 (bottom), 310, 311 (top), 311 (bottom), 315 (top), 315 (bottom right), 319, 334, 343, 347, 349 (top), 351 (top), 351 (bottom), 354, 355, 356, 357, 360, 361, 362 (bottom left), 362 (bottom right), 363, 364, 367, 368, 374, 378 (top), 378 (bottom), 380, 381 (bottom), 382 (top), 383 (top), 383 (bottom), 385 (top), 385 (bottom), 386, 387 (middle-top), 387 (middle-bottom), 387 (bottom), 393, 394, 395, 396 (bottom), 398, 403 (top right), 403 (middle left), 403 (middle right), 403 (top right), 403 (middle left), 403 (middle right), 403 (bottom), 404 (top left), 404 (top right), 404 middle), 404 (bottom left), 404 (bottom right), 407, 409 (top), 409 (middle right), 410, 411, 415 (top left), 415 (top right), 415 (bottom left), 415 (bottom right), 416, 417, 423, 426, 429 (top), 429 (bottom), 431, 432, 436, 441 (top), 442 (top), 444 (top left), 444 (top right), 444 (bottom left), 444 (bottom right), 445 (top right), 445 (middle right), 448, 451, 454 (top left), 454 (top right), 454 (bottom left), 454 (bottom right), 457 (top left), 457 (top right), 457 (bottom), 458, 459, 460 (top), 460 (bottom), 461 (top), 461 (bottom), 462 (top), 462 (bottom), 463 (top), 463 (bottom), 465 (top left), 465 (top right), 468 (top left), 468 (top right), 468 (bottom right), 469 (bottom)

D Appendices

APPENDIX 1

CHAPTER 3

THE ENTRANCE GARDEN AND THE STUDIO GARDEN

Ten Favorites from the Studio Garden

Because it would be inappropriate to discuss each kind of herbaceous plant used here, I think it only fair to focus on 10 of the hardy herbaceous plants that have become subjects of particular affection in this garden. These special friends are:

1. *Hosta sieboldii* f. *kabitan* has been in this garden almost from the beginning and has been divided many times. There are now two major sweeps of this plant. Its bright yellow tips push out of the ground at the same time as the foliage tips of tulips, *Narcissus*, and *Muscari*. As this hosta's leaves mature, they are the very essence of spring chartreuse. I especially love them with the white trumpets of *Narcissus* 'Beersheba'. The small hosta foliage makes a very successful carpet throughout the season, when the leaf colors are more muted.

2. *Lathyrus vernus* (spring vetchling). This European wildflower produces incredibly beautiful flowers for a very brief period during tulip season. They are bicolor—a blue and a mauve made to be seen together. Although they never set fertile seed and they fuss about being divided, I wouldn't want to be without them.

3. *Polygonatum humile* (formerly *P. falcatum*) came as a gift from my special friend that great garden promoter Jerry Eaton. Stoloniferous, it has a maximum height of 10 inches, but it is often

shorter. The white flowers are large enough to be entirely visible, even though the stems grow close together and the leaves are closely spaced. Everyone who sees *Polygonatum humile* falls in love with it ("that cute little thing" syndrome). Unfortunately, although the plant is entirely perennial, the foliage often dies down as early as late June. But for May and most of June, it is absolutely charming and totally unique.

4. *Iris graminea* (from Central and Southeastern Europe to the Caucasus) arrived here in 1978, a gift of Linc Foster, an admirable and dedicated rock gardener. The narrow, dark green leaves form a tight clump, which expands horizontally with age. Diminutive bicolor (dark blue and purple) blossoms are partly submerged in the foliage, with just enough of the flowers showing above it to beckon you closer. At that point the fragrance takes over. As I have mentioned (in Chapter 14), the British call this the plum tart iris, because its aroma closely resembles that of its freshly baked namesake. Although plum tarts are not exactly common in American homes, no one over here could possibly want to give this plant up once he or she has tried it. It is luscious. Ours grows in a raised bed just where one goes out the east side of the garden. In early May, nobody fails to stop.

5. *Thalictrum rochenbruneanum* (from Japan) was first purchased for this garden in 1983. I'm convinced that it is the best of the meadow rues for our area. The tall stems and branches are narrow in diameter but wiry and strong; the leaves are divided into small blue green ovals and heavily clustered at the base, the overall effect is ferny. Its inflorescences are large open panicles of diminutive violet flowers with yellow stamens, appearing in late May, June, and July. This plant occasionally seeds itself in our

garden, and such self-sown-seedlings always perform better than transplants from a nursery. Surprisingly, the spots that *T. rochenbruneanum* picks to seed itself almost always turn out to be where it fits the design scheme best! Its height, often to seven to eight feet, may seem large for such a small-scale garden. But because this is what many gardeners call a scrim plant, it works. The haze of sparkling flowers enhances everything nearby. A lone person strolling in the garden feels the warmth of close friends, without the bulk of human bodies.

6. *Pardancanda norisii* is a bi-generic hybrid (*Pardanthopsis* x *Pardancanda norisii*) made during my gardening lifetime. It has the overall appearance of the old fashioned blackberry lily (*Belamcanda chinensis*): German irislike leaves, a four-foot stem branching near its top above the foliage to support a single flower of four petals, orange with black spots. The hybrid is a little more vigorous and offers a wide color range to choose from. In 1982 we grew a packet of seeds of a Park Seed Company hybrid and were delighted with the colors. One with eggplant-colored flowers struck our fancy, and it has played an important part in our garden life ever since.

7. *Phlox paniculata*, the summer bloomer of our grandparents' gardens, gives off an incredibly wonderful fragrance on warm summer evenings, as long as it has not been overly hybridized. In 1989 Nancy and I were enjoying a late evening visit with friends in their recently acquired 19th-century farmhouse. We were sitting on a screened-in porch with darkness all around us, enjoying the sensual night sounds of crickets and other country fauna, when we noticed a marvelously seductive fragrance. After

borrowing a flashlight, I followed my nose to a deep pink summer phlox dramatically more fragrant than its nearby brothers and sisters. Not long after that we received a division from its owner, which we planted just below the larger Studio Garden terrace and near our bedroom window. Its scent continues to delight all who encounter it, and we have privately named this treasure *P. paniculata* 'Ezio', after the generous donor.

8. *Liriope muscari* 'Royal Purple'. Many years ago, when *L. muscari* and its various cultivars first came into use in this area, I jumped on the bandwagon. More recently, a friend told me about 'Royal Purple'. It is truly better than any *L. muscari* I have grown. Whereas the flowers on most cultivars are partly tucked within the foliage, extending only two inches above it, the flower spikes on 'Royal Purple' begin five inches above the foliage, revealing a complete "flower on a stem." The narrow leaves are a good dark green. The flower is a rich lavender randomly spotted with very small white spots, which help to electrify the whole picture. The most distinctive quality of all is the color of the stems. Within the flower spike itself, the stem is the same lavender as the blossoms; a little farther down, however, the stem turns a deep black purple. Having grown 'Royal Purple' here since 1991, we take ever greater delight in its presence in late August and early September, normally a dull time in Delaware gardens.

9. *Tricyrtis* 'Sinonome' reached us in 1996, and it remains this garden's most attractive and satisfactorily performing toad lily. Our clump, which starts blooming in mid-September, stands 38 inches tall with about 20 stems arching toward the most light. The alternate, pointed leaves are a healthy clear green

with the flower buds clustered at their tips. There are often 12 or more buds per stem, and the zigzag stems themselves possess a special charm. Anyone seeing the blossoms for the first time may think "orchid." The $1^5/_8$-inch flowers with six narrow petals are enchanting. Purple dots and blotches spot the petals' white background, sometimes sharply distinct and sometimes bleeding into one another. No two petals display the same pattern. In the center of each flower is a tube within a tube, the pistil rising as high as the petals are long and opening into tiny forked structures that open outward. The outer tube opens (at a lower level) into familiar looking anthers and stamens. This central feature of the flower is less spotted and more consistently purple, but instead of having a smooth texture, it is ever so slightly hairy. The overall effect is that of a piece of jewelry, and I react with the same pleasure every year when it blooms.

10. *Vinca minor* 'Aurea'. This ground cover fills the rectangular area that surrounds the Henry Loustau sculpture. Since we first planted the *V. minor* more than 10 years ago it has made a dense mat four to five inches high. The "gold" of the new growth is not quite so important a feature as the vendor suggested. Even though whatever variegation it has disappears very quickly during the growing season, it is this plant's vigor that I like most. The plant is, indeed, robust and always a dependable glossy dark green. I know of no other *V. minor* as satisfactory in this respect.

APPENDIX 2
CHAPTER 9
GREEN AND WHITE PATH

Downhill (South) Side of Green and White Path

The following eight plantings lie behind and close to the *Taxus* hedge. They are seen between pairs of *Hibiscus syriacus* 'Diana' as one walks from west to east. Asterisks indicate "events" detailed in note 9.10, page 241.

Between *Hibiscus* standards #2 and #3:
Most handsome specimen of *Ilex* x *aquipernyi* 'Meschick' Dragon Lady® (1¬ plant)
Cornus kousa 'Milky Way' (1)

Between *Hibiscus* #3 and #4:
Chamaecyparis obtusa 'Breviramea' (1)
Part of planting of *Miscanthus sinensis* 'Morning Light'
Half of planting of *Stewartia koreana*

Between *Hibiscus* #4 and #5*:
Balance of *Stewartia* and *Miscanthus* plantings
Eleutherococcus sieboldianus 'Variegatus' (syn. *Acanthopanax sieboldianus* 'Variegatus')(1)
Cornus alternifolia 'Variegata' (1)

Between *Hibiscus* #5 and #6:
Ilex x *aquipernyi* 'San Jose' (Dudley #4) (1)
Cornus kousa 'Milky Way' (1)
Abies firma (1)

Between *Hibiscus* #6 and #7:
Chamaecyparis obtusa 'Dainty Doll'
Intersection with back drive
Heptacodium miconioides (1)
Miscanthus sinensis 'Variegata' (1)

Between *Hibiscus* #7 and #8:
Buxus sempervirens (Longwood resistant) (1)
Juniperus 'Grey Owl' (5)
Lilium filipinense var. *formosanum* (6)
Vitex agnus-castus 'Silver Spire' (1)
Cornus kousa 'Milky Way' (1)
Philadelphus 'Burkwoodii' (1)
Hydrangea arborescens 'Annabelle' (3)

Between *Hibiscus* #8 and #9:
Stewartia koreana (3)
Cornus alba 'Elegantissima' (1)

After *Hibiscus* #9:
Baptisia alba (1)
Ilex x *aquipernyi* 'San Jose' (Dudley #4) (1)
Salix alba 'Regalis' (1)

APPENDIX 3
CHAPTER 9
GREEN AND WHITE PATH

Uphill (North) Side of Green and White Path

Plantings in five bays of ground cover-based plantings of particularly stimulating interest. Asterisks indicate "events" detailed in note 9.10, page 241.

Bay #1
Ground cover of *Stachys byzantina*
Dark green *Ilex* x *meserveae* 'Mesid' Blue Maid®, behind specimen
Salix elaeagnos
Miscanthus sinensis 'Variegatus' (2)
Crambe cordifolia (several)
Eryngium yuccifolium (rattlesnake plantain) (several)
Lilium 'Black Dragon' (several)
Dividers:
  Buxus sempervirens (Longwood Resistant) (5)
  Juniperus 'Grey Owl' (9)
  Ilex 'Meschick' Dragon Lady® (1)
  Chamaecyparis obtusa 'Nana Gracilis' (1)

Bay #2
Shaded by *Cornus kousa* 'Milky Way' (1)*
Ballota acetabulosa
Antennaria parlinii subsp. *fallax* (syn. *Antennaria plantaginifolia* var. *ambigens*) with
Begonia grandis 'Alba'

From bank above roadway behind bay:

Rubus cockburnianus—showing gray foliage through *Cornus kousa* branches in the summertime, white stems in the winter

Dividers:

   Chamaecyparis obtusa 'Nana Gracilis' (1)

   Taxus baccata 'Repandens' (several)

Bay #3*

Deutzia chunii (2)

Crambe cordifolia (several)

Silybum marianum (several)

Onopordum acanthium (1 or 2)

At the rear:

Hydrangea paniculata 'White Tiara' (several)

Dividers:

   Taxus baccata 'Repandens' (several)

   Vitex agnus castus 'Silver Spire' (1)

   Hydrangea paniculata 'White Tiara' (1)

Bay #4

Stachys byzantina ground cover

Ilex x meserveae 'Conablu' (Blue Princess®) and *Taxus baccata* 'Repandens' in background

Cornus kousa 'Milky Way' (1) underplanted with *Liriope muscari* 'Monroe White' (contained in steel edging)

Salix alba var. *sericea* (1)

Ilex 'Meschick' Dragon Lady® (1)

Yucca flaccida (Henry Selection) (5+3)

Dividers:

   Chamaecyparis obtusa 'Breviramea' (2)

   Picea orientalis 'Procumbens' (1)

Bay #5*

Stachys byzantina as ground cover

Salix alba var. *sericea* (2) in background

Juniperus 'Gray Owl' (8)

Taxus baccata 'Repandens' (6)

Ilex x *aquipernyi* 'San Jose' (Dudley #4) (1)

Ligustrum quihoui (1)

Paeonia 'White Ivory' (37)

Hydrangea paniculata 'White Tiara' (several)

Lilium 'Black Dragon' (14)

Vitex agnus-castus 'Silver Spire' (1)

Miscanthus sinensis 'Cabaret' (1)

Cornus kousa 'Milky Way' (1) underplanted with *Liriope muscari* 'Monroe White'

Onopordum acanthium (7)

Verbascum chaixii 'Album' and *Anemone* x *hybrida* 'Honorine Jobert' underplanted with *Chrysanthemum weyrichii* 'White Bomb' *Allium stipitatum* 'White Giant'

Dividers:

Chamaecyparis obtusa 'Nana Gracilis' (2)

Ilex crenata 'Helleri' (9)

Yucca flaccida (Henry Selection) (3)

Miscanthus sinensis 'Variegatus' (2)

APPENDIX 4

CHAPTER 11

WISTERIA LAWN AND ROSE PATH

Roses Noted on 1980 Visit to Garden of Roses of Legend and Romance in Wooster, Ohio

Years at beginnings of entries record planting dates at Ashland Hollow; years at ends of entries indicate when these roses were introduced, followed by breeders' names, if known, in parentheses.

1982   *Rosa* 'Crested Moss' (syn. 'Chapeau de Napoléon') (Moss (Centifolia)—light pink; fragrant; a must because of extreme mossiness, in spite of floppy habit; 1827 (Vibert)

R. glauca (syn. *R. rubrifolia*) (Species)—medium pink; single; thornless; 1789

R. 'Lillian Gibson' (Shrub, Hybrid Blanda) medium pink; fragrant; dense but rangy habit; 5 to 6 feet; thornless; 1938 (Hansen)

R. roxburghii forma *normalis* (burr rose, single chestnut rose) (Species)—single; light pink; handsome bark; large bush to 15 by 15 feet; 1908

R. x *centifolia* (Provence rose, cabbage rose)—medium pink; fragrant; 4 feet; 1596

1982+86 *Rosa* 'Alice Vena' (Gallica/Hybrid China)—dark purple to old-rose color; 1867(?)

1982+93 *R.* 'Sarah van Fleet' (Hybrid Rugosa)—light rose and pink; fragrant;1926 (Van Fleet)

1983	R. 'Reine des Violettes' ('Queen of the Violets') (Hybrid Perpetual)—mauve and mauve blend; fragrant; 1860
	R. rubiginosa (syn. R. eglanteria) (eglantine, sweetbriar) (Species)—single; light pink; foliage has fragrance of green apples; 10 feet by 10 feet; 1753 (possibly 1551)
	R. rugosa—double; purple pink; excellent habit; not in Combined Rose List 2006
1984	R. 'Henri Martin' (Moss)—medium red; fragrant; 1862 (Laffay)
1984+96	R. 'The Bishop' (R. x centifolia)—quartered; rose pink; extremely fragrant; good habit; 4 feet; date unknown
1985	R. 'Adeline' (Alba)—semidouble; pink; very graceful habit; 5 feet; not in Combined Rose List 2006
1986	R. 'Capitaine John Ingram' (Moss)—mauve and mauve blend, very fragrant; 1855 (Laffay)
1987+93 +05	R. 'Roseraie de l'Haÿ' (Hybrid Rugosa)—red and mauve blend; very fragrant; 1901 and 2005 (Cochet-Cochet)

APPENDIX 5

Expanded Rose List after Wooster Visit
(Part of 1980s Planting)

Years and breeders' names noted as in Appendix 4.

1982   *Rosa* 'Amélie Gravereaux' (Hybrid Rugosa)—medium
red; 1903 (Gravereaux)

            R. 'Belle Poitevine' (Hybrid Rugosa)—medium pink;
very fragrant; 1894 (Bruant)

            R. 'Delicata' (Hybrid Rugosa)—light pink (mauve and
mauve blend); fragrant; 1898 (Cooling)

            R. 'Hansa' (Hybrid Rugosa)—mauve and mauve
blend); fragrant; 1905 (Schaum & Vantol)

            R. rugosa 'Rubra' (Species)—single; mauve and mauve
blend (Combined Rose List terms it deep pink);
fragrant; CRL: "No date; very old"

            R. x ? —pink; from the French home of Pierre Samuel
du Pont de Nemours; cutting brought back to the
U.S., rooted, and distributed to interested du Pont
descendants by Wilhelmina du Pont Ross

1982+86   *R.* 'Charles de Mills' (syn. 'Bizarre Triumphant')
(Gallica)—mauve; fragrant

1983   R. 'Catherine Seyton' (Eglanteria hybrid)—light pink,
single; 1894 (Penzance); not in *CRL 2006*

1983+93	*R.* 'Variegata di Bologna' (Bourbon)—red blend; striped; fragrant; 1909 (Bonfiglioli)
1983+93 +05	*R.* 'Highdownensis' (Shrub, Hybrid Moyesii)—single; medium red; 1928 (Sir Frederick Stern)
	R. 'Rose à Parfum de l'Haÿ' (Hybrid Rugosa)—medium red; highly fragrant; 1901 (Gravereaux)
1985	*R.* 'Doorenbos Selection' (Hybrid Spinosissima)—Case Estates, Shrub Garden (gift of Patrick Willoughby), from Kalmthout Arboretum; no date (Doorenbos)
1987	*R.* 'Deuil de Paul Fontaine' (Moss)—mauve and mauve blend; 1873 (Fontaine)
	R. moyesii 'Superba'; in *Combined Rose List* I could find only (Rugosa Hybrid) 'Scabrosa' cross-reference from 'Superba'; nothing under *moyesii*.
	R. rugosa (Stonington)(Eglanteria Hybrid)—single, light pink; 1894 (Penzance)
1987+90 +93	*R.* 'Mme. Isaac Pereire'(syn. 'Le Bienheureux de la Salle') (Bourbon)—deep pink; very fragrant; shaggy purple, enormous flowers"; 1881 (Garçon)
1987+99	*R. moyesii* (Species)—medium red; 1894

APPENDIX 6
CHAPTER 11
WISTERIA LAWN AND ROSE PATH

Rosa Rugosa *Hybrids*

I have extracted these from Appendices 1 and 2 to illustrate
the extent to which *Rosa rugosa* (native to China and Japan;
Zone 2) has been used in hybridization. After trying all of these
over a long period of time at Ashland Hollow, I can say that, with
two exceptions—noted with asterisks below—they have not
performed well in mid-Atlantic conditions. Their performance is
quite likely better in New England, judging from what I see on
vacation in Maine.

Rosa 'Amélie Gravereaux'	
R. 'Belle Poitevine'	1894
R. 'Delicata'	1898
R. 'Hansa'	1903
* R. 'Roseraie de L'Haÿ'	1901
R. *rugosa* (double)	
R. *rugosa* 'Rubra'	
R. 'Rose à Parfum de l'Haÿ'	1901
* R. 'Sarah Van Fleet'	1926

Plants Whose Season of Greatest Interest
Precedes Rose and Wisteria Season

Chionodoxa luciliae

Dicentra spectabilis

Galanthus nivalis 'Charlockii'

Helleborus x *orientalis* (Royal Heritage Strain)

H. x *orientalis* (Skyland's Pink seedlings)

H. x *orientalis* (Winterthur seedlings)

Iris 'Eleanor Roosevelt' This plant has turned out to be a very successful ground cover. Its *Iris germanica*-like rhizomes make a tight mat, keeping weeds out. The shorter foliage stays dense and disease free. These virtues, combined with short-stemmed rich, deep purple blue blossoms make this iris a winner.*

Muscari azureum

M. latifolia

M. armeniacum 'Valerie Finnis'

Phlox subulata 'Tamsin'

Symphytum 'Belsay Gold'

* *Iris* 'Eleanor Roosevelt' came here as a gift of Joanna Reed, a very special gardening friend. Joanna's understanding of plants was excellent, and her understanding of people, without equal. Few came away from her enchanting garden uninspired and without a special plant to cherish.

APPENDIX 8

CHAPTER 11

WISTERIA LAWN AND ROSE PATH

Plants Whose Season of Greatest Interest
Follows Rose and Wisteria Season

Summer

Acanthus spinosissimus (for its foliage)

Allium cernuum

Calamintha nepeta

Clematis heracleifolia

Corydalis sempervirens

Dierama pulcherrimum

Foeniculum vulgare 'Purpureum'

Indigofera 'Rose Carpet'

Phlox paniculata 'Franz Schubert'

P. pilosa subsp. *ozarkana*

Verbascum 'Southern Charm'

Fall

Amsonia hubrichtii (for its golden foliage)

Anemone hupehensis (unnamed gift from Paul Skibinski)

Begonia grandis

Calamintha nepeta

Chrysanthemum 'Ryan's Pink'

Lespedeza thunbergii 'Gibraltar'

APPENDIX 9
CHAPTER 13

PAUL I

Summer Interns by Year

1974	Stephen H. Hampson
1975	Marc B. Willson, Brian Allman
1976	James McCready, Allen Reeves
1977	Avery Cook
1978	Mark Schneider
1979	Andrew Durham
1980	Robert Curtis
1981	Raymond Pohl
1982	David Baker, Mark McAteer
1983	Tim Weiler, Richard Greback
1984	Barbara Coulston, Richard Epps
1985	Walt Lumley
1986	Mark Beauchamp
1987	Mark Gormel
1988	Robert Couch
1989	Frances T. Marquis
1990	Troy Banks
1991	Laurie Mack
1992	Tres Fromme
1993	Laurel Rimmer
1994	Chad Nelson
1995	Deborah Bowen
1996	Steven Barrett
1997	Jerry Parmenter
1998	Ryan Case
1999	Tina Duperron
2000	Julie Cassels
2001	Casey Taylor

APPENDIX 10

CHAPTER 14

PAUL II

Bedding Plants—2006 Season

(List made in May)

Studio Garden Beds

Ageratum 'Hawaii Blue'

Alternanthera sessilis 'Rubra'

Angelonia angustifolia 'Anblauzwei' (Angel Face® Blue)

Asclepias curassavica

Asparagus densiflorus 'Myersii'

Caladium 'Tom-Tom'

Canna (Belize seedling)

Canna warszewiczii

Delphinium 'Blue Butterfly'

Emilia coccinea

Eucomis 'Van der Merwei'

Gomphrena haageana 'Strawberry Fields'

Heliotropium 'Marine'

Hibiscus acetosella 'Red Shield'

Impatiens 'Bruno Red'

I. 'Bruno Violet'

I. 'Dazzler Apricot'

I. 'Dazzler Deep Orange'

I. auricoma 'Jungle Gold'

I. 'Orange over Apricot'

I. (New Guinea) 'Salmon'

I. (New Guinea) 'True Red'

Ipomoea tricolor 'Heavenly Blue'

Iresine 'Purple Lady'

Nicotiana langsdorfii

N. 'Merlin Magic'

N. 'Tinkerbell'

Ornithogalum saundersiae

Oxalis vulcanicola 'Copper Glow'

Oxypetalum caeruleum

Petunia 'Purple Wave'

Phygelius rectus 'New Sensation'

Salvia chiapensis

S. farinacea 'Victoria Blue'

S. guaranitica 'Black and Blue'

S. guaranitica 'Kobalt'

Solenostemon scutellarioides 'Giant Exhibition Limelight'

S. scutellarioides 'Giant Exhibition Palisandra'

Stipa arundinacea

Strobilanthes dyerianus

Talinum paniculatum 'Kingswood Gold'

Tetrapanax papyrifera

Torenia 'Blue Panda'

T. 'Summer Wave'

Tradescantia pallida (syn. *Setcreasea pallida*)

Xanthosoma sagittifolium 'Lime Zinger' (syn. 'Chartreuse Giant')

Swimming Pool Garden Bed and Fence

Alocasia 'Calidora'

Caladium 'Tom-Tom'

Cobaea scandens

Euphorbia cotinifolia

Hamelia patens

Heliotropium 'Marine'

Hibiscus acetosella 'Red Shield'

Impatiens balsamina (magenta form)

I. 'Dazzler Deep Orange'

I. (New Guinea) 'Orange over Apricot'

Ipomoea tricolor 'Heavenly Blue'

Mina lobata

Nicotiana 'Merlin Magic'

Ricinus communis 'Zanzibariensis' (red selection)

Salvia farinacea 'Victoria Blue'

S. guaranitica

Talinum paniculatum 'Kingswood Gold'

Tibouchina urvilleana 'Edwards'

Torenia 'Summer Wave'

Verbascum 'Harkness Hybrid'

V. 'Vega'

Vigna caracalla

APPENDIX 11

CHAPTER 14

PAUL II

Tubbed and Potted Plants—2006 Season

(List made in May)

Entry Garden, Courtyard, and Front Hall

Begonia boliviensis 'Bertini'

Caladium 'Gingerland'

Clerodendrum wallichii

Coprosma 'Karo Red'

Impatiens auricoma 'Jungle Gold'

Studio Garden Containers

Brunfelsia pilosa

Canna (gift of Dean Rossman)

Corynephorus canescens 'Spiky Blue'

Dicliptera suberecta

Epiphyllum oxypetalum

Hamelia patens

Hibiscus sinensis (double peach)

Impatiens 'Paradise Salmon'

Oxypetalum coeruleum

Plumbago auriculata 'Imperial Blue' (syn. *Plumbago capensis*
    'Imperial Blue')

Rotheca myricoides (syn. *Clerodendrum ugandensis*)

Sanchezia speciosa

Solenostemon scutellarioides 'Giant Exhibition Palisandra'

Strobilanthes dyerianus

Syngonium poelophyllum var. *albescens*

Swimming Pool Containers

Asparagus densiflorus 'Myersii'

Cestrum nocturnum

Citrus limon (Wilson's House Lemon)

Colocasia esculenta 'Black Magic'

Duranta erecta var. *grandiflora*

Gladiolus murielae (syn. Acidanthera bicolor)

Heliotropium 'Marine'

Impatiens 'Paradise Salmon'

Iochroma cyaneum

Isolepis cernua (syn. Scirpus cernuus)

Jacaranda mimosifolia

Lysimachia nummularia 'Aurea'

Nassella tenuissima (syn. *Stipa tenuissima*)

Oryza sativa 'Red Dragon'

Pentas lanceolata 'Cranberry Punch'

Plectranthus argentatus 'Silver Shield'

Stipa arundinacea

Teucrium fruticans

Tibouchina urvilleana 'Edwards'

Xanthosoma sagittifolium 'Lime Zinger' (syn. *X.* 'Chartreuse Giant')

APPENDIX 12

American Hollies Planted in the Winter Garden

Ilex opaca 'Arden' (1 plant)	1971
I. opaca 'Arden' (26)	1976
I. opaca 'Clark' (5)	1971
I. opaca 'Clarissa' (1)	1979
I. opaca (yellow-berried) (3)	1971
I. opaca 'Gertrude' (1)	1971
I. opaca 'Hedgeholly' (Paul Bosley hybrid) (1)	1980
I. opaca 'Jersey Princess' (8)	1979
I. opaca 'Judge Brown' (4)	1971
I. opaca 'Mae' (5)	1971
I. opaca 'Nancy' (4)	1971
I. opaca 'Red Velvet' (1)	1971
I. opaca (staminate) (1)	1971
I. opaca (staminate) (1)	1976
I. opaca name unknown (1)	1971

APPENDIX 13

Deciduous Hollies Planted in the Winter Garden

Ilex 'Autumn Glow' (2 plants)

I. 'Harvest Red' (1)

I. verticillata 'Jim Dandy' (staminate) (1)

I. verticillata 'Red Sprite' (2)

I. verticillata 'Rhett Butler' (staminate) (1)

I. verticillata 'Scarlett O'Hara' (2)

I. 'Sparkleberry' (1)

I. verticillata 'Winter Red' (1)

APPENDIX 14

Salix *Chronology and Sources*

Dates record when these plants arrived at Ashland Hollow.

1961   *Salix repens* subsp. *arenaria* (syn. var. *argentea*): from Gulf Stream Nursery (transplanted from our prior residence)

1981   *S. gracilistyla*: Scott Arboretum (via Delaware Center for Horticulture Rare Plant Auction)

1981   *S. gracilistyla* 'Melanostachys': Melinger Nursery

1982   *S. humilis* var. *tristis* (syn. var. *microphylla*): Polly Hill, Bernard's Inn Farm

1982   *S. daphnoides* 'Aglaia': British friend (propagation courtesy Dick Lighty)

1983   *S. acutifolia* 'Longifolia': Willow wood Arboretum (propagation courtesy Tom Buchter)

1986   *S. x rubra* 'Eugenei': first seen at 1982 Royal Horticultural Society Show (propagation courtesy Dick Lighty)

1986   *S. chaenomeloides*: Brookside Gardens (propagation courtesy Tom Buchter)

1987   *S. repens* var. *arenaria* (syn. var. *argentea*): Gulf Stream Nursery

1992   *S. aegyptiaca*: first seen at Kew Gardens with John Simmons (propagation courtesy Dick Lighty)

1999   *S. bockii*: gift of Louis Bauer

APPENDIX 15

Hamamelis *Added after 1982*

1986	*Hamamelis* x *intermedia* 'Pallida'
1988	*H.* x *intermedia* 'Diane'
	H. x *intermedia* 'Primavera'
1990	*H.* x *intermedia* 'Pallida'
1992	*H.* x *intermedia* 'Jelena'
	H. x *intermedia* 'Primavera'
1993	*H.* x *intermedia* 'Arnold Promise'
2007	*H.* x *vernalis* 'Carnea'
	H. x *intermedia* 'Princeton Gold'

E Garden Plan Index

In order of appearance in text

GARDEN PLAN NAME	CHAPTER	PAGE

F Plant Index

PLANT NAME	ALTERNATE PLANT NAME	CHAPTER	PAGE
Abeliophyllum distichum		Chapter 12, 18	326, 444, 466
Abies firma		Chapter 8, 9, Appendix #2	214, 228, 240, 487
Abies nordmanniana		Chapter 5, 9	122, 124, 125, 228
Acanthopanax sieboldianus 'Variegatus'	*Eleutherococcus sieboldianus* 'Variegatus'	Chapter 9, Appendix #2	240, 241, 487
Acanthus spinosissimus		Chapter 11, Appendix #8	297, 498
Acer griseum		Chapter 8, 18	217, 444
Acer palmatum		Chapter 1	4
Acer palmatum 'West Grove'		Chapter 3, 14	67, 356
Acer platanoides		Chapter 1	15
Acer rubrum		Chapter 4	100
Acidanthera bicolor	*Gladiolus murielae*	Appendix #11	504
Acorus gramineus 'Ogon'		Chapter 6	142
Actinidia kolomikta		Chapter 14	352
Adina rubella		Chapter 3, 14	72, 356
Adonis amurensis		Chapter 18	461
Adonis amurensis 'Fukujukai'		Chapter 18	460, 461, 462, 463, 472
Aesculus pavia		Chapter 3	86
Ageratum 'Hawaii Blue'		Appendix #10	500
Agropyron repens		Chapter 14	370
Alcea rugosa		Chapter 10	268
Allium cernuum		Appendix #8	498
Allium giganteum 'Mt. Blanc'		Chapter 9	238, 240
Allium 'Mount Everest'		Chapter 9	230
Allium 'Purple Sensation'		Chapter 3, 11	73, 277, 280
Allium stipitatum 'White Giant'		Chapter 9, Appendix #3	230, 238, 240, 491
Allium tricoccum		Chapter 17	428
Allium tuberosum		Chapter 3	80
Alocasia 'Calidora'		Chapter 6, Appendix #10	166, 502
Alternanthera sessilis 'Rubra'		Appendix #10	500
American arborvitae	*Thuja occidentalis*	Chapter 1	4
American beech	*Fagus grandifolia*	Chapter 4, 6, 7, 17	100, 140, 170, 428
American holly	*Ilex opaca*	Chapter 1, 8, 15, 16, 18	4, 214, 379, 389, 394, 419, 441
Amsonia hubrichtii		Chapter 11, Appendix #8	277, 280, 296, 498
Amsonia tabernaemontana		Chapter 7	176
Andropogon virginicus		Chapter 8	201

PLANT NAME	ALTERNATE PLANT NAME	CHAPTER	PAGE
anemone		Chapter 14	356
Anemone blanda		Chapter 18	467
Anemone blanda 'White Splendour'		Chapter 9	240
Anemone hupehensis		Appendix #8	498
Anemone x hybrida 'Honorine Jobert'		Chapter 9, Appendix #3	242, 491
Angelonia angustifolia 'Anblauzwei' Angel Face® Blue		Appendix #10	500
angel's fishing rod	*Dierama pulcherrimum*	Chapter 11	297
Anisostichus capreolata	*Bignonia capreolata*	Chapter 6	158
Antennaria parlinii subsp. *fallax*		Chapter 9, Appendix #3	240, 242, 489
Antennaria plantaginifolia var. *ambigens*	*Antennaria parlinil* subsp. *fallax*	Chapter 9, Appendix #3	240, 242, 489
apple		Chapter 6	136, 138
Aquilegia canadensis		Chapter 15	396
Aralia elata		Chapter 6	151, 152
arborvitae		Chapter 10	246, 247, 260
Arum italicum 'Marmoratum'		Chapter 18	444
Arum italicum 'Pictum'	*Arum italicum* 'Marmoratum'	Chapter 12	326
Aruncus aethusifolius		Chapter 7	197
Arundinaria virdistriata		Chapter 6, 14	154, 356
Arundo donax		Chapter 1, 6	14, 15, 16, 151, 153
Asclepias curassavica		Appendix #10	500
Asclepias tuberosa		Chapter 8	203
ash		Chapter 15	391
Asiatic spice bush	*Lindera angustifolia*	Chapter 16	402
asparagus		Chapter 12	315, 321
Asparagus densiflorus 'Myersii'		Appendix #10, #11	500, 504
Asphodeline lutea		Chapter 10	258
aster		Chapter 6, 16	165, 417
Aster cordifolius	*Symphyotrichum cordifolium*	Chapter 7, 15, 16	171, 397, 414
Aster tataricus		Chapter 10	255, 263, 268
Astilboides tabularis		Chapter 17	435
Athyrium goeringianum 'Pictum'		Chapter 7	179
Athyrium niponicum var. *pictum*	*Athyrium goeringianum* 'Pictum'	Chapter 7	179
atlas cedar	*Cedrus atlantica* 'Glauca'	Chapter 1	4
Austrian pine	*Pinus nigra*	Chapter 1	4
azalea		Chapter 1, 3, 5, 6, 7, 10, 11, 13, 15	4, 7, 88, 121, 127, 129, 132, 151, 179, 249, 253, 255, 262, 266, 273, 274, 279, 338, 396, 397

PLANT NAME	ALTERNATE PLANT NAME	CHAPTER	PAGE
Azalea arborescens	*Rhododendron arborescens*	Chapter 3	58
Azalea canescens	*Rhododendron canescens*	Chapter 3	53, 57
Azalea ledifolia var. alba	*Rhododendron mucronatum*	Chapter 1	4
Azalea pontica	*Rhododendron luteum*	Chapter 6	163
azalea-Kurume hybrid		Chapter 1	4
Ballota acetabulosa		Chapter 9, Appendix #3	240, 241, 242, 489
balloon vine	*Cardiospermum halicacabum*	Chapter 6	159
Baltic ivy	*Hedera helix 'Baltica'*	Chapter 4, 5	109, 114
bamboo		Chapter 18	447
Baptisia alba		Chapter 9, Appendix #2	240, 488
Baptisia australis		Chapter 11	291, 292
bears' britches	*Acanthus spinosissimus*	Chapter 11	297
beautyberry	*Callicarpa dichotoma, Callicarpa japonica*	Chapter 1, 10	4, 253, 255, 257
beauty-bush	*Kolkwitzia amabilis*	Chapter 1	4
beech		Chapter 2, 7, 15	32, 173, 395, 399
beets		Chapter 12	321
Begonia boliviensis 'Bertini'		Appendix #11	503
Begonia grandis		Appendix #8	498
Begonia grandis 'Alba'		Chapter 9, Appendix #3	234, 240, 242, 489
Belamcanda		Appendix #1	484
Belamcanda chinensis		Appendix #1	484
Berberis thunbergii		Chapter 1	4
Berberis thunbergii 'Autropurpurea Nana'		Chapter 6, 11, 14	150, 291, 352
Berberis thunbergii 'Crimson Pygmy'	*Berberis thunbergii 'Autropurpurea Nana'*	Chapter 11	279, 291
Berberis thunbergii forma atropurpurea		Chapter 10, 11	249, 277
Berberis vulgaris 'Royal Cloak'		Chapter 10	249
Bergenia 'Sunningdale'		Chapter 8, 10	217, 260
Bermuda grass		Chapter 1	24
Betula nigra		Chapter 12, 18	326, 441
Betula pendula		Chapter 1	4
Betula platyphylla var. japonica		Chapter 16	408, 418
Bignonia capreolata		Chapter 6, 14	158, 159, 351
Bignonia capreolata 'Tangerine Beauty'		Chapter 6, 14	158, 351
bird's nest spruce	*Picea abies 'Nidiformis'*	Chapter 3, 10	87, 253
black haw viburnum	*Viburnum prunifolium*	Chapter 2, 8	40, 198, 202, 214
black locust	*Robinia pseudoaccia 'Dean Rossman'*	Chapter 15	379, 394, 399
black oak		Chapter 15	395
black walnut	*Juglans nigra*	Chapter 3, 14, 15, 17	88, 370, 379, 394, 426

PLANT NAME	ALTERNATE PLANT NAME	CHAPTER	PAGE
blackberry-lily	*Belamcanda chinensis*	Appendix #1	484
bleeding heart	*Dicentra spectabilis*	Chapter 11	277
Bletilla striata		Chapter 11	294
blue atlas cedar	*Cedrus atlantica* 'Glauca'	Chapter 3	74
blue clematis		Chapter 3	54
blue spruce	*Picea pungens*	Chapter 1	4
boxwood		Chapter 1	5
Brandywine bluebells	*Mertensia virginica*	Chapter 6	143, 144
bridal wreath	*Spiraea prunifolia*	Chapter 1	4
broom-sedge	*Andropogon virginicus*	Chapter 8	201, 202
Brunfelsia pilosa		Appendix #11	503
Buddleja alternifolia		Chapter 11	291
Buddleja davidii		Chapter 3	84
Buddleja davidii 'Black Knight'		Chapter 3, 14	84, 355
Buddleja davidii 'Opera'		Chapter 3, 14	84, 355
Buddleja davidii 'Potter's Purple'		Chapter 3, 14	84, 355
Buddleja davidii 'Princeton Purple'		Chapter 3, 14	84, 355
burgundy-colored European beech	*Fagus sylvatica* 'Riversii'	Chapter 9, 12	224, 326
Burkwood daphne	*Daphne* x *burkwoodii* 'Carol Mackie'	Chapter 3	57
burkwood's hybrid osmanthus	*Osmanthus burkwoodii*	Chapter 3	57
burr rose	*Rosa roxburghii forma normalis*	Chapter 11	288
buttercup		Chapter 2	33
butterfly bush	*Buddleja davidii*	Chapter 3	70, 84
butterfly weed	*Asclepias tuberosa*	Chapter 8	203
Buxus 'Green Gem'		Chapter 3, 12, 14, 18	67, 68, 326, 357, 444, 472
Buxus microphylla var. *japonica*		Chapter 1	4
Buxus 'Morris Dwarf'		Chapter 12	326
Buxus sempervirens (Longwood resistant)		Chapter 9, Appendix #2, #3	240, 241, 488, 489
Buxus sempervirens 'Suffuticosa'		Chapter 1	5
Caladium 'Gingerland'		Appendix #11	503
Caladium 'Tom-Tom'		Chapter 6, Appendix #10	166, 500, 502
Calamagrostis arundinacea var. *brachytricha*		Chapter 7	197
Calamagrostis x *acutiflora* 'Karl Foerster'		Chapter 6	154
Calamintha nepeta		Appendix #8	498
Callicarpa dichotoma		Chapter 10, 14	253, 255, 257, 355
Callicarpa japonica		Chapter 1	4
Calocedrus decurrens		Chapter 1, 4, 10	16, 95, 263
Caltha palustris		Chapter 7	190
Caltha palustris var. *polypetala*		Chapter 7	191

PLANT NAME	ALTERNATE PLANT NAME	CHAPTER	PAGE
Chaenomeles x *superba* 'Perfecta'		Chapter 12	308, 309
Chaenomeles x *superba* 'Rowallane'		Chapter 3	60, 72
Chaenomles speciosa (Winterthur #1)		Chapter 12	309
Chaenomles speciosa 'Apple Blossom'		Chapter 12	309
Chaenomles speciosa 'Cameo'		Chapter 12	310
Chaenomles speciosa 'Hollandia'		Chapter 12	310
Chamaecyparis		Chapter 9	228
Chamaecyparis obtusa 'Breviramea'		Chapter 9, Appendix #2, #3	240, 487, 490
Chamaecyparis obtusa 'Dainty Doll'		Chapter 9, Appendix #2	240, 488
Chamaecyparis obtusa 'Gracilis'		Chapter 9	240
Chamaecyparis obtusa 'Nana Gracilis'		Chapter 9, 14, Appendix #3	240, 241, 352, 489, 490, 491
chestnut rose	*Rosa roxburghii forma normalis*	Chapter 11, Appendix #4	288, 492
Chimonanthus praecox		Chapter 3	52, 57
China-fir	*Cunninghamia lanceolata*	Chapter 1	4
Chinese witch-hazel	*Hamamelis mollis*	Chapter 18	450, 454, 472
Chinese woodbine	*Lonicera tragophylla*	Chapter 3	58
Chionanthus virginicus		Chapter 1, 3	4, 73, 74
Chionodoxa luciliae		Appendix #7	497
Chionodoxa luciliae 'Alba'		Chapter 18	461, 464, 466
choke cherry	*Prunus serotina*	Chapter 14	370
Christmas fern	*Polystichum acrostichoides*	Chapter 17	434
Christmas-rose	*Helleborus niger*	Chapter 6	140
chrysanthemum		Chapter 6, 14	165, 356
Chrysanthemum 'Clara Curtis'		Chapter 10	268
Chrysanthemum coreanum	*Chrysanthemum zawadskii*	Chapter 10	268
Chrysanthemum 'Pink Procession'		Chapter 10	268
Chrysanthemum rubellum	*Chrysanthemum zawadskii* subsp. *latilobum*	Chapter 10	268
Chrysanthemum 'Ryan's Pink'		Appendix #8	498
Chrysanthemum weyrichii 'White Bomb'		Chapter 9, Appendix #3	240, 242, 491
Chrysanthemum x *morifolium*		Chapter 10	268
Chrysanthemum zawadskii		Chapter 10	268
Chrysanthemum zawadskii subsp. *latilobum*		Chapter 10	268
Chyrsanthemum 'Mary Stocker'		Chapter 10	268
Cirsium arvense		Chapter 14	370
Citrus		Chapter 3	54
Citrus limon		Appendix #11	504
Clematis		Chapter 3	54
Clematis 'Betty Corning' (Viticella Group)		Chapter 3, 14	69, 351

PLANT NAME	ALTERNATE PLANT NAME	CHAPTER	PAGE
Corylopsis 'Longwood Chimes'		Chapter 16	418
Corylopsis platypetala	*Corylopsis sinensis* var. *calvescens*	Chapter 16	406
Corylopsis sinensis		Chapter 16	418
Corylopsis sinensis var. *calvescens*		Chapter 16	406, 418
Corylopsis 'Winterthur'		Chapter 16	418
Corylus colurna		Chapter 16	418
Corynephorus canescens 'Spiky Blue'		Appendix #11	503
Cotinus coggygria 'Purple Supreme'		Chapter 11, 14	277, 355, 356
Cotoneaster adpressus var. *praecox*		Chapter 10	262, 263
Cotoneaster divaricatus		Chapter 1	4
Cotoneaster salicifolius		Chapter 1	4
crab apple	*Malus floribunda*	Chapter 6	136
Crambe cordifolia		Chapter 9, Appendix #3	230, 240, 489, 490
Crataegus		Chapter 1, 2, 15	4, 40, 399
Crataegus crus-galli		Chapter 15	399
Crataegus viridis 'Winter King'		Chapter 16	418
creeping phlox	*Phlox* 'Millstream Jupiter'	Chapter 12	308, 310
crested iris	*Iris cristata*	Chapter 5	119, 129
crimson pygmy barberry	*Berberis thunbergii* 'Autropurpurea Nana'	Chapter 5, 6, 7, 11	118, 127, 146, 150, 154, 156, 163, 165, 181, 279, 291
Crocus ancyrensis 'Golden Bunch'		Chapter 18	467
Crocus chrysanthus 'Blue Pearl'		Chapter 14	366
Crocus chrysanthus 'Prinses Beatrix'		Chapter 14	366
Crocus 'Ruby Giant'		Chapter 7	171
Crocus sieberi 'Firefly'		Chapter 18	466
Crocus 'Taplow Ruby'		Chapter 7	171
Crocus tommasinianus		Chapter 5, 7	132, 171, 172
Crocus tommasinianus 'Whitewell Purple'		Chapter 18	460, 462, 463, 466
cross vine	*Bignonia capreolata*	Chapter 6	158
Crucianella stylosa	*Phuopsis stylosa*	Chapter 11	292
Cryptomeria japonica 'Lobbii'		Chapter 1	4
Cunninghamia lanceolata		Chapter 1	4, 5
cup and saucer vine	*Cobaea scandens*	Chapter 6	159
Cupressus sempervirens		Chapter 8	211
cut-leaf European beech		Chapter 8	217
Cyclamen coum		Chapter 8, 18	217, 456
Cyclamen europaeum	*Cyclamen purpurascens*	Chapter 5	119
Cyclamen hederifolium		Chapter 5	119
Cyclamen purpurascens		Chapter 5	119
Cynara cardunculus		Chapter 9	240

PLANT NAME	ALTERNATE PLANT NAME	CHAPTER	PAGE
eglantine rose	*Rosa rubiginosa*	Chapter 11, Appendix #4	286, 493
Elaeagnus pungens 'Fruitlandii'		Chapter 3, 14	58, 349
Elaeagnus pungens 'Maculata'		Chapter 3, 8, 14	71, 217, 349
Eleutherococcus sieboldianus 'Variegatus'		Appendix #2	487
Emilia coccinea	*Emilia flammea*	Chapter 7, Appendix #10	180, 500
Emilia flammea		Chapter 7	180
Endymion hispanicus	*Hyacinthoides hispanica*	Chapter 3, 10	79, 257
English beech	*Fagus sylvatica* 'Riversii'	Chapter 3	86
English holly	*Ilex aquifolium*	Chapter 9, 11	240, 297
English yew	*Taxus baccata*	Chapter 8	209
Epiphyllum oxypetalum		Appendix #11	503
Equisetum hyemale 'Robustrum'	*Equisetum hyemale* var. *affine*	Chapter 7	195
Equisetum hyemale var. *affine*		Chapter 7	195
Eranthis hyemalis		Chapter 18	458, 460, 461, 463, 464, 472
Eranthis x *tubergenii* 'Guinea Gold'		Chapter 18	461, 463, 464, 466
Ernest Wilson's Chinese house lemon	*Citrus*	Chapter 3	54
Eryngium giganteum		Chapter 9	240
Eryngium yuccifolium		Chapter 9, Appendix #3	240, 489
Erythronium 'Pagoda'		Chapter 5	119, 121
Eucomis 'Van der Merwei'		Appendix #10	500
Euonymus alatus		Chapter 1, 7, 10, 15	4, 175, 253, 255, 380, 389, 392, 393
Euonymus alatus 'Monstrosus'		Chapter 3, 14, 15	85, 359, 393
Euonymus fortunei 'Emerald Gaiety'		Chapter 9	240
Euonymus fortunei 'Gracilis'		Chapter 9	240
Euonymus sachalinensis		Chapter 16	418
Euonymus yedoensis		Chapter 1	4
Euphorbia amygdaloides var. *robbiae*		Chapter 3	84
Euphorbia cotinifolia		Appendix #10	502
Euphorbia dulcis 'Chameleon'		Chapter 11	292
European bird cherry	*Prunus avium* 'Plena'	Chapter 15	386
European white birch	*Betula pendula*	Chapter 1	4
evergreen azalea		Chapter 4, 10, 14	109, 249, 357, 358
Fagus grandifolia		Chapter 4, 6, 7, 15	100, 140, 170, 399
Fagus sylvatica 'Laciniata'		Chapter 18	445
Fagus sylvatica 'Pendula'		Chapter 6	149
Fagus sylvatica 'Riversii'		Chapter 3, 9, 10, 14	66, 224, 249, 352, 357, 522
fall crocus	*Sternbergia lutea*	Chapter 6	165

PLANT NAME	ALTERNATE PLANT NAME	CHAPTER	PAGE
heather	*Erica*	Chapter 1	27
Hedera colchica 'Dentata'		Chapter 10	264, 266, 267
Hedera helix 'Baltica'		Chapter 4, Chapter 9	109, 240
Hedera helix 'Buttercup'		Chapter 3, 14	68, 351
Hedera pastuchovii		Chapter 9	240
hedge apple	*Maclura pomifera*	Chapter 2, 3, 16	40, 56, 410, 411
Hedyotis caerulea	*Houstonia caerulea*	Chapter 5	118
Helianthus mollis		Chapter 8	203
Heliopsis helianthoides 'Karat'		Chapter 6	154
Heliopsis helianthoides 'Venus'		Chapter 6	162
Heliotropium 'Marine'		Appendix #10, #11	500, 502, 504
Helleborus foetidus		Chapter 10, 18	265, 266, 444
Helleborus niger		Chapter 6, 17	140, 142, 426
Helleborus x hybridus (Royal Heritage strain)		Appendix #7	497
Helleborus x hybridus (Skyland's pink seedling)		Appendix #7	497
Helleborus x hybridus (Winterthur seedlings)		Appendix #7	497
Hemerocallis		Chapter 10	255
Hemerocallis 'Aten'		Chapter 10	266
Hemerocallis 'Autumn Minaret'		Chapter 10	259
Hemerocallis 'Autumn Prince'		Chapter 6	157
Hemerocallis 'Hyperion'		Chapter 6	150
Hemerocallis minor		Chapter 7	182
Hemerocallis 'Serene Madonna'		Chapter 9	240
Hemerocallis 'Spellbinder'		Chapter 10	250, 253, 259, 266, 267
Hemerocallis 'Spiderman'		Chapter 7	192
hemlock	*Tsuga canadensis*	Chapter 1	4
Hepatica americana		Chapter 15	399
Heptacodium miconioides		Chapter 9, 11, Appendix #2	236, 240, 280, 488
Hesperis matronalis		Chapter 10, 14	258, 362
Hetz Wintergreen arborvitae		Chapter 10	260
Hibiscus acetosella 'Red Shield'		Chapter 6, Appendix #10	166, 500, 502
Hibiscus coccineus		Chapter 7	191, 192
Hibiscus sinensis (double peach)		Appendix #11	503
Hibiscus syriacus 'Blue Bird'		Chapter 3, 14	70, 349
Hibiscus syriacus 'Diana'		Chapter 9, 14, Appendix #2	218, 227, 228, 234, 240, 357, 491
Hick's yew	*Taxus media* 'Hicksii'	Chapter 1	4
Higan cherry	*Prunus x subhirtella*	Chapter 11	280

PLANT NAME	ALTERNATE PLANT NAME	CHAPTER	PAGE
Himalayan rhubarb		Chapter 1	27
Hindu datura	*Datura metal*	Chapter 1	14
Hohman's golden dogwood	*Cornus florida 'Hohman's Gold'*	Chapter 10	255, 264, 265
hollyhock	*Alcea rugosa*	Chapter 10	268
horse chestnut	*Aesculus pavia*	Chapter 3	86
Hosta clausa		Chapter 5	120, 121
Hosta sieboldiana 'Caerulea'		Chapter 6	157
Hosta sieboldii f. kabitan		Chapter 3, Appendix #1	60, 72, 482
Hosta venusta		Chapter 7	182
Houstonia caerulea		Chapter 5	118, 119, 129
hyacinth-bean	*Dolichos lablab*	Chapter 6	159
Hyacinthoides hispanica		Chapter 10	257
Hyacinthoides hispanica 'Excelsior'		Chapter 10	257
hybrid boxwood	*Buxus 'Green Gem'*	Chapter 3	67, 68
hybrid tea roses	*Rosa*	Chapter 1	5
hybrid winter aconite	*Eranthis x tubergenii 'Guinea Gold'*	Chapter 18	461, 463
Hydrangea		Chapter 1	4
Hydrangea arborescens 'Annabelle'		Chapter 9, Appendix #2	240, 241, 488
Hydrangea aspera subsp. *sargentiana*		Chapter 3	52, 53
Hydrangea paniculata 'White Tiara'		Chapter 9, Appendix #3	234, 240, 242, 490, 491
Hydrangea quercifolia		Chapter 7	175, 176
Idesia polycarpa		Chapter 12	320
Ilex		Chapter 9	228
Ilex aquifolium		Chapter 9	240
Ilex 'Autumn Glow'		Chapter 8, Appendix #13	214, 506
Ilex crenata		Chapter 1	4
Ilex crenata 'Helleri'		Chapter 9, Appendix #3	240, 491
Ilex glabra		Chapter 8	217
Ilex 'Harvest Red'		Chapter 8, Appendix #13	214, 506
Ilex opaca		Chapter 1, 18, Appendix #12	4, 441, 505
Ilex opaca (staminate)		Appendix #12	505
Ilex opaca (yellow-berried)		Appendix #12	505
Ilex opaca 'Arden'		Appendix #12	505
Ilex opaca 'Clarissa'		Appendix #12	505
Ilex opaca 'Clark'		Appendix #12	505
Ilex opaca 'Gertrude'		Appendix #12	505

PLANT NAME	ALTERNATE PLANT NAME	CHAPTER	PAGE
Impatiens 'Dazzler Deep Orange'		Appendix #10	500, 502
Impatiens 'Orange over Apricot'		Appendix #10	500, 502
Impatiens 'Paradise Salmon'		Appendix #11	503, 504
Impatiens 'Tango'		Chapter 3	80
incense-cedar	*Calocedrus decurrens*	Chapter 1, 4, 10	16, 95, 263, 264
Indigofera 'Rose Carpet'		Chapter 11, Appendix #8	297, 298, 498
Inula helenium		Chapter 6	157, 162
Iochroma cyaneum		Appendix #11	504
Ipomoea purpurea 'Kniola's Purple-black'		Chapter 6	159
Ipomoea tricolor 'Heavenly Blue'		Appendix #10	501, 502
Iresine 'Purple Lady'		Appendix #10	501
iris		Chapter 1	6, 7
Iris 'Cantab'		Chapter 18	467
Iris cristata		Chapter 5	119, 121, 129
Iris 'Eleanor Roosevelt'		Appendix #7	497
Iris ensata var. *spontanea*		Chapter 7	190, 191, 192, 197
Iris 'George'		Chapter 18	466
Iris germanica		Chapter 3, Appendix #7	73, 497
Iris graminea		Chapter 14, Appendix #1	366, 483
Iris 'Grapesicle'		Chapter 3	77
Iris 'Happy Birthday'		Chapter 3	84
Iris 'Harmony'		Chapter 18	467
Iris histrioides 'Major'		Chapter 18	467
Iris orientalis 'Shelford Giant'		Chapter 6	154
Iris pseudacorus		Chapter 7, 17	191, 192, 435
Iris sibirica		Chapter 11	294
Iris sibirica 'Maranatha'		Chapter 10	249, 260
Iris sibirica 'Ausable River'		Chapter 11	291, 292
Iris sibirica 'Orville Fay'		Chapter 11	294
Irish yew	*Taxus baccata* 'Fastigiata'	Chapter 8	209
Isolepis cernua		Chapter 6, Appendix #11	158, 504
Italian cypress	*Cupressus sempervirens*	Chapter 8	211
Itea virginica 'Henry's Garnet'		Chapter 6	162
Jacaranda mimosifolia		Appendix #11	504
Japanese barberry	*Berberis thunbergii*	Chapter 1	4
Japanese box	*Buxus microphylla* var. *japonica*	Chapter 1	4
Japanese holly	*Ilex crenata*	Chapter 1	4
Japanese honeysuckle	*Lonicera japonica* 'Halliana', *Lonicera japonica*	Chapter 8, 14	202, 370

PLANT NAME	ALTERNATE PLANT NAME	CHAPTER	PAGE
Japanese maple	*Acer palmatum*	Chapter 1	4
Japanese red maple	*Acer palmatum* 'West Grove'	Chapter 3	67
Japanese silver fern	*Athyrium goeringianum* 'Pictum'	Chapter 7	179
Japanese snowbell	*Styrax japonicus* 'Carillon'	Chapter 7	175
Japanese torreya	*Torreya nucifera*	Chapter 16	402, 405, 406, 407, 411, 413, 416
Japanese tree wisteria	*Wisteria floribunda*	Chapter 4, 7, 10, 13, 14	96, 183, 249, 273, 290, 294, 299, 342, 355, 356
Japanese umbrella-pine	*Sciadopitys verticillata*	Chapter 2, 5, 6, 7, 12, 14	43, 115, 117, 118, 160, 161, 183, 186, 188, 189, 192, 196, 290, 320, 358
Japanese white pine	*Pinus parviflora* 'Glauca'	Chapter 5	125, 126
Japanese witch-hazel	*Hamamelis japonica*	Chapter 18	450
Japanese yew	*Taxus cuspidata*	Chapter 1, 8	4, 209
Jasminum nudiflorum		Chapter 18	445
Jerusalem artichokes		Chapter 12	321, 324
Juglans nigra		Chapter 3, 14, 15, 17	88, 370, 379, 394, 426
Juniperus 'Gray Owl'		Chapter 9, Appendix #2, #3	228, 240, 241, 242, 488, 489, 491
Juniperus virginiana	red cedar	Chapter 2, 4, 5, 6, 7, 14, 15	40, 43, 100, 115, 116, 126, 148, 183, 352, 379, 389, 393, 394, 396, 399
Kentucky coffee tree	*Gymnocladus dioicus*	Chapter 15	379, 393
Kerria japonica		Chapter 18	445
Kerria japonica 'Golden Guinea'		Chapter 8	217
Koelreuteria paniculata		Chapter 18	472
Kolkwitzia amabilis		Chapter 1	4
Korean chrysanthemum		Chapter 10	255, 263, 268
Korean dogwood	*Cornus kousa* 'Milky Way'	Chapter 9	230, 240, 241, 242
Korean pine	*Pinus koraiensis*	Chapter 5	125
Korean rhododendron	*Rhododendron mucronulatum* 'Cornell Pink'	Chapter 18	466
Korean stewartia	*Stewartia koreana*	Chapter 11	281, 290
kousa dogwood	*Cornus kousa*	Chapter 1	4
Kwanzan cherry	*Prunus serrulata* 'Kwanzan'	Chapter 1	15
Lablab purpureus	*Dolichos lablab*	Chapter 6	159
Laburnum x *watereri* 'Vossii'		Chapter 10	262
lacebark pine	*Pinus bungeana*	Chapter 5	125
lace cap hydrangea		Chapter 4	103
lamb's ear	*Stachys byzantina*	Chapter 9, 13	226, 227, 238, 242, 338

PLANT NAME	ALTERNATE PLANT NAME	CHAPTER	PAGE
Nordman's fir	*Abies nordmanniana*	Chapter 5	124, 125
Norway maple	*Acer platanoides*	Chapter 1	15
Norway spruce	*Picea abies*	Chapter 5	124
Nymphaea 'Helvola'		Chapter 7	192
Nyssa sylvatica		Chapter 15	394, 397
oakleaf hydrangea	*Hydrangea quercifolia*	Chapter 7	175, 176
Oenothera perennis		Chapter 1	6
old shrub roses		Chapter 11	282, 283, 285, 286, 288, 289, 290, 291, 296
Onopordum acanthium		Chapter 9, 14, Appendix #3	230, 233, 240, 242, 362, 490, 491
Ophiopogon japonicus		Chapter 3	56
Ophiopogon japonicus 'Nanus'		Chapter 3	56
orchid		Appendix #1	486
Oriental bittersweet	*Celastrus orbiculatus*	Chapter 8, 14	202, 370
Oriental spruce	*Picea orientalis*	Chapter 5	124, 125
Ornithogalum saundersiae		Appendix #10	501
Oryza sativa 'Red Dragon'		Appendix #11	504
osage orange	*Maclura pomifera*	Chapter 2, 3, 16	40, 56, 410
Osmanthus burkwoodii		Chapter 3	57
ostrich fern	*Matteuccia struthiopteris*	Chapter 17	434
Oxalis vulcanicolo 'Copper Glow'		Appendix #10	501
Oxypetalum caeruleum		Chapter 3, Appendix #10, #11	78, 501, 503
Pachysandra terminalis 'Green Sheen'		Chapter 8, 18	217, 445
Paeonia 'Festiva Maxima'		Chapter 9	228, 230, 240, 242
Paeonia 'Gauguin'		Chapter 11	294
Paeonia 'Joseph Rock'		Chapter 6	162
Paeonia 'Mt. Everest'		Chapter 9	230
Paeonia 'Rock's Variety'	*Paeonia* 'Joseph Rock'	Chapter 6	166
Paeonia suffruticosa		Chapter 1, 6	7, 162
Paeonia suffruticosa subsp. *rockii*	*Paeonia* 'Joseph Rock'	Chapter 6	165
Paeonia 'White Ivory'		Chapter 9, Appendix #3	230, 240, 242, 491
pansies		Chapter 3	76
paperbark maple	*Acer griseum*	Chapter 8	217
Pardanthopsis		Appendix #1	484
Parrotia persica		Chapter 18	445
Parthenocissus quinquefolia 'Monham' (Star Showers™)		Chapter 9	240
Patrinia scabrosifolia		Chapter 10	268
Pennisetum alopecuroides		Chapter 6, 7	154, 191

PLANT NAME	ALTERNATE PLANT NAME	CHAPTER	PAGE
Pentas lanceolata 'Cranberry Punch'		Chapter 6, Appendix #11	158, 504
peonies		Chapter 1	6
persimmon		Chapter 16	410
Petunia 'Purple Wave'		Appendix #10	505
Philadelphus		Chapter 1	4
Philadelphus 'Burkwoodii'		Chapter 9, Appendix #2	230, 240, 241, 488
Philadelphus 'Etoile Rose'		Chapter 9	240
Philadelphus 'Virginata'		Chapter 9	240
Phlox divaricata		Chapter 11	292
Phlox 'Millstream Jupiter'		Chapter 12	308, 310
Phlox paniculata		Appendix #1	484
Phlox paniculata 'Ezio'		Appendix #1	485
Phlox paniculata 'Franz Schubert'		Appendix #8	498
Phlox pilosa subsp. *ozarkana*		Chapter 11, Appendix #8	292, 498
Phlox subulata 'Tamsin'		Appendix #7	497
Photinia davidiana var. *undulata* 'Prostrata'	*Stranvaesia davidiana* var. *undulata* 'Prostrata'	Chapter 5	118
Phuopsis stylosa		Chapter 11	292
Phygelius rectus 'New Sensation'		Appendix #10	501
Phyllostachys aureosulcata		Chapter 6	152, 153, 154, 166
Physostegia virginiana		Chapter 1	6
Phytolacca americana		Chapter 14	370
Picea abies		Chapter 5	124
Picea abies 'Nidiformis'		Chapter 3, 10	87, 253
Picea orientalis		Chapter 5	124, 125
Picea orientalis 'Procumbens'		Appendix #3	490
Picea polita		Chapter 1	4
Picea pungens		Chapter 1	4
pigsqueak	*Bergenia* 'Sunningdale'	Chapter 10	260
Pinus ayacahuite		Chapter 5, 9	125, 228
Pinus bungeana		Chapter 5	125
Pinus cembra		Chapter 5, 15	125, 382
Pinus densiflora 'Umbraculifera'		Chapter 5, 15	125, 387
Pinus flexilis		Chapter 5	125
Pinus koraiensis		Chapter 5	125
Pinus mugo var. *mugo*		Chapter 1	4
Pinus nigra		Chapter 1	4
Pinus parviflora 'Glauca'		Chapter 5, 9	125, 228
Pinus strobus		Chapter 5, 9	124, 125, 228

PLANT NAME	ALTERNATE PLANT NAME	CHAPTER	PAGE
Prunus serrulata 'Kwanzan'		Chapter 1	15
Prunus serrulata 'Ojochin'		Chapter 15	384
Prunus serrulata 'Taihaku'		Chapter 15	382
Prunus x *subhirtella*		Chapter 15	380, 382, 384, 385, 386
Prunus x *subhirtella* "Scott early"		Chapter 11, 12, 15	280, 290, 291, 305, 307, 308, 309, 310, 384
Prunus x *subhirtella* 'Autumnalis'		Chapter 5, 14	118, 119, 129, 365
Prunus x *subhirtella* 'Pendula'		Chapter 15	386
Prunus x *subhirtella* 'Rosy Cloud'		Chapter 15	384, 386
Prunus x *yedoensis*		Chapter 8, 15	214, 382, 384, 386
Pseudolarix amabilis		Chapter 3, 9, 10	84, 85, 240, 253
Pseudolarix kaempferi	*Pseudolarix amabilis*	Chapter 3, 10	84, 253
Pseudomuscari azureum 'Alba'	*Muscari azureum* 'Album'	Chapter 14	366
Punica granatum		Chapter 3	52
Pyracantha		Chapter 1	4
Pyrus 'Chojuro'		Chapter 6	136
Pyrus communis		Chapter 8	202
Pyrus 'Seuri'		Chapter 6	136
quack grass	*Agropyron repens*	Chapter 10, 14	263, 266, 370
Quaker ladies	*Houstonia caerulea*	Chapter 5	118, 119, 129
Quercus alba		Chapter 4, 15	95, 379, 381
Quercus rubra		Chapter 4, 15	100, 379, 389
quince		Chapter 12	307, 308, 310
ramps	*Allium tricoccum*	Chapter 17	428
Ranunculus ficaria 'Flore Pleno'		Chapter 6	142
raspberry		Chapter 12	315, 316, 321, 322
rattlesnake plantain	*Eryngium yuccifolium*	Appendix #3	489
red cardinal flower	*Lobelia cardinalis*	Chapter 4	109
red oak	*Quercus rubra*	Chapter 4, 15	100, 379, 389
redbud	*Cercis canadensis*	Chapter 7	179
red cedar	*Juniperus virginiana*	Chapter 2, 4, 5, 6, 7, 15	40, 43, 100, 102, 115, 147, 183, 186, 188, 379, 389, 393, 394, 396
redleaf barberry	*Berberis thunbergii* forma *atropurpurea*	Chapter 11	277
redleaf smoke bush		Chapter 11	277
red-twig dogwood	*Cornus sericea* 'Bloodgood'	Chapter 8	217
rhododendron		Chapter 1, 16	7, 418
Rhododendron 'Amoenum'		Chapter 5	129
Rhododendron arborescens		Chapter 3	58
Rhododendron 'Azura'		Chapter 17	431
Rhododendron 'Bo-Peep'		Chapter 5	129

PLANT NAME	ALTERNATE PLANT NAME	CHAPTER	PAGE
Salix gracilistyla 'Melanostachys'		Chapter 18, Appendix #14	449, 507
Salix humilis var. *microphylla*	*Salix humilis* var. *tristis*	Chapter 18, Appendix #14	449, 507
Salix humilis var. *tristis*		Chapter 18, Appendix #14	449, 507
Salix repens var. *arenaria*		Chapter 18, Appendix #14	449, 507
Salix repens var. *argentea*	*Salix repens* var. *arenaria*	Chapter 18, Appendix #14	449, 507
Salix x rubra 'Eugenei'		Chapter 18, Appendix #14	447, 449, 507
salsify		Chapter 12	321
Salvia chiapensis		Appendix #10	501
Salvia coccinea 'Lady in Red'		Chapter 6	158
Salvia farinacea 'Victoria Blue'		Chapter 6, Appendix #10	166, 501, 502
Salvia guaranitica		Chapter 6, Appendix #10	166, 502
Salvia guaranitica 'Black and Blue'		Appendix #10	501
Salvia guaranitica 'Kobalt'		Appendix #10	501
Salvia haematodes 'Indigo'		Chapter 11	280, 293
Salvia praetensis 'Indigo'	*Salvia haematodes* 'Indigo'	Chapter 11	293
Sanchezia speciosa		Appendix #11	503
sand pear	*Pyrus* 'Chojuro'	Chapter 6	136
Sanguinaria canadensis 'Multiplex'		Chapter 9	238, 240
Sargent's hydrangea	*Hydrangea aspera* subsp. *sargentiana*	Chapter 3	52, 53
Sargent's weeping hemlock	*Tsuga canadensis* 'Pendula'	Chapter 3, 10	87, 253
Sasa veitchii		Chapter 14, 16, 17	356, 405, 435
Sassafras		Chapter 15	394, 396, 397
saxifrage		Chapter 3	79
Schizophragma hydrangeoides 'Moonlight'		Chapter 14	351
Sciadopitys verticillata		Chapter 5, 12 14	115, 116, 117, 118, 133, 320, 358
Scilla campanulata	*Hyacinthoides hispanica*	Chapter 10	257
Scilla hispanica	*Hyacinthoides hispanica*	Chapter 10	257
Scilla siberica		Chapter 6, 18	142, 461, 464, 466
Scilla siberica (Winterthur Selection)		Chapter 18	467
Scirpus		Chapter 7	195
Scirpus cernuus	*Isolepis cernua*	Appendix #11	504
Scirpus schoenoplectus		Chapter 7	192
Scirpus tabernamontana 'Albescens'	*Scirpus schoenoplectus*	Chapter 7	192
Scotch broom	*Cytisus scoparius*	Chapter 1	4

PLANT NAME	ALTERNATE PLANT NAME	CHAPTER	PAGE
spinach		Chapter 12	321
Spiraea prunifolia		Chapter 1	4
Spiraea vanhouttei		Chapter 1	4
spreading cotoneaster	*Cotoneaster divaricatus*	Chapter 1	4
spring snowflake	*Leucojum vernum*	Chapter 18	472
spring vetchling	*Lathyrus vernus*	Appendix #1	486
St. Mary's milk	*Silybum marianum*	Chapter 9	242
Stachys byzantina		Chapter 9, Appendix #3	226, 240, 242, 493, 494, 494
Stachys 'Countess Helen von Stein'		Chapter 9	240
Stephanandra incisa 'Crispa'		Chapter 16	412
Sternbergia lutea		Chapter 6	165
Stewartia koreana		Chapter 9, 11, 14, Appendix #2	230, 240, 241, 281, 290, 298, 352, 487, 488
Stipa arundinacea		Appendix #10, #11	501, 504
Stipa tenuissima	*Nassella tenuissima*	Appendix #11	504
Stranvaesia davidiana var. *undulata* 'Prostrata'		Chapter 5	118
Strobilanthes dyerianus		Appendix #10, #11	501, 503
Styrax japonicus 'Carillon'		Chapter 7	175
swamp magnolia	*Magnolia virginiana*	Chapter 3	52, 56, 57
swamp maple	*Acer rubrum*	Chapter 2, 4	45, 100
sweet gum	*Liquidambar styraciflua* 'Corky'	Chapter 16	409
sweetbriar rose	*Rosa rubiginosa*	Chapter 11, Appendix #4	286, 493
Swiss mountain pine	*Pinus mugo* var. *mugo*	Chapter 1	4
Swiss stone pine	*Pinus cembra*	Chapter 5, 15	125, 126, 382
sycamore	*Platanus, Platanus occidentalis*	Chapter 2, 17	32, 426
Symphyotrichum cordifolium		Chapter 7, 15, 16	171, 397, 414
Symphytum 'Belsay Gold'		Appendix #7	497
Symplocarpus foetidus		Chapter 6	141
Syngonium poelophyllum var. *albescens*		Appendix #11	503
Syringa laciniata		Chapter 6	160, 162
Syringa microphylla		Chapter 1	4
Syringa patula		Chapter 11	273
Syringa vulgaris	lilac	Chapter 15	380
Syringa vulgaris 'Charles Joly'		Chapter 1	4
Syringa vulgaris 'Edward J. Gardner'		Chapter 15	389, 390, 392
Syringa vulgaris 'Firmament'		Chapter 15	389, 390, 392
Syringa vulgaris 'Ludwig Spaeth'		Chapter 15	389, 390, 392

PLANT NAME	ALTERNATE PLANT NAME	CHAPTER	PAGE
Tricyrtis 'Sinonome'		Chapter 3, Appendix #1	80, 485
Tsuga canadensis 'Pendula'		Chapter 3	67
Tsuga canadensis		Chapter 1	4
Tsuga caroliniana		Chapter 1	4
Tulipa 'Cum Laude'		Chapter 3	77
Tulipa 'Day Dream'		Chapter 3	76
Tulipa humilis 'Violacea'		Chapter 14	366
Tulipa 'King's Blood'		Chapter 3	60
Tulipa kolpakowskiana		Chapter 3	77
Tulipa 'Lightning Sun'		Chapter 3	76, 77
Tulipa linifolia		Chapter 3	77
Tulipa pulchella 'Violacea'	*Tulipa humilis* 'Violacea'	Chapter 14	366
Tulipa 'Queen of the Night'		Chapter 3	76
Tulipa 'Sancerre'		Chapter 3	77
Tulipa sylvestris		Chapter 10	256
Tulipa 'Temple of Beauty'		Chapter 3	77
Tulipa 'West Point'		Chapter 3	76
tulip poplar	*Liriodendron tulipifera*	Chapter 4, 14	100, 101, 358
tulips		Chapter 3, 17, Appendix #1	72, 73, 76, 422, 482
Turksih filbert	*Corylus colurna*	Chapter 16	418
Verbascum chaixii 'Album'		Chapter 9, Appendix #3	233, 240, 242, 491
Verbascum densiflorum		Chapter 14	375
Verbascum 'Harkness Hybrid'		Chapter 6, 14, Appendix #10	154, 362, 502
Verbascum longifolium var. *pannosum*	*Verbascum olympicum*	Chapter 14	375
Verbascum olympicum		Chapter 14	375
Verbascum 'Snow Maiden'		Chapter 9	240
Verbascum 'Southern Charm'		Appendix #8	498
Verbascum thapsiforme	*Verbascum densiflorum*	Chapter 14	375
Verbascum 'Vega'		Appendix #10	502
Verbena bonariensis		Chapter 7	182
viburnum		Chapter 1, 14, 18	7, 357, 443
Viburnum acerifolium		Chapter 17	434
Viburnum carlesii		Chapter 1, 3	4, 88
Viburnum macrocephalum forma *macrocephalum*		Chapter 3, 12, 14	69, 308, 310, 349
Viburnum opulus 'Aureum'		Chapter 15	391, 392, 399
Viburnum prunifolium		Chapter 8, 12, 15	201, 202, 214, 318, 396
Viburnum x burkwoodii		Chapter 1	4

G General Index

NAME	PAGE
House - trial bridge	35
Hunt Botanical Library	11
Huntington, John	247
Innisfree (Chinese Cup Garden)	26
Jacobsen, Arne	27, 66
Jellicoe, Susan and Geoffrey	27
Jellicoe, Geoffrey	221
Johnson, Phillip	17
Johnston, Lawrence	21
Kalmthout	452, 472
Kassler, Elizabeth	17
Klehm, Roy	462
Lancaster, Roy	447
Landforms	32, 36, 41, 42
Lawrence, George	11
Le Corbusier	17
Lennen, Jaap	138
Liberty Hyde Bailey Hortorium	11
Lighty, Richard W.	190, 197
Lilacs	390-392
Lindtner, Peter	166
Lloyd, Nathaniel	21
Lloyd, Christopher	21
Longwood Gardens, Inc.	301, 418
Loustau, Henry	67, 68
Loustau, Henry - Gate	429
Loustau, Henry - Priapus	430, 432, 436
Lowther Estate	6
Lutyens, Edwin	17, 21
Manus, Therman	196
McCormack, Marie	340
Meserve, Kathleen	240, 260
Millais, Sir John Everett	467
Millcreek Nursery	3, 13
Modern Gardens, Praeger, 1954	17
Modern Gardens and the Landscape Doubleday,1963	17
Modern Private Gardens, 1968	27
Mortier, P.	164
Mulrooney, Robert	133
Museum of Modern Art	17
Myers, Russell	391
Nearing, Guy	418